Stormweaver The Goatman Lives

Stormweaver The Goatman Lives

Doug Hensley

Ingram spark

CONTENTS

Stormweaver
The Goatman Lives
By
Doug Hensley
Table Of Contents

Chapter 1: The Unknown Encounter

- A group of friends on a camping trip
- Mysterious noises in the woods at night

Chapter 2: Whispering Shadows

- Strange occurrences escalate
- Unsettling whispers heard in the darkness

Chapter 3: The Legend Unveiled

- Local tales of the Goatman shared around the campfire
- Skepticism and unease among the group

Chapter 4: A Fateful Decision

- The group decides to investigate the legend

- Deep into the forest, the atmosphere thickens

Chapter 5: Signs of the Goatman

- Disturbing symbols and tracks discovered
- Tension grows as reality sets in

Chapter 6: Disappearing Act

- One member of the group goes missing
- Panic and fear grip the others

Chapter 7: Unholy Alliance

- Remaining friends unite to find the missing person
- A pact to face the Goatman together

Chapter 8: Haunting Memories

- Flashbacks reveal past encounters with the Goatman
- Characters confront their own fears

Chapter 9: Night of the Full Moon

- The group faces the Goatman for the first time
- A terrifying chase through the woods ensues

Chapter 10: The Goatman's Curse

- Survivor guilt and paranoia set in
- The Goatman's curse becomes evident

Chapter 11: The Unseen Stalker

- Unexplained phenomena haunt the group
- A feeling of being constantly watched

Chapter 12: The Goatman's Lair

- Discover a hidden lair deep in the woods
- A horrifying revelation awaits

Chapter 13: Descent into Madness

- Characters grapple with their sanity
- Unexplainable events intensify

Chapter 14: The Goatman's Call

- A hypnotic call draws the group deeper
- Internal conflicts escalate

Chapter 15: Sacrificial Night

- The group faces a choice to save themselves or succumb to the Goatman's curse
- Tension peaks as the night unfolds

Chapter 16: Midnight Ritual

- Ritualistic elements unfold
- The Goatman's power grows stronger

Chapter 17: The Final Confrontation

- Confrontation with the Goatman in a climactic battle
- Sacrifices made to break the curse

Chapter 18: Lingering Shadows

- The aftermath of the confrontation
- The group struggles to return to normalcy

Chapter 19: Epilogue of Fear

- Lingering fears and unanswered questions
- Hints that the Goatman may still be out there

Chapter 20: The Legend Lives On

- Closing with a new group stumbling upon the same legend
- The cycle continues, leaving the ending open-ended and unsettling

Chapter 1: The Unknown Encounter

The dense forest canopy loomed overhead, casting eerie shadows as the group of friends, led by the adventurous spirit of Mark, ventured deeper into the wilderness. A cool breeze rustled the leaves, creating an ominous symphony that echoed through the trees. Their laughter filled the air, a stark contrast to the quiet unease that settled with the setting sun.

As darkness embraced the forest, the friends gathered around a crackling campfire. The flickering flames danced to the rhythm of their hushed conversations. An unsettling feeling hung in the air,

unnoticed by most, except for Emily, who couldn't shake off the sensation that they were not alone.

Unknown to the group, distant whispers intertwined with the nocturnal symphony, carried by the wind. Mark, the leader of the expedition, dismissed them as the rustling of leaves or the murmur of the night creatures. Little did they know that these whispers were the first ominous notes of a malevolent tune.

As the night wore on, the friends shared stories, trying to drown out the disconcerting sounds around them. In the midst of laughter, a sudden silence fell upon the group, broken only by the distant howl of a lone wolf. They exchanged uneasy glances, their camaraderie momentarily fractured.

The crackling fire cast eerie shadows on the surrounding trees, creating grotesque shapes that seemed to watch the friends with malevolent intent. An inexplicable tension wrapped itself around them, tightening like a coil. Emily's gaze flickered nervously between the dancing flames and the dark recesses of the forest.

The once vibrant atmosphere now carried an undertone of dread. Mark, attempting to dispel the growing unease, suggested exploring the nearby trails. Reluctantly, the group ventured into the heart of the woods, guided only by dim flashlights that struggled to penetrate the thick darkness.

As they meandered through the labyrinthine paths, the night seemed to swallow them whole. The moon cast an eerie glow, revealing twisted branches that resembled skeletal fingers reaching out from the shadows. Unbeknownst to the friends, unseen eyes observed their every move.

The distant echoes of footsteps, not matching the rhythm of their own, reverberated through the night. A cold shiver ran down Emily's spine as she whispered to Mark, "Did you hear that?" He

dismissed it as their imagination playing tricks, but doubt lingered in his eyes.

The trail, once familiar, now felt like an ever-twisting maze. Panic set in as the friends realized they were lost. The forest seemed to conspire against them, distorting their perception of time and space. Anxiety gripped the group, amplifying the unsettling aura that clung to the night.

A blood-curdling scream shattered the silence, sending shockwaves through the group. Fear etched deep lines on their faces as they turned toward the source. In the suffocating darkness, a silhouette moved swiftly, disappearing among the gnarled trees.

Panic took hold, and the friends sprinted back towards the campsite, fueled by a primal instinct to survive. The once-familiar surroundings now felt alien and menacing. The forest, alive with unseen malevolence, seemed to mock their feeble attempts to escape.

The crackling campfire welcomed them back, but the safety it once provided now felt like a fragile illusion. The missing member, a specter in their midst, cast a long shadow over the group. The night, far from over, held secrets that would unravel as the friends clung to the flickering flames, unaware of the terror that awaited them in the heart of the haunted woods.

Chapter 2: Whispering Shadows

The remnants of their once-jovial campfire flickered in the oppressive darkness. Unsettled by the earlier scream, the friends huddled close, their faces etched with fear. Mark, the bravest among them, attempted to lighten the mood with nervous jokes, but the unease lingered like a thick fog.

As they sat in the ominous stillness, the haunting whispers returned. The friends exchanged anxious glances, realizing the sounds were more than mere forest murmurs. The words, though

unintelligible, seemed to crawl beneath their skin, instilling a primal fear that transcended rationality.

Emily, the most sensitive to the otherworldly, clutched her ears, desperate to block out the spectral voices. The whispers intertwined with the wind, creating an otherworldly melody that resonated through the haunted woods. Shadows danced menacingly, morphing into grotesque forms that seemed to mimic the torment in the friends' hearts.

Mark, determined to maintain a semblance of control, suggested investigating the source of the whispers. Armed with flashlights, the group ventured into the inky darkness, guided by the haunting voices that seemed to lead them deeper into the heart of the haunted woods.

The forest, now transformed into a realm of spectral uncertainty, played tricks on their senses. Trees twisted into nightmarish shapes, their branches reaching out like skeletal fingers. Each step felt like a descent into an abyss, and the whispers grew louder, forming an otherworldly chorus that resonated through the friends' minds.

A surreal fog enveloped the path, distorting reality. Shadows detached from the trees, taking on a sinister life of their own. Unseen eyes followed the group's every move, and the air became dense with an otherworldly energy that made it difficult to breathe.

Amidst the disorienting whispers, a distant figure materialized before them. The friends froze, their flashlights trembling in their hands. The silhouette seemed to flicker between the shadows, an elusive presence that defied comprehension. Panic gripped the group as the figure approached with an otherworldly grace.

With each step, the whispers intensified, revealing fragments of a haunting narrative. The legend of the Goatman, an entity that blurred the line between man and beast, echoed through the spectral voices. Dread tightened its grip on the friends as they realized

they were entangled in a story that surpassed the boundaries of the known.

A sudden gust of wind extinguished their flashlights, plunging them into pitch darkness. The whispers crescendoed into an unsettling cacophony, weaving a narrative that spoke of ancient curses and forbidden rituals. The friends stumbled blindly, guided only by the haunting voices that seemed to mock their feeble attempts to escape the encroaching nightmare.

As they fumbled through the labyrinthine paths, the forest itself seemed to conspire against them. Trees leaned menacingly, forming an impenetrable barrier that distorted their perception of space. Panic reached its zenith when the friends realized they were caught in a malevolent force beyond their understanding.

In the heart of the haunted woods, the whispers reached a deafening climax. The spectral figure, now a manifestation of pure terror, revealed itself as the harbinger of an ancient curse. The friends, paralyzed by fear, witnessed the birth of a nightmare that transcended the realm of the living.

The haunting voices echoed a chilling prophecy, sealing the friends' fate as pawns in a cosmic game. As the shadows enveloped them, the whispers faded into an ominous silence, leaving the group suspended in the chilling realization that they were now entwined with the legendary Goatman, and their journey into terror had only just begun.

Chapter 3: The Legend Unveiled

The haunted woods bore witness to the friends' descent into an abyss of fear, their breaths visible in the chilling air as they stood at the precipice of the unknown. Mark, the once-confident leader, now felt the weight of uncertainty press upon him, his eyes flickering nervously between the faces of his friends.

The chilling echoes of the Goatman's curse lingered, a sinister resonance that seeped into their very souls. As the group gathered around the remnants of their campfire, a shadowy figure materialized within the shifting shadows, a grotesque manifestation of the legend they had dismissed as mere folklore.

An air of disbelief hung heavy as the friends exchanged uneasy glances. Emily's wide eyes mirrored the terror reflected in the faces of the others. The whispers, now reduced to a haunting murmur, seemed to emanate from the very core of the forest, weaving a tapestry of dread that ensnared the group in an inescapable nightmare.

Against the backdrop of encroaching darkness, Mark attempted to rationalize the situation, attributing the spectral figure to mere illusions. However, the disconcerting reality betrayed his attempts at reassurance. The forest, alive with an otherworldly energy, pulsated with the ancient heartbeat of a malevolent force.

Doubt gnawed at the edges of the friends' minds as the whispers intensified. The spectral figure, now a tangible presence, beckoned them into the heart of the woods. The group, caught in the gravitational pull of an insidious force, hesitated on the brink of a decision that would seal their fate.

Reluctantly, they followed the elusive silhouette, their path illuminated by the pale glow of the moon. The forest, now a labyrinth of twisted shadows, seemed to breathe in tandem with the ethereal whispers that guided their journey. Unseen eyes observed their every move as they delved deeper into the legend that had come to life.

The friends stumbled upon an ancient clearing, adorned with eerie symbols etched into the earth. Mark, ever the skeptic, dismissed them as mere remnants of forgotten rituals. However, the others felt an otherworldly pull, an invisible thread connecting them to a malevolent past.

As the group examined the haunting symbols, the whispers coalesced into a narrative, recounting the tale of the Goatman—a creature that straddled the boundary between man and beast, a cursed entity bound by ancient rites. The friends, ensnared in the unfolding nightmare, now faced a reality that surpassed the confines of reason.

The spectral figure, a conduit of the Goatman's curse, revealed itself as a harbinger of impending doom. The friends, caught in the snare of a supernatural force, realized the legend was no mere folktale but a living nightmare that demanded their acknowledgment.

The moon cast an otherworldly glow upon the clearing as the group, paralyzed by a mixture of awe and terror, bore witness to the manifestation of the Goatman. A creature of nightmares stood before them, its eyes gleaming with an otherworldly intelligence that transcended the animalistic form it wore.

The atmosphere thickened with a palpable malevolence as the Goatman's presence dominated the clearing. Its form seemed to shift and contort, a grotesque dance that defied the laws of nature. The friends, gripped by an ancient fear, trembled as the Goatman spoke through the whispers, weaving a fate that intertwined with their very essence.

The friends, now bound by an unbreakable covenant, stood on the precipice of an unholy alliance. The Goatman, an embodiment of primordial terror, extended a spectral hand, inviting the group to embrace the curse that lurked within the shadows. Their destinies, forever altered, collided with the inexorable force of the legend, and the haunted woods echoed with the ominous laughter of a malevolent entity that reveled in the unfolding nightmare.

Chapter 4: A Fateful Decision

The haunted clearing pulsated with an otherworldly energy as the friends faced the enigmatic presence of the Goatman. The air

grew dense with the weight of an ancient curse, and the friends, caught between reason and the supernatural, found themselves at a crossroads that would define their destiny.

Mark, ever the voice of skepticism, hesitated. His logical mind resisted the pull of the unknown, urging him to reject the spectral hand that extended toward them. But the allure of the Goatman's power, shrouded in the whispers that echoed through the clearing, whispered promises of understanding and dominion over the mysterious forces that governed their existence.

Emily, sensitive to the ethereal currents, felt an irresistible draw. The whispers, now a seductive lullaby, caressed her consciousness, weaving visions of forbidden knowledge and a connection to realms beyond mortal comprehension. The choice lay before them, a perilous gambit that promised either enlightenment or descent into the abyss.

As the group teetered on the precipice of decision, the forest itself seemed to hold its breath. Unseen eyes observed their every move, and the shadows twisted in anticipation. The Goatman, a creature of the ancient woods, watched with an intelligence that transcended the animalistic facade it presented.

A cold wind whispered through the gnarled branches, carrying echoes of the past and the future. The choice, suspended in the eerie silence, would echo through the corridors of time, leaving an indelible mark on the souls of the friends who dared to confront the unknown.

In the midst of this spectral tableau, a memory surfaced in the recesses of Mark's mind—a childhood tale of a friend who disappeared in mysterious circumstances, whispered to be a victim of the Goatman's curse. The realization struck him like a bolt of lightning, igniting a primal fear that pulsed through his veins.

The haunting whispers morphed into chilling laughter, echoing Mark's internal turmoil. The Goatman, sensing the doubt, pressed its advantage, its eyes gleaming with an ancient malevolence. The clearing became a battleground of wills, where the tangible and intangible clashed in a dance of shadows.

As the friends deliberated, the forest responded to the rising tension. The ancient trees groaned, their branches contorting into grotesque forms. The whispers, now laced with impatience, intensified, urging the group to make their choice. The boundary between reality and nightmare blurred, and the friends found themselves ensnared in a surreal dreamscape.

Emily, tormented by the visions, trembled as conflicting emotions wrestled within her. The allure of forbidden knowledge clashed with an instinctual fear that warned of the consequences of tampering with forces beyond mortal understanding. The Goatman's eyes bore into her soul, a silent plea that transcended the limitations of spoken language.

Amidst the inner turmoil, a distant sound reverberated through the clearing—a mournful howl that cut through the spectral tension. The friends, momentarily distracted, turned toward the source. Shadows danced on the periphery of the clearing, and an unseen presence circled them like a predatory force.

The Goatman's form flickered, its patience wearing thin. The friends, aware of the imminent choice, felt the weight of the decision settle upon them like a suffocating cloak. The clearing, a stage for the cosmic drama, held its breath as the friends confronted the inevitable.

In a moment of collective resolve, the group stepped back from the outstretched hand of the Goatman. The whispers, now a discordant symphony of disappointment, echoed through the haunted

woods. The spectral figure, once a harbinger of alliance, recoiled into the shadows, its eyes aflame with an ancient ire.

As the friends retreated from the clearing, the forest sighed with relief. The ethereal tension dissipated, and the haunted woods returned to a semblance of stillness. The friends, marked by the encounter, stumbled back into the labyrinth of the forest, haunted by the knowledge that they had narrowly evaded a fate entwined with the Goatman's curse.

Yet, the shadows clung to their every step, and the whispers lingered, a reminder that the legend, far from defeated, awaited its next encounter with unsuspecting souls who dared to tread the boundary between the known and the supernatural. The night, pregnant with uncertainty, unfolded its mysteries as the friends navigated the haunted woods, forever changed by the fateful decision that spared them from the Goatman's insidious embrace.

T

Chapter 5: Signs of the Goatman

The haunted woods, having witnessed the friends' rejection of the Goatman's enticement, stirred with an ancient restlessness. The air crackled with latent energy as the group, still shaken from their encounter, navigated the twisting trails. The forest, once familiar, now seemed to shift and contort, its very essence reacting to the disturbance in the supernatural equilibrium.

Unspoken tension hung between the friends as they threaded through the labyrinth of shadows. The whispers, subdued but undeterred, lingered on the periphery of their consciousness. Emily, especially, felt the ethereal threads tugging at the edges of her sanity, weaving a tapestry of unnerving visions that threatened to unravel the fabric of her understanding.

A subtle rustling in the underbrush echoed through the stillness, sending a shiver down the spines of the friends. The forest seemed to

respond to their every step, alive with an unseen force that observed their every move. Paranoia took root, and the group cast nervous glances over their shoulders, half-expecting the Goatman's grotesque figure to materialize from the shadows.

Mark, burdened by the weight of his past and the consequences of the group's rejection, led the way with a furrowed brow. The once-confident leader now grappled with doubt, haunted by the memory of his childhood friend who had vanished into the clutches of the Goatman's curse. The forest, sensing his internal conflict, seemed to feed on his insecurities, twisting the trees into macabre forms that mirrored the tendrils of fear constricting his heart.

As they pressed forward, the trail revealed unsettling signs—twisted branches forming crude symbols, the earth marked with enigmatic patterns, and distant echoes that mimicked the mournful cries of the spectral creature they had narrowly evaded. The friends, unable to escape the omnipresent gaze of the haunted woods, exchanged wary glances as the realization dawned that the legend of the Goatman was far from a mere tale.

The group stumbled upon a clearing bathed in an eerie moonlit glow, its center dominated by a gnarled tree that bore the unmistakable markings of the supernatural. Emily, drawn by an invisible force, approached the ancient tree, her fingers tracing the symbols etched into its bark. The whispers, now a ghostly murmur, beckoned her to decipher the cryptic language of the Goatman's curse.

As Emily touched the symbols, the forest responded with a sudden surge of energy. The air crackled with an otherworldly charge, and the friends, captivated by a force beyond their control, witnessed the roots of the ancient tree twitch and writhe. The earth itself seemed to pulse with an unholy heartbeat as the symbols glowed with an ethereal light.

A ghostly apparition materialized before them, an echo of the Goatman's presence. Its eyes gleamed with an otherworldly intelligence, and a spectral voice resonated through the clearing. The friends, entranced by the unfolding spectacle, listened as the Goatman's tale unfolded—a story of ancient curses, forbidden pacts, and the insatiable hunger that bound it to the haunted woods.

As the spectral apparition spoke, the friends felt the tendrils of the Goatman's influence worming their way into their minds. Visions of torment and cosmic malevolence unfolded, weaving a narrative that blurred the boundaries between reality and nightmare. Emily, caught in the vortex of the supernatural revelation, glimpsed the unfathomable depths of the Goatman's ancient origins.

The whispers crescendoed, their words weaving an intricate web that ensnared the friends in a surreal dance of fate. The forest, now an extension of the Goatman's domain, pulsed with an ominous energy. The group, teetering on the precipice of enlightenment and damnation, faced the haunting reality that the legend had claimed them as unwilling participants in its insidious narrative.

In the midst of the ethereal revelation, a distant howl echoed through the clearing—a mournful cry that reverberated through the haunted woods. The spectral Goatman, its form flickering like a dying flame, receded into the shadows. The ancient tree, its roots once animated, settled into an eerie stillness.

The friends, released from the trance, stumbled backward, their minds reeling from the forbidden knowledge bestowed upon them. The clearing, now devoid of the Goatman's presence, returned to a deceptive calm. The haunted woods, however, retained the scars of their encounter, the symbols etched into the ancient tree serving as a chilling reminder that they were forever bound to the unfolding nightmare.

As the group retreated from the clearing, the forest whispered its secrets—a haunting lament that echoed through the shadows. The friends, marked by the signs of the Goatman, ventured deeper into the heart of the haunted woods, their destinies entwined with the ancient curse that refused to release its grip. The spectral whispers lingered, a spectral chorus that foretold of the terrors yet to unfold in the labyrinth of nightmares they now called home.

Chapter 6: Disappearing Act

The haunted woods, now saturated with the residual energy of the Goatman's revelation, clung to the friends like a suffocating shroud. The symbols etched into the ancient tree continued to glow with an otherworldly radiance, casting an eerie glow upon the path ahead. The air, thick with the weight of forbidden knowledge, pressed down on the group as they pressed forward, their fate intricately woven into the fabric of the supernatural.

Mark, haunted by the ghostly memories of his childhood friend's disappearance, felt an invisible force tugging at the edges of his consciousness. The whispers, once distant murmurs, now reverberated through his mind with an unsettling clarity. He strained to maintain composure, masking his internal turmoil behind a façade of false bravado. Unbeknownst to him, the haunted woods, sentient and malevolent, fed on his fear like a ravenous entity.

The trail, twisted and labyrinthine, seemed to shift with a will of its own. The friends, ensnared by the spectral threads that bound them to the Goatman's curse, navigated the surreal landscape with trepidation. The shadows played tricks on their senses, morphing into phantasmal shapes that seemed to watch with unseen eyes.

As the group delved deeper into the heart of the haunted woods, a palpable tension threaded through their camaraderie. Emily, marked by the spectral encounter at the ancient tree, felt an inexorable pull toward the unknown. The whispers, now a constant companion,

murmured secrets that transcended the realm of mortal understanding. Her eyes, once bright with curiosity, now reflected the unsettling wisdom bestowed upon her by the Goatman's revelation.

A distant howl echoed through the woods, a mournful cry that reverberated with a haunting resonance. The friends, halted by the spectral sound, exchanged uneasy glances. The Goatman's influence, a malevolent force that defied the natural order, now seemed to guide their every step. The path ahead, obscured by a foreboding mist, beckoned them into the heart of the supernatural enigma.

The trail, fraught with unseen perils, led the friends to a clearing bathed in an ethereal glow. A spectral figure materialized before them, its eyes gleaming with an otherworldly intelligence. The Goatman, a manifestation of cosmic dread, stood as a sentinel at the crossroads of their destiny.

In a voice that echoed through the haunted woods, the Goatman spoke, its words a haunting melody that resonated with the friends' deepest fears. The choices made, the destinies entwined, the group stood as unwitting participants in a cosmic drama that unfolded with a relentless momentum. The Goatman, a puppeteer of fate, reveled in the dance of shadows that played out in the haunted clearing.

As the spectral figure spoke, the surroundings warped into a surreal dreamscape. Reality and nightmare merged, and the friends found themselves suspended in a liminal space where time seemed to lose its meaning. Visions of the Goatman's cursed legacy unfolded—a tapestry of despair woven with threads of ancient malevolence.

Mark, tormented by memories of his lost friend, witnessed haunting scenes from the past. The woods became a theater of spectral apparitions, replaying moments of anguish and despair. The Goatman's voice, a spectral undertone, whispered forgotten secrets that clawed at the edges of his sanity.

Emily, sensitive to the ethereal currents, glimpsed glimpses of the future—a mosaic of tormented landscapes and spectral encounters. The haunted woods, now a maze of interconnected destinies, revealed a nightmarish tableau that unfolded with an inexorable inevitability.

As the visions played out, the friends, paralyzed by the supernatural revelation, became mere spectators in their own existential drama. The Goatman, a harbinger of cosmic terror, reveled in the torment it unleashed upon their minds. The clearing, a stage for the unfolding nightmare, pulsated with an otherworldly energy.

Suddenly, the visions ceased, and the friends, released from the spectral trance, found themselves standing in the clearing once more. The Goatman, its form flickering like a dying ember, faded into the shadows. The ancient tree, now devoid of the supernatural glow, stood as a silent witness to the cosmic theater that unfolded beneath its twisted branches.

The friends, disoriented and haunted by the echoes of the Goatman's revelations, staggered away from the clearing. The haunted woods, now a sentient labyrinth, seemed to rearrange itself, guiding the group deeper into the heart of the supernatural enigma.

As they pressed forward, a cold wind whispered through the twisted branches, carrying with it a chilling echo of the Goatman's laughter. The friends, caught in a cycle of existential dread, stumbled through the haunted woods, forever marked by the disappearing act that unfolded in the surreal clearing. The night, pregnant with cosmic uncertainty, stretched before them like an endless abyss, and the friends, ensnared by the spectral forces that governed their fate, plunged further into the inescapable nightmare that awaited in the shadowed depths of the ancient forest.

Chapter 7: Unholy Alliance

The haunted woods, now a realm of spectral uncertainty, closed in around the friends as they stumbled through the labyrinthine trails. The air was thick with an oppressive tension, and the whispers, once distant murmurs, reverberated through the trees with an unsettling urgency. Mark, Emily, and the rest of the group were mere pawns in a cosmic game, ensnared by the Goatman's curse, and each step they took seemed to propel them deeper into the heart of an insidious nightmare.

The trail, twisted and sinuous, led the friends to the edge of an ancient clearing. Moonlight filtered through the gnarled branches, casting an ethereal glow on the uneven ground. The clearing, marked by a series of grotesque symbols etched into the earth, seemed to pulse with a malevolent energy. Unseen eyes watched from the shadows as the friends hesitated at the threshold of the supernatural stage.

Emily, the once-curious soul now burdened by the weight of forbidden knowledge, felt an invisible force drawing her toward the center of the clearing. The whispers, now an incessant chorus, beckoned her to unravel the mysteries encoded in the symbols. A compulsion, an otherworldly pull, guided her steps as she approached the enigmatic patterns etched into the earth.

Mark, torn between the rational skepticism that had defined him and the growing influence of the Goatman's curse, cast wary glances at the symbols. The haunted woods, responsive to the internal struggles of the friends, seemed to warp and contort with a will of its own. Shadows danced in grotesque patterns, and the clearing became a stage for a supernatural spectacle.

The group, teetering on the brink of an abyss, gathered at the center of the clearing. Emily traced her fingers over the symbols, her touch unlocking a latent energy that pulsed through the earth. The whispers intensified, their spectral voices weaving a narrative

that echoed through the haunted woods—a tale of ancient alliances, cosmic conspiracies, and the inexorable dance between the living and the supernatural.

As Emily deciphered the symbols, the clearing transformed into a spectral panorama. Visions of the Goatman's cursed legacy unfolded, revealing a tapestry of intertwined destinies that stretched across epochs. The friends, now mere spectators in the cosmic drama, glimpsed fragments of the entity's tormented existence.

The Goatman, a creature bound by an unholy alliance with forces beyond mortal understanding, emerged as a tragic figure—a victim of a cosmic imbalance that demanded appeasement through unspeakable rituals and sacrifices. Its eyes, once gleaming with malevolence, now reflected a profound sadness that transcended the bestial form it wore.

The friends, ensnared in the unfolding revelation, witnessed scenes from the Goatman's past—a time when the ancient woods echoed with primal magic, and forbidden pacts were forged beneath the watchful gaze of eldritch entities. The haunted woods, a nexus of supernatural energies, became a stage for an age-old conflict that transcended the boundaries of time.

Mark, grappling with the conflicting forces that tore at his sanity, saw glimpses of the Goatman's interactions with lost souls—a spectral procession of individuals who had been entangled in the cosmic machinations of the ancient curse. The forest, a witness to centuries of suffering, whispered tales of tormented souls and unspeakable horrors that lurked in the shadowed depths.

The friends, released from the spectral visions, found themselves standing in the clearing once more. The symbols, now infused with a latent energy, pulsed with an otherworldly radiance. The Goatman, its form flickering between the grotesque and the tragic,

remained at the periphery of their perception, a spectral guardian of the haunted woods.

As the friends retreated from the clearing, a mournful howl echoed through the trees—a sound that transcended the natural world. The spectral alliance between the friends and the Goatman, forged by the revelation in the clearing, had sealed their destinies in an unholy covenant. The whispers, now a constant companion, guided them deeper into the labyrinth of the supernatural, their fates entwined with the spectral forces that governed the haunted woods.

The group, marked by the spectral encounter, pressed forward with a newfound awareness. The haunted woods, now an extension of the Goatman's domain, seemed to anticipate their every move. Shadows clung to the friends like a malevolent fog, and the air pulsed with an otherworldly energy that heightened the senses to the unseen threats that lurked in the shadows.

As they traversed the twisted trails, the group became acutely aware of an invisible tether connecting them to the Goatman's curse. The forest, alive with spectral currents, responded to their presence with a symphony of ethereal whispers. The alliance, forged in the clearing, propelled them toward a convergence of cosmic forces that awaited in the heart of the supernatural enigma.

The night, pregnant with uncertainty, stretched before the friends like an endless abyss. The haunted woods, a realm of shifting shadows and spectral whispers, beckoned them into the heart of the supernatural enigma. The Goatman, now an unseen puppeteer of their destinies, watched with an otherworldly intelligence as the group delved deeper into the spectral dance that awaited them in the shadowed depths.

Chapter 8: The Dance of Shadows

The haunted woods, now an extension of the Goatman's dominion, closed in around the friends as they ventured deeper into the labyrinth of shadows. The spectral alliance forged in the clearing bound them to the ancient curse, and with each step, the ethereal whispers seemed to guide their path. Mark, Emily, and the rest of the group were caught in a cosmic dance, their destinies entwined with the malevolent forces that governed the supernatural enigma.

The twisted trails led the friends to a secluded grove bathed in an otherworldly glow. Moonlight filtered through the gnarled branches, casting an ethereal pallor on the ground. The air crackled with latent energy, and the shadows played tricks on their senses. Unseen eyes observed their every move as the group hesitated at the edge of the spectral grove.

Emily, the unwitting conduit of forbidden knowledge, felt an invisible force pulling her toward the center of the grove. The whispers, now a spectral symphony, urged her to unravel the mysteries concealed within the ancient symbols etched into the earth. A compulsion, an otherworldly call, guided her steps as she approached the enigmatic patterns that pulsed with latent power.

Mark, torn between the skepticism that defined him and the growing influence of the Goatman's curse, cast wary glances at the symbols. The haunted woods, responsive to the internal struggles of the friends, seemed to warp and contort with a will of its own. Shadows danced in grotesque patterns, and the grove became a stage for a supernatural spectacle.

The rest of the group, caught in the gravitational pull of the Goatman's influence, gathered around Emily. The clearing, a nexus of spectral energies, hummed with an ominous resonance. Unseen forces coalesced, and the grove transformed into a gateway to the unknown.

As Emily traced her fingers over the symbols, the grove became a canvas for ethereal visions. The ancient curse, woven into the fabric of the haunted woods, unfolded before the friends like a nightmarish tapestry. The Goatman, a tragic figure shackled by an unholy alliance, emerged from the shadows, its form flickering with a spectral radiance.

The friends, ensnared in the unfolding revelation, witnessed scenes from the Goatman's existence—a journey through epochs marked by cosmic pacts, eldritch rituals, and the insatiable hunger that bound the entity to the supernatural realm. The grove, now a theater of spectral memories, echoed with the haunting cries of lost souls and the tormented echoes of ancient rites.

Mark, tormented by the conflicting forces that tore at his sanity, saw glimpses of the Goatman's interactions with souls who had been entangled in the cosmic machinations of the ancient curse. The forest, a silent witness to centuries of suffering, whispered tales of tormented spirits and unspeakable horrors that lurked in the shadowed depths.

Emily, sensitive to the ethereal currents, glimpsed fragments of the future—an ominous tableau that unfolded with an inexorable inevitability. The haunted woods, now a mosaic of interconnected destinies, revealed a nightmarish dance between the living and the spectral.

As the visions played out, the friends, released from the spectral trance, found themselves standing in the grove once more. The symbols, now infused with a latent energy, pulsed with an otherworldly radiance. The Goatman, its form flickering between the grotesque and the tragic, remained at the periphery of their perception, a spectral guardian of the haunted woods.

The friends, marked by the spectral encounter, retreated from the grove. The symbols, now charged with a malevolent force,

lingered in their consciousness like a haunting echo. The haunted woods, sentient and malevolent, responded to their presence with an unsettling intensity.

As the group pressed forward, the forest itself seemed to conspire against them. The twisted trails became a labyrinth, shifting with a will of their own. The spectral currents guided the friends deeper into the heart of the supernatural enigma, and the whispers, now an incessant chorus, reverberated through the haunted woods.

A sudden gust of wind whispered through the gnarled branches, carrying with it the mournful howl of the Goatman. The spectral alliance, forged in the grove, propelled the friends toward a convergence of cosmic forces that awaited in the shadowed depths. The night, fraught with unseen perils, stretched before them like an endless abyss, and the friends, ensnared by the spectral forces that governed their fate, plunged further into the inescapable dance of shadows that awaited in the ancient forest.

The twisted trails, illuminated by an otherworldly glow, led the group to the heart of the haunted woods. The whispers, now a cacophony of spectral voices, guided their every step, and the air pulsated with an ethereal energy that heightened the senses to the unseen threats that lurked in the shadows.

As the friends delved deeper, the forest itself seemed to morph into a surreal dreamscape. Trees contorted into nightmarish shapes, and the ground undulated like the surface of an otherworldly sea. Unseen eyes watched from the darkness, and the haunted woods, now a living entity, responded to their presence with a symphony of spectral echoes.

The group, now caught in a cosmic ballet, reached a clearing bathed in an otherworldly radiance. Symbols etched into the earth pulsed with an ancient power, and the whispers intensified, their spectral voices reaching a deafening crescendo. In the center of the

clearing stood a spectral figure—a manifestation of the Goatman's curse, its eyes gleaming with an otherworldly intelligence.

The friends, paralyzed by the unfolding spectacle, felt the air thicken with a malevolent force. The Goatman, now a puppeteer of their destinies, extended a spectral hand, inviting the group to join the cosmic dance. Mark, Emily, and the rest stood at the precipice of a choice that would seal their fate—a decision that transcended mortal understanding.

As the spectral figure beckoned, the haunted woods echoed with the haunting laughter of the Goatman. The friends, ensnared in the dance of shadows, stood at the nexus of the supernatural enigma, their destinies entwined with the ancient curse that governed the heart of the forest.

The night, fraught with cosmic uncertainty, stretched before the friends like an infinite canvas. The spectral grove, now a gateway to the unknown, beckoned them into the inescapable dance that awaited in the shadowed depths. The friends, marked by the ethereal revelations and the spectral alliance, plunged further into the heart of the haunted woods, where the Goatman's malevolent influence

Chapter 9: Pact with Shadows

The friends, standing on the precipice of the spectral clearing, felt the oppressive weight of the Goatman's influence bearing down upon them. The ethereal radiance cast an eerie glow on the symbols that pulsed with an otherworldly energy. The whispers, now an unrelenting cacophony, echoed through the haunted woods, urging the group to surrender to the cosmic dance that awaited.

Mark, the once-skeptical leader, hesitated, his eyes darting between the spectral figure and his companions. The forest, now a sentient entity, seemed to respond to his internal struggle, twisting the trees into grotesque forms that mirrored the tendrils of doubt

constricting his heart. Emily, sensitive to the ethereal currents, trembled as conflicting emotions wrestled within her.

The Goatman's eyes, gleaming with an ancient intelligence, bore into the souls of the friends. The haunted clearing became a battleground of wills, where the tangible and intangible clashed in a dance of shadows. Unseen forces whispered promises of enlightenment and power, luring the friends toward an unholy pact that defied the natural order.

In the face of the spectral invitation, the group felt a collective unease. The air crackled with tension, and the haunted woods, alive with spectral currents, seemed to conspire against them. The choice, a perilous gambit that promised either dominion over the supernatural or descent into eternal torment, hung in the balance.

As the friends deliberated, the grove transformed into a surreal dreamscape. Reality and nightmare merged, and the spectral figure at the center of the clearing became an ever-shifting enigma. The whispers, now a dissonant symphony, intensified, urging the group to embrace the Goatman's curse and become conduits for the malevolent forces that pulsed through the heart of the forest.

Emily, tormented by the conflicting forces that tugged at her soul, felt an irresistible pull toward the outstretched hand of the Goatman. The symbols etched into the earth seemed to respond to her internal turmoil, glowing with an intensity that mirrored the tumult within her consciousness. The friends, caught in the gravitational pull of an insidious force, stood at the crossroads of their destinies.

In a moment of collective resolve, the group stepped back from the spectral figure. The Goatman's eyes, once filled with a gleaming anticipation, narrowed with disappointment. The whispers, now a discordant lament, echoed through the haunted woods. The spectral figure, a harbinger of alliance, receded into the shadows, leaving

the friends standing in the clearing, marked by the weight of their choice.

The haunted woods, now a tapestry of shifting shadows and spectral echoes, responded to the rejection with a sinister sigh. The grove, once a gateway to the unknown, settled into an eerie stillness. The friends, released from the immediate threat, felt a mixture of relief and lingering dread.

As the group retreated from the clearing, the symbols etched into the earth seemed to pulse with a fading energy. The whispers, now reduced to a haunting murmur, lingered on the fringes of their consciousness. The haunted woods, while momentarily subdued, retained the scars of the friends' encounter, and the night unfolded with an ominous uncertainty.

The group, bound by the spectral alliance but defiant in the face of the Goatman's influence, ventured deeper into the labyrinth of shadows. The twisted trails, now a maze of spectral illusions, seemed to shift with a malevolent intent. The friends, caught in the ebb and flow of the supernatural currents, pressed forward with a cautious determination.

As they navigated the haunted woods, the spectral echoes intensified. Unseen eyes watched from the shadows, and the air became charged with an otherworldly energy. The friends, marked by the spectral encounter, felt the weight of the ancient curse lingering like a palpable presence. The night, pregnant with the unknown, whispered secrets that reverberated through the twisted branches.

Suddenly, a mournful howl echoed through the trees—a sound that transcended the natural world. The spectral alliance, though rejected in the clearing, continued to bind the friends to the Goatman's curse. The haunted woods, now a sentient entity, responded to their presence with an unsettling intensity.

The friends stumbled upon an ancient altar, hidden within the depths of the forest. The symbols engraved upon it mirrored those in the clearing, and the air pulsed with an otherworldly resonance. The whispers, now a siren's call, beckoned them to approach the altar, promising a communion with the supernatural forces that governed the haunted woods.

Mark, haunted by the memories of his lost friend and the consequences of the group's rejection, grappled with the inexorable pull toward the altar. The friends, caught between the desire for understanding and the fear of the unknown, hesitated at the threshold of the spectral enclave.

As they approached, the symbols on the altar glowed with an intensity that mirrored the ethereal currents within the haunted woods. The whispers, now a seductive melody, caressed their minds, weaving visions of power and transcendence. The Goatman's presence, though momentarily distant, lingered like a shadow cast upon the spectral canvas.

A choice loomed before the friends—a choice that would either cement their unholy alliance with the Goatman or cast them further into the abyss of the unknown. The haunted woods, alive with a malevolent energy, awaited the outcome of the cosmic dance that unfolded beneath its twisted canopy.

In a moment of collective hesitation, the friends stood at the edge of the altar, the symbols pulsating with an otherworldly radiance. The whispers, now a haunting serenade, reverberated through the haunted woods, weaving a narrative that transcended mortal understanding. The group, teetering on the brink of enlightenment and damnation, faced the haunting reality that the legend of the Goatman had claimed them as unwilling participants in its insidious narrative.

The night, draped in an ethereal mist, enveloped the friends as they stood at the crossroads of their destinies. The haunted woods, a realm of shifting shadows and spectral echoes, watched with an otherworldly intelligence as the group, bound by an unspoken pact, ventured further into the heart of the supernatural enigma. The night, now a canvas for the dance of shadows, whispered of terrors yet to unfold as the friends pressed forward, their footsteps echoing through the labyrinth of nightmares that awaited in the ancient forest.

Chapter 10: Veil of Shadows

The haunted woods, a labyrinth of shifting shadows and spectral echoes, enveloped the friends as they ventured deeper into the heart of the supernatural enigma. The spectral alliance, though rejected at the clearing, lingered like an unseen shroud, binding the group to the Goatman's curse. The twisted trails, now a maze of spectral illusions, seemed to warp with a malevolent intent, guiding the friends toward an unknown destination.

As the group pressed forward, the spectral echoes intensified. Unseen eyes watched from the shadows, and the air crackled with an otherworldly energy. The haunted woods, sentient and malevolent, responded to their presence with an unsettling intensity. The friends, marked by the spectral encounter, felt the weight of the ancient curse lingering like a palpable presence.

The whispers, once a dissonant symphony, now coalesced into a haunting serenade that reverberated through the twisted branches. Emily, sensitive to the ethereal currents, found herself caught in the ebb and flow of spectral energies. Visions of the Goatman's cursed legacy danced before her eyes—a tapestry of ancient alliances, forbidden pacts, and the insatiable hunger that bound the entity to the supernatural realm.

Mark, tormented by the memories of his lost friend and the consequences of their rejection, grappled with an internal struggle. The twisted trails seemed to twist with a will of their own, mirroring the tumult within his consciousness. The haunted woods, responsive to the friends' internal conflicts, conspired against them with a malevolent glee.

The friends stumbled upon an ancient altar, hidden within the depths of the forest. The symbols engraved upon it mirrored those in the clearing, and the air pulsed with an otherworldly resonance. The whispers, now a seductive melody, caressed their minds, weaving visions of power and transcendence. The Goatman's presence, though momentarily distant, lingered like a shadow cast upon the spectral canvas.

A choice loomed before the friends—a choice that would either cement their unholy alliance with the Goatman or cast them further into the abyss of the unknown. The haunted woods, alive with a malevolent energy, awaited the outcome of the cosmic dance that unfolded beneath its twisted canopy.

In a moment of collective hesitation, the friends stood at the edge of the altar, the symbols pulsating with an otherworldly radiance. The whispers, now a haunting serenade, reverberated through the haunted woods, weaving a narrative that transcended mortal understanding. The group, teetering on the brink of enlightenment and damnation, faced the haunting reality that the legend of the Goatman had claimed them as unwilling participants in its insidious narrative.

The night, draped in an ethereal mist, enveloped the friends as they stood at the crossroads of their destinies. The haunted woods, a realm of shifting shadows and spectral echoes, watched with an otherworldly intelligence as the group, bound by an unspoken pact, ventured further into the heart of the supernatural enigma. The

night, now a canvas for the dance of shadows, whispered of terrors yet to unfold as the friends pressed forward, their footsteps echoing through the labyrinth of nightmares that awaited in the ancient forest.

The twisted trails, illuminated by an otherworldly glow, led the group to the heart of the haunted woods. The whispers, now an incessant chorus, guided their every step, and the air pulsated with an ethereal energy that heightened the senses to the unseen threats that lurked in the shadows.

As the friends delved deeper, the forest itself seemed to morph into a surreal dreamscape. Trees contorted into nightmarish shapes, and the ground undulated like the surface of an otherworldly sea. Unseen eyes watched from the darkness, and the haunted woods, now a living entity, responded to their presence with a symphony of spectral echoes.

The group, now caught in a cosmic ballet, reached a clearing bathed in an otherworldly radiance. Symbols etched into the earth pulsed with an ancient power, and the whispers intensified, their spectral voices reaching a deafening crescendo. In the center of the clearing stood a spectral figure—a manifestation of the Goatman's curse, its eyes gleaming with an otherworldly intelligence.

The friends, paralyzed by the unfolding spectacle, felt the air thicken with a malevolent force. The Goatman, now a puppeteer of their destinies, extended a spectral hand, inviting the group to join the cosmic dance. Mark, Emily, and the rest stood at the precipice of a choice that would seal their fate—a decision that transcended mortal understanding.

As the spectral figure beckoned, the haunted woods echoed with the haunting laughter of the Goatman. The friends, ensnared in the dance of shadows, stood at the nexus of the supernatural enigma,

their destinies entwined with the ancient curse that governed the heart of the forest.

The night, fraught with cosmic uncertainty, stretched before the friends like an infinite canvas. The spectral grove, now a gateway to the unknown, beckoned them into the inescapable dance that awaited in the shadowed depths. The friends, marked by the ethereal revelations and the spectral alliance, plunged further into the heart of the haunted woods, where the Goatman's malevolent influence awaited.

The twisted trails, now a spectral tapestry, led the friends to a clearing bathed in an ethereal glow. Symbols etched into the earth pulsated with an otherworldly radiance, and the whispers, now a ghostly chorus, guided them to the center of the supernatural stage. The spectral figure, a manifestation of the Goatman's curse, awaited with eyes that gleamed with ancient knowledge.

In a moment of collective resolve, the friends stepped forward, surrendering to the cosmic dance that unfolded in the haunted clearing. The symbols, now infused with a latent energy, glowed with an intensity that mirrored the ethereal currents within the haunted woods. The whispers, a symphony of spectral voices, reached a crescendo, weaving a narrative that transcended mortal comprehension.

As the friends embraced the spectral invitation, the clearing transformed into a surreal dreamscape. Reality and nightmare merged, and the friends found themselves suspended in a liminal space where time seemed to lose its meaning. Visions of the Goatman's cursed legacy unfolded—a tapestry of intertwined destinies and cosmic malevolence.

Mark, tormented by the memories of his lost friend, witnessed haunting scenes from the past. The woods became a theater of spectral apparitions, replaying moments of anguish and despair. The

Goatman's voice, a spectral undertone, whispered forgotten secrets that clawed at the edges of his sanity.

Emily, sensitive to the ethereal currents, glimpsed fragments of the future—an ominous tableau that unfolded with an inexorable inevitability. The haunted woods, now a mosaic of interconnected destinies, revealed a nightmarish dance between the living and the spectral.

As the visions played out, the friends, paralyzed by the supernatural revelation, became mere spectators in their own existential drama. The Goatman, a harbinger of cosmic terror, reveled in the torment it unleashed upon their minds. The clearing, a stage for the unfolding nightmare, pulsated with an otherworldly energy.

Suddenly, the visions ceased, and the friends, released from the spectral trance, found themselves standing in the clearing once more. The Goatman, its form flickering like a

dying ember, faded into the shadows. The ancient tree, now devoid of the supernatural glow, stood as a silent witness to the cosmic theater that unfolded beneath its twisted branches.

The friends, disoriented and haunted by the echoes of the Goatman's revelations, stumbled away from the clearing. The haunted woods, now a sentient labyrinth, seemed to rearrange itself, guiding the group deeper into the heart of the supernatural enigma. The air, thick with the residue of spectral energy, clung to them like an intangible shroud.

As they pressed forward, a cold wind whispered through the twisted branches, carrying with it a chilling echo of the Goatman's laughter. The friends, caught in a cycle of existential dread, stumbled through the haunted woods, forever marked by the disappearing act that unfolded in the surreal clearing. The night, pregnant with cosmic uncertainty, stretched before them like an endless abyss.

The spectral alliance, rejected at the altar, continued to bind the friends to the Goatman's curse. The twisted trails, now a spectral tapestry, guided them with an otherworldly intelligence. Shadows clung to the group like a malevolent fog, and the air pulsed with an ethereal energy that heightened their senses to the unseen threats that lurked in the shadows.

As they traversed the haunted woods, the group became acutely aware of an invisible tether connecting them to the Goatman's curse. The forest, alive with spectral currents, responded to their presence with a symphony of ethereal whispers. The alliance, forged in the clearing, propelled them toward a convergence of cosmic forces that awaited in the heart of the supernatural enigma.

The night, fraught with unseen perils, stretched before the friends like an endless abyss. The haunted woods, a realm of shifting shadows and spectral whispers, beckoned them into the heart of the supernatural enigma. The Goatman, now an unseen puppeteer of their destinies, watched with an otherworldly intelligence as the group delved deeper into the spectral dance that awaited them in the shadowed depths.

The twisted trails, illuminated by an otherworldly glow, led the friends to an ancient ruin hidden within the depths of the haunted woods. The spectral echoes intensified, and the air crackled with an otherworldly energy. Unseen eyes watched from the darkness as the group hesitated at the threshold of the supernatural enclave.

Emily, sensitive to the ethereal currents, felt an invisible force drawing her toward the heart of the ruins. The whispers, now an incessant chorus, urged her to unravel the mysteries concealed within the ancient stones. A compulsion, an otherworldly pull, guided her steps as she approached the spectral threshold.

Mark, torn between rational skepticism and the growing influence of the Goatman's curse, cast wary glances at the ancient ruin.

The haunted woods, responsive to the internal struggles of the friends, seemed to warp and contort with a will of its own. Shadows danced in grotesque patterns, and the ruins became a stage for a supernatural spectacle.

The rest of the group, ensnared by the spectral forces that governed their fate, gathered around Emily. The ruins, a nexus of spectral energies, hummed with an ominous resonance. Unseen forces coalesced, and the ancient stones transformed into conduits for the ethereal currents that pulsed through the heart of the forest.

As Emily traced her fingers over the weathered stones, the ruins became a canvas for ethereal visions. The ancient curse, woven into the fabric of the haunted woods, unfolded before the friends like a nightmarish tapestry. The Goatman, a tragic figure shackled by an unholy alliance, emerged from the shadows, its form flickering with a spectral radiance.

The friends, ensnared in the unfolding revelation, witnessed scenes from the Goatman's existence—a journey through epochs marked by cosmic pacts, eldritch rituals, and the insatiable hunger that bound the entity to the supernatural realm. The ruins, now a theater of spectral memories, echoed with the haunting cries of lost souls and the tormented echoes of ancient rites.

Mark, tormented by the conflicting forces that tore at his sanity, saw glimpses of the Goatman's interactions with lost souls—a spectral procession of individuals who had been entangled in the cosmic machinations of the ancient curse. The forest, a silent witness to centuries of suffering, whispered tales of tormented spirits and unspeakable horrors that lurked in the shadowed depths.

Emily, sensitive to the ethereal currents, glimpsed fragments of the future—an ominous tableau that unfolded with an inexorable inevitability. The haunted woods, now a mosaic of interconnected

destinies, revealed a nightmarish dance between the living and the spectral.

As the visions played out, the friends, paralyzed by the supernatural revelation, became mere spectators in their own existential drama. The Goatman, a harbinger of cosmic terror, reveled in the torment it unleashed upon their minds. The ruins, a stage for the unfolding nightmare, pulsated with an otherworldly energy.

Suddenly, the visions ceased, and the friends, released from the spectral trance, found themselves standing in the ruins once more. The Goatman, its form flickering between the grotesque and the tragic, remained at the periphery of their perception, a spectral guardian of the haunted woods.

The friends, disoriented and haunted by the echoes of the Goatman's revelations, stumbled away from the ruins. The haunted woods, now a sentient labyrinth, seemed to rearrange itself, guiding the group deeper into the heart of the supernatural enigma. The air, thick with the residue of spectral energy, clung to them like an intangible shroud.

As they pressed forward, a cold wind whispered through the twisted branches, carrying with it a chilling echo of the Goatman's laughter. The friends, caught in a cycle of existential dread, stumbled through the haunted woods, forever marked by the disappearing act that unfolded in the surreal clearing. The night, pregnant with cosmic uncertainty, stretched before them like an endless abyss.

The spectral alliance, rejected at the ruins, continued to bind the friends to the Goatman's curse. The twisted trails, now a spectral tapestry, guided them with an otherworldly intelligence. Shadows clung to the group like a malevolent fog, and the air pulsed with an ethereal energy that heightened their senses to the unseen threats that lurked in the shadows.

As they traversed the haunted woods, the group became acutely aware of an invisible tether connecting them to the Goatman's curse. The forest, alive with spectral currents, responded to their presence with a symphony of ethereal whispers. The alliance, forged in the ruins, propelled them toward a convergence of cosmic forces that awaited in the heart of the supernatural enigma.

The night, fraught with unseen perils, stretched before the friends like an endless abyss. The haunted woods, a realm of shifting shadows and spectral whispers, beckoned them into the heart of the supernatural enigma. The Goatman, now an unseen puppeteer of their destinies, watched with an otherworldly intelligence as the group delved deeper into the spectral dance that awaited them in the shadowed depths.

The twisted trails, illuminated by an otherworldly glow, led the friends to an ancient grove concealed within the heart of the haunted woods. The spectral echoes intensified, and the air crackled with an otherworldly energy. Unseen eyes watched from the darkness as the group hesitated at the threshold of the supernatural enclave.

Emily, sensitive to the ethereal currents, felt an invisible force pulling her toward the center of the grove. The whispers, now an incessant chorus, urged her to unravel the mysteries concealed within the ancient trees. A compulsion, an otherworldly call, guided her steps as she approached the spectral threshold.

Mark, torn between rational skepticism and the growing influence of the Goatman's curse, cast wary glances at the ancient grove. The haunted woods, responsive to the internal struggles of the friends, seemed to warp and contort with a will of its own. Shadows danced in grotesque patterns, and the grove became a stage for a supernatural spectacle.

The rest of the group, ensnared by the spectral forces that governed their fate, gathered around Emily. The grove, a nexus

of spectral energies, hummed with an ominous resonance. Unseen forces coalesced, and the ancient trees transformed into conduits for the ethereal currents that pulsed through the heart of the forest.

As Emily traced her fingers over the gnarled bark, the grove became a canvas for ethereal visions. The ancient curse, woven into the fabric of the haunted woods, unfolded before the friends like a nightmarish tapestry. The Goatman, a tragic figure shackled by an unholy alliance, emerged from the shadows, its form flickering with a spectral radiance.

The friends, ensnared in the unfolding revelation, witnessed scenes from the Goatman's existence—a journey through epochs marked by cosmic pacts, eldritch rituals, and the insatiable hunger that bound the entity to the supernatural realm. The grove, now a theater of spectral memories, echoed with the haunting cries of lost souls and the tormented echoes of ancient rites.

Mark, tormented by the conflicting forces that tore at his sanity, saw glimpses of the Goatman's interactions with lost souls—a spectral procession of individuals who had been entangled in the cosmic machinations of the ancient curse. The forest, a silent witness to centuries of suffering, whispered tales of tormented spirits and unspeakable horrors that lurked in the shadowed depths.

Emily, sensitive to the ethereal currents, glimpsed fragments of the future—an ominous tableau that unfolded with an inexorable inevitability. The haunted woods, now a mosaic of interconnected destinies, revealed a nightmarish dance between the living and the spectral.

As the visions played out, the friends, paralyzed by the supernatural revelation, became mere spectators in their own existential drama. The Goatman, a harbinger of cosmic terror, reveled in the torment it unleashed upon their minds. The grove, a stage for the unfolding nightmare, pulsated with an otherworldly energy.

Suddenly, the visions ceased, and the friends, released from the spectral trance, found themselves standing in the grove once more. The Goatman, its form flickering between the grotesque and the tragic, remained at the periphery of their perception, a spectral guardian of the haunted woods.

The friends, disoriented and haunted by the echoes of the Goatman's revelations, stumbled away from the grove. The haunted woods, now a sentient labyrinth, seemed to rearrange itself, guiding the group deeper into the heart of the supernatural enigma. The air, thick with the residue of spectral energy, clung to them like an intangible shroud.

As they pressed forward, a cold wind whispered through the twisted branches, carrying with it a chilling echo of the Goatman's laughter. The friends, caught in a cycle of existential dread, stumbled through the haunted woods, forever marked by the disappearing act that unfolded in the surreal clearing. The night, pregnant with cosmic uncertainty, stretched before them like an endless abyss.

The spectral alliance, rejected at the grove, continued to bind the friends to the Goatman's curse. The twisted trails, now a spectral tapestry, guided them with an otherworldly intelligence. Shadows clung to the group like a malevolent fog, and the air pulsed with an ethereal energy that heightened their senses to the unseen threats that lurked in the shadows.

As they traversed the haunted woods, the group became acutely aware of

an invisible tether connecting them to the Goatman's curse. The forest, alive with spectral currents, responded to their presence with a symphony of ethereal whispers. The alliance, forged in the grove, propelled them toward a convergence of cosmic forces that awaited in the heart of the supernatural enigma.

The night, fraught with unseen perils, stretched before the friends like an endless abyss. The haunted woods, a realm of shifting shadows and spectral whispers, beckoned them into the heart of the supernatural enigma. The Goatman, now an unseen puppeteer of their destinies, watched with an otherworldly intelligence as the group delved deeper into the spectral dance that awaited them in the shadowed depths.

The twisted trails, illuminated by an otherworldly glow, led the friends to an ancient burial ground hidden within the heart of the haunted woods. The spectral echoes intensified, and the air crackled with an otherworldly energy. Unseen eyes watched from the darkness as the group hesitated at the threshold of the supernatural enclave.

Emily, sensitive to the ethereal currents, felt an invisible force pulling her toward the center of the burial ground. The whispers, now an incessant chorus, urged her to unravel the mysteries concealed within the ancient gravestones. A compulsion, an otherworldly call, guided her steps as she approached the spectral threshold.

Mark, torn between rational skepticism and the growing influence of the Goatman's curse, cast wary glances at the ancient burial ground. The haunted woods, responsive to the internal struggles of the friends, seemed to warp and contort with a will of its own. Shadows danced in grotesque patterns, and the burial ground became a stage for a supernatural spectacle.

The rest of the group, ensnared by the spectral forces that governed their fate, gathered around Emily. The burial ground, a nexus of spectral energies, hummed with an ominous resonance. Unseen forces coalesced, and the ancient gravestones transformed into conduits for the ethereal currents that pulsed through the heart of the forest.

As Emily traced her fingers over the weathered stones, the burial ground became a canvas for ethereal visions. The ancient curse, woven into the fabric of the haunted woods, unfolded before the friends like a nightmarish tapestry. The Goatman, a tragic figure shackled by an unholy alliance, emerged from the shadows, its form flickering with a spectral radiance.

The friends, ensnared in the unfolding revelation, witnessed scenes from the Goatman's existence—a journey through epochs marked by cosmic pacts, eldritch rituals, and the insatiable hunger that bound the entity to the supernatural realm. The burial ground, now a theater of spectral memories, echoed with the haunting cries of lost souls and the tormented echoes of ancient rites.

Mark, tormented by the conflicting forces that tore at his sanity, saw glimpses of the Goatman's interactions with lost souls—a spectral procession of individuals who had been entangled in the cosmic machinations of the ancient curse. The forest, a silent witness to centuries of suffering, whispered tales of tormented spirits and unspeakable horrors that lurked in the shadowed depths.

Emily, sensitive to the ethereal currents, glimpsed fragments of the future—an ominous tableau that unfolded with an inexorable inevitability. The haunted woods, now a mosaic of interconnected destinies, revealed a nightmarish dance between the living and the spectral.

As the visions played out, the friends, paralyzed by the supernatural revelation, became mere spectators in their own existential drama. The Goatman, a harbinger of cosmic terror, reveled in the torment it unleashed upon their minds. The burial ground, a stage for the unfolding nightmare, pulsated with an otherworldly energy.

Suddenly, the visions ceased, and the friends, released from the spectral trance, found themselves standing in the burial ground once more. The Goatman, its form flickering between the grotesque and

the tragic, remained at the periphery of their perception, a spectral guardian of the haunted woods.

The friends, disoriented and haunted by the echoes of the Goatman's revelations, stumbled away from the burial ground. The haunted woods, now a sentient labyrinth, seemed to rearrange itself, guiding the group deeper into the heart of the supernatural enigma. The air, thick with the residue of spectral energy, clung to them like an intangible shroud.

As they pressed forward, a cold wind whispered through the twisted branches, carrying with it a chilling echo of the Goatman's laughter. The friends, caught in a cycle of existential dread, stumbled through the haunted woods, forever marked by the disappearing act that unfolded in the surreal clearing. The night, pregnant with cosmic uncertainty, stretched before them like an endless abyss.

The spectral alliance, rejected at the burial ground, continued to bind the friends to the Goatman's curse. The twisted trails, now a spectral tapestry, guided them with an otherworldly intelligence. Shadows clung to the group like a malevolent fog, and the air pulsed with an ethereal energy that heightened their senses to the unseen threats that lurked in the shadows.

As they traversed the haunted woods, the group became acutely aware of an invisible tether connecting them to the Goatman's curse. The forest, alive with spectral currents, responded to their presence with a symphony of ethereal whispers. The alliance, forged in the burial ground, propelled them toward a convergence of cosmic forces that awaited in the heart of the supernatural enigma.

The night, fraught with unseen perils, stretched before the friends like an endless abyss. The haunted woods, a realm of shifting shadows and spectral whispers, beckoned them into the heart of the supernatural enigma. The Goatman, now an unseen puppeteer of their destinies, watched with an otherworldly intelligence as the

group delved deeper into the spectral dance that awaited them in the shadowed depths.

The twisted trails, illuminated by an otherworldly glow, led the friends to an ancient altar concealed within the heart of the haunted woods. The spectral echoes intensified, and the air crackled with an otherworldly energy. Unseen eyes watched from the darkness as the group hesitated at the threshold of the supernatural enclave.

Emily, sensitive to the ethereal currents, felt an invisible force pulling her toward the center of the altar. The whispers, now an incessant chorus, urged her to unravel the mysteries concealed within the ancient symbols. A compulsion, an otherworldly call, guided her steps as she approached the spectral threshold.

Mark, torn between rational skepticism and the growing influence of the Goatman's curse, cast wary glances at the ancient altar. The haunted woods, responsive to the internal struggles of the friends, seemed to warp and contort with a will of its own. Shadows danced in grotesque patterns, and the altar became a stage for a supernatural spectacle.

The rest of the group, ensnared by the spectral forces that governed their fate, gathered around Emily. The altar, a nexus of spectral energies, hummed with an ominous resonance. Unseen forces coalesced, and the ancient symbols transformed into conduits for the ethereal currents that pulsed through the heart of the forest.

As Emily traced her fingers over the weathered symbols, the altar became a canvas for ethereal visions. The ancient curse, woven into the fabric of the haunted woods, unfolded before the friends like a nightmarish tapestry. The Goatman, a tragic figure shackled by an unholy alliance, emerged from the shadows, its form flickering with a spectral radiance.

The friends, ensnared in the unfolding revelation, witnessed scenes from the Goatman's existence—a journey through epochs

marked by cosmic pacts, eldritch rituals, and the insatiable hunger that bound the entity to the supernatural realm. The altar, now a theater of spectral memories, echoed with the haunting cries of lost souls and the tormented echoes of ancient rites.

Mark, tormented by the conflicting forces that tore at his sanity, saw glimpses of the Goatman's interactions with lost souls—a spectral procession of individuals who had been entangled in the cosmic machinations of the ancient curse. The forest, a silent witness to centuries of suffering, whispered tales of tormented spirits and unspeakable horrors that lurked in the shadowed depths.

Emily, sensitive to the ethereal currents, glimpsed fragments of the future—an ominous tableau that unfolded with an inexorable inevitability. The haunted woods, now a mosaic of interconnected destinies, revealed a nightmarish dance between the living and the spectral.

As the visions played out, the friends, paralyzed by the supernatural revelation, became mere spectators in their own existential drama. The Goatman, a harbinger of cosmic terror, reveled in the torment it unleashed upon their minds. The altar, a stage for the unfolding nightmare, pulsated with an otherworldly energy.

Suddenly, the visions ceased, and the friends, released from the spectral trance, found themselves standing before the altar once more. The Goatman, its form flickering between the grotesque and the tragic, remained at the periphery of their perception, a spectral guardian of the haunted woods.

The friends, disoriented and haunted by the echoes of the Goatman's revelations, stumbled away from the altar. The haunted woods, now a sentient labyrinth, seemed to rearrange itself, guiding the group deeper into the heart of the supernatural enigma. The air, thick with the residue of spectral energy, clung to them like an intangible shroud.

As they pressed forward, a cold wind whispered through the twisted branches, carrying with it a chilling echo of the Goatman's laughter. The friends, caught in a cycle of existential dread, stumbled through the haunted woods, forever marked by the disappearing act that unfolded in the surreal clearing. The night, pregnant with cosmic uncertainty, stretched before them like an endless abyss.

The spectral alliance, rejected at the altar, continued to bind the friends to the Goatman's curse. The twisted trails, now a spectral tapestry, guided them with an otherworldly intelligence. Shadows clung to the group like a malevolent fog, and the air pulsed with an ethereal energy that heightened their senses to the unseen threats that lurked in the shadows.

As they traversed the haunted woods, the group became acutely aware of an invisible tether connecting them to the Goatman's curse. The forest, alive with spectral currents, responded to their presence with a symphony of ethereal whispers. The alliance, forged in the altar, propelled them toward a convergence of cosmic forces that awaited in the heart of the supernatural enigma.

Chapter 11: Echoes of Betrayal

The haunted woods, now pulsating with an otherworldly energy, closed in around the friends like a malevolent embrace. The spectral alliance, an invisible tether, bound them to the Goatman's curse, and the twisted trails led them deeper into the heart of the supernatural enigma. Each step resonated with an eerie echo, as if the forest itself whispered tales of ancient treacheries.

The air, thick with a palpable tension, seemed to vibrate with the echoes of spectral voices. Unseen eyes watched from the shadows, and the friends felt the weight of the Goatman's malevolent gaze upon them. Emily, still sensitive to the ethereal currents, shivered as the whispers intensified, weaving a narrative of betrayal and impending doom.

Mark, haunted by the memories of his lost friend and the shifting allegiances within the group, struggled to maintain a semblance of composure. The haunted woods, now a labyrinth of twisted shadows, seemed to mirror the turmoil within his mind. Visions of the Goatman's cursed legacy clashed with the reality of their journey, blurring the lines between nightmare and waking.

As the friends ventured further, the twisted trails guided them to an ancient grove bathed in an unnatural glow. The spectral echoes intensified, and the air crackled with an otherworldly energy. Symbols etched into the trees pulsed with an ethereal radiance, casting grotesque shadows that danced with a life of their own.

In the center of the grove stood a spectral figure—a manifestation of the Goatman's curse, its eyes gleaming with an otherworldly intelligence. The friends, transfixed by the haunting presence, felt the weight of an unspoken invitation. The grove, now a stage for a cosmic drama, beckoned them to confront the echoes of betrayal that lingered in the shadows.

Emily, driven by a compulsion she could not resist, approached the spectral figure. The whispers, now a dissonant symphony, reverberated through the grove, casting a haunting spell upon the group. The friends, their senses heightened by the spectral energy, became acutely aware of the invisible threads that connected them to the Goatman's curse.

As Emily reached out, the spectral figure extended a ghostly hand. A surge of ancient memories flooded her consciousness—a tapestry of betrayals and alliances that transcended mortal understanding. The Goatman's voice, a haunting undertone, whispered forgotten secrets that clawed at the edges of her sanity.

Mark, torn between the mistrust within the group and the allure of the Goatman's promises, grappled with an internal tempest. Shadows cast by the ethereal glow contorted into grotesque shapes,

mirroring the conflicting emotions that tormented him. The grove, now a battleground of spectral forces, awaited the resolution of the internal strife that threatened to tear the group apart.

The rest of the friends, ensnared by the spectral drama, watched with a mixture of fear and fascination. The grove, bathed in an otherworldly radiance, became a theater for the unfolding nightmare. The Goatman's laughter, a haunting melody, echoed through the ancient trees, marking the friends as unwilling participants in its cosmic play.

Suddenly, the spectral figure and Emily recoiled as if struck by an unseen force. The grove, now plunged into an eerie silence, seemed to hold its breath. The spectral alliance, momentarily disrupted, cast a shadow of uncertainty upon the friends.

A voice, neither human nor spectral, resonated through the grove—a chorus of ancient whispers that spoke of broken pacts and the consequences of defiance. The friends, still caught in the ethereal web, felt the weight of the Goatman's judgment looming over them.

The grove, once a sanctuary of spectral revelations, became a battleground between the friends and the malevolent forces that sought to manipulate their destinies. The twisted trails, now obscured by shifting shadows, led the group deeper into the heart of the haunted woods, where the echoes of betrayal whispered of darker truths yet to unfold.

As the friends pressed forward, the spectral alliance tightened its grip, binding them to the Goatman's curse with an unbreakable resolve. The haunted woods, now a realm of shifting shadows and unseen perils, seemed to anticipate their every move. Each step echoed with the weight of ancient choices, and the air pulsed with an otherworldly energy that foretold of imminent horrors.

The twisted trails, like serpentine veins, guided the friends to an ancient ruin hidden within the depths of the haunted woods.

Symbols etched into the stones glowed with an ethereal radiance, and the air hummed with a spectral resonance. Unseen eyes watched from the darkness, and the ruins became a threshold to the unknown.

As the friends hesitated at the entrance, the whispers intensified, forming a cacophony of spectral voices that spoke of forgotten oaths and the inevitable descent into darkness. Emily, still bearing the weight of the spectral revelation, felt a compulsion to unravel the mysteries concealed within the ruins.

Mark, his trust shattered by the echoes of betrayal, cast wary glances at the ancient stones. The haunted woods, now alive with a malevolent energy, seemed to pulse with the heartbeat of an ancient evil. Shadows danced upon the ruins, casting ominous shapes that hinted at the horrors waiting within.

The rest of the group, caught in the web of the Goatman's curse, gathered around Emily. The ruins, a nexus of spectral energies, beckoned them to confront the consequences of their choices. The ancient stones, infused with an otherworldly power, awaited the unfolding of a cosmic drama that transcended the boundaries of mortal understanding.

As Emily traced her fingers over the weathered symbols, the ruins became a canvas for ethereal visions. The ancient curse, woven into the fabric of the haunted woods, unfolded before the friends like a nightmarish tapestry. The Goatman, a tragic figure shackled by an unholy alliance, emerged from the shadows, its form flickering with a spectral radiance.

The friends, ensnared in the unfolding revelation, witnessed scenes from the Goatman's existence—a journey through epochs marked by cosmic pacts, eldritch rituals, and the insatiable hunger that bound the entity to the supernatural realm. The ruins, now a

theater of spectral memories, echoed with the haunting cries of lost souls and the tormented echoes of ancient rites.

Mark, tormented by the conflicting forces that tore at his sanity, saw glimpses of the Goatman's interactions with lost souls—a spectral procession of individuals who had been entangled in the cosmic machinations of the ancient curse. The forest, a silent witness to centuries of suffering, whispered tales of tormented spirits and unspeakable horrors that lurked in the shadowed depths.

Emily, sensitive to the ethereal currents, glimpsed fragments of the future—an ominous tableau that unfolded with an inexorable inevitability. The haunted woods, now a mosaic of interconnected destinies, revealed a nightmarish dance between the living and the spectral.

As the visions played out, the friends, paralyzed by the supernatural revelation, became mere spectators in their own existential drama. The Goatman, a harbinger of cosmic terror, reveled in the torment it unleashed upon their minds. The ruins, a stage for the unfolding nightmare, pulsated with an otherworldly energy.

Suddenly, the visions ceased, and the friends, released from the spectral trance, found themselves standing within the ancient ruins once more. The Goatman, its form flickering between the grotesque and the tragic, remained a spectral presence at the periphery of their perception. The ruins, now silent and foreboding, seemed to anticipate the next chapter in the cosmic drama.

The friends, shaken by the spectral revelations, exchanged uneasy glances. The twisted trails, like a river of shadows, beckoned them deeper into the heart of the haunted woods. The air, heavy with the residue of ethereal energy, clung to them as a constant reminder of the supernatural forces that governed their fate.

As they ventured forth, the ruins behind them, the haunted woods seemed to close in, its twisted branches forming an impenetrable

canopy above. Shadows danced along the gnarled trunks, and the ground beneath their feet pulsed with an otherworldly heartbeat. The friends, now bound by the unseen threads of the Goatman's curse, pressed on with a mixture of dread and determination.

The twisted trails led them to a clearing bathed in an eerie, spectral light. In the center stood an ancient altar, adorned with symbols that seemed to writhe and shift in the dim illumination. The air became charged with an unsettling energy, and the friends felt the weight of the Goatman's gaze upon them once more.

Emily, still influenced by the ethereal currents, approached the altar with a sense of inevitability. The whispers, now a haunting chorus, seemed to guide her every step. The friends, unable to resist the unseen forces that governed their journey, gathered around the ancient stone structure.

As Emily reached out to touch the symbols, the altar responded with a surge of spectral energy. Visions unfolded before her eyes—scenes of ancient rituals, cosmic pacts, and the intertwining destinies of those who had crossed paths with the Goatman. The friends, ensnared in the ethereal spectacle, witnessed the tragic tales of souls bound to an ancient curse.

Mark, his skepticism eroded by the relentless onslaught of supernatural revelations, saw the threads of fate weaving around the group. The haunted woods, now a stage for cosmic machinations, echoed with the tormented cries of lost souls and the spectral laughter of the Goatman. The air crackled with an ominous resonance, and the ground seemed to shift beneath their feet.

The rest of the group, caught in the spectral current, felt the altar's power enveloping them. Shadows danced upon their faces, mirroring the ancient struggles playing out in the unseen realms. The Goatman, a puppeteer of destinies, reveled in the unfolding

drama as the friends teetered on the precipice of their own cosmic unraveling.

A voice, echoing from the depths of the haunted woods, resonated through the clearing—a haunting lamentation that spoke of betrayal, cosmic bargains, and the unrelenting hunger that bound the Goatman to its cursed existence. The friends, now witnesses to the unfolding tragedy, felt the weight of their choices bearing down upon them.

Emily, guided by an otherworldly compulsion, spoke words that seemed to echo with ancient power. The symbols on the altar glowed brighter, and the spectral light enveloped the friends. The haunted woods, alive with the energy of forgotten pacts, seemed to respond to Emily's invocation, and the air crackled with an ethereal electricity.

The friends, now connected by an invisible web of fate, felt the boundaries between the living and the spectral blur. The clearing transformed into a surreal tableau—a nexus of cosmic energies that defied mortal comprehension. The Goatman, its spectral form looming large, became a focal point in the unfolding ritual.

As the spectral light reached its zenith, the haunted woods seemed to hold its breath. The air became charged with an otherworldly tension, and the friends braced themselves for the unknown. Shadows, twisted and contorted, converged upon the clearing, forming a veil between the mortal realm and the supernatural forces that lurked beyond.

Suddenly, the spectral light extinguished, plunging the clearing into darkness. The friends, disoriented and surrounded by an oppressive silence, found themselves standing in the aftermath of the ritual. The Goatman's laughter echoed through the haunted woods, mocking the futility of mortal endeavors.

The twisted trails, now obscured by the lingering shadows, beckoned the friends deeper into the heart of the supernatural enigma. The air, thick with the residue of spectral energies, clung to them as a spectral shroud. The haunted woods, a labyrinth of cosmic horrors, seemed to whisper tales of their impending doom.

As the friends pressed forward, the spectral alliance tightening its grip, they became unwitting participants in a nightmare woven from the threads of ancient curses and cosmic machinations. The Goatman, a spectral puppeteer, reveled in the torment it unleashed upon their minds. The haunted woods, a realm of shifting shadows and unseen perils, awaited the next chapter in the unfolding cosmic drama.

Chapter 12: Whispers in the Shadows

The twisted trails guided the friends through the haunted woods, a realm now saturated with the lingering echoes of the ritual. The air crackled with an unsettling energy, and the shadows seemed to writhe with a newfound malevolence. The Goatman's curse, an invisible tether, bound them tighter as they delved deeper into the heart of the supernatural enigma.

The friends, haunted by the spectral revelations and the unsettling ritual, pressed on with a sense of trepidation. Each step through the dense undergrowth echoed with an ominous resonance, and the twisted branches overhead formed a canopy that blocked out the moonlight. The darkness seemed to pulse with a life of its own, and unseen eyes watched their every move.

As they traversed the haunted woods, Mark's gaze darted nervously between the shifting shadows. The Goatman's laughter lingered in the air, a haunting reminder of their entanglement with cosmic forces beyond their understanding. Doubt gnawed at Mark's sanity, and the trust between the friends strained under the weight of unseen horrors.

Emily, still influenced by the ethereal currents, walked with a purpose that seemed guided by forces beyond her control. The whispers, now a dissonant symphony, surrounded her like a spectral aura. The friends, ensnared in the spectral web, followed Emily as the twisted trails led them to a clearing bathed in an otherworldly glow.

In the center of the clearing stood a dilapidated mansion, its decaying façade casting eerie shadows in the spectral light. The air hummed with a haunting melody, and the friends felt an inexplicable compulsion to enter the mansion. The Goatman's curse, now a palpable force, seemed to emanate from the ancient structure.

As they approached the mansion, its doors creaked open with a ghostly wail. The interior, shrouded in darkness, exuded a malevolent energy. Unseen whispers echoed through the halls, recounting the tragic tales of those who had crossed paths with the Goatman within these haunted walls.

The friends hesitated at the threshold, a silent acknowledgment of the impending horrors awaiting them. Emily, still under the influence of the spectral forces, stepped forward with an unwavering determination. The mansion seemed to welcome her, its walls pulsating with an unseen heartbeat.

As the friends entered, the doors slammed shut behind them, sealing their fate within the spectral confines of the mansion. The air grew colder, and the walls whispered tales of betrayal, sacrifice, and the unrelenting hunger that bound the Goatman to its cursed existence. Shadows danced along the corridors, casting grotesque silhouettes that seemed to mock the intruders.

The mansion, a labyrinth of forgotten memories and spectral horrors, unfolded its secrets with each creaking floorboard and echoing whisper. The friends, now prisoners of the spectral drama, ventured deeper into the heart of the ancient structure. The Goatman's

laughter, a sinister undertone, reverberated through the halls, guiding them toward an inevitable confrontation.

Rooms adorned with dusty relics told stories of a bygone era, where the mansion was once a place of decadence and opulence. Now, draped in an ethereal gloom, the grandeur had given way to a pervading sense of decay. Paintings on the walls seemed to watch the intruders with hollow eyes, capturing moments of torment and despair.

Emily, compelled by unseen forces, led the group to a grand hall adorned with a twisted chandelier that cast eerie patterns of light. In the center stood a forgotten altar, covered in cryptic symbols. The air thickened with a spectral presence, and the friends felt the weight of unseen eyes upon them.

As Emily approached the altar, the whispers intensified, forming a cacophony that echoed through the mansion. Visions of ancient rituals played out before the friends, a tapestry of eldritch ceremonies and sacrificial rites. The Goatman's curse, woven into the very fabric of the mansion, revealed its darkest secrets.

Mark, his skepticism now replaced by a growing dread, watched as the spectral energy coalesced around Emily. Shadows danced upon the walls, forming grotesque figures that seemed to writhe in agony. The grand hall became a theater for the unfolding nightmare, with the friends as unwilling actors in a cosmic play.

The rest of the group, caught in the spectral current, stood as witnesses to the ancient forces that manipulated their destinies. The Goatman, now a looming presence within the grand hall, revealed itself with a spectral radiance. The air crackled with an otherworldly electricity as the friends braced themselves for the climax of the haunting spectacle.

Emily, her eyes now reflecting the eerie glow of the altar, spoke words that resonated with ancient power. The symbols etched into

the stone seemed to come alive, glowing brighter with each incantation. The grand hall pulsed with a spectral energy, and the friends felt the very fabric of reality unraveling around them.

A rift, a tear in the fabric of the supernatural, opened before the altar. From the depths emerged the Goatman, its form flickering with a malevolent radiance. The friends, now faced with the spectral entity, felt a chill that transcended the physical realm. The Goatman's laughter, a haunting melody, echoed through the grand hall.

The friends, caught in the grip of the Goatman's curse, were now mere pawns in its cosmic machinations. The mansion, a stage for the unfolding nightmare, seemed to warp and contort with the weight of ancient malevolence. Shadows, now animated with spectral life, closed in around the group, forming a suffocating shroud.

The Goatman, its voice echoing through the halls, spoke of cosmic bargains and the inevitable descent into darkness. The grand hall became a battleground for the friends' sanity as the Goatman's words clawed at the edges of their minds. The spectral currents, now a tempest of unseen forces, whipped through the mansion with an otherworldly fury.

As the friends stood before the altar, a choice loomed in the shadows—an offering to the Goatman or a futile attempt to defy the cosmic forces that bound them. The air crackled with an impending doom, and the grand hall seemed to hold its breath in anticipation of the friends' decision.

Emily, now a conduit for the Goatman's curse, faced the friends with hollow eyes. The whispers, once a dissonant symphony, became a unified chorus urging them toward the inevitable. The spectral threads tightened, pulling the friends into the cosmic dance that awaited its final act within the haunted mansion.

The friends, their fates entwined with the Goatman's curse, stood at the precipice of their own unraveling. The grand hall, a

silent witness to centuries of spectral torment, seemed to echo with the cries of lost souls and the laughter of an entity that defied mortal understanding.

The twisted trails, once a path through the haunted woods, now extended into the very fabric of their existence. The spectral alliance, an unbreakable bond, bound them to the Goatman's curse with an inescapable resolve. The friends, now faced with a choice that would seal their destinies, braced themselves for the next chapter in the cosmic nightmare that unfolded within the walls of the haunted mansion.

Chapter 13: Pact with the Shadows

The grand hall, now a stage for the unfolding cosmic drama, held its breath as the friends stood before the ancient altar. The Goatman, its spectral form flickering with malevolent radiance, loomed over them like a puppeteer orchestrating the final act of a nightmarish play. The air crackled with ethereal energy, and shadows clung to the walls, whispering tales of ancient pacts and unspeakable horrors.

Emily, a conduit for the Goatman's curse, raised her arms as if guided by unseen hands. The symbols on the altar pulsed with an otherworldly glow, and the friends felt the spectral currents intensify. The grand hall seemed to warp, its dimensions shifting in response to the cosmic forces at play. The Goatman's laughter echoed through the mansion, a haunting melody that heralded the imminent climax.

The friends, ensnared by the spectral alliance, felt the weight of the Goatman's gaze upon them. Unseen threads tightened, binding them to the ancient curse that now permeated the very fabric of the mansion. Mark, tormented by doubt and the shadows of betrayal, struggled to comprehend the unfolding nightmare. The grand hall, once a sanctuary of opulence, now exuded a malevolent aura that seeped into the marrow of their bones.

As Emily spoke the incantations, the spectral energy coalesced into a swirling vortex above the altar. The rift, a tear in the fabric of reality, widened, revealing glimpses of a cosmic void that defied mortal comprehension. The Goatman's voice, now a chorus of haunting whispers, echoed through the rift, speaking of forbidden knowledge and the inevitability of their entanglement with the supernatural.

The friends, caught in the grip of the Goatman's curse, felt an inexorable pull toward the cosmic void. Shadows danced upon the edges of the rift, forming grotesque figures that seemed to beckon them into the unknown. The grand hall, now a gateway to cosmic horrors, awaited the friends' choice—submit to the Goatman's influence or defy the cosmic forces that sought to unravel their existence.

Mark, his mind a tempest of conflicting emotions, looked to the other friends. Their faces mirrored the uncertainty that gnawed at his sanity. The Goatman's laughter, a maddening cacophony, intensified as the rift pulsed with an otherworldly glow. The decision, an irreversible pact with the shadows, loomed before them like a specter of doom.

Emily, her eyes hollow and distant, uttered words that seemed to resonate with the very fabric of the supernatural. The friends, compelled by unseen forces, stepped closer to the rift. The grand hall seemed to blur, its boundaries dissolving as the spectral energies surged around them.

Suddenly, the mansion trembled as if in response to an ancient power. The Goatman's laughter, once triumphant, faltered for a moment. The friends, caught in the grip of the cosmic tempest, felt a shift in the spectral currents. The rift, now a pulsating maw, cast an eerie glow upon their faces.

A voice, neither human nor spectral, reverberated through the grand hall—a lamentation that spoke of cosmic balance and the

consequences of meddling with forces beyond mortal understanding. The Goatman, its spectral form recoiling as if struck by an unseen force, hissed with an otherworldly fury.

The friends, momentarily released from the ethereal trance, found themselves standing at the precipice of the rift. The grand hall, now a battleground between cosmic entities, seemed to hold its breath in anticipation of the friends' next move.

Mark, his rational mind clashing with the supernatural forces that surrounded him, hesitated. The Goatman's curse, now weakened but far from defeated, still pulsed through the mansion. Shadows, like tendrils of malevolence, reached out from the walls, whispering promises of forbidden knowledge and unspeakable power.

The other friends, their faces etched with the struggle of internal conflicts, looked to Mark as if seeking guidance. The grand hall, a silent witness to their existential torment, seemed to echo with the cries of lost souls and the laughter of entities that defied mortal comprehension.

In that moment of hesitation, the Goatman's laughter resurged with a renewed malevolence. The spectral currents, like an invisible tide, surged forward, pulling the friends closer to the rift. Shadows clung to them, entwining with the unseen threads that bound them to the ancient curse.

Emily, still under the influence of the Goatman's influence, stepped closer to the rift. The grand hall, now a surreal tableau of cosmic conflict, seemed to warp and contort with the weight of ancient malevolence. The air, thick with the residue of spectral energy, clung to them as a suffocating shroud.

Mark, torn between defiance and the allure of forbidden power, felt the weight of the Goatman's gaze upon him. The rift, a gateway to the unknown, beckoned with a promise of cosmic revelations.

The friends, now at the mercy of supernatural forces, stood on the brink of a choice that would seal their destinies.

As Emily extended her hand toward the rift, the grand hall vibrated with an otherworldly resonance. The Goatman, its form flickering with a desperate fury, hissed with a spectral voice that echoed through the very fabric of the mansion. The friends, caught in the cosmic struggle, felt a surge of unseen forces that threatened to tear their souls asunder.

A voice, ancient and authoritative, cut through the chaos. It spoke of cosmic balance and the need for mortals to resist the temptations that lurked within the shadows. The rift, now a swirling maelstrom of spectral energy, seemed to respond to the authoritative voice.

The Goatman's laughter waned, replaced by an eerie silence. The friends, their minds still entangled in the ethereal web, witnessed the rift's transformation. The cosmic void, once a gateway to the unknown, now shimmered with a tranquil luminescence. Shadows receded, revealing the grand hall in its original state.

The friends, released from the spectral trance, found themselves standing in the mansion's grand hall. The Goatman, its presence diminished but not vanquished, lingered at the periphery of their perception. The air, now devoid of the suffocating spectral shroud, held a sense of uneasy calm.

The authoritative voice, a guiding force that had intervened in the cosmic struggle, echoed through the mansion. It spoke of the friends' resilience in the face of cosmic temptation and the importance of maintaining the delicate balance between the mortal realm and the supernatural. The grand hall, now free from the oppressive malevolence that had gripped it, seemed to regain a semblance of its former opulence. Paintings on the walls, once twisted depictions of torment, now appeared as mere artistic renderings. The dilapidated

mansion, bathed in an otherworldly glow, retained an eerie beauty that hinted at a history shrouded in mystery.

The friends, their senses returning to them, exchanged uncertain glances. The Goatman, a diminished presence, retreated further into the shadows, its spectral form flickering like a dying ember. The authoritative voice continued to resonate, guiding the friends toward a newfound understanding of the cosmic forces that governed their existence.

Mark, his mind a battlefield between reason and supernatural influence, struggled to reconcile the surreal events that had unfolded. The grand hall, once a chamber of horrors, now felt almost serene. The spectral currents, while still present, seemed to ebb away, leaving behind an uneasy calm.

The friends, guided by the authoritative voice, explored the mansion with a newfound sense of purpose. Rooms that had once harbored spectral terrors now revealed forgotten artifacts and relics of a bygone era. The Goatman's curse, now a fading echo, no longer held the mansion in its suffocating grip.

As they ventured deeper into the mansion, the authoritative voice spoke of ancient rituals, cosmic guardians, and the delicate balance that must be maintained to prevent the malevolence of the supernatural from overwhelming the mortal realm. The friends, their minds now attuned to the guiding force, began to understand the significance of their journey.

In a forgotten library, they discovered tomes that chronicled the history of the Goatman—a tragic entity bound by an unholy alliance forged in the shadows of cosmic realms. The authoritative voice explained that the friends' defiance had disrupted the spectral equilibrium, offering a chance to tip the balance away from the malevolence that had plagued the haunted woods.

Mark, grappling with the revelations, felt a weight lifting from his shoulders. The Goatman, now a vanquished specter, no longer held sway over his mind. The friends, united by their shared struggle, delved deeper into the mansion's secrets, guided by the authoritative voice toward a resolution that would safeguard both the mortal and supernatural realms.

In a chamber hidden beneath the mansion, they discovered an ancient artifact—an amulet pulsating with ethereal energy. The authoritative voice explained that the amulet had the power to seal the remnants of the Goatman's curse and restore balance to the haunted woods. The friends, now entrusted with a cosmic responsibility, prepared for a final confrontation.

The grand hall, once witness to cosmic struggles, became a staging ground for the friends' decisive act. The amulet, held by Emily, radiated with a soothing luminescence. The Goatman, its diminished form lingering in the shadows, hissed with a fading defiance.

As Emily approached the spectral remnants of the Goatman's curse, the authoritative voice guided her in a ritual of sealing. Symbols etched into the floor glowed with an otherworldly radiance. The friends, standing in a circle around the amulet, channeled their collective energy into the cosmic task before them.

The mansion trembled as the ritual unfolded, and the Goatman's laughter echoed one last time through the grand hall. Shadows, now devoid of malevolence, danced with a newfound serenity. The friends, their resolve unbroken, witnessed the ethereal currents converging toward the amulet, sealing the remnants of the Goatman's curse within its crystalline core.

A blinding light enveloped the grand hall, and the mansion seemed to transcend the boundaries of time and space. The friends felt a cosmic energy surging through them, connecting them to the very essence of the supernatural. The authoritative voice, now a

benevolent guide, spoke of the friends' triumph over cosmic malevolence and the restoration of equilibrium.

As the light subsided, the grand hall returned to its former state of faded grandeur. The Goatman, its spectral form extinguished, became a mere memory. The haunted woods, once a realm of cosmic nightmares, seemed to breathe with newfound vitality. The friends, now free from the spectral alliance that had bound them, emerged from the mansion with a sense of accomplishment.

The authoritative voice, a fading echo, spoke its final words of gratitude and guidance. The friends, forever changed by their ordeal, walked out of the haunted woods into the moonlit night. The spectral currents, now a gentle breeze, whispered tales of ancient struggles and cosmic resolutions.

As they exited the woods, the haunted realm seemed to recede into the shadows. The Goatman's curse, sealed within the amulet, no longer held dominion over the supernatural enclave. The friends, marked by their journey through cosmic horrors, carried the weight of their experiences as a testament to the delicate balance between the mortal and supernatural realms.

The haunted woods, now a tranquil grove bathed in moonlight, stood as a testament to the friends' resilience. The spectral alliance, once a malevolent force, had been disrupted, and the cosmic equilibrium restored. The friends, forever bonded by their shared struggle, left the haunted woods behind, their footsteps echoing with the echoes of ancient tales and the triumphant resolution of cosmic mysteries.

As they ventured further from the haunted woods, the moonlit path guided them back to the realm of the living. The friends, still processing the surreal events, found solace in the gentle rustle of leaves and the calming night breeze. The amulet, now a relic of

their cosmic triumph, radiated with a subtle glow, a testament to the balance they had restored.

The authoritative voice, its echoes fading into the night, left the friends with a lingering sense of purpose. The haunted mansion, once a chamber of spectral horrors, disappeared from their view. The spectral currents, now harmonized with the natural energies of the world, whispered tales of ancient guardians and cosmic safeguards.

Mark, his mind now free from the haunting influence, looked at his friends with a mixture of relief and gratitude. The journey through the haunted woods had forged bonds that transcended the boundaries of the mundane. The friends, forever changed by their cosmic ordeal, shared an unspoken understanding that went beyond the realm of mortal comprehension.

As they walked, the moon casting a silver glow on their path, the friends reflected on the cosmic mysteries they had encountered. The haunted woods, once a realm of malevolence, had become a sanctuary of cosmic balance. The amulet, now a symbol of their resilience, dangled from Emily's neck, a reminder of the unseen forces that bound them together.

In the distance, the haunted woods receded into the night, its secrets hidden once more within the shadows. The friends, now free from the spectral alliance, emerged into the world with a newfound appreciation for the delicate interplay between the known and the unknown. The cosmic forces, once a source of terror, had become guardians of a delicate equilibrium.

Days turned into nights, and the friends continued their journey, forever marked by the spectral ordeal. The haunted woods, now a distant memory, left an indelible imprint on their souls. The amulet, a silent guardian against malevolence, resonated with the cosmic energies that flowed through their veins.

As they reached the outskirts of a nearby town, the friends paused to gaze back at the moonlit horizon. The haunted woods, a realm of cosmic nightmares, remained hidden in the distance. The amulet, now a talisman of cosmic balance, glowed with a reassuring warmth.

The friends, bound by the shared secrets of the supernatural, moved forward into the tapestry of their lives. The authoritative voice, a distant echo, whispered final words of guidance, fading into the realm of forgotten cosmic tales. The haunted mansion, once a chamber of horrors, became a relic in their collective memory.

The moon, a silent witness to their cosmic journey, cast its light upon the friends as they continued their way. The spectral currents, now a gentle presence, whispered tales of ancient guardians watching over the boundaries between realms. The friends, now guardians in their own right, carried the weight of their cosmic triumph as they embraced the unknown that lay ahead.

The moonlit night, with its secrets and mysteries, enveloped the friends in a comforting embrace. The haunted woods, once a crucible of terror, became a distant chapter in the ever-expanding cosmic narrative. The friends, forever intertwined by the unseen threads of their shared ordeal, moved forward into the mysteries that awaited them, their footsteps echoing with the echoes of ancient tales and the triumphant resolution of cosmic enigmas.

Chapter 14: Echoes of the Unknown

The town at the outskirts offered a semblance of normalcy, but the friends couldn't shake the echoes of the haunted woods that lingered in the recesses of their minds. The amulet, now a silent guardian against unseen forces, emitted a subtle glow as they navigated the streets. The authoritative voice, a distant whisper, continued to guide them with cryptic assurances.

In the heart of the town, they stumbled upon an ancient bookstore. The shelves were lined with weathered tomes containing forgotten knowledge of the supernatural. The friends, still haunted by their cosmic journey, felt an irresistible pull toward the musty volumes that hinted at untold mysteries.

As they delved into the books, the words on the pages seemed to come alive, recounting tales of forgotten rituals, eldritch entities, and the delicate balance that tethered the mortal and supernatural realms. The amulet, attuned to the ancient energies, pulsed with an otherworldly resonance as if acknowledging the truths within the pages.

One particular book caught their attention—an ancient grimoire that spoke of cosmic gateways and the consequences of disrupting the equilibrium between realms. The authoritative voice, now a comforting presence, guided them to a passage that foretold of a looming cosmic disturbance tied to their recent ordeal.

The friends, gripped by a sense of urgency, sought answers from the cryptic text. The grimoire spoke of a cosmic entity known as the Veilstitcher—an ancient force responsible for mending the fabric of reality when disrupted by mortal meddling. The disrupted equilibrium in the haunted woods had awakened the Veilstitcher, and its influence now extended beyond the spectral enclave.

A foreboding realization set in—the friends' actions in the haunted woods had not only disrupted the Goatman's curse but had also set in motion a cosmic chain reaction. The Veilstitcher, a guardian of the cosmic balance, now sought to mend the fabric of reality by any means necessary.

The town, once a refuge, now became a battleground between the Veilstitcher's influence and the friends' struggle for understanding. Shadows seemed to dance with a newfound malevolence, and

the air vibrated with an otherworldly tension. The authoritative voice, now urgent, guided the friends toward a cosmic reckoning.

As night fell, the friends found themselves drawn to an abandoned mansion on the outskirts of the town—a structure that resonated with the cosmic energies emanating from the awakened Veilstitcher. The amulet, now glowing with an intensity that mirrored the urgency of their mission, led them through the moonlit streets toward the looming edifice.

The mansion, a spectral relic like the one in the haunted woods, exuded an ethereal glow. The Veilstitcher's influence seemed to warp the very fabric of reality within its walls. The friends, their minds attuned to the cosmic energies, hesitated at the threshold, knowing that their actions within might determine the fate of both the mortal and supernatural realms.

As they entered, the mansion revealed itself as a nexus of cosmic energies. The authoritative voice, now resonating with a somber tone, explained that the Veilstitcher, once a dormant guardian, had been stirred by the friends' disruption of the cosmic equilibrium. The mansion, a convergence point of realities, now stood as a battleground for their cosmic destiny.

The rooms within the mansion, adorned with symbols that pulsed with cosmic significance, told tales of forgotten rituals and eldritch pacts. Shadows, animated by the Veilstitcher's influence, seemed to observe the intruders with an ominous awareness. The friends, guided by the amulet and the authoritative voice, navigated the twisting corridors toward the heart of the cosmic disturbance.

In a grand chamber, they discovered an ancient portal—a tear in the fabric of reality itself. The Veilstitcher, a spectral entity with threads of cosmic energy weaving around it, stood at the center. The authoritative voice, now a desperate plea, urged the friends to

confront the awakened guardian and seek a resolution that could prevent the unraveling of reality.

The friends, their minds burdened by the weight of cosmic responsibility, faced the Veilstitcher. Its presence, a maelstrom of spectral energies, seemed to scrutinize their very essence. The amulet, now radiating with an otherworldly brilliance, resonated with the Veilstitcher's influence.

The authoritative voice spoke of a cosmic choice—a pact with the Veilstitcher to mend the fabric of reality or a defiance that could unleash untold cosmic consequences. The friends, bound by the unseen threads of their shared journey, exchanged uneasy glances as the Veilstitcher's influence pulsed around them.

Emily, still attuned to the cosmic currents, stepped forward with a sense of purpose. The amulet, now a conduit for cosmic energies, seemed to respond to her presence. The Veilstitcher, its spectral form shifting with an otherworldly grace, communicated in a language of cosmic vibrations that transcended mortal comprehension.

As Emily spoke, her words resonated with the Veilstitcher's energies. The symbols around the portal glowed with an ethereal luminescence, and the grand chamber seemed to ripple with unseen forces. The friends, caught between cosmic choices, felt the weight of their destinies hanging in the balance.

The Veilstitcher, now engaged in a cosmic dialogue, revealed the consequences of its awakening. Reality, torn by the disruption in the haunted woods, threatened to unravel unless a cosmic pact was forged. The friends, their minds a battleground between mortal instincts and cosmic responsibilities, listened to the Veilstitcher's revelations.

Mark, still grappling with the echoes of the haunted woods, questioned the Veilstitcher's motives. The authoritative voice, now a spectral whisper, explained that the awakened guardian sought to

preserve the delicate balance disrupted by mortal interference. The Veilstitcher's influence, while imposing, was a necessary force to prevent cosmic chaos.

The friends, now faced with an impossible choice, deliberated their next move. The Veilstitcher, its spectral form exuding a sense of inevitability, awaited their decision. The amulet, a silent witness to the cosmic drama, pulsed with an intensity that mirrored the urgency of the situation.

As the friends reached a collective decision, the Veilstitcher's influence intensified. The grand chamber seemed to tremble with unseen forces as cosmic energies converged around the portal. Shadows, now imbued with the guardian's essence, danced along the walls, casting grotesque silhouettes.

The Veilstitcher, its spectral form resonating with a somber luminescence, spoke words that transcended mortal comprehension. The friends, guided by the authoritative voice and the amulet's influence, entered into a cosmic pact with the awakened guardian. The symbols on the portal glowed brighter, and reality seemed to shift as the pact was forged.

The town outside, once caught in the grip of the Veilstitcher's influence, returned to a semblance of normalcy. The cosmic energies, now harmonized by the friends' choice, resonated with a tranquil hum. The mansion, a nexus of cosmic disturbances, faded into the shadows as the portal closed behind them.

The authoritative voice, a fading echo, expressed gratitude for the friends' sacrifice in preserving the cosmic equilibrium. The amulet, now a symbol of their cosmic pact, emitted a subdued glow. The Veilstitcher's influence, while still present, now felt more like a benevolent current flowing through the friends' veins. The cosmic energies, once turbulent, settled into a harmonious resonance that connected the mortal and supernatural realms.

The friends, their minds still echoing with the cosmic dialogue, emerged from the grand chamber. The mansion, now devoid of spectral disturbances, felt like a sanctuary of forgotten cosmic truths. The town, released from the Veilstitcher's influence, embraced a serene calm that hinted at the delicate balance that had been restored.

As the friends walked through the moonlit streets, the amulet pulsed with a gentle radiance. The authoritative voice, now a comforting whisper, spoke of the friends' role as guardians of the cosmic equilibrium. The Veilstitcher, its spectral presence lingering in the background, communicated an unspoken assurance that their sacrifice had averted a cosmic catastrophe.

Days turned into nights, and the friends found themselves drawn to the ancient bookstore once again. The tomes that had once spoken of cosmic disturbances now revealed passages about cosmic guardians and the delicate dance between realms. The friends, now more attuned to the cosmic energies, sought further understanding of their newfound responsibilities.

In the bookstore, they discovered a hidden chamber that housed an ancient artifact—a celestial map that depicted the interconnected realms of existence. The authoritative voice guided them to specific constellations that represented cosmic gateways and unseen forces that governed the fabric of reality.

As the friends studied the celestial map, the Veilstitcher's influence resonated with the symbols, creating an ethereal connection between the mortal and supernatural realms. The amulet, now an instrument of cosmic awareness, hummed with a resonant frequency that mirrored the cosmic energies depicted on the map.

The authoritative voice explained that the friends, having forged a cosmic pact with the Veilstitcher, now held the key to maintaining the delicate balance between realms. Their journey, once a

harrowing ordeal, had transformed into a cosmic responsibility to safeguard the cosmic equilibrium.

Guided by the celestial map and the amulet, the friends embarked on a journey that transcended the boundaries of the known. They visited ancient sites, long-forgotten temples, and mystical landscapes that resonated with cosmic energies. The Veilstitcher's influence, now a guiding force, revealed hidden truths about the interconnected nature of existence.

In their cosmic travels, the friends encountered otherworldly entities—guardians, cosmic spirits, and ethereal beings that watched over the boundaries between realms. Each encounter deepened their understanding of the cosmic forces at play and reinforced the importance of their role as guardians of the equilibrium.

The celestial map, now a cosmic compass, led them to a sacred grove bathed in starlight. The Veilstitcher's influence pulsed through the ancient trees, and the amulet resonated with a sublime luminescence. The authoritative voice, now a guiding presence, spoke of a cosmic convergence that required the friends' attention.

In the heart of the sacred grove, a cosmic portal shimmered with an otherworldly radiance. The symbols on the portal echoed the constellations on the celestial map. The friends, their minds attuned to the Veilstitcher's influence, recognized the significance of the cosmic convergence.

As they approached the portal, the Veilstitcher's spectral form materialized, its presence now a harmonious dance of cosmic energies. The amulet, imbued with the friends' cosmic journey, resonated with the portal's energies. The authoritative voice spoke of a cosmic event that would test their resolve and strengthen the bonds between realms.

The friends, guided by their newfound cosmic awareness, stepped through the portal. The celestial map, now a guide through the

cosmic convergence, revealed a breathtaking tapestry of interconnected realms. The Veilstitcher's influence, once a source of cosmic disturbance, now merged seamlessly with the cosmic currents that flowed through the tapestry.

As they traversed the cosmic convergence, the friends encountered celestial phenomena—shifting realities, ethereal landscapes, and manifestations of cosmic energies that transcended mortal comprehension. The amulet, now a conduit for their shared cosmic journey, pulsed with a vibrant energy that mirrored the celestial wonders around them.

The authoritative voice, a guiding presence in the cosmic expanse, explained the friends' role in maintaining the delicate balance between realms during the convergence. The Veilstitcher, its spectral form intertwining with the cosmic currents, communicated an unspoken assurance that their cosmic pact had prepared them for this pivotal moment.

In the cosmic tapestry, the friends witnessed the Veilstitcher's influence harmonizing with other cosmic guardians. The celestial convergence, a sublime dance of energies, echoed with the echoes of ancient tales and cosmic resolutions. The friends, now guardians of the equilibrium, embraced their role with a sense of cosmic purpose.

As the cosmic convergence reached its zenith, the friends felt a profound connection to the very fabric of existence. The Veilstitcher's influence, now a benevolent force, guided them through the celestial wonders. The amulet, a symbol of their cosmic journey, radiated with a brilliance that mirrored the cosmic energies that flowed through the tapestry.

As the friends emerged from the cosmic convergence, they found themselves back in the sacred grove bathed in starlight. The portal closed behind them, leaving a lingering sense of cosmic awareness. The Veilstitcher's spectral form, now a distant presence, conveyed

a silent gratitude for the friends' guardianship of the cosmic equilibrium.

The celestial map, still in their possession, revealed new constellations that represented the friends' cosmic journey. The authoritative voice, a fading echo, spoke of the friends' transformation from seekers of the unknown to guardians of cosmic balance. The amulet, now a relic imbued with cosmic energies, pulsed with a steady resonance.

The friends, forever changed by their cosmic ordeal, looked to the night sky with a newfound understanding. The echoes of the unknown, once a source of terror, now whispered tales of cosmic guardianship and the delicate dance between realms. The Veilstitcher's influence, though distant, remained a guiding force in their cosmic journey.

As the friends ventured back into the mortal realm, the town at the outskirts welcomed them with a tranquil calm. The echoes of the haunted woods and the cosmic convergence became part of their collective memory. The amulet, now a timeless artifact, symbolized their connection to the cosmic forces that governed existence.

The Veilstitcher, a guardian in the cosmic expanse, continued its silent vigil over the delicate balance between realms. The friends, now stewards of the equilibrium, embraced their cosmic responsibilities with a sense of purpose. The cosmic tapestry, woven with threads of celestial wonders, echoed with the echoes of ancient tales and the triumphant resolution of cosmic enigmas.

Guided by the celestial map, the friends embarked on a journey to further understand and strengthen their cosmic abilities. The amulet, now an integral part of their existence, resonated with the energies of the interconnected realms. The Veilstitcher's influence, though no longer a constant presence, lingered as a silent assurance in the background.

As they delved into their newfound cosmic awareness, the friends discovered hidden sanctuaries and ancient sites where the fabric of reality seemed thin. Each encounter with cosmic phenomena deepened their understanding of the delicate balance they upheld. The celestial map, now a well-worn guide, led them to forgotten realms where cosmic secrets awaited revelation.

The friends encountered other guardians—ethereal beings who watched over specific aspects of the cosmic equilibrium. These cosmic sentinels imparted ancient wisdom and shared tales of cosmic struggles that transcended mortal lifetimes. The amulet, responding to the cosmic revelations, pulsed with an ethereal glow that mirrored the wisdom they gained.

In one such realm, the friends faced a cosmic trial—an otherworldly challenge that tested their resilience and understanding of the interconnected tapestry. The Veilstitcher's influence, once again a guiding force, whispered encouragement as the friends navigated through shifting realities and celestial puzzles. The amulet, a source of cosmic strength, resonated with a brilliance that defied mortal comprehension.

As they emerged victorious from the cosmic trial, the friends felt a surge of cosmic energy coursing through them. The celestial map, now adorned with new constellations, reflected their triumph. The Veilstitcher's spectral form, a distant but benevolent presence, communicated a silent acknowledgment of their growth as cosmic stewards.

The friends, now attuned to the cosmic rhythms, realized that their journey had become a perpetual quest to maintain the balance between realms. The Veilstitcher's influence guided them toward cosmic disturbances that threatened to disrupt the delicate equilibrium. The amulet, a cosmic compass, pulsed with urgency as the friends embraced their roles as cosmic guardians.

In one particularly perilous encounter, the friends faced an entity that sought to unravel the threads of reality. The cosmic disturbance, a malevolent force that defied comprehension, manifested in shifting shadows and ethereal echoes. The Veilstitcher's influence, now an active guide, directed the friends in a cosmic battle against the encroaching chaos.

As the friends confronted the cosmic disturbance, the amulet resonated with a fierce brilliance. The celestial map, now animated with cosmic energies, revealed the weaknesses in the malevolent force. Guided by the Veilstitcher's influence, the friends channeled their cosmic abilities to weave threads of stability into the fabric of reality.

The cosmic battle unfolded in a surreal dance of energies, with the friends wielding the amulet as a conduit for their newfound cosmic powers. The Veilstitcher's spectral form, a silent overseer, observed their efforts with a sense of approval. The celestial map, now a source of tactical insight, guided the friends through the intricate maneuvers needed to restore cosmic equilibrium.

As the malevolent force recoiled under the friends' cosmic onslaught, the cosmic disturbance began to dissipate. The Veilstitcher's influence, intertwined with the amulet's radiant glow, sealed the weakened threads of reality. The friends, exhausted but triumphant, stood amidst the cosmic aftermath, their cosmic abilities now more refined and potent.

The Veilstitcher's spectral form approached, its essence resonating with a profound serenity. The amulet, still glowing with the aftermath of the cosmic battle, conveyed a sense of fulfillment. The celestial map, though marked by the recent cosmic disturbance, hinted at the friends' ongoing journey as cosmic guardians.

As the friends left the disrupted realm, the Veilstitcher's influence lingered as a silent companion. The amulet, now a vessel of cosmic

energies, pulsed with a steady rhythm. The celestial map, enriched by the recent experiences, reflected the intricate dance of cosmic forces that shaped their cosmic journey.

In the wake of the cosmic battle, the friends continued their exploration of interconnected realms. The Veilstitcher's influence, though less prominent, remained a guiding force in their cosmic endeavors. The amulet, now a symbol of their cosmic mastery, resonated with a harmonious energy that connected them to the very essence of the cosmic tapestry.

The friends' travels took them to celestial landscapes, ancient observatories, and cosmic sanctuaries where the boundaries between realms blurred. The Veilstitcher's influence guided them toward cosmic phenomena that demanded their attention. The amulet, now an instrument of cosmic balance, pulsed with an ethereal glow as they upheld their cosmic responsibilities.

Through their cosmic journey, the friends encountered beings of cosmic wisdom and entities that embodied the intricate dance of existence. The Veilstitcher's spectral form, though distant, communicated a sense of approval as the friends navigated through celestial wonders and unearthed forgotten truths.

As the friends embraced their roles as cosmic guardians, the Veilstitcher's influence gradually withdrew, leaving them with a sense of empowerment and cosmic purpose. The amulet, now an artifact infused with cosmic energies, became a symbol of their journey—an enduring testament to their triumphs over cosmic disturbances.

The celestial map, adorned with constellations representing their cosmic victories, guided the friends toward new realms and cosmic challenges. The echoes of the unknown, once a source of terror, now whispered tales of cosmic guardianship and the delicate dance between realms. The friends, forever bound by their shared cosmic

journey, embraced the ongoing mysteries that awaited them in the interconnected tapestry of existence.

As the friends ventured further into the cosmic unknown, the Veilstitcher's spectral form faded into the cosmic expanse, its influence becoming a timeless part of their cosmic legacy. The amulet, a luminous beacon of cosmic mastery, pulsed with the echoes of ancient tales and the triumphant resolution of cosmic enigmas. The celestial map, now a guide through the cosmic realms, unfolded new constellations that beckoned the friends toward their next cosmic adventure—a perpetual odyssey that transcended the boundaries of the known and embraced the infinite possibilities of the cosmic tapestry.

Chapter 15: Cosmic Odyssey

Guided by the celestial map, the friends embarked on a cosmic odyssey that traversed realms beyond mortal comprehension. The interconnected tapestry of existence unfolded before them, revealing celestial wonders, ethereal landscapes, and cosmic phenomena that defied explanation.

The Veilstitcher's influence, though a distant echo, resonated in the cosmic energies that enveloped the friends. The amulet, a radiant beacon of their cosmic mastery, pulsed with an ever-present glow. The celestial map, now adorned with constellations representing their cosmic victories, guided them toward new frontiers in the cosmic expanse.

Their cosmic journey led them to an astral city suspended in the fabric of reality—a nexus where cosmic beings congregated to exchange wisdom and share tales of cosmic struggles. The friends, now revered as cosmic guardians, were welcomed into the celestial enclave. The Veilstitcher's influence, a silent companion, conveyed a sense of pride in their cosmic achievements.

In the astral city, the friends encountered beings of transcendent wisdom—entities that embodied the very essence of cosmic existence. The Veilstitcher's spectral form, though unseen, communicated with the celestial beings in a language of cosmic vibrations. The amulet, resonating with the celestial energies, marked the friends as stewards of the delicate balance between realms.

As they communed with cosmic sages and explored the astral city's ethereal architecture, the friends learned of ancient prophecies that foretold cosmic challenges yet to come. The celestial map, now revealing constellations depicting future cosmic disturbances, guided them toward their next cosmic mission.

The Veilstitcher's influence, now a guiding force in their cosmic endeavors, urged the friends to embrace their roles as cosmic guardians with renewed determination. The amulet, a conduit for cosmic energies, hummed with a harmonious resonance that mirrored the celestial symphony around them.

Their cosmic odyssey led them to a realm where time flowed in paradoxical currents and spatial dimensions intertwined. The celestial map, now navigating through temporal anomalies, revealed cosmic disturbances that threatened to disrupt the cosmic equilibrium. The Veilstitcher's influence, though subtle, guided the friends toward a cosmic anomaly that transcended the boundaries of temporal understanding.

As they entered the realm of temporal paradoxes, the friends encountered echoes of past, present, and future cosmic events. The Veilstitcher's spectral form, now a temporal observer, guided them through the intricacies of temporal anomalies. The amulet, attuned to the temporal energies, pulsed with a rhythmic cadence that marked the ebb and flow of cosmic time.

In their cosmic exploration, the friends faced temporal challenges that tested their understanding of the interconnected tapestry. The

celestial map, now a guide through the temporal labyrinth, revealed constellations representing pivotal moments in cosmic history. The Veilstitcher's influence, intertwined with the amulet's radiant glow, whispered insights into the delicate dance between temporal forces.

As they navigated through temporal currents and faced paradoxical trials, the friends felt the weight of cosmic responsibility. The Veilstitcher's spectral form, a temporal overseer, communicated a sense of urgency in preserving the cosmic equilibrium across all timelines. The amulet, a temporal anchor, resonated with a steady frequency that harmonized with the cosmic time stream.

Their triumph over temporal challenges marked a pivotal moment in their cosmic journey. The Veilstitcher's influence, though bound by temporal constraints, conveyed a sense of approval. The amulet, now a temporal artifact, bore the imprints of their cosmic victories in the temporal realm.

The celestial map, enriched by their experiences in the realm of temporal paradoxes, guided the friends toward new frontiers in the cosmic tapestry. The Veilstitcher's spectral form, though distant, remained a silent companion in their cosmic odyssey. The amulet, now a relic infused with temporal energies, pulsed with the echoes of ancient tales and the triumphant resolution of temporal enigmas.

As the friends ventured further into the cosmic unknown, the celestial map unfolded new constellations representing uncharted realms. The Veilstitcher's influence, now a timeless presence, guided them toward cosmic phenomena that transcended mortal understanding. The amulet, an ever-present source of cosmic awareness, resonated with a luminous brilliance that mirrored the cosmic wonders around them.

Their cosmic odyssey continued, weaving through realms of surreal beauty, cosmic challenges, and ancient mysteries. The Veilstitcher's spectral form, now an ethereal companion, communicated

a sense of purpose in their ongoing quest to uphold the delicate balance between realms. The amulet, a cosmic talisman, pulsed with an enduring glow that marked the friends as eternal stewards of the cosmic equilibrium.

As the friends embraced the infinite possibilities of the cosmic tapestry, the echoes of the unknown whispered tales of cosmic guardianship and the intricate dance between realms. The Veilstitcher's influence, though timeless, remained an ever-watchful guide in their perpetual cosmic adventure. The amulet, a radiant symbol of their cosmic journey, continued to resonate with the echoes of ancient tales and the triumphant resolution of cosmic enigmas.

In the vast expanse of the interconnected tapestry, the friends' cosmic odyssey unfolded like an eternal saga—an ongoing exploration of the unknown, a journey that transcended the boundaries of the known, and a testament to the enduring bond between mortal souls and the cosmic forces that shaped their destinies.

Chapter 15: The Abyss of Cosmic Dread

As the friends delved deeper into the cosmic expanse, guided by the celestial map, they sensed an ominous shift in the fabric of reality. The Veilstitcher's influence, once a reassuring presence, now vibrated with an undercurrent of cosmic dread. The amulet, usually radiant with cosmic energies, flickered with an unsettling uncertainty as they approached a realm shrouded in cosmic shadows.

The astral city, which had once welcomed them as revered cosmic guardians, now revealed a darker underbelly. Celestial beings, their ethereal forms distorted by an unseen malevolence, whispered foreboding prophecies of an impending cosmic catastrophe. The Veilstitcher's spectral form, still present but veiled in cosmic dread, communicated a sense of urgency that sent shivers through the friends' cosmic awareness.

The celestial map, now marked by constellations that seemed to writhe with cosmic unease, directed them toward an abyssal rift—an anomaly in the fabric of existence that emitted an unsettling resonance. As they approached the cosmic abyss, the amulet pulsed with an erratic energy, reflecting the growing cosmic disturbance that threatened to unravel the delicate balance between realms.

As they entered the abyssal rift, the friends felt an overwhelming sense of existential dread. The Veilstitcher's influence, usually a guiding force, now manifested as haunting whispers that echoed through the cosmic void. Shadows danced with a malevolent glee, and the celestial map, once a source of guidance, seemed to lead them deeper into the cosmic abyss.

In the depths of the rift, the friends encountered cosmic horrors that defied mortal comprehension. Entities of cosmic malevolence, their forms twisted by the abyssal energies, sought to consume the very essence of their cosmic being. The Veilstitcher's spectral form, dimmed by the cosmic dread, conveyed a silent plea for the friends to resist the encroaching darkness.

The amulet, struggling against the oppressive forces of the abyss, emitted flashes of dim light that barely illuminated the cosmic horrors that lurked in the shadows. The celestial map, now distorted by the abyssal energies, led the friends through maddening labyrinths where reality itself seemed to unravel.

As they faced the cosmic horrors, the friends felt the weight of existential terror bearing down upon them. The Veilstitcher's spectral form, now a flickering beacon in the cosmic abyss, urged them to confront the source of the malevolence that threatened to rupture the fabric of reality. The amulet, their only source of cosmic defense, resonated with the desperate pulses of their fear-stricken hearts.

In their cosmic struggle against the abyssal forces, the friends discovered ancient ruins—remnants of a forgotten civilization that

had succumbed to the same cosmic dread. The celestial map, though tainted by the abyssal energies, revealed inscriptions that spoke of rituals to appease eldritch entities and the consequences of cosmic disturbances left unchecked.

The Veilstitcher's spectral form, now dimmed by the encroaching darkness, communicated the dire implications of the abyssal rift's existence. If not sealed, it threatened to become a cosmic tear that could unleash unspeakable horrors upon the interconnected tapestry. The friends, gripped by terror and determination, understood the gravity of their cosmic mission.

As they ventured deeper into the ruins, the abyssal energies twisted the very fabric of reality. Cosmic echoes whispered tales of the doomed civilization that had once thrived in the cosmic abyss. The amulet, now a fragile shield against the abyssal forces, flickered with the desperate hope that the friends could prevent a similar fate.

In the heart of the ruins, the friends discovered a cosmic altar—a focal point for the abyssal energies that pulsed through the rift. Eldritch symbols adorned the altar, resonating with malevolence that sent shivers down their spines. The celestial map, now a guide through the madness, directed them toward a cosmic ritual that could seal the abyssal rift and avert the impending cosmic catastrophe.

As they prepared to enact the ritual, the friends felt the oppressive weight of the abyssal energies bearing down upon them. Whispers of cosmic horrors echoed in their minds, and the Veilstitcher's spectral form, barely visible amidst the cosmic dread, communicated the urgency of completing the ritual before the fabric of reality unraveled completely.

The amulet, now strained to its cosmic limits, emitted a feeble glow as the friends channeled their cosmic abilities into the ritual. Shadows, animated by the abyssal forces, writhed in protest as the

celestial map guided them through the intricate steps of the cosmic sealing. The Veilstitcher's spectral form, though barely discernible, resonated with the friends' determination to defy the encroaching cosmic dread.

In the midst of the ritual, the friends felt the cosmic abyss resisting their efforts. Eldritch energies surged, threatening to overwhelm their sanity. The Veilstitcher's influence, now a beacon in the cosmic storm, lent its spectral strength to their cosmic struggle. The amulet, teetering on the brink of cosmic exhaustion, emitted a final burst of radiant light that merged with the celestial energies of the sealing ritual.

As the last cosmic incantation echoed through the ruins, a profound stillness settled over the abyssal rift. The cosmic dread that had permeated the very fabric of reality began to recede. The Veilstitcher's spectral form, now visible in a dim luminescence, conveyed a silent acknowledgment of the friends' success in averting the cosmic catastrophe.

The amulet, though dimmed and worn, retained a subdued glow—a testament to the friends' resilience against the abyssal forces. The celestial map, now cleared of the malevolent constellations, revealed a new cosmic equilibrium that mirrored the triumph over the cosmic dread that had threatened to consume the interconnected tapestry.

As the friends emerged from the ruins, the abyssal rift sealed behind them, the Veilstitcher's spectral form regained its ethereal brilliance. The amulet, though scarred by the cosmic struggle, pulsed with a renewed vitality. The celestial map, now restored to its cosmic clarity, guided them toward realms untouched by the malevolent forces that had lurked in the cosmic abyss.

The friends, forever changed by their harrowing encounter with the abyssal forces, continued their cosmic odyssey with a heightened

awareness of the cosmic horrors that lurked in the vast expanse. The Veilstitcher's influence, now a vigilant guardian, accompanied them as a guiding force. The amulet, a resilient artifact that bore the scars of their cosmic ordeal, resonated with a luminous brilliance that symbolized their triumph over the abyssal dread.

The celestial map, once tainted by malevolence, now guided the friends toward realms where cosmic wonders awaited discovery. The echoes of the unknown, though still haunting, whispered tales of cosmic resilience and the indomitable spirit that defied the abyssal forces. The friends, forever entwined by the shared horrors they had faced, embraced the mysteries that awaited them in the uncharted territories of the interconnected tapestry.

Their cosmic odyssey, now marked by the echoes of cosmic dread and triumphant resilience, unfolded like a cosmic epic—an eternal saga that transcended mortal fears and celebrated the enduring bond between mortal souls and the cosmic forces that shaped their destinies.

Chapter 16: Shadows of the Celestial Betrayal

As the friends ventured further into the cosmic unknown, guided by the celestial map, they found themselves in a realm cloaked in unsettling shadows. The Veilstitcher's influence, though a constant presence, seemed to waver as they approached an ancient observatory atop a desolate cosmic peak. The amulet, typically radiant with cosmic energies, emitted a dim glow that reflected the ominous atmosphere that pervaded the celestial landscape.

The observatory, a structure that bore witness to eons of cosmic phenomena, now echoed with whispers of a celestial betrayal that had cast a dark shadow over the interconnected tapestry. The Veilstitcher's spectral form, a silhouette against the cosmic gloom, communicated a tale of treachery that had resonated through the celestial realms.

The celestial map, now displaying constellations that seemed to writhe in cosmic agony, directed the friends toward the heart of the celestial betrayal. As they ascended the cosmic peak, the shadows deepened, and the amulet pulsed with a disconcerting rhythm that mirrored the cosmic unease.

In the observatory's inner sanctum, the friends discovered a cosmic artifact—a relic of ancient power that had been corrupted by the tendrils of celestial betrayal. Eldritch symbols adorned the artifact, resonating with malevolence that sent shivers down their spines. The Veilstitcher's influence, though shrouded in cosmic sorrow, urged them to unravel the mysteries of the celestial betrayal that had tainted the very essence of the interconnected tapestry.

As the friends examined the corrupted artifact, the shadows within the observatory seemed to come alive. Cosmic entities, twisted by the influence of celestial betrayal, materialized in ghostly forms. The Veilstitcher's spectral form, now obscured by the cosmic gloom, whispered warnings of the malevolent entities that guarded the secrets of the celestial betrayal.

The amulet, sensing the encroaching cosmic malevolence, emitted a protective aura that shielded the friends from the ghostly entities' influence. The celestial map, though distorted by the shadows, revealed inscriptions that chronicled the ancient pact that had led to the celestial betrayal and the cosmic consequences that followed.

In their exploration of the observatory, the friends faced spectral guardians—entities that embodied the malevolent echoes of celestial betrayal. Shadows danced with a haunting grace as the Veilstitcher's influence guided them through cosmic trials that tested their resolve. The amulet, a luminous beacon against the cosmic darkness, resonated with a determination to uncover the truth behind the celestial betrayal.

As they delved deeper into the observatory's mysteries, the whispers of the celestial betrayal grew more pronounced. The Veilstitcher's spectral form, now a spectral guide in the cosmic shadows, conveyed a sense of cosmic sorrow that mirrored the anguish of ancient cosmic entities. The amulet, their only defense against the encroaching malevolence, flickered with a resilient glow that defied the cosmic despair.

In the observatory's inner chambers, the friends uncovered an ancient cosmic chronicle—an illuminated manuscript that chronicled the events leading to the celestial betrayal. The celestial map, now revealing constellations that depicted cosmic alliances shattered by treachery, guided them through the cosmic revelations that awaited.

The Veilstitcher's influence, though shrouded in cosmic sorrow, narrated a tale of celestial beings bound by a sacred covenant to uphold the cosmic equilibrium. Betrayal, driven by cosmic ambition, had fractured the bonds of trust and unleashed cosmic disturbances that reverberated through the interconnected tapestry.

As the friends immersed themselves in the cosmic chronicle, they witnessed cosmic battles, treacherous alliances, and the tragic fall of celestial beings consumed by their desires for power. The celestial map, now marked by constellations that depicted the celestial betrayal in vivid detail, guided them toward the heart of the observatory where the corrupted artifact held the key to understanding the cosmic transgressions.

In the inner sanctum, the friends faced a spectral guardian—an embodiment of the celestial betrayal that had tainted the artifact with malevolent energies. The Veilstitcher's spectral form, now a solemn observer, conveyed a sense of sorrow as the friends confronted the echoes of ancient cosmic treachery. The amulet, resonating with the cosmic revelations, emitted a luminous glow that mirrored the

friends' determination to cleanse the artifact and unravel the mysteries of the celestial betrayal.

The celestial map, now pulsating with the cosmic consequences of the ancient transgressions, guided the friends through a ritual to purify the corrupted artifact. Shadows writhed with resistance, and the spectral guardian unleashed cosmic energies in a desperate attempt to prevent the redemption of the tainted relic. The Veilstitcher's influence, though veiled in cosmic sorrow, whispered words of encouragement as the friends channeled their cosmic abilities into the purification ritual.

In the midst of the cosmic struggle, the artifact resonated with celestial energies, and the shadows within the observatory recoiled. The Veilstitcher's spectral form, now visible in a dim luminescence, conveyed a sense of approval as the purification ritual reached its zenith. The amulet, though strained by the cosmic exertion, emitted a final burst of radiant light that merged with the purified energies of the artifact.

As the celestial energies enveloped the observatory, a profound stillness settled over the cosmic peak. The shadows dissipated, and the celestial map, now cleared of the malevolent constellations, revealed a new cosmic equilibrium that reflected the friends' triumph over the celestial betrayal. The Veilstitcher's spectral form, though still tinged with cosmic sorrow, conveyed a silent acknowledgment of their success in redeeming the corrupted artifact.

The amulet, though scarred by the cosmic struggle, retained a subdued glow—a testament to the friends' resilience against the malevolent forces of celestial betrayal. The celestial map, now restored to its cosmic clarity, guided them toward realms where the echoes of ancient treachery had been silenced.

As the friends emerged from the observatory, the celestial betrayal purged behind them, the Veilstitcher's spectral form regained

its ethereal brilliance. The amulet, though dimmed and worn, pulsed with a renewed vitality. The celestial map, now cleared of the malevolent constellations, guided them toward new frontiers in the interconnected tapestry.

The friends, forever changed by their harrowing encounter with the celestial betrayal, continued their cosmic odyssey with a heightened awareness of the cosmic transgressions that could threaten the delicate balance between realms. The Veilstitcher's influence, now a vigilant guardian, accompanied them as a guiding force. The amulet, a resilient artifact that bore the scars of their cosmic ordeal, resonated with a luminous brilliance that symbolized their triumph over the shadows of ancient treachery.

The celestial map, once tainted by malevolence, now guided the friends toward realms where cosmic wonders awaited discovery. The echoes of the unknown, though still haunting, whispered tales of cosmic resilience and the indomitable spirit that defied the shadows of celestial betrayal. The friends, forever entwined by the shared horrors they had faced, embraced the mysteries that awaited them in the uncharted territories of the interconnected tapestry.

Their cosmic odyssey, now marked by the echoes of celestial betrayal and triumphant resilience, unfolded like a cosmic epic—an eternal saga that transcended mortal fears and celebrated the enduring bond between mortal souls and the cosmic forces that shaped their destinies.

Chapter 17: Whispers of the Cosmic Abyss

As the friends continued their cosmic odyssey, guided by the celestial map, they found themselves drawn to a realm shrouded in enigmatic whispers—the remnants of cosmic echoes that hinted at an ancient cosmic abyss. The Veilstitcher's influence, a vigilant guardian, resonated with a somber resonance as they approached the threshold of this mysterious cosmic chasm. The amulet, though

usually radiant with cosmic energies, emitted an ethereal glow that reflected the unsettling atmosphere surrounding the abyss.

The celestial map, now marked by constellations that seemed to ripple like cosmic waves, directed the friends toward the edge of the cosmic abyss. As they descended into its depths, the shadows deepened, and the amulet pulsed with an eerie luminosity that mirrored the cosmic uncertainties that lay ahead.

In the cosmic abyss, the friends encountered surreal landscapes where the fabric of reality seemed to unravel. Ethereal whispers, echoing from the depths of the abyss, conveyed tales of ancient cosmic entities that had succumbed to the allure of forbidden knowledge. The Veilstitcher's spectral form, now a solemn guide, warned of the cosmic perils that lurked in the abyssal depths.

As they navigated through the cosmic echoes, the friends faced spectral manifestations—entities born from the lingering remnants of cosmic entities that had unraveled in the abyss. Shadows danced with an otherworldly grace, and the celestial map, now flickering with cosmic uncertainties, guided them through trials that tested their resilience against the cosmic abyss.

The Veilstitcher's influence, though a steadfast companion, communicated a sense of caution as the friends delved deeper into the cosmic unknown. The amulet, their cosmic beacon, emitted a protective aura that shielded them from the haunting forces that sought to entice them into the cosmic abyss's alluring depths.

In the heart of the abyss, the friends discovered an ancient cosmic library—a repository of forbidden knowledge that had driven cosmic entities to madness. Eldritch tomes, adorned with celestial symbols, whispered cosmic secrets that reverberated through the friends' consciousness. The celestial map, now etched with constellations depicting cosmic entities succumbing to the abyssal allure, guided them through the cosmic archives.

The Veilstitcher's spectral form, now a spectral librarian, communicated the dire consequences of delving too deeply into the forbidden knowledge within the cosmic library. The amulet, resonating with the echoes of cosmic entities lost to the abyss, pulsed with a cautionary rhythm that mirrored the friends' trepidation.

As they deciphered the celestial symbols within the tomes, the friends uncovered the tale of an ancient cosmic entity—an entity that had sought to unravel the mysteries of the cosmos but had succumbed to the cosmic abyss's seductive whispers. The celestial map, now revealing constellations that mirrored the entity's descent into madness, guided them toward the entity's resting place within the abyss.

The Veilstitcher's influence, now a solemn guide in the cosmic library, urged the friends to tread carefully as they approached the entity's lair. Shadows, animated by the abyssal energies, seemed to writhe with anticipation, and the amulet emitted a subdued glow that signaled their entry into the heart of the cosmic abyss.

In the presence of the ancient cosmic entity, echoes of madness reverberated through the abyss. The entity's spectral form, twisted by the allure of forbidden knowledge, manifested in surreal splendor. The Veilstitcher's spectral form, a spectral witness to the entity's tragic fate, communicated the profound sorrow that accompanied the entity's descent into the cosmic abyss.

The friends, now confronted by the entity's spectral manifestation, felt the weight of cosmic madness bearing down upon them. The celestial map, now depicting constellations that mirrored the entity's cosmic unraveling, guided them through a cosmic trial that tested their sanity. The amulet, their only defense against the abyssal forces, emitted a protective aura that resonated with a determination to resist the cosmic allure.

In their cosmic struggle against the entity's spectral manifestation, the friends uncovered the cosmic truths that had driven the entity to madness. Forbidden knowledge, woven into the very fabric of the cosmic abyss, whispered cosmic secrets that defied mortal comprehension. The Veilstitcher's spectral form, a witness to the unfolding cosmic drama, conveyed a sense of empathy for the entity's tragic journey.

The amulet, attuned to the cosmic revelations, emitted pulses of resonant light that harmonized with the celestial map's guidance. As the friends faced the entity's spectral manifestation, the cosmic abyss seemed to echo with the collective sorrow of entities lost to the seductive whispers of forbidden knowledge.

In a moment of cosmic clarity, the friends realized that the only way to quell the entity's spectral madness was to weave threads of cosmic understanding into the fabric of the abyss. The Veilstitcher's spectral form, now a spectral weaver, guided them through a cosmic ritual that sought to restore the entity's fractured consciousness.

As they channeled their cosmic abilities into the ritual, the cosmic abyss responded with an ethereal symphony. Shadows, once animated by madness, now danced with a melancholic grace. The celestial map, now pulsating with threads of cosmic understanding, guided the friends through the intricate maneuvers needed to mend the entity's cosmic essence.

In the cosmic aftermath of the ritual, the entity's spectral manifestation transformed. Madness gave way to a serene luminescence, and the abyssal energies seemed to retreat. The Veilstitcher's influence, now a cosmic weaver of understanding, conveyed a sense of resolution as the friends witnessed the entity's spectral form find peace within the cosmic abyss.

The amulet, though worn by the cosmic struggle, emitted a radiant glow that mirrored the friends' triumph over the abyssal allure.

The celestial map, now cleared of constellations depicting madness, revealed a new cosmic equilibrium that reflected the friends' ability to navigate the cosmic abyss and emerge unscathed.

As the friends ascended from the cosmic abyss, the Veilstitcher's spectral form regained its ethereal brilliance. The amulet, though scarred by the cosmic ordeal, pulsed with a renewed vitality. The celestial map, now cleared of the cosmic uncertainties, guided them toward new frontiers in the interconnected tapestry.

The friends, forever changed by their harrowing encounter with the cosmic abyss, continued their cosmic odyssey with a heightened awareness of the cosmic perils that lurked in the vast expanse. The Veilstitcher's influence, now a cosmic weaver of understanding, accompanied them as a guiding force. The amulet, a resilient artifact that bore the scars of their cosmic ordeal, resonated with a luminous brilliance that symbolized their triumph over the shadows of the cosmic abyss.

The celestial map, once tainted by cosmic uncertainties, now guided the friends toward realms where cosmic wonders awaited discovery. The echoes of the unknown, though still haunting, whispered tales of cosmic resilience and the indomitable spirit that defied the allure of the cosmic abyss. The friends, forever entwined by the shared horrors they had faced, embraced the mysteries that awaited them in the uncharted territories of the interconnected tapestry.

Their cosmic odyssey, now marked by the echoes of the cosmic abyss and triumphant resilience, unfolded like a cosmic epic—an eternal saga that transcended mortal fears and celebrated the enduring bond between mortal souls and the cosmic forces that shaped their destinies.

Chapter 18: Symphony of Celestial Woe

As the friends continued their cosmic journey, guided by the celestial map, they found themselves drawn to a realm where celestial

forces clashed in a symphony of woe. The Veilstitcher's influence, ever watchful, resonated with a sense of foreboding as they approached an ethereal battleground where cosmic entities engaged in an otherworldly conflict. The amulet, typically radiant with cosmic energies, flickered with an ominous luminosity that mirrored the discordant atmosphere surrounding the celestial battleground.

The celestial map, now marked by constellations that seemed to clash in celestial strife, directed the friends toward the epicenter of the cosmic conflict. As they ventured deeper into the celestial battleground, the cosmic energies pulsated with an unsettling intensity, and the amulet emitted an erratic glow that reflected the cosmic turbulence that surrounded them.

In the midst of the celestial clash, the friends witnessed cosmic entities locked in a dance of ethereal combat. Celestial beings, once guardians of cosmic harmony, now clashed in discordant symphonies that reverberated through the interconnected tapestry. The Veilstitcher's spectral form, a spectral witness to the celestial woe, communicated a tale of ancient grievances that had ignited the cosmic conflict.

The celestial map, now revealing constellations that depicted celestial entities entwined in celestial strife, guided the friends through the celestial battleground. Shadows danced with malevolent glee, and the amulet emitted a protective aura that shielded them from the cosmic energies unleashed in the celestial clash.

As they navigated through the cosmic battlefield, the friends encountered spectral remnants—echoes of celestial entities consumed by the warring energies. The Veilstitcher's influence, though a vigilant observer, conveyed a sense of cosmic sorrow as the friends witnessed the tragic consequences of the celestial conflict. The amulet, their cosmic protector, resonated with a determination to understand the origins of the celestial woe.

In the heart of the celestial battleground, the friends discovered an ancient cosmic artifact—a relic of power that had become a focal point for the warring energies. Eldritch symbols adorned the artifact, resonating with the echoes of ancient grievances that fueled the celestial conflict. The celestial map, now etched with constellations that depicted the artifact's role in the celestial strife, guided them toward understanding the artifact's significance.

The Veilstitcher's spectral form, now a spectral historian, communicated the cosmic tale of how the artifact had become a catalyst for the celestial woe. Betrayals, vendettas, and cosmic vendettas had intertwined in a cosmic dance that threatened to unravel the very fabric of the interconnected tapestry. The amulet, resonating with the cosmic revelations, emitted a luminescent glow that mirrored the friends' determination to quell the celestial conflict.

As they approached the cosmic artifact, the friends faced celestial guardians—entities consumed by the warring energies that emanated from the relic. Shadows, animated by ancient grievances, seemed to materialize in ethereal forms, and the Veilstitcher's spectral form guided them through trials that tested their resolve against the celestial woe.

The amulet, their cosmic defense, emitted a protective aura that shimmered with radiant light. The celestial map, now pulsating with constellations that depicted the celestial guardians in moments of cosmic despair, guided the friends through the celestial trials. The Veilstitcher's influence, though tinged with cosmic sorrow, urged them to confront the spectral remnants and restore cosmic harmony.

In their cosmic struggle against the celestial guardians, the friends uncovered the origins of the ancient vendettas that had fueled the celestial conflict. Betrayals, forged alliances, and cosmic vendettas had intertwined in a cosmic dance that threatened to consume the

celestial battleground. The Veilstitcher's spectral form, a witness to the unfolding cosmic drama, conveyed a sense of urgency as the friends unraveled the cosmic grievances that fueled the celestial woe.

The amulet, attuned to the cosmic revelations, emitted pulses of resonant light that harmonized with the celestial map's guidance. As the friends faced the celestial guardians, the cosmic energies seemed to shift in response to their cosmic understanding. Shadows, once animated by warring energies, now flickered with moments of celestial harmony.

In a pivotal moment of the celestial struggle, the friends realized that the only way to quell the celestial conflict was to sever the ties that bound the ancient vendettas. The Veilstitcher's spectral form, now a cosmic arbitrator, guided them through a celestial ritual that sought to break the cosmic cycles of vengeance and restore the celestial entities' understanding.

As they channeled their cosmic abilities into the ritual, the cosmic energies responded with an ethereal symphony. Shadows, once animated by ancient grievances, now danced in a harmonious ballet. The celestial map, now pulsating with threads of cosmic understanding, guided the friends through the intricate maneuvers needed to mend the celestial entities' fractured consciousness.

In the cosmic aftermath of the ritual, the celestial guardians transformed. The cosmic vendettas that had fueled their spectral existence seemed to dissipate, and the celestial energies responded with a serene luminescence. The Veilstitcher's influence, now a cosmic mediator, conveyed a sense of resolution as the friends witnessed the celestial entities find peace within the cosmic battleground.

The amulet, though worn by the cosmic struggle, emitted a radiant glow that mirrored the friends' triumph over the celestial woe. The celestial map, now cleared of constellations depicting discord, revealed a new cosmic equilibrium that reflected the friends'

ability to mediate the celestial conflict and bring about a cosmic understanding.

As the friends ascended from the celestial battleground, the Veilstitcher's spectral form regained its ethereal brilliance. The amulet, though scarred by the cosmic ordeal, pulsed with a renewed vitality. The celestial map, now cleared of the cosmic disharmony, guided them toward new frontiers in the interconnected tapestry.

The friends, forever changed by their harrowing encounter with the celestial woe, continued their cosmic odyssey with a heightened awareness of the cosmic perils that lurked in the vast expanse. The Veilstitcher's influence, now a cosmic mediator, accompanied them as a guiding force. The amulet, a resilient artifact that bore the scars of their cosmic ordeal, resonated with a luminous brilliance that symbolized their triumph over the discordant echoes of the celestial woe.

The celestial map, once tainted by cosmic disharmony, now guided the friends toward realms where cosmic wonders awaited discovery. The echoes of the unknown, though still haunting, whispered tales of cosmic resilience and the indomitable spirit that defied the discord of the celestial woe. The friends, forever entwined by the shared horrors they had faced, embraced the mysteries that awaited them in the uncharted territories of the interconnected tapestry.

Their cosmic odyssey, now marked by the echoes of the celestial woe and triumphant resilience, unfolded like a cosmic epic—an eternal saga that transcended mortal fears and celebrated the enduring bond between mortal souls and the cosmic forces that shaped their destinies.

Chapter 19: The Veil's Unraveling

In the wake of their triumph over the celestial woe, the friends felt a profound shift in the cosmic fabric as the celestial map guided them towards the heart of an impending cosmic catastrophe. The

Veilstitcher's influence, though a steadfast companion, resonated with an urgency that transcended the cosmic echoes. The amulet, usually radiant with cosmic energies, emitted a flickering glow that mirrored the unsettling atmosphere surrounding them.

The celestial map, now marked by constellations that seemed to spiral in cosmic distress, directed the friends towards an ancient cosmic observatory—a place where the threads of reality and the cosmic veil converged. As they approached the observatory, the shadows deepened, and the amulet pulsed with an ominous luminosity that hinted at the cosmic perils that awaited them.

In the observatory's sacred chambers, the friends discovered an ancient cosmic artifact—an unraveling veil that bound the threads of the interconnected tapestry. Eldritch symbols adorned the artifact, resonating with an unsettling energy that sent shivers down their spines. The Veilstitcher's spectral form, now a solemn guide, communicated a tale of cosmic imbalance that threatened to rupture the very fabric of reality.

The celestial map, now etched with constellations that depicted the cosmic veil's unraveling, guided the friends through the cosmic observatory. Shadows danced with malevolent glee, and the amulet emitted a protective aura that shielded them from the cosmic disturbances that emanated from the artifact.

As they explored the observatory's depths, the friends faced cosmic guardians—entities tasked with protecting the artifact that held the threads of the cosmic veil. The Veilstitcher's influence, though tinged with cosmic sorrow, urged them to confront the guardians and understand the source of the cosmic imbalance. The amulet, their cosmic shield, resonated with a determination to prevent the impending catastrophe.

In the heart of the observatory, the friends discovered celestial inscriptions that chronicled the artifact's role in maintaining the

cosmic equilibrium. The celestial map, now revealing constellations that depicted the threads of reality woven into the cosmic veil, guided them towards an understanding of the artifact's significance. The Veilstitcher's spectral form, now a cosmic historian, conveyed the dire consequences of the cosmic veil's unraveling.

As they deciphered the celestial inscriptions, the friends learned of an ancient cosmic entity—the Weaver of Realms—who had crafted the cosmic veil to ensure the harmony of the interconnected tapestry. Betrayals and vendettas had driven the cosmic entity to an abyss of despair, leading to a cosmic curse that now threatened to shatter the delicate threads of reality.

The Veilstitcher's spectral form, now a cosmic weaver, guided the friends through a ritual to commune with the Weaver of Realms and understand the cosmic curse that had befallen the artifact. The amulet, resonating with the cosmic revelations, emitted a luminescent glow that mirrored the friends' determination to mend the unraveling cosmic veil.

As they channeled their cosmic abilities into the ritual, the cosmic observatory responded with ethereal energies. Shadows, once animated by cosmic imbalance, now seemed to waver in a cosmic dance. The celestial map, now pulsating with threads of cosmic understanding, guided the friends through the intricate maneuvers needed to commune with the Weaver of Realms.

In the cosmic communion, the friends glimpsed the Weaver of Realms—a spectral entity consumed by cosmic despair. The Veilstitcher's spectral form, now a compassionate guide, urged them to unravel the cosmic curse that bound the Weaver and restore balance to the interconnected tapestry. The amulet, attuned to the cosmic revelations, emitted pulses of resonant light that harmonized with the celestial map's guidance.

As the friends faced the Weaver of Realms, the cosmic entity conveyed the tale of its descent into cosmic despair. Betrayals and vendettas had shattered the cosmic harmony it sought to maintain, leading to a curse that now threatened to unravel the very fabric of reality. The Veilstitcher's influence, now a cosmic mediator, urged the friends to break the chains of despair and restore hope to the Weaver.

In a pivotal moment of cosmic communion, the friends realized that the only way to mend the cosmic veil was to heal the Weaver of Realms' cosmic despair. The Veilstitcher's spectral form, now a cosmic healer, guided them through a celestial ritual that sought to break the cosmic curse and bring solace to the beleaguered cosmic entity.

As they channeled their cosmic abilities into the ritual, the cosmic observatory responded with an ethereal symphony. Shadows, once animated by cosmic despair, now seemed to waver in a harmonious ballet. The celestial map, now pulsating with threads of cosmic understanding, guided the friends through the intricate maneuvers needed to heal the Weaver of Realms.

In the cosmic aftermath of the ritual, the Weaver of Realms' spectral form transformed. Despair gave way to a serene luminescence, and the cosmic energies responded with a harmonious resonance. The Veilstitcher's influence, now a cosmic healer, conveyed a sense of resolution as the friends witnessed the Weaver find peace within the cosmic observatory.

The amulet, though worn by the cosmic struggle, emitted a radiant glow that mirrored the friends' triumph over the cosmic despair. The celestial map, now cleared of constellations depicting the cosmic curse, revealed a new cosmic equilibrium that reflected the friends' ability to mend the unraveling threads of the cosmic veil.

As the friends ascended from the cosmic observatory, the Veilstitcher's spectral form regained its ethereal brilliance. The amulet, though scarred by the cosmic ordeal, pulsed with a renewed vitality. The celestial map, now cleared of the cosmic imbalance, guided them toward new frontiers in the interconnected tapestry.

The friends, forever changed by their harrowing encounter with the unraveling cosmic veil, continued their cosmic odyssey with a heightened awareness of the cosmic perils that lurked in the vast expanse. The Veilstitcher's influence, now a cosmic healer, accompanied them as a guiding force. The amulet, a resilient artifact that bore the scars of their cosmic ordeal, resonated with a luminous brilliance that symbolized their triumph over the cosmic despair.

The celestial map, once tainted by cosmic imbalance, now guided the friends toward realms where cosmic wonders awaited discovery. The echoes of the unknown, though still haunting, whispered tales of cosmic resilience and the indomitable spirit that defied the cosmic despair. The friends, forever entwined by the shared horrors they had faced, embraced the mysteries that awaited them in the uncharted territories of the interconnected tapestry.

Their cosmic odyssey, now marked by the mending of the cosmic veil and triumphant resilience, unfolded like a cosmic epic—an eternal saga that transcended mortal fears and celebrated the enduring bond between mortal souls and the cosmic forces that shaped their destinies.

As the friends ventured forth from the cosmic observatory, a newfound clarity enveloped the interconnected tapestry. The Veilstitcher's spectral form, once a guardian in cosmic despair, radiated with a luminous brilliance that mirrored the cosmic healing they had achieved. The amulet, though marked by the trials of unraveling cosmic threads, retained a resilient glow—a testament to their ability to mend the cosmic veil.

The celestial map, now cleared of constellations depicting imbalance, guided the friends towards realms where cosmic wonders awaited discovery. The echoes of the unknown, though still haunting, whispered tales of cosmic resilience and the indomitable spirit that defied the cosmic despair. The friends, forever entwined by the shared horrors they had faced, embraced the mysteries that awaited them in the uncharted territories of the interconnected tapestry.

Their cosmic odyssey, now marked by the mending of the cosmic veil and triumphant resilience, unfolded like a cosmic epic—an eternal saga that transcended mortal fears and celebrated the enduring bond between mortal souls and the cosmic forces that shaped their destinies.

As they ventured into unexplored cosmic realms, the friends encountered celestial wonders that seemed to shimmer with a renewed vitality. The Veilstitcher's influence, now a beacon of cosmic healing, guided them through realms where echoes of their cosmic deeds resonated with celestial echoes. The amulet, a cosmic artifact infused with the power of mended threads, pulsed with a rhythmic glow that echoed the harmony they had restored.

The celestial map, now revealing constellations that depicted the friends as cosmic healers, guided them towards realms where their presence was needed. Shadows, once animated by cosmic despair, now seemed to retreat in the wake of their cosmic healing. The friends, now custodians of celestial balance, embraced their role in preserving the interconnected tapestry.

In their cosmic journey, the friends encountered celestial beings whose threads of reality had frayed. The Veilstitcher's spectral form, now a cosmic guide in mending, urged them to extend their healing touch to those ensnared by cosmic disarray. The amulet, resonating with the threads of cosmic understanding, emitted a gentle glow that mirrored their commitment to restoring celestial harmony.

As they traversed through realms touched by cosmic imbalance, the friends faced cosmic trials that tested their newfound abilities as healers of the interconnected tapestry. The Veilstitcher's influence, now a cosmic mentor, guided them through rituals that sought to mend the threads of reality and restore balance to celestial entities caught in the throes of cosmic disarray.

The amulet, a conduit of cosmic energies, emitted pulses of healing light that harmonized with the celestial map's guidance. Shadows, once animated by cosmic despair, now seemed to dissipate as the friends embraced their cosmic roles as healers. The echoes of their cosmic deeds reverberated through the interconnected tapestry, leaving a trail of celestial balance in their wake.

In a celestial sanctuary, the friends encountered a cosmic entity—a guardian of the celestial realms whose threads of reality had become entangled in cosmic disarray. The Veilstitcher's spectral form, now a cosmic healer, communicated with the entity in a language of cosmic understanding. The amulet, resonating with the threads of mended reality, emitted a soothing aura that calmed the entity's cosmic unrest.

As the friends performed a cosmic ritual to heal the guardian's threads, the celestial sanctuary responded with ethereal energies. The Veilstitcher's influence, now a cosmic conductor, guided them through the intricate maneuvers needed to mend the celestial guardian's frayed threads. The amulet, attuned to the cosmic revelations, emitted pulses of resonant light that harmonized with the celestial map's guidance.

In the cosmic aftermath of the ritual, the celestial guardian's spectral form transformed. Threads once entangled in cosmic disarray now shimmered with a serene luminescence. The Veilstitcher's influence, now a cosmic healer, conveyed a sense of fulfillment as

the friends witnessed the guardian find peace within the celestial sanctuary.

The amulet, though worn by the cosmic struggle, emitted a radiant glow that mirrored the friends' triumph as cosmic healers. The celestial map, now cleared of constellations depicting cosmic disarray, revealed a new cosmic equilibrium that reflected the friends' ability to extend their healing touch to the interconnected tapestry.

As the friends continued their cosmic journey, the Veilstitcher's spectral form, now a cosmic mentor, guided them towards realms where celestial entities awaited their healing touch. The amulet, a beacon of cosmic balance, pulsed with a rhythmic glow that echoed the harmonious resonance they had restored. The celestial map, now revealing constellations that depicted the friends as cosmic healers, guided them towards realms where their presence was needed.

Their cosmic odyssey, now marked by the mending of celestial threads and triumphant resilience, unfolded like a cosmic epic—an eternal saga that transcended mortal fears and celebrated the enduring bond between mortal souls and the cosmic forces that shaped their destinies.

Chapter 20: The Cosmic Reckoning

In the final leg of their cosmic odyssey, the friends sensed a gathering cosmic storm—a tempest that threatened to unravel the very fabric of reality. The Veilstitcher's influence, a vigilant beacon, resonated with a profound urgency that transcended the echoes of their past encounters. The amulet, though resilient, emitted a pulsating glow that mirrored the unsettling cosmic energies that surrounded them.

The celestial map, now marked by constellations that seemed to writhe in cosmic distress, guided the friends towards the epicenter of the looming cosmic tempest. As they approached, the shadows deepened, and the cosmic storm manifested in swirling patterns of

ethereal chaos. The Veilstitcher's spectral form, now a harbinger of cosmic reckoning, communicated a dire prophecy of an ancient cosmic entity—the Stormweaver—whose fury threatened to engulf the interconnected tapestry.

In the heart of the cosmic storm, the friends confronted an ethereal vortex—a manifestation of the Stormweaver's wrath. Eldritch symbols adorned the vortex, resonating with an ominous energy that sent shivers down their spines. The celestial map, now etched with constellations that depicted the Stormweaver's fury, guided them towards understanding the origin of the cosmic tempest.

The Veilstitcher's spectral form, now a cosmic seer, revealed the tale of the Stormweaver—an ancient cosmic entity imprisoned by the threads of reality in ages past. Betrayals and vendettas had fueled the Stormweaver's rage, and its spectral essence now sought to unleash cosmic chaos upon the interconnected tapestry. The amulet, resonating with the cosmic revelations, emitted a luminescent glow that mirrored the friends' determination to quell the cosmic reckoning.

As they ventured into the heart of the cosmic vortex, the friends faced celestial guardians—entities corrupted by the Stormweaver's malevolent influence. The Veilstitcher's influence, though tinged with cosmic sorrow, urged them to confront the guardians and understand the depths of the cosmic tempest's power. The amulet, their cosmic shield, resonated with a determination to resist the impending catastrophe.

In the cosmic battleground, the friends encountered remnants of cosmic entities ensnared by the Stormweaver's malevolent influence. Shadows, animated by cosmic fury, seemed to writhe with an otherworldly malevolence. The Veilstitcher's spectral form guided them through trials that tested their resolve against the impending cosmic reckoning.

The celestial map, now revealing constellations that depicted the enslaved cosmic entities, guided the friends through the cosmic trials. The amulet, emitting a protective aura, shimmered with a resilient light that mirrored their commitment to resist the cosmic tempest's onslaught.

As they navigated through the cosmic chaos, the friends uncovered an ancient cosmic prison—an ethereal cage that held the Stormweaver's spectral essence. Eldritch symbols adorned the prison, resonating with the echoes of ancient grievances that fueled the cosmic reckoning. The celestial map, now etched with constellations that depicted the prison's significance, guided them towards understanding the key to subduing the Stormweaver's fury.

The Veilstitcher's spectral form, now a cosmic keybearer, communicated a ritual to unlock the prison and confront the Stormweaver. The amulet, resonating with the cosmic revelations, emitted a luminescent glow that mirrored the friends' determination to face the ancient cosmic entity. As they channeled their cosmic abilities into the ritual, the cosmic prison responded with an ethereal symphony.

Shadows, once animated by cosmic fury, now seemed to waver in a discordant ballet. The celestial map, now pulsating with threads of cosmic understanding, guided the friends through the intricate maneuvers needed to unlock the ancient prison. The Veilstitcher's influence, now a cosmic guide, urged them to unravel the Stormweaver's malevolent influence and restore balance to the interconnected tapestry.

In the cosmic aftermath of the ritual, the ancient prison released the Stormweaver's spectral essence. The friends, now confronted by the embodiment of cosmic fury, felt the weight of the impending reckoning bearing down upon them. The Veilstitcher's spectral form, now a cosmic defender, communicated a sense of urgency as the friends prepared to face the Stormweaver's wrath.

The celestial map, now depicting constellations that mirrored the Stormweaver's cosmic fury, guided the friends through a cosmic trial that tested their resilience against the impending reckoning. The amulet, their only defense against the cosmic tempest, emitted a protective aura that shimmered with a determination to resist the ancient entity's onslaught.

In their cosmic struggle against the Stormweaver's spectral essence, the friends uncovered the origins of the ancient grievances that had fueled the cosmic reckoning. Betrayals, vendettas, and cosmic vendettas had intertwined in a malevolent dance that threatened to consume the interconnected tapestry. The Veilstitcher's spectral form, a witness to the unfolding cosmic drama, conveyed a sense of urgency as the friends unraveled the ancient cosmic entity's malevolent influence.

The amulet, attuned to the cosmic revelations, emitted pulses of resonant light that harmonized with the celestial map's guidance. As the friends faced the Stormweaver's spectral essence, the cosmic tempest seemed to shift in response to their cosmic understanding. Shadows, once animated by cosmic fury, now flickered with moments of cosmic discord.

In a pivotal moment of the cosmic struggle, the friends realized that the only way to quell the Stormweaver's wrath was to break the chains of ancient grievances. The Veilstitcher's spectral form, now a cosmic arbitrator, guided them through a celestial ritual that sought to sever the cosmic cycles of vengeance and restore the ancient entity's fractured consciousness.

As they channeled their cosmic abilities into the ritual, the cosmic tempest responded with an ethereal symphony. Shadows, once animated by cosmic fury, now seemed to waver in a harmonious ballet. The celestial map, now pulsating with threads of cosmic

understanding, guided the friends through the intricate maneuvers needed to mend the Stormweaver's spectral essence.

In the cosmic aftermath of the ritual, the Stormweaver's spectral essence transformed. Fury gave way to a serene luminescence, and the cosmic tempest seemed to retreat. The Veilstitcher's influence, now a cosmic mediator, conveyed a sense of resolution as the friends witnessed the ancient entity find peace within the interconnected tapestry.

The amulet, though worn by the cosmic struggle, emitted a radiant glow that mirrored the friends' triumph over the impending reckoning. The celestial map, now cleared of constellations depicting discord, revealed a new cosmic equilibrium that reflected the friends' ability to confront the ancient cosmic entity and emerge unscathed.

As the friends ascended from the cosmic battleground, the Veilstitcher's spectral form regained its ethereal brilliance. The amulet, though scarred by the cosmic ordeal, pulsed with a renewed vitality. The celestial map, now cleared of the cosmic turmoil, guided them towards new frontiers in the interconnected tapestry.

The friends, forever changed by their harrowing encounter with the cosmic reckoning, continued their cosmic odyssey with a heightened awareness of the cosmic perils that lurked in the vast expanse. The Veilstitcher's influence, now a cosmic mediator, accompanied them as a guiding force. The amulet, a resilient artifact that bore the scars of their cosmic ordeal, resonated with a luminous brilliance that symbolized their triumph over the impending reckoning.

The celestial map, once tainted by the cosmic turmoil, now guided the friends toward realms where cosmic wonders awaited discovery. The echoes of the unknown, though still haunting, whispered tales of cosmic resilience and the indomitable spirit that defied the cosmic tempest. The friends, forever entwined by the shared

horrors they had faced, embraced the mysteries that awaited them in the uncharted territories of the interconnected tapestry.

Their cosmic odyssey, now marked by the triumphant resolution of the cosmic reckoning, unfolded like a cosmic epic—an eternal saga that transcended mortal fears and celebrated the enduring bond between mortal souls and the cosmic forces that shaped their destinies.

As they journeyed into the unexplored cosmic realms, the friends encountered celestial wonders that seemed to radiate with the echoes of their victorious struggle. The Veilstitcher's influence, now a beacon of cosmic resolution, guided them through realms where echoes of their cosmic deeds resonated with celestial echoes. The amulet, a cosmic artifact infused with the power of triumphant threads, pulsed with a rhythmic glow that echoed the harmony they had restored.

The celestial map, now revealing constellations that depicted the friends as cosmic defenders, guided them toward realms where their presence was needed. Shadows, once animated by cosmic fury, now seemed to retreat in the wake of their cosmic triumph. The friends, now guardians of celestial balance, embraced their role in preserving the interconnected tapestry.

In their cosmic journey, the friends encountered celestial beings whose threads of reality had been freed from the shackles of ancient grievances. The Veilstitcher's spectral form, now a cosmic liberator, urged them to extend their cosmic influence to those freed from the burden of cosmic turmoil. The amulet, resonating with the threads of triumphant reality, emitted a radiant glow that mirrored their commitment to safeguarding the celestial realms.

As they traversed through realms touched by cosmic liberation, the friends faced cosmic trials that tested their newfound abilities as defenders of the interconnected tapestry. The Veilstitcher's

influence, now a cosmic mentor, guided them through rituals that sought to fortify the threads of reality and preserve balance in celestial entities freed from ancient shackles.

The amulet, a conduit of cosmic energies, emitted pulses of protective light that harmonized with the celestial map's guidance. Shadows, once animated by cosmic turmoil, now seemed to dissipate as the friends embraced their cosmic roles as defenders. The echoes of their cosmic deeds reverberated through the interconnected tapestry, leaving a trail of celestial balance in their wake.

In a celestial sanctuary, the friends encountered a cosmic entity—a guardian of the celestial realms whose threads of reality had been freed from ancient shackles. The Veilstitcher's spectral form, now a cosmic liberator, communicated with the entity in a language of cosmic understanding. The amulet, resonating with the threads of triumphant reality, emitted a soothing aura that celebrated the entity's cosmic liberation.

As the friends reveled in the cosmic liberation, the celestial sanctuary responded with ethereal energies. The Veilstitcher's influence, now a cosmic conductor of harmony, guided them through the intricate maneuvers needed to celebrate the celestial guardian's newfound freedom. The amulet, attuned to the cosmic revelations, emitted pulses of resonant light that harmonized with the celestial map's guidance.

In the cosmic aftermath of the celebration, the celestial guardian's spectral form radiated with joy. Threads once bound by ancient grievances now shimmered with a serene luminescence. The Veilstitcher's influence, now a cosmic celebrant, conveyed a sense of fulfillment as the friends witnessed the guardian revel in newfound peace within the celestial sanctuary.

The amulet, though worn by the cosmic struggle, emitted a radiant glow that mirrored the friends' triumph as cosmic liberators.

The celestial map, now cleared of constellations depicting ancient shackles, revealed a new cosmic equilibrium that reflected the friends' ability to free celestial entities from the burden of cosmic turmoil.

As the friends continued their cosmic journey, the Veilstitcher's spectral form, now a cosmic celebrant, guided them toward realms where celestial entities awaited their liberating touch. The amulet, a beacon of cosmic liberation, pulsed with a rhythmic glow that echoed the joy they had spread. The celestial map, now revealing constellations that depicted the friends as cosmic liberators, guided them toward realms where their presence was needed.

Their cosmic odyssey, now marked by the celebration of cosmic liberation and triumphant resolution, unfolded like a cosmic epic—an eternal saga that transcended mortal fears and celebrated the enduring bond between mortal souls and the cosmic forces that shaped their destinies.

Stormweaver
The Goatman Lives
By
Doug Hensley
Table Of Contents

Chapter 1: The Unknown Encounter

- A group of friends on a camping trip
- Mysterious noises in the woods at night

Chapter 2: Whispering Shadows

- Strange occurrences escalate
- Unsettling whispers heard in the darkness

Chapter 3: The Legend Unveiled

- Local tales of the Goatman shared around the campfire
- Skepticism and unease among the group

Chapter 4: A Fateful Decision

- The group decides to investigate the legend

- Deep into the forest, the atmosphere thickens

Chapter 5: Signs of the Goatman

- Disturbing symbols and tracks discovered
- Tension grows as reality sets in

Chapter 6: Disappearing Act

- One member of the group goes missing
- Panic and fear grip the others

Chapter 7: Unholy Alliance

- Remaining friends unite to find the missing person
- A pact to face the Goatman together

Chapter 8: Haunting Memories

- Flashbacks reveal past encounters with the Goatman
- Characters confront their own fears

Chapter 9: Night of the Full Moon

- The group faces the Goatman for the first time
- A terrifying chase through the woods ensues

Chapter 10: The Goatman's Curse

- Survivor guilt and paranoia set in
- The Goatman's curse becomes evident

Chapter 11: The Unseen Stalker

- Unexplained phenomena haunt the group
- A feeling of being constantly watched

Chapter 12: The Goatman's Lair

- Discover a hidden lair deep in the woods
- A horrifying revelation awaits

Chapter 13: Descent into Madness

- Characters grapple with their sanity
- Unexplainable events intensify

Chapter 14: The Goatman's Call

- A hypnotic call draws the group deeper
- Internal conflicts escalate

Chapter 15: Sacrificial Night

- The group faces a choice to save themselves or succumb to the Goatman's curse
- Tension peaks as the night unfolds

Chapter 16: Midnight Ritual

- Ritualistic elements unfold
- The Goatman's power grows stronger

Chapter 17: The Final Confrontation

- Confrontation with the Goatman in a climactic battle
- Sacrifices made to break the curse

Chapter 18: Lingering Shadows

- The aftermath of the confrontation
- The group struggles to return to normalcy

Chapter 19: Epilogue of Fear

- Lingering fears and unanswered questions
- Hints that the Goatman may still be out there

Chapter 20: The Legend Lives On

- Closing with a new group stumbling upon the same legend
- The cycle continues, leaving the ending open-ended and unsettling

Chapter 1: The Unknown Encounter

The dense forest canopy loomed overhead, casting eerie shadows as the group of friends, led by the adventurous spirit of Mark, ventured deeper into the wilderness. A cool breeze rustled the leaves, creating an ominous symphony that echoed through the trees. Their laughter filled the air, a stark contrast to the quiet unease that settled with the setting sun.

As darkness embraced the forest, the friends gathered around a crackling campfire. The flickering flames danced to the rhythm of their hushed conversations. An unsettling feeling hung in the air,

unnoticed by most, except for Emily, who couldn't shake off the sensation that they were not alone.

Unknown to the group, distant whispers intertwined with the nocturnal symphony, carried by the wind. Mark, the leader of the expedition, dismissed them as the rustling of leaves or the murmur of the night creatures. Little did they know that these whispers were the first ominous notes of a malevolent tune.

As the night wore on, the friends shared stories, trying to drown out the disconcerting sounds around them. In the midst of laughter, a sudden silence fell upon the group, broken only by the distant howl of a lone wolf. They exchanged uneasy glances, their camaraderie momentarily fractured.

The crackling fire cast eerie shadows on the surrounding trees, creating grotesque shapes that seemed to watch the friends with malevolent intent. An inexplicable tension wrapped itself around them, tightening like a coil. Emily's gaze flickered nervously between the dancing flames and the dark recesses of the forest.

The once vibrant atmosphere now carried an undertone of dread. Mark, attempting to dispel the growing unease, suggested exploring the nearby trails. Reluctantly, the group ventured into the heart of the woods, guided only by dim flashlights that struggled to penetrate the thick darkness.

As they meandered through the labyrinthine paths, the night seemed to swallow them whole. The moon cast an eerie glow, revealing twisted branches that resembled skeletal fingers reaching out from the shadows. Unbeknownst to the friends, unseen eyes observed their every move.

The distant echoes of footsteps, not matching the rhythm of their own, reverberated through the night. A cold shiver ran down Emily's spine as she whispered to Mark, "Did you hear that?" He

dismissed it as their imagination playing tricks, but doubt lingered in his eyes.

The trail, once familiar, now felt like an ever-twisting maze. Panic set in as the friends realized they were lost. The forest seemed to conspire against them, distorting their perception of time and space. Anxiety gripped the group, amplifying the unsettling aura that clung to the night.

A blood-curdling scream shattered the silence, sending shockwaves through the group. Fear etched deep lines on their faces as they turned toward the source. In the suffocating darkness, a silhouette moved swiftly, disappearing among the gnarled trees.

Panic took hold, and the friends sprinted back towards the campsite, fueled by a primal instinct to survive. The once-familiar surroundings now felt alien and menacing. The forest, alive with unseen malevolence, seemed to mock their feeble attempts to escape.

The crackling campfire welcomed them back, but the safety it once provided now felt like a fragile illusion. The missing member, a specter in their midst, cast a long shadow over the group. The night, far from over, held secrets that would unravel as the friends clung to the flickering flames, unaware of the terror that awaited them in the heart of the haunted woods.

Chapter 2: Whispering Shadows

The remnants of their once-jovial campfire flickered in the oppressive darkness. Unsettled by the earlier scream, the friends huddled close, their faces etched with fear. Mark, the bravest among them, attempted to lighten the mood with nervous jokes, but the unease lingered like a thick fog.

As they sat in the ominous stillness, the haunting whispers returned. The friends exchanged anxious glances, realizing the sounds were more than mere forest murmurs. The words, though

unintelligible, seemed to crawl beneath their skin, instilling a primal fear that transcended rationality.

Emily, the most sensitive to the otherworldly, clutched her ears, desperate to block out the spectral voices. The whispers intertwined with the wind, creating an otherworldly melody that resonated through the haunted woods. Shadows danced menacingly, morphing into grotesque forms that seemed to mimic the torment in the friends' hearts.

Mark, determined to maintain a semblance of control, suggested investigating the source of the whispers. Armed with flashlights, the group ventured into the inky darkness, guided by the haunting voices that seemed to lead them deeper into the heart of the haunted woods.

The forest, now transformed into a realm of spectral uncertainty, played tricks on their senses. Trees twisted into nightmarish shapes, their branches reaching out like skeletal fingers. Each step felt like a descent into an abyss, and the whispers grew louder, forming an otherworldly chorus that resonated through the friends' minds.

A surreal fog enveloped the path, distorting reality. Shadows detached from the trees, taking on a sinister life of their own. Unseen eyes followed the group's every move, and the air became dense with an otherworldly energy that made it difficult to breathe.

Amidst the disorienting whispers, a distant figure materialized before them. The friends froze, their flashlights trembling in their hands. The silhouette seemed to flicker between the shadows, an elusive presence that defied comprehension. Panic gripped the group as the figure approached with an otherworldly grace.

With each step, the whispers intensified, revealing fragments of a haunting narrative. The legend of the Goatman, an entity that blurred the line between man and beast, echoed through the spectral voices. Dread tightened its grip on the friends as they realized

they were entangled in a story that surpassed the boundaries of the known.

A sudden gust of wind extinguished their flashlights, plunging them into pitch darkness. The whispers crescendoed into an unsettling cacophony, weaving a narrative that spoke of ancient curses and forbidden rituals. The friends stumbled blindly, guided only by the haunting voices that seemed to mock their feeble attempts to escape the encroaching nightmare.

As they fumbled through the labyrinthine paths, the forest itself seemed to conspire against them. Trees leaned menacingly, forming an impenetrable barrier that distorted their perception of space. Panic reached its zenith when the friends realized they were caught in a malevolent force beyond their understanding.

In the heart of the haunted woods, the whispers reached a deafening climax. The spectral figure, now a manifestation of pure terror, revealed itself as the harbinger of an ancient curse. The friends, paralyzed by fear, witnessed the birth of a nightmare that transcended the realm of the living.

The haunting voices echoed a chilling prophecy, sealing the friends' fate as pawns in a cosmic game. As the shadows enveloped them, the whispers faded into an ominous silence, leaving the group suspended in the chilling realization that they were now entwined with the legendary Goatman, and their journey into terror had only just begun.

Chapter 3: The Legend Unveiled

The haunted woods bore witness to the friends' descent into an abyss of fear, their breaths visible in the chilling air as they stood at the precipice of the unknown. Mark, the once-confident leader, now felt the weight of uncertainty press upon him, his eyes flickering nervously between the faces of his friends.

The chilling echoes of the Goatman's curse lingered, a sinister resonance that seeped into their very souls. As the group gathered around the remnants of their campfire, a shadowy figure materialized within the shifting shadows, a grotesque manifestation of the legend they had dismissed as mere folklore.

An air of disbelief hung heavy as the friends exchanged uneasy glances. Emily's wide eyes mirrored the terror reflected in the faces of the others. The whispers, now reduced to a haunting murmur, seemed to emanate from the very core of the forest, weaving a tapestry of dread that ensnared the group in an inescapable nightmare.

Against the backdrop of encroaching darkness, Mark attempted to rationalize the situation, attributing the spectral figure to mere illusions. However, the disconcerting reality betrayed his attempts at reassurance. The forest, alive with an otherworldly energy, pulsated with the ancient heartbeat of a malevolent force.

Doubt gnawed at the edges of the friends' minds as the whispers intensified. The spectral figure, now a tangible presence, beckoned them into the heart of the woods. The group, caught in the gravitational pull of an insidious force, hesitated on the brink of a decision that would seal their fate.

Reluctantly, they followed the elusive silhouette, their path illuminated by the pale glow of the moon. The forest, now a labyrinth of twisted shadows, seemed to breathe in tandem with the ethereal whispers that guided their journey. Unseen eyes observed their every move as they delved deeper into the legend that had come to life.

The friends stumbled upon an ancient clearing, adorned with eerie symbols etched into the earth. Mark, ever the skeptic, dismissed them as mere remnants of forgotten rituals. However, the others felt an otherworldly pull, an invisible thread connecting them to a malevolent past.

As the group examined the haunting symbols, the whispers coalesced into a narrative, recounting the tale of the Goatman—a creature that straddled the boundary between man and beast, a cursed entity bound by ancient rites. The friends, ensnared in the unfolding nightmare, now faced a reality that surpassed the confines of reason.

The spectral figure, a conduit of the Goatman's curse, revealed itself as a harbinger of impending doom. The friends, caught in the snare of a supernatural force, realized the legend was no mere folktale but a living nightmare that demanded their acknowledgment.

The moon cast an otherworldly glow upon the clearing as the group, paralyzed by a mixture of awe and terror, bore witness to the manifestation of the Goatman. A creature of nightmares stood before them, its eyes gleaming with an otherworldly intelligence that transcended the animalistic form it wore.

The atmosphere thickened with a palpable malevolence as the Goatman's presence dominated the clearing. Its form seemed to shift and contort, a grotesque dance that defied the laws of nature. The friends, gripped by an ancient fear, trembled as the Goatman spoke through the whispers, weaving a fate that intertwined with their very essence.

The friends, now bound by an unbreakable covenant, stood on the precipice of an unholy alliance. The Goatman, an embodiment of primordial terror, extended a spectral hand, inviting the group to embrace the curse that lurked within the shadows. Their destinies, forever altered, collided with the inexorable force of the legend, and the haunted woods echoed with the ominous laughter of a malevolent entity that reveled in the unfolding nightmare.

Chapter 4: A Fateful Decision

The haunted clearing pulsated with an otherworldly energy as the friends faced the enigmatic presence of the Goatman. The air

grew dense with the weight of an ancient curse, and the friends, caught between reason and the supernatural, found themselves at a crossroads that would define their destiny.

Mark, ever the voice of skepticism, hesitated. His logical mind resisted the pull of the unknown, urging him to reject the spectral hand that extended toward them. But the allure of the Goatman's power, shrouded in the whispers that echoed through the clearing, whispered promises of understanding and dominion over the mysterious forces that governed their existence.

Emily, sensitive to the ethereal currents, felt an irresistible draw. The whispers, now a seductive lullaby, caressed her consciousness, weaving visions of forbidden knowledge and a connection to realms beyond mortal comprehension. The choice lay before them, a perilous gambit that promised either enlightenment or descent into the abyss.

As the group teetered on the precipice of decision, the forest itself seemed to hold its breath. Unseen eyes observed their every move, and the shadows twisted in anticipation. The Goatman, a creature of the ancient woods, watched with an intelligence that transcended the animalistic facade it presented.

A cold wind whispered through the gnarled branches, carrying echoes of the past and the future. The choice, suspended in the eerie silence, would echo through the corridors of time, leaving an indelible mark on the souls of the friends who dared to confront the unknown.

In the midst of this spectral tableau, a memory surfaced in the recesses of Mark's mind—a childhood tale of a friend who disappeared in mysterious circumstances, whispered to be a victim of the Goatman's curse. The realization struck him like a bolt of lightning, igniting a primal fear that pulsed through his veins.

The haunting whispers morphed into chilling laughter, echoing Mark's internal turmoil. The Goatman, sensing the doubt, pressed its advantage, its eyes gleaming with an ancient malevolence. The clearing became a battleground of wills, where the tangible and intangible clashed in a dance of shadows.

As the friends deliberated, the forest responded to the rising tension. The ancient trees groaned, their branches contorting into grotesque forms. The whispers, now laced with impatience, intensified, urging the group to make their choice. The boundary between reality and nightmare blurred, and the friends found themselves ensnared in a surreal dreamscape.

Emily, tormented by the visions, trembled as conflicting emotions wrestled within her. The allure of forbidden knowledge clashed with an instinctual fear that warned of the consequences of tampering with forces beyond mortal understanding. The Goatman's eyes bore into her soul, a silent plea that transcended the limitations of spoken language.

Amidst the inner turmoil, a distant sound reverberated through the clearing—a mournful howl that cut through the spectral tension. The friends, momentarily distracted, turned toward the source. Shadows danced on the periphery of the clearing, and an unseen presence circled them like a predatory force.

The Goatman's form flickered, its patience wearing thin. The friends, aware of the imminent choice, felt the weight of the decision settle upon them like a suffocating cloak. The clearing, a stage for the cosmic drama, held its breath as the friends confronted the inevitable.

In a moment of collective resolve, the group stepped back from the outstretched hand of the Goatman. The whispers, now a discordant symphony of disappointment, echoed through the haunted

woods. The spectral figure, once a harbinger of alliance, recoiled into the shadows, its eyes aflame with an ancient ire.

As the friends retreated from the clearing, the forest sighed with relief. The ethereal tension dissipated, and the haunted woods returned to a semblance of stillness. The friends, marked by the encounter, stumbled back into the labyrinth of the forest, haunted by the knowledge that they had narrowly evaded a fate entwined with the Goatman's curse.

Yet, the shadows clung to their every step, and the whispers lingered, a reminder that the legend, far from defeated, awaited its next encounter with unsuspecting souls who dared to tread the boundary between the known and the supernatural. The night, pregnant with uncertainty, unfolded its mysteries as the friends navigated the haunted woods, forever changed by the fateful decision that spared them from the Goatman's insidious embrace.

T

Chapter 5: Signs of the Goatman

The haunted woods, having witnessed the friends' rejection of the Goatman's enticement, stirred with an ancient restlessness. The air crackled with latent energy as the group, still shaken from their encounter, navigated the twisting trails. The forest, once familiar, now seemed to shift and contort, its very essence reacting to the disturbance in the supernatural equilibrium.

Unspoken tension hung between the friends as they threaded through the labyrinth of shadows. The whispers, subdued but undeterred, lingered on the periphery of their consciousness. Emily, especially, felt the ethereal threads tugging at the edges of her sanity, weaving a tapestry of unnerving visions that threatened to unravel the fabric of her understanding.

A subtle rustling in the underbrush echoed through the stillness, sending a shiver down the spines of the friends. The forest seemed to

respond to their every step, alive with an unseen force that observed their every move. Paranoia took root, and the group cast nervous glances over their shoulders, half-expecting the Goatman's grotesque figure to materialize from the shadows.

Mark, burdened by the weight of his past and the consequences of the group's rejection, led the way with a furrowed brow. The once-confident leader now grappled with doubt, haunted by the memory of his childhood friend who had vanished into the clutches of the Goatman's curse. The forest, sensing his internal conflict, seemed to feed on his insecurities, twisting the trees into macabre forms that mirrored the tendrils of fear constricting his heart.

As they pressed forward, the trail revealed unsettling signs—twisted branches forming crude symbols, the earth marked with enigmatic patterns, and distant echoes that mimicked the mournful cries of the spectral creature they had narrowly evaded. The friends, unable to escape the omnipresent gaze of the haunted woods, exchanged wary glances as the realization dawned that the legend of the Goatman was far from a mere tale.

The group stumbled upon a clearing bathed in an eerie moonlit glow, its center dominated by a gnarled tree that bore the unmistakable markings of the supernatural. Emily, drawn by an invisible force, approached the ancient tree, her fingers tracing the symbols etched into its bark. The whispers, now a ghostly murmur, beckoned her to decipher the cryptic language of the Goatman's curse.

As Emily touched the symbols, the forest responded with a sudden surge of energy. The air crackled with an otherworldly charge, and the friends, captivated by a force beyond their control, witnessed the roots of the ancient tree twitch and writhe. The earth itself seemed to pulse with an unholy heartbeat as the symbols glowed with an ethereal light.

A ghostly apparition materialized before them, an echo of the Goatman's presence. Its eyes gleamed with an otherworldly intelligence, and a spectral voice resonated through the clearing. The friends, entranced by the unfolding spectacle, listened as the Goatman's tale unfolded—a story of ancient curses, forbidden pacts, and the insatiable hunger that bound it to the haunted woods.

As the spectral apparition spoke, the friends felt the tendrils of the Goatman's influence worming their way into their minds. Visions of torment and cosmic malevolence unfolded, weaving a narrative that blurred the boundaries between reality and nightmare. Emily, caught in the vortex of the supernatural revelation, glimpsed the unfathomable depths of the Goatman's ancient origins.

The whispers crescendoed, their words weaving an intricate web that ensnared the friends in a surreal dance of fate. The forest, now an extension of the Goatman's domain, pulsed with an ominous energy. The group, teetering on the precipice of enlightenment and damnation, faced the haunting reality that the legend had claimed them as unwilling participants in its insidious narrative.

In the midst of the ethereal revelation, a distant howl echoed through the clearing—a mournful cry that reverberated through the haunted woods. The spectral Goatman, its form flickering like a dying flame, receded into the shadows. The ancient tree, its roots once animated, settled into an eerie stillness.

The friends, released from the trance, stumbled backward, their minds reeling from the forbidden knowledge bestowed upon them. The clearing, now devoid of the Goatman's presence, returned to a deceptive calm. The haunted woods, however, retained the scars of their encounter, the symbols etched into the ancient tree serving as a chilling reminder that they were forever bound to the unfolding nightmare.

As the group retreated from the clearing, the forest whispered its secrets—a haunting lament that echoed through the shadows. The friends, marked by the signs of the Goatman, ventured deeper into the heart of the haunted woods, their destinies entwined with the ancient curse that refused to release its grip. The spectral whispers lingered, a spectral chorus that foretold of the terrors yet to unfold in the labyrinth of nightmares they now called home.

Chapter 6: Disappearing Act

The haunted woods, now saturated with the residual energy of the Goatman's revelation, clung to the friends like a suffocating shroud. The symbols etched into the ancient tree continued to glow with an otherworldly radiance, casting an eerie glow upon the path ahead. The air, thick with the weight of forbidden knowledge, pressed down on the group as they pressed forward, their fate intricately woven into the fabric of the supernatural.

Mark, haunted by the ghostly memories of his childhood friend's disappearance, felt an invisible force tugging at the edges of his consciousness. The whispers, once distant murmurs, now reverberated through his mind with an unsettling clarity. He strained to maintain composure, masking his internal turmoil behind a façade of false bravado. Unbeknownst to him, the haunted woods, sentient and malevolent, fed on his fear like a ravenous entity.

The trail, twisted and labyrinthine, seemed to shift with a will of its own. The friends, ensnared by the spectral threads that bound them to the Goatman's curse, navigated the surreal landscape with trepidation. The shadows played tricks on their senses, morphing into phantasmal shapes that seemed to watch with unseen eyes.

As the group delved deeper into the heart of the haunted woods, a palpable tension threaded through their camaraderie. Emily, marked by the spectral encounter at the ancient tree, felt an inexorable pull toward the unknown. The whispers, now a constant companion,

murmured secrets that transcended the realm of mortal understanding. Her eyes, once bright with curiosity, now reflected the unsettling wisdom bestowed upon her by the Goatman's revelation.

A distant howl echoed through the woods, a mournful cry that reverberated with a haunting resonance. The friends, halted by the spectral sound, exchanged uneasy glances. The Goatman's influence, a malevolent force that defied the natural order, now seemed to guide their every step. The path ahead, obscured by a foreboding mist, beckoned them into the heart of the supernatural enigma.

The trail, fraught with unseen perils, led the friends to a clearing bathed in an ethereal glow. A spectral figure materialized before them, its eyes gleaming with an otherworldly intelligence. The Goatman, a manifestation of cosmic dread, stood as a sentinel at the crossroads of their destiny.

In a voice that echoed through the haunted woods, the Goatman spoke, its words a haunting melody that resonated with the friends' deepest fears. The choices made, the destinies entwined, the group stood as unwitting participants in a cosmic drama that unfolded with a relentless momentum. The Goatman, a puppeteer of fate, reveled in the dance of shadows that played out in the haunted clearing.

As the spectral figure spoke, the surroundings warped into a surreal dreamscape. Reality and nightmare merged, and the friends found themselves suspended in a liminal space where time seemed to lose its meaning. Visions of the Goatman's cursed legacy unfolded—a tapestry of despair woven with threads of ancient malevolence.

Mark, tormented by memories of his lost friend, witnessed haunting scenes from the past. The woods became a theater of spectral apparitions, replaying moments of anguish and despair. The Goatman's voice, a spectral undertone, whispered forgotten secrets that clawed at the edges of his sanity.

Emily, sensitive to the ethereal currents, glimpsed glimpses of the future—a mosaic of tormented landscapes and spectral encounters. The haunted woods, now a maze of interconnected destinies, revealed a nightmarish tableau that unfolded with an inexorable inevitability.

As the visions played out, the friends, paralyzed by the supernatural revelation, became mere spectators in their own existential drama. The Goatman, a harbinger of cosmic terror, reveled in the torment it unleashed upon their minds. The clearing, a stage for the unfolding nightmare, pulsated with an otherworldly energy.

Suddenly, the visions ceased, and the friends, released from the spectral trance, found themselves standing in the clearing once more. The Goatman, its form flickering like a dying ember, faded into the shadows. The ancient tree, now devoid of the supernatural glow, stood as a silent witness to the cosmic theater that unfolded beneath its twisted branches.

The friends, disoriented and haunted by the echoes of the Goatman's revelations, staggered away from the clearing. The haunted woods, now a sentient labyrinth, seemed to rearrange itself, guiding the group deeper into the heart of the supernatural enigma.

As they pressed forward, a cold wind whispered through the twisted branches, carrying with it a chilling echo of the Goatman's laughter. The friends, caught in a cycle of existential dread, stumbled through the haunted woods, forever marked by the disappearing act that unfolded in the surreal clearing. The night, pregnant with cosmic uncertainty, stretched before them like an endless abyss, and the friends, ensnared by the spectral forces that governed their fate, plunged further into the inescapable nightmare that awaited in the shadowed depths of the ancient forest.

Chapter 7: Unholy Alliance

The haunted woods, now a realm of spectral uncertainty, closed in around the friends as they stumbled through the labyrinthine trails. The air was thick with an oppressive tension, and the whispers, once distant murmurs, reverberated through the trees with an unsettling urgency. Mark, Emily, and the rest of the group were mere pawns in a cosmic game, ensnared by the Goatman's curse, and each step they took seemed to propel them deeper into the heart of an insidious nightmare.

The trail, twisted and sinuous, led the friends to the edge of an ancient clearing. Moonlight filtered through the gnarled branches, casting an ethereal glow on the uneven ground. The clearing, marked by a series of grotesque symbols etched into the earth, seemed to pulse with a malevolent energy. Unseen eyes watched from the shadows as the friends hesitated at the threshold of the supernatural stage.

Emily, the once-curious soul now burdened by the weight of forbidden knowledge, felt an invisible force drawing her toward the center of the clearing. The whispers, now an incessant chorus, beckoned her to unravel the mysteries encoded in the symbols. A compulsion, an otherworldly pull, guided her steps as she approached the enigmatic patterns etched into the earth.

Mark, torn between the rational skepticism that had defined him and the growing influence of the Goatman's curse, cast wary glances at the symbols. The haunted woods, responsive to the internal struggles of the friends, seemed to warp and contort with a will of its own. Shadows danced in grotesque patterns, and the clearing became a stage for a supernatural spectacle.

The group, teetering on the brink of an abyss, gathered at the center of the clearing. Emily traced her fingers over the symbols, her touch unlocking a latent energy that pulsed through the earth. The whispers intensified, their spectral voices weaving a narrative

that echoed through the haunted woods—a tale of ancient alliances, cosmic conspiracies, and the inexorable dance between the living and the supernatural.

As Emily deciphered the symbols, the clearing transformed into a spectral panorama. Visions of the Goatman's cursed legacy unfolded, revealing a tapestry of intertwined destinies that stretched across epochs. The friends, now mere spectators in the cosmic drama, glimpsed fragments of the entity's tormented existence.

The Goatman, a creature bound by an unholy alliance with forces beyond mortal understanding, emerged as a tragic figure—a victim of a cosmic imbalance that demanded appeasement through unspeakable rituals and sacrifices. Its eyes, once gleaming with malevolence, now reflected a profound sadness that transcended the bestial form it wore.

The friends, ensnared in the unfolding revelation, witnessed scenes from the Goatman's past—a time when the ancient woods echoed with primal magic, and forbidden pacts were forged beneath the watchful gaze of eldritch entities. The haunted woods, a nexus of supernatural energies, became a stage for an age-old conflict that transcended the boundaries of time.

Mark, grappling with the conflicting forces that tore at his sanity, saw glimpses of the Goatman's interactions with lost souls—a spectral procession of individuals who had been entangled in the cosmic machinations of the ancient curse. The forest, a witness to centuries of suffering, whispered tales of tormented souls and unspeakable horrors that lurked in the shadowed depths.

The friends, released from the spectral visions, found themselves standing in the clearing once more. The symbols, now infused with a latent energy, pulsed with an otherworldly radiance. The Goatman, its form flickering between the grotesque and the tragic,

remained at the periphery of their perception, a spectral guardian of the haunted woods.

As the friends retreated from the clearing, a mournful howl echoed through the trees—a sound that transcended the natural world. The spectral alliance between the friends and the Goatman, forged by the revelation in the clearing, had sealed their destinies in an unholy covenant. The whispers, now a constant companion, guided them deeper into the labyrinth of the supernatural, their fates entwined with the spectral forces that governed the haunted woods.

The group, marked by the spectral encounter, pressed forward with a newfound awareness. The haunted woods, now an extension of the Goatman's domain, seemed to anticipate their every move. Shadows clung to the friends like a malevolent fog, and the air pulsed with an otherworldly energy that heightened the senses to the unseen threats that lurked in the shadows.

As they traversed the twisted trails, the group became acutely aware of an invisible tether connecting them to the Goatman's curse. The forest, alive with spectral currents, responded to their presence with a symphony of ethereal whispers. The alliance, forged in the clearing, propelled them toward a convergence of cosmic forces that awaited in the heart of the supernatural enigma.

The night, pregnant with uncertainty, stretched before the friends like an endless abyss. The haunted woods, a realm of shifting shadows and spectral whispers, beckoned them into the heart of the supernatural enigma. The Goatman, now an unseen puppeteer of their destinies, watched with an otherworldly intelligence as the group delved deeper into the spectral dance that awaited them in the shadowed depths.

Chapter 8: The Dance of Shadows

The haunted woods, now an extension of the Goatman's dominion, closed in around the friends as they ventured deeper into the labyrinth of shadows. The spectral alliance forged in the clearing bound them to the ancient curse, and with each step, the ethereal whispers seemed to guide their path. Mark, Emily, and the rest of the group were caught in a cosmic dance, their destinies entwined with the malevolent forces that governed the supernatural enigma.

The twisted trails led the friends to a secluded grove bathed in an otherworldly glow. Moonlight filtered through the gnarled branches, casting an ethereal pallor on the ground. The air crackled with latent energy, and the shadows played tricks on their senses. Unseen eyes observed their every move as the group hesitated at the edge of the spectral grove.

Emily, the unwitting conduit of forbidden knowledge, felt an invisible force pulling her toward the center of the grove. The whispers, now a spectral symphony, urged her to unravel the mysteries concealed within the ancient symbols etched into the earth. A compulsion, an otherworldly call, guided her steps as she approached the enigmatic patterns that pulsed with latent power.

Mark, torn between the skepticism that defined him and the growing influence of the Goatman's curse, cast wary glances at the symbols. The haunted woods, responsive to the internal struggles of the friends, seemed to warp and contort with a will of its own. Shadows danced in grotesque patterns, and the grove became a stage for a supernatural spectacle.

The rest of the group, caught in the gravitational pull of the Goatman's influence, gathered around Emily. The clearing, a nexus of spectral energies, hummed with an ominous resonance. Unseen forces coalesced, and the grove transformed into a gateway to the unknown.

As Emily traced her fingers over the symbols, the grove became a canvas for ethereal visions. The ancient curse, woven into the fabric of the haunted woods, unfolded before the friends like a nightmarish tapestry. The Goatman, a tragic figure shackled by an unholy alliance, emerged from the shadows, its form flickering with a spectral radiance.

The friends, ensnared in the unfolding revelation, witnessed scenes from the Goatman's existence—a journey through epochs marked by cosmic pacts, eldritch rituals, and the insatiable hunger that bound the entity to the supernatural realm. The grove, now a theater of spectral memories, echoed with the haunting cries of lost souls and the tormented echoes of ancient rites.

Mark, tormented by the conflicting forces that tore at his sanity, saw glimpses of the Goatman's interactions with souls who had been entangled in the cosmic machinations of the ancient curse. The forest, a silent witness to centuries of suffering, whispered tales of tormented spirits and unspeakable horrors that lurked in the shadowed depths.

Emily, sensitive to the ethereal currents, glimpsed fragments of the future—an ominous tableau that unfolded with an inexorable inevitability. The haunted woods, now a mosaic of interconnected destinies, revealed a nightmarish dance between the living and the spectral.

As the visions played out, the friends, released from the spectral trance, found themselves standing in the grove once more. The symbols, now infused with a latent energy, pulsed with an otherworldly radiance. The Goatman, its form flickering between the grotesque and the tragic, remained at the periphery of their perception, a spectral guardian of the haunted woods.

The friends, marked by the spectral encounter, retreated from the grove. The symbols, now charged with a malevolent force,

lingered in their consciousness like a haunting echo. The haunted woods, sentient and malevolent, responded to their presence with an unsettling intensity.

As the group pressed forward, the forest itself seemed to conspire against them. The twisted trails became a labyrinth, shifting with a will of their own. The spectral currents guided the friends deeper into the heart of the supernatural enigma, and the whispers, now an incessant chorus, reverberated through the haunted woods.

A sudden gust of wind whispered through the gnarled branches, carrying with it the mournful howl of the Goatman. The spectral alliance, forged in the grove, propelled the friends toward a convergence of cosmic forces that awaited in the shadowed depths. The night, fraught with unseen perils, stretched before them like an endless abyss, and the friends, ensnared by the spectral forces that governed their fate, plunged further into the inescapable dance of shadows that awaited in the ancient forest.

The twisted trails, illuminated by an otherworldly glow, led the group to the heart of the haunted woods. The whispers, now a cacophony of spectral voices, guided their every step, and the air pulsated with an ethereal energy that heightened the senses to the unseen threats that lurked in the shadows.

As the friends delved deeper, the forest itself seemed to morph into a surreal dreamscape. Trees contorted into nightmarish shapes, and the ground undulated like the surface of an otherworldly sea. Unseen eyes watched from the darkness, and the haunted woods, now a living entity, responded to their presence with a symphony of spectral echoes.

The group, now caught in a cosmic ballet, reached a clearing bathed in an otherworldly radiance. Symbols etched into the earth pulsed with an ancient power, and the whispers intensified, their spectral voices reaching a deafening crescendo. In the center of the

clearing stood a spectral figure—a manifestation of the Goatman's curse, its eyes gleaming with an otherworldly intelligence.

The friends, paralyzed by the unfolding spectacle, felt the air thicken with a malevolent force. The Goatman, now a puppeteer of their destinies, extended a spectral hand, inviting the group to join the cosmic dance. Mark, Emily, and the rest stood at the precipice of a choice that would seal their fate—a decision that transcended mortal understanding.

As the spectral figure beckoned, the haunted woods echoed with the haunting laughter of the Goatman. The friends, ensnared in the dance of shadows, stood at the nexus of the supernatural enigma, their destinies entwined with the ancient curse that governed the heart of the forest.

The night, fraught with cosmic uncertainty, stretched before the friends like an infinite canvas. The spectral grove, now a gateway to the unknown, beckoned them into the inescapable dance that awaited in the shadowed depths. The friends, marked by the ethereal revelations and the spectral alliance, plunged further into the heart of the haunted woods, where the Goatman's malevolent influence

Chapter 9: Pact with Shadows

The friends, standing on the precipice of the spectral clearing, felt the oppressive weight of the Goatman's influence bearing down upon them. The ethereal radiance cast an eerie glow on the symbols that pulsed with an otherworldly energy. The whispers, now an unrelenting cacophony, echoed through the haunted woods, urging the group to surrender to the cosmic dance that awaited.

Mark, the once-skeptical leader, hesitated, his eyes darting between the spectral figure and his companions. The forest, now a sentient entity, seemed to respond to his internal struggle, twisting the trees into grotesque forms that mirrored the tendrils of doubt

constricting his heart. Emily, sensitive to the ethereal currents, trembled as conflicting emotions wrestled within her.

The Goatman's eyes, gleaming with an ancient intelligence, bore into the souls of the friends. The haunted clearing became a battleground of wills, where the tangible and intangible clashed in a dance of shadows. Unseen forces whispered promises of enlightenment and power, luring the friends toward an unholy pact that defied the natural order.

In the face of the spectral invitation, the group felt a collective unease. The air crackled with tension, and the haunted woods, alive with spectral currents, seemed to conspire against them. The choice, a perilous gambit that promised either dominion over the supernatural or descent into eternal torment, hung in the balance.

As the friends deliberated, the grove transformed into a surreal dreamscape. Reality and nightmare merged, and the spectral figure at the center of the clearing became an ever-shifting enigma. The whispers, now a dissonant symphony, intensified, urging the group to embrace the Goatman's curse and become conduits for the malevolent forces that pulsed through the heart of the forest.

Emily, tormented by the conflicting forces that tugged at her soul, felt an irresistible pull toward the outstretched hand of the Goatman. The symbols etched into the earth seemed to respond to her internal turmoil, glowing with an intensity that mirrored the tumult within her consciousness. The friends, caught in the gravitational pull of an insidious force, stood at the crossroads of their destinies.

In a moment of collective resolve, the group stepped back from the spectral figure. The Goatman's eyes, once filled with a gleaming anticipation, narrowed with disappointment. The whispers, now a discordant lament, echoed through the haunted woods. The spectral figure, a harbinger of alliance, receded into the shadows, leaving

the friends standing in the clearing, marked by the weight of their choice.

The haunted woods, now a tapestry of shifting shadows and spectral echoes, responded to the rejection with a sinister sigh. The grove, once a gateway to the unknown, settled into an eerie stillness. The friends, released from the immediate threat, felt a mixture of relief and lingering dread.

As the group retreated from the clearing, the symbols etched into the earth seemed to pulse with a fading energy. The whispers, now reduced to a haunting murmur, lingered on the fringes of their consciousness. The haunted woods, while momentarily subdued, retained the scars of the friends' encounter, and the night unfolded with an ominous uncertainty.

The group, bound by the spectral alliance but defiant in the face of the Goatman's influence, ventured deeper into the labyrinth of shadows. The twisted trails, now a maze of spectral illusions, seemed to shift with a malevolent intent. The friends, caught in the ebb and flow of the supernatural currents, pressed forward with a cautious determination.

As they navigated the haunted woods, the spectral echoes intensified. Unseen eyes watched from the shadows, and the air became charged with an otherworldly energy. The friends, marked by the spectral encounter, felt the weight of the ancient curse lingering like a palpable presence. The night, pregnant with the unknown, whispered secrets that reverberated through the twisted branches.

Suddenly, a mournful howl echoed through the trees—a sound that transcended the natural world. The spectral alliance, though rejected in the clearing, continued to bind the friends to the Goatman's curse. The haunted woods, now a sentient entity, responded to their presence with an unsettling intensity.

The friends stumbled upon an ancient altar, hidden within the depths of the forest. The symbols engraved upon it mirrored those in the clearing, and the air pulsed with an otherworldly resonance. The whispers, now a siren's call, beckoned them to approach the altar, promising a communion with the supernatural forces that governed the haunted woods.

Mark, haunted by the memories of his lost friend and the consequences of the group's rejection, grappled with the inexorable pull toward the altar. The friends, caught between the desire for understanding and the fear of the unknown, hesitated at the threshold of the spectral enclave.

As they approached, the symbols on the altar glowed with an intensity that mirrored the ethereal currents within the haunted woods. The whispers, now a seductive melody, caressed their minds, weaving visions of power and transcendence. The Goatman's presence, though momentarily distant, lingered like a shadow cast upon the spectral canvas.

A choice loomed before the friends—a choice that would either cement their unholy alliance with the Goatman or cast them further into the abyss of the unknown. The haunted woods, alive with a malevolent energy, awaited the outcome of the cosmic dance that unfolded beneath its twisted canopy.

In a moment of collective hesitation, the friends stood at the edge of the altar, the symbols pulsating with an otherworldly radiance. The whispers, now a haunting serenade, reverberated through the haunted woods, weaving a narrative that transcended mortal understanding. The group, teetering on the brink of enlightenment and damnation, faced the haunting reality that the legend of the Goatman had claimed them as unwilling participants in its insidious narrative.

The night, draped in an ethereal mist, enveloped the friends as they stood at the crossroads of their destinies. The haunted woods, a realm of shifting shadows and spectral echoes, watched with an otherworldly intelligence as the group, bound by an unspoken pact, ventured further into the heart of the supernatural enigma. The night, now a canvas for the dance of shadows, whispered of terrors yet to unfold as the friends pressed forward, their footsteps echoing through the labyrinth of nightmares that awaited in the ancient forest.

Chapter 10: Veil of Shadows

The haunted woods, a labyrinth of shifting shadows and spectral echoes, enveloped the friends as they ventured deeper into the heart of the supernatural enigma. The spectral alliance, though rejected at the clearing, lingered like an unseen shroud, binding the group to the Goatman's curse. The twisted trails, now a maze of spectral illusions, seemed to warp with a malevolent intent, guiding the friends toward an unknown destination.

As the group pressed forward, the spectral echoes intensified. Unseen eyes watched from the shadows, and the air crackled with an otherworldly energy. The haunted woods, sentient and malevolent, responded to their presence with an unsettling intensity. The friends, marked by the spectral encounter, felt the weight of the ancient curse lingering like a palpable presence.

The whispers, once a dissonant symphony, now coalesced into a haunting serenade that reverberated through the twisted branches. Emily, sensitive to the ethereal currents, found herself caught in the ebb and flow of spectral energies. Visions of the Goatman's cursed legacy danced before her eyes—a tapestry of ancient alliances, forbidden pacts, and the insatiable hunger that bound the entity to the supernatural realm.

Mark, tormented by the memories of his lost friend and the consequences of their rejection, grappled with an internal struggle. The twisted trails seemed to twist with a will of their own, mirroring the tumult within his consciousness. The haunted woods, responsive to the friends' internal conflicts, conspired against them with a malevolent glee.

The friends stumbled upon an ancient altar, hidden within the depths of the forest. The symbols engraved upon it mirrored those in the clearing, and the air pulsed with an otherworldly resonance. The whispers, now a seductive melody, caressed their minds, weaving visions of power and transcendence. The Goatman's presence, though momentarily distant, lingered like a shadow cast upon the spectral canvas.

A choice loomed before the friends—a choice that would either cement their unholy alliance with the Goatman or cast them further into the abyss of the unknown. The haunted woods, alive with a malevolent energy, awaited the outcome of the cosmic dance that unfolded beneath its twisted canopy.

In a moment of collective hesitation, the friends stood at the edge of the altar, the symbols pulsating with an otherworldly radiance. The whispers, now a haunting serenade, reverberated through the haunted woods, weaving a narrative that transcended mortal understanding. The group, teetering on the brink of enlightenment and damnation, faced the haunting reality that the legend of the Goatman had claimed them as unwilling participants in its insidious narrative.

The night, draped in an ethereal mist, enveloped the friends as they stood at the crossroads of their destinies. The haunted woods, a realm of shifting shadows and spectral echoes, watched with an otherworldly intelligence as the group, bound by an unspoken pact, ventured further into the heart of the supernatural enigma. The

night, now a canvas for the dance of shadows, whispered of terrors yet to unfold as the friends pressed forward, their footsteps echoing through the labyrinth of nightmares that awaited in the ancient forest.

The twisted trails, illuminated by an otherworldly glow, led the group to the heart of the haunted woods. The whispers, now an incessant chorus, guided their every step, and the air pulsated with an ethereal energy that heightened the senses to the unseen threats that lurked in the shadows.

As the friends delved deeper, the forest itself seemed to morph into a surreal dreamscape. Trees contorted into nightmarish shapes, and the ground undulated like the surface of an otherworldly sea. Unseen eyes watched from the darkness, and the haunted woods, now a living entity, responded to their presence with a symphony of spectral echoes.

The group, now caught in a cosmic ballet, reached a clearing bathed in an otherworldly radiance. Symbols etched into the earth pulsed with an ancient power, and the whispers intensified, their spectral voices reaching a deafening crescendo. In the center of the clearing stood a spectral figure—a manifestation of the Goatman's curse, its eyes gleaming with an otherworldly intelligence.

The friends, paralyzed by the unfolding spectacle, felt the air thicken with a malevolent force. The Goatman, now a puppeteer of their destinies, extended a spectral hand, inviting the group to join the cosmic dance. Mark, Emily, and the rest stood at the precipice of a choice that would seal their fate—a decision that transcended mortal understanding.

As the spectral figure beckoned, the haunted woods echoed with the haunting laughter of the Goatman. The friends, ensnared in the dance of shadows, stood at the nexus of the supernatural enigma,

their destinies entwined with the ancient curse that governed the heart of the forest.

The night, fraught with cosmic uncertainty, stretched before the friends like an infinite canvas. The spectral grove, now a gateway to the unknown, beckoned them into the inescapable dance that awaited in the shadowed depths. The friends, marked by the ethereal revelations and the spectral alliance, plunged further into the heart of the haunted woods, where the Goatman's malevolent influence awaited.

The twisted trails, now a spectral tapestry, led the friends to a clearing bathed in an ethereal glow. Symbols etched into the earth pulsated with an otherworldly radiance, and the whispers, now a ghostly chorus, guided them to the center of the supernatural stage. The spectral figure, a manifestation of the Goatman's curse, awaited with eyes that gleamed with ancient knowledge.

In a moment of collective resolve, the friends stepped forward, surrendering to the cosmic dance that unfolded in the haunted clearing. The symbols, now infused with a latent energy, glowed with an intensity that mirrored the ethereal currents within the haunted woods. The whispers, a symphony of spectral voices, reached a crescendo, weaving a narrative that transcended mortal comprehension.

As the friends embraced the spectral invitation, the clearing transformed into a surreal dreamscape. Reality and nightmare merged, and the friends found themselves suspended in a liminal space where time seemed to lose its meaning. Visions of the Goatman's cursed legacy unfolded—a tapestry of intertwined destinies and cosmic malevolence.

Mark, tormented by the memories of his lost friend, witnessed haunting scenes from the past. The woods became a theater of spectral apparitions, replaying moments of anguish and despair. The

Goatman's voice, a spectral undertone, whispered forgotten secrets that clawed at the edges of his sanity.

Emily, sensitive to the ethereal currents, glimpsed fragments of the future—an ominous tableau that unfolded with an inexorable inevitability. The haunted woods, now a mosaic of interconnected destinies, revealed a nightmarish dance between the living and the spectral.

As the visions played out, the friends, paralyzed by the supernatural revelation, became mere spectators in their own existential drama. The Goatman, a harbinger of cosmic terror, reveled in the torment it unleashed upon their minds. The clearing, a stage for the unfolding nightmare, pulsated with an otherworldly energy.

Suddenly, the visions ceased, and the friends, released from the spectral trance, found themselves standing in the clearing once more. The Goatman, its form flickering like a

dying ember, faded into the shadows. The ancient tree, now devoid of the supernatural glow, stood as a silent witness to the cosmic theater that unfolded beneath its twisted branches.

The friends, disoriented and haunted by the echoes of the Goatman's revelations, stumbled away from the clearing. The haunted woods, now a sentient labyrinth, seemed to rearrange itself, guiding the group deeper into the heart of the supernatural enigma. The air, thick with the residue of spectral energy, clung to them like an intangible shroud.

As they pressed forward, a cold wind whispered through the twisted branches, carrying with it a chilling echo of the Goatman's laughter. The friends, caught in a cycle of existential dread, stumbled through the haunted woods, forever marked by the disappearing act that unfolded in the surreal clearing. The night, pregnant with cosmic uncertainty, stretched before them like an endless abyss.

The spectral alliance, rejected at the altar, continued to bind the friends to the Goatman's curse. The twisted trails, now a spectral tapestry, guided them with an otherworldly intelligence. Shadows clung to the group like a malevolent fog, and the air pulsed with an ethereal energy that heightened their senses to the unseen threats that lurked in the shadows.

As they traversed the haunted woods, the group became acutely aware of an invisible tether connecting them to the Goatman's curse. The forest, alive with spectral currents, responded to their presence with a symphony of ethereal whispers. The alliance, forged in the clearing, propelled them toward a convergence of cosmic forces that awaited in the heart of the supernatural enigma.

The night, fraught with unseen perils, stretched before the friends like an endless abyss. The haunted woods, a realm of shifting shadows and spectral whispers, beckoned them into the heart of the supernatural enigma. The Goatman, now an unseen puppeteer of their destinies, watched with an otherworldly intelligence as the group delved deeper into the spectral dance that awaited them in the shadowed depths.

The twisted trails, illuminated by an otherworldly glow, led the friends to an ancient ruin hidden within the depths of the haunted woods. The spectral echoes intensified, and the air crackled with an otherworldly energy. Unseen eyes watched from the darkness as the group hesitated at the threshold of the supernatural enclave.

Emily, sensitive to the ethereal currents, felt an invisible force drawing her toward the heart of the ruins. The whispers, now an incessant chorus, urged her to unravel the mysteries concealed within the ancient stones. A compulsion, an otherworldly pull, guided her steps as she approached the spectral threshold.

Mark, torn between rational skepticism and the growing influence of the Goatman's curse, cast wary glances at the ancient ruin.

The haunted woods, responsive to the internal struggles of the friends, seemed to warp and contort with a will of its own. Shadows danced in grotesque patterns, and the ruins became a stage for a supernatural spectacle.

The rest of the group, ensnared by the spectral forces that governed their fate, gathered around Emily. The ruins, a nexus of spectral energies, hummed with an ominous resonance. Unseen forces coalesced, and the ancient stones transformed into conduits for the ethereal currents that pulsed through the heart of the forest.

As Emily traced her fingers over the weathered stones, the ruins became a canvas for ethereal visions. The ancient curse, woven into the fabric of the haunted woods, unfolded before the friends like a nightmarish tapestry. The Goatman, a tragic figure shackled by an unholy alliance, emerged from the shadows, its form flickering with a spectral radiance.

The friends, ensnared in the unfolding revelation, witnessed scenes from the Goatman's existence—a journey through epochs marked by cosmic pacts, eldritch rituals, and the insatiable hunger that bound the entity to the supernatural realm. The ruins, now a theater of spectral memories, echoed with the haunting cries of lost souls and the tormented echoes of ancient rites.

Mark, tormented by the conflicting forces that tore at his sanity, saw glimpses of the Goatman's interactions with lost souls—a spectral procession of individuals who had been entangled in the cosmic machinations of the ancient curse. The forest, a silent witness to centuries of suffering, whispered tales of tormented spirits and unspeakable horrors that lurked in the shadowed depths.

Emily, sensitive to the ethereal currents, glimpsed fragments of the future—an ominous tableau that unfolded with an inexorable inevitability. The haunted woods, now a mosaic of interconnected

destinies, revealed a nightmarish dance between the living and the spectral.

As the visions played out, the friends, paralyzed by the supernatural revelation, became mere spectators in their own existential drama. The Goatman, a harbinger of cosmic terror, reveled in the torment it unleashed upon their minds. The ruins, a stage for the unfolding nightmare, pulsated with an otherworldly energy.

Suddenly, the visions ceased, and the friends, released from the spectral trance, found themselves standing in the ruins once more. The Goatman, its form flickering between the grotesque and the tragic, remained at the periphery of their perception, a spectral guardian of the haunted woods.

The friends, disoriented and haunted by the echoes of the Goatman's revelations, stumbled away from the ruins. The haunted woods, now a sentient labyrinth, seemed to rearrange itself, guiding the group deeper into the heart of the supernatural enigma. The air, thick with the residue of spectral energy, clung to them like an intangible shroud.

As they pressed forward, a cold wind whispered through the twisted branches, carrying with it a chilling echo of the Goatman's laughter. The friends, caught in a cycle of existential dread, stumbled through the haunted woods, forever marked by the disappearing act that unfolded in the surreal clearing. The night, pregnant with cosmic uncertainty, stretched before them like an endless abyss.

The spectral alliance, rejected at the ruins, continued to bind the friends to the Goatman's curse. The twisted trails, now a spectral tapestry, guided them with an otherworldly intelligence. Shadows clung to the group like a malevolent fog, and the air pulsed with an ethereal energy that heightened their senses to the unseen threats that lurked in the shadows.

As they traversed the haunted woods, the group became acutely aware of an invisible tether connecting them to the Goatman's curse. The forest, alive with spectral currents, responded to their presence with a symphony of ethereal whispers. The alliance, forged in the ruins, propelled them toward a convergence of cosmic forces that awaited in the heart of the supernatural enigma.

The night, fraught with unseen perils, stretched before the friends like an endless abyss. The haunted woods, a realm of shifting shadows and spectral whispers, beckoned them into the heart of the supernatural enigma. The Goatman, now an unseen puppeteer of their destinies, watched with an otherworldly intelligence as the group delved deeper into the spectral dance that awaited them in the shadowed depths.

The twisted trails, illuminated by an otherworldly glow, led the friends to an ancient grove concealed within the heart of the haunted woods. The spectral echoes intensified, and the air crackled with an otherworldly energy. Unseen eyes watched from the darkness as the group hesitated at the threshold of the supernatural enclave.

Emily, sensitive to the ethereal currents, felt an invisible force pulling her toward the center of the grove. The whispers, now an incessant chorus, urged her to unravel the mysteries concealed within the ancient trees. A compulsion, an otherworldly call, guided her steps as she approached the spectral threshold.

Mark, torn between rational skepticism and the growing influence of the Goatman's curse, cast wary glances at the ancient grove. The haunted woods, responsive to the internal struggles of the friends, seemed to warp and contort with a will of its own. Shadows danced in grotesque patterns, and the grove became a stage for a supernatural spectacle.

The rest of the group, ensnared by the spectral forces that governed their fate, gathered around Emily. The grove, a nexus

of spectral energies, hummed with an ominous resonance. Unseen forces coalesced, and the ancient trees transformed into conduits for the ethereal currents that pulsed through the heart of the forest.

As Emily traced her fingers over the gnarled bark, the grove became a canvas for ethereal visions. The ancient curse, woven into the fabric of the haunted woods, unfolded before the friends like a nightmarish tapestry. The Goatman, a tragic figure shackled by an unholy alliance, emerged from the shadows, its form flickering with a spectral radiance.

The friends, ensnared in the unfolding revelation, witnessed scenes from the Goatman's existence—a journey through epochs marked by cosmic pacts, eldritch rituals, and the insatiable hunger that bound the entity to the supernatural realm. The grove, now a theater of spectral memories, echoed with the haunting cries of lost souls and the tormented echoes of ancient rites.

Mark, tormented by the conflicting forces that tore at his sanity, saw glimpses of the Goatman's interactions with lost souls—a spectral procession of individuals who had been entangled in the cosmic machinations of the ancient curse. The forest, a silent witness to centuries of suffering, whispered tales of tormented spirits and unspeakable horrors that lurked in the shadowed depths.

Emily, sensitive to the ethereal currents, glimpsed fragments of the future—an ominous tableau that unfolded with an inexorable inevitability. The haunted woods, now a mosaic of interconnected destinies, revealed a nightmarish dance between the living and the spectral.

As the visions played out, the friends, paralyzed by the supernatural revelation, became mere spectators in their own existential drama. The Goatman, a harbinger of cosmic terror, reveled in the torment it unleashed upon their minds. The grove, a stage for the unfolding nightmare, pulsated with an otherworldly energy.

Suddenly, the visions ceased, and the friends, released from the spectral trance, found themselves standing in the grove once more. The Goatman, its form flickering between the grotesque and the tragic, remained at the periphery of their perception, a spectral guardian of the haunted woods.

The friends, disoriented and haunted by the echoes of the Goatman's revelations, stumbled away from the grove. The haunted woods, now a sentient labyrinth, seemed to rearrange itself, guiding the group deeper into the heart of the supernatural enigma. The air, thick with the residue of spectral energy, clung to them like an intangible shroud.

As they pressed forward, a cold wind whispered through the twisted branches, carrying with it a chilling echo of the Goatman's laughter. The friends, caught in a cycle of existential dread, stumbled through the haunted woods, forever marked by the disappearing act that unfolded in the surreal clearing. The night, pregnant with cosmic uncertainty, stretched before them like an endless abyss.

The spectral alliance, rejected at the grove, continued to bind the friends to the Goatman's curse. The twisted trails, now a spectral tapestry, guided them with an otherworldly intelligence. Shadows clung to the group like a malevolent fog, and the air pulsed with an ethereal energy that heightened their senses to the unseen threats that lurked in the shadows.

As they traversed the haunted woods, the group became acutely aware of

an invisible tether connecting them to the Goatman's curse. The forest, alive with spectral currents, responded to their presence with a symphony of ethereal whispers. The alliance, forged in the grove, propelled them toward a convergence of cosmic forces that awaited in the heart of the supernatural enigma.

The night, fraught with unseen perils, stretched before the friends like an endless abyss. The haunted woods, a realm of shifting shadows and spectral whispers, beckoned them into the heart of the supernatural enigma. The Goatman, now an unseen puppeteer of their destinies, watched with an otherworldly intelligence as the group delved deeper into the spectral dance that awaited them in the shadowed depths.

The twisted trails, illuminated by an otherworldly glow, led the friends to an ancient burial ground hidden within the heart of the haunted woods. The spectral echoes intensified, and the air crackled with an otherworldly energy. Unseen eyes watched from the darkness as the group hesitated at the threshold of the supernatural enclave.

Emily, sensitive to the ethereal currents, felt an invisible force pulling her toward the center of the burial ground. The whispers, now an incessant chorus, urged her to unravel the mysteries concealed within the ancient gravestones. A compulsion, an otherworldly call, guided her steps as she approached the spectral threshold.

Mark, torn between rational skepticism and the growing influence of the Goatman's curse, cast wary glances at the ancient burial ground. The haunted woods, responsive to the internal struggles of the friends, seemed to warp and contort with a will of its own. Shadows danced in grotesque patterns, and the burial ground became a stage for a supernatural spectacle.

The rest of the group, ensnared by the spectral forces that governed their fate, gathered around Emily. The burial ground, a nexus of spectral energies, hummed with an ominous resonance. Unseen forces coalesced, and the ancient gravestones transformed into conduits for the ethereal currents that pulsed through the heart of the forest.

As Emily traced her fingers over the weathered stones, the burial ground became a canvas for ethereal visions. The ancient curse, woven into the fabric of the haunted woods, unfolded before the friends like a nightmarish tapestry. The Goatman, a tragic figure shackled by an unholy alliance, emerged from the shadows, its form flickering with a spectral radiance.

The friends, ensnared in the unfolding revelation, witnessed scenes from the Goatman's existence—a journey through epochs marked by cosmic pacts, eldritch rituals, and the insatiable hunger that bound the entity to the supernatural realm. The burial ground, now a theater of spectral memories, echoed with the haunting cries of lost souls and the tormented echoes of ancient rites.

Mark, tormented by the conflicting forces that tore at his sanity, saw glimpses of the Goatman's interactions with lost souls—a spectral procession of individuals who had been entangled in the cosmic machinations of the ancient curse. The forest, a silent witness to centuries of suffering, whispered tales of tormented spirits and unspeakable horrors that lurked in the shadowed depths.

Emily, sensitive to the ethereal currents, glimpsed fragments of the future—an ominous tableau that unfolded with an inexorable inevitability. The haunted woods, now a mosaic of interconnected destinies, revealed a nightmarish dance between the living and the spectral.

As the visions played out, the friends, paralyzed by the supernatural revelation, became mere spectators in their own existential drama. The Goatman, a harbinger of cosmic terror, reveled in the torment it unleashed upon their minds. The burial ground, a stage for the unfolding nightmare, pulsated with an otherworldly energy.

Suddenly, the visions ceased, and the friends, released from the spectral trance, found themselves standing in the burial ground once more. The Goatman, its form flickering between the grotesque and

the tragic, remained at the periphery of their perception, a spectral guardian of the haunted woods.

The friends, disoriented and haunted by the echoes of the Goatman's revelations, stumbled away from the burial ground. The haunted woods, now a sentient labyrinth, seemed to rearrange itself, guiding the group deeper into the heart of the supernatural enigma. The air, thick with the residue of spectral energy, clung to them like an intangible shroud.

As they pressed forward, a cold wind whispered through the twisted branches, carrying with it a chilling echo of the Goatman's laughter. The friends, caught in a cycle of existential dread, stumbled through the haunted woods, forever marked by the disappearing act that unfolded in the surreal clearing. The night, pregnant with cosmic uncertainty, stretched before them like an endless abyss.

The spectral alliance, rejected at the burial ground, continued to bind the friends to the Goatman's curse. The twisted trails, now a spectral tapestry, guided them with an otherworldly intelligence. Shadows clung to the group like a malevolent fog, and the air pulsed with an ethereal energy that heightened their senses to the unseen threats that lurked in the shadows.

As they traversed the haunted woods, the group became acutely aware of an invisible tether connecting them to the Goatman's curse. The forest, alive with spectral currents, responded to their presence with a symphony of ethereal whispers. The alliance, forged in the burial ground, propelled them toward a convergence of cosmic forces that awaited in the heart of the supernatural enigma.

The night, fraught with unseen perils, stretched before the friends like an endless abyss. The haunted woods, a realm of shifting shadows and spectral whispers, beckoned them into the heart of the supernatural enigma. The Goatman, now an unseen puppeteer of their destinies, watched with an otherworldly intelligence as the

group delved deeper into the spectral dance that awaited them in the shadowed depths.

The twisted trails, illuminated by an otherworldly glow, led the friends to an ancient altar concealed within the heart of the haunted woods. The spectral echoes intensified, and the air crackled with an otherworldly energy. Unseen eyes watched from the darkness as the group hesitated at the threshold of the supernatural enclave.

Emily, sensitive to the ethereal currents, felt an invisible force pulling her toward the center of the altar. The whispers, now an incessant chorus, urged her to unravel the mysteries concealed within the ancient symbols. A compulsion, an otherworldly call, guided her steps as she approached the spectral threshold.

Mark, torn between rational skepticism and the growing influence of the Goatman's curse, cast wary glances at the ancient altar. The haunted woods, responsive to the internal struggles of the friends, seemed to warp and contort with a will of its own. Shadows danced in grotesque patterns, and the altar became a stage for a supernatural spectacle.

The rest of the group, ensnared by the spectral forces that governed their fate, gathered around Emily. The altar, a nexus of spectral energies, hummed with an ominous resonance. Unseen forces coalesced, and the ancient symbols transformed into conduits for the ethereal currents that pulsed through the heart of the forest.

As Emily traced her fingers over the weathered symbols, the altar became a canvas for ethereal visions. The ancient curse, woven into the fabric of the haunted woods, unfolded before the friends like a nightmarish tapestry. The Goatman, a tragic figure shackled by an unholy alliance, emerged from the shadows, its form flickering with a spectral radiance.

The friends, ensnared in the unfolding revelation, witnessed scenes from the Goatman's existence—a journey through epochs

marked by cosmic pacts, eldritch rituals, and the insatiable hunger that bound the entity to the supernatural realm. The altar, now a theater of spectral memories, echoed with the haunting cries of lost souls and the tormented echoes of ancient rites.

Mark, tormented by the conflicting forces that tore at his sanity, saw glimpses of the Goatman's interactions with lost souls—a spectral procession of individuals who had been entangled in the cosmic machinations of the ancient curse. The forest, a silent witness to centuries of suffering, whispered tales of tormented spirits and unspeakable horrors that lurked in the shadowed depths.

Emily, sensitive to the ethereal currents, glimpsed fragments of the future—an ominous tableau that unfolded with an inexorable inevitability. The haunted woods, now a mosaic of interconnected destinies, revealed a nightmarish dance between the living and the spectral.

As the visions played out, the friends, paralyzed by the supernatural revelation, became mere spectators in their own existential drama. The Goatman, a harbinger of cosmic terror, reveled in the torment it unleashed upon their minds. The altar, a stage for the unfolding nightmare, pulsated with an otherworldly energy.

Suddenly, the visions ceased, and the friends, released from the spectral trance, found themselves standing before the altar once more. The Goatman, its form flickering between the grotesque and the tragic, remained at the periphery of their perception, a spectral guardian of the haunted woods.

The friends, disoriented and haunted by the echoes of the Goatman's revelations, stumbled away from the altar. The haunted woods, now a sentient labyrinth, seemed to rearrange itself, guiding the group deeper into the heart of the supernatural enigma. The air, thick with the residue of spectral energy, clung to them like an intangible shroud.

As they pressed forward, a cold wind whispered through the twisted branches, carrying with it a chilling echo of the Goatman's laughter. The friends, caught in a cycle of existential dread, stumbled through the haunted woods, forever marked by the disappearing act that unfolded in the surreal clearing. The night, pregnant with cosmic uncertainty, stretched before them like an endless abyss.

The spectral alliance, rejected at the altar, continued to bind the friends to the Goatman's curse. The twisted trails, now a spectral tapestry, guided them with an otherworldly intelligence. Shadows clung to the group like a malevolent fog, and the air pulsed with an ethereal energy that heightened their senses to the unseen threats that lurked in the shadows.

As they traversed the haunted woods, the group became acutely aware of an invisible tether connecting them to the Goatman's curse. The forest, alive with spectral currents, responded to their presence with a symphony of ethereal whispers. The alliance, forged in the altar, propelled them toward a convergence of cosmic forces that awaited in the heart of the supernatural enigma.

Chapter 11: Echoes of Betrayal

The haunted woods, now pulsating with an otherworldly energy, closed in around the friends like a malevolent embrace. The spectral alliance, an invisible tether, bound them to the Goatman's curse, and the twisted trails led them deeper into the heart of the supernatural enigma. Each step resonated with an eerie echo, as if the forest itself whispered tales of ancient treacheries.

The air, thick with a palpable tension, seemed to vibrate with the echoes of spectral voices. Unseen eyes watched from the shadows, and the friends felt the weight of the Goatman's malevolent gaze upon them. Emily, still sensitive to the ethereal currents, shivered as the whispers intensified, weaving a narrative of betrayal and impending doom.

Mark, haunted by the memories of his lost friend and the shifting allegiances within the group, struggled to maintain a semblance of composure. The haunted woods, now a labyrinth of twisted shadows, seemed to mirror the turmoil within his mind. Visions of the Goatman's cursed legacy clashed with the reality of their journey, blurring the lines between nightmare and waking.

As the friends ventured further, the twisted trails guided them to an ancient grove bathed in an unnatural glow. The spectral echoes intensified, and the air crackled with an otherworldly energy. Symbols etched into the trees pulsed with an ethereal radiance, casting grotesque shadows that danced with a life of their own.

In the center of the grove stood a spectral figure—a manifestation of the Goatman's curse, its eyes gleaming with an otherworldly intelligence. The friends, transfixed by the haunting presence, felt the weight of an unspoken invitation. The grove, now a stage for a cosmic drama, beckoned them to confront the echoes of betrayal that lingered in the shadows.

Emily, driven by a compulsion she could not resist, approached the spectral figure. The whispers, now a dissonant symphony, reverberated through the grove, casting a haunting spell upon the group. The friends, their senses heightened by the spectral energy, became acutely aware of the invisible threads that connected them to the Goatman's curse.

As Emily reached out, the spectral figure extended a ghostly hand. A surge of ancient memories flooded her consciousness—a tapestry of betrayals and alliances that transcended mortal understanding. The Goatman's voice, a haunting undertone, whispered forgotten secrets that clawed at the edges of her sanity.

Mark, torn between the mistrust within the group and the allure of the Goatman's promises, grappled with an internal tempest. Shadows cast by the ethereal glow contorted into grotesque shapes,

mirroring the conflicting emotions that tormented him. The grove, now a battleground of spectral forces, awaited the resolution of the internal strife that threatened to tear the group apart.

The rest of the friends, ensnared by the spectral drama, watched with a mixture of fear and fascination. The grove, bathed in an otherworldly radiance, became a theater for the unfolding nightmare. The Goatman's laughter, a haunting melody, echoed through the ancient trees, marking the friends as unwilling participants in its cosmic play.

Suddenly, the spectral figure and Emily recoiled as if struck by an unseen force. The grove, now plunged into an eerie silence, seemed to hold its breath. The spectral alliance, momentarily disrupted, cast a shadow of uncertainty upon the friends.

A voice, neither human nor spectral, resonated through the grove—a chorus of ancient whispers that spoke of broken pacts and the consequences of defiance. The friends, still caught in the ethereal web, felt the weight of the Goatman's judgment looming over them.

The grove, once a sanctuary of spectral revelations, became a battleground between the friends and the malevolent forces that sought to manipulate their destinies. The twisted trails, now obscured by shifting shadows, led the group deeper into the heart of the haunted woods, where the echoes of betrayal whispered of darker truths yet to unfold.

As the friends pressed forward, the spectral alliance tightened its grip, binding them to the Goatman's curse with an unbreakable resolve. The haunted woods, now a realm of shifting shadows and unseen perils, seemed to anticipate their every move. Each step echoed with the weight of ancient choices, and the air pulsed with an otherworldly energy that foretold of imminent horrors.

The twisted trails, like serpentine veins, guided the friends to an ancient ruin hidden within the depths of the haunted woods.

Symbols etched into the stones glowed with an ethereal radiance, and the air hummed with a spectral resonance. Unseen eyes watched from the darkness, and the ruins became a threshold to the unknown.

As the friends hesitated at the entrance, the whispers intensified, forming a cacophony of spectral voices that spoke of forgotten oaths and the inevitable descent into darkness. Emily, still bearing the weight of the spectral revelation, felt a compulsion to unravel the mysteries concealed within the ruins.

Mark, his trust shattered by the echoes of betrayal, cast wary glances at the ancient stones. The haunted woods, now alive with a malevolent energy, seemed to pulse with the heartbeat of an ancient evil. Shadows danced upon the ruins, casting ominous shapes that hinted at the horrors waiting within.

The rest of the group, caught in the web of the Goatman's curse, gathered around Emily. The ruins, a nexus of spectral energies, beckoned them to confront the consequences of their choices. The ancient stones, infused with an otherworldly power, awaited the unfolding of a cosmic drama that transcended the boundaries of mortal understanding.

As Emily traced her fingers over the weathered symbols, the ruins became a canvas for ethereal visions. The ancient curse, woven into the fabric of the haunted woods, unfolded before the friends like a nightmarish tapestry. The Goatman, a tragic figure shackled by an unholy alliance, emerged from the shadows, its form flickering with a spectral radiance.

The friends, ensnared in the unfolding revelation, witnessed scenes from the Goatman's existence—a journey through epochs marked by cosmic pacts, eldritch rituals, and the insatiable hunger that bound the entity to the supernatural realm. The ruins, now a

theater of spectral memories, echoed with the haunting cries of lost souls and the tormented echoes of ancient rites.

Mark, tormented by the conflicting forces that tore at his sanity, saw glimpses of the Goatman's interactions with lost souls—a spectral procession of individuals who had been entangled in the cosmic machinations of the ancient curse. The forest, a silent witness to centuries of suffering, whispered tales of tormented spirits and unspeakable horrors that lurked in the shadowed depths.

Emily, sensitive to the ethereal currents, glimpsed fragments of the future—an ominous tableau that unfolded with an inexorable inevitability. The haunted woods, now a mosaic of interconnected destinies, revealed a nightmarish dance between the living and the spectral.

As the visions played out, the friends, paralyzed by the supernatural revelation, became mere spectators in their own existential drama. The Goatman, a harbinger of cosmic terror, reveled in the torment it unleashed upon their minds. The ruins, a stage for the unfolding nightmare, pulsated with an otherworldly energy.

Suddenly, the visions ceased, and the friends, released from the spectral trance, found themselves standing within the ancient ruins once more. The Goatman, its form flickering between the grotesque and the tragic, remained a spectral presence at the periphery of their perception. The ruins, now silent and foreboding, seemed to anticipate the next chapter in the cosmic drama.

The friends, shaken by the spectral revelations, exchanged uneasy glances. The twisted trails, like a river of shadows, beckoned them deeper into the heart of the haunted woods. The air, heavy with the residue of ethereal energy, clung to them as a constant reminder of the supernatural forces that governed their fate.

As they ventured forth, the ruins behind them, the haunted woods seemed to close in, its twisted branches forming an impenetrable

canopy above. Shadows danced along the gnarled trunks, and the ground beneath their feet pulsed with an otherworldly heartbeat. The friends, now bound by the unseen threads of the Goatman's curse, pressed on with a mixture of dread and determination.

The twisted trails led them to a clearing bathed in an eerie, spectral light. In the center stood an ancient altar, adorned with symbols that seemed to writhe and shift in the dim illumination. The air became charged with an unsettling energy, and the friends felt the weight of the Goatman's gaze upon them once more.

Emily, still influenced by the ethereal currents, approached the altar with a sense of inevitability. The whispers, now a haunting chorus, seemed to guide her every step. The friends, unable to resist the unseen forces that governed their journey, gathered around the ancient stone structure.

As Emily reached out to touch the symbols, the altar responded with a surge of spectral energy. Visions unfolded before her eyes— scenes of ancient rituals, cosmic pacts, and the intertwining destinies of those who had crossed paths with the Goatman. The friends, ensnared in the ethereal spectacle, witnessed the tragic tales of souls bound to an ancient curse.

Mark, his skepticism eroded by the relentless onslaught of supernatural revelations, saw the threads of fate weaving around the group. The haunted woods, now a stage for cosmic machinations, echoed with the tormented cries of lost souls and the spectral laughter of the Goatman. The air crackled with an ominous resonance, and the ground seemed to shift beneath their feet.

The rest of the group, caught in the spectral current, felt the altar's power enveloping them. Shadows danced upon their faces, mirroring the ancient struggles playing out in the unseen realms. The Goatman, a puppeteer of destinies, reveled in the unfolding

drama as the friends teetered on the precipice of their own cosmic unraveling.

A voice, echoing from the depths of the haunted woods, resonated through the clearing—a haunting lamentation that spoke of betrayal, cosmic bargains, and the unrelenting hunger that bound the Goatman to its cursed existence. The friends, now witnesses to the unfolding tragedy, felt the weight of their choices bearing down upon them.

Emily, guided by an otherworldly compulsion, spoke words that seemed to echo with ancient power. The symbols on the altar glowed brighter, and the spectral light enveloped the friends. The haunted woods, alive with the energy of forgotten pacts, seemed to respond to Emily's invocation, and the air crackled with an ethereal electricity.

The friends, now connected by an invisible web of fate, felt the boundaries between the living and the spectral blur. The clearing transformed into a surreal tableau—a nexus of cosmic energies that defied mortal comprehension. The Goatman, its spectral form looming large, became a focal point in the unfolding ritual.

As the spectral light reached its zenith, the haunted woods seemed to hold its breath. The air became charged with an otherworldly tension, and the friends braced themselves for the unknown. Shadows, twisted and contorted, converged upon the clearing, forming a veil between the mortal realm and the supernatural forces that lurked beyond.

Suddenly, the spectral light extinguished, plunging the clearing into darkness. The friends, disoriented and surrounded by an oppressive silence, found themselves standing in the aftermath of the ritual. The Goatman's laughter echoed through the haunted woods, mocking the futility of mortal endeavors.

The twisted trails, now obscured by the lingering shadows, beckoned the friends deeper into the heart of the supernatural enigma. The air, thick with the residue of spectral energies, clung to them as a spectral shroud. The haunted woods, a labyrinth of cosmic horrors, seemed to whisper tales of their impending doom.

As the friends pressed forward, the spectral alliance tightening its grip, they became unwitting participants in a nightmare woven from the threads of ancient curses and cosmic machinations. The Goatman, a spectral puppeteer, reveled in the torment it unleashed upon their minds. The haunted woods, a realm of shifting shadows and unseen perils, awaited the next chapter in the unfolding cosmic drama.

Chapter 12: Whispers in the Shadows

The twisted trails guided the friends through the haunted woods, a realm now saturated with the lingering echoes of the ritual. The air crackled with an unsettling energy, and the shadows seemed to writhe with a newfound malevolence. The Goatman's curse, an invisible tether, bound them tighter as they delved deeper into the heart of the supernatural enigma.

The friends, haunted by the spectral revelations and the unsettling ritual, pressed on with a sense of trepidation. Each step through the dense undergrowth echoed with an ominous resonance, and the twisted branches overhead formed a canopy that blocked out the moonlight. The darkness seemed to pulse with a life of its own, and unseen eyes watched their every move.

As they traversed the haunted woods, Mark's gaze darted nervously between the shifting shadows. The Goatman's laughter lingered in the air, a haunting reminder of their entanglement with cosmic forces beyond their understanding. Doubt gnawed at Mark's sanity, and the trust between the friends strained under the weight of unseen horrors.

Emily, still influenced by the ethereal currents, walked with a purpose that seemed guided by forces beyond her control. The whispers, now a dissonant symphony, surrounded her like a spectral aura. The friends, ensnared in the spectral web, followed Emily as the twisted trails led them to a clearing bathed in an otherworldly glow.

In the center of the clearing stood a dilapidated mansion, its decaying façade casting eerie shadows in the spectral light. The air hummed with a haunting melody, and the friends felt an inexplicable compulsion to enter the mansion. The Goatman's curse, now a palpable force, seemed to emanate from the ancient structure.

As they approached the mansion, its doors creaked open with a ghostly wail. The interior, shrouded in darkness, exuded a malevolent energy. Unseen whispers echoed through the halls, recounting the tragic tales of those who had crossed paths with the Goatman within these haunted walls.

The friends hesitated at the threshold, a silent acknowledgment of the impending horrors awaiting them. Emily, still under the influence of the spectral forces, stepped forward with an unwavering determination. The mansion seemed to welcome her, its walls pulsating with an unseen heartbeat.

As the friends entered, the doors slammed shut behind them, sealing their fate within the spectral confines of the mansion. The air grew colder, and the walls whispered tales of betrayal, sacrifice, and the unrelenting hunger that bound the Goatman to its cursed existence. Shadows danced along the corridors, casting grotesque silhouettes that seemed to mock the intruders.

The mansion, a labyrinth of forgotten memories and spectral horrors, unfolded its secrets with each creaking floorboard and echoing whisper. The friends, now prisoners of the spectral drama, ventured deeper into the heart of the ancient structure. The Goatman's

laughter, a sinister undertone, reverberated through the halls, guiding them toward an inevitable confrontation.

Rooms adorned with dusty relics told stories of a bygone era, where the mansion was once a place of decadence and opulence. Now, draped in an ethereal gloom, the grandeur had given way to a pervading sense of decay. Paintings on the walls seemed to watch the intruders with hollow eyes, capturing moments of torment and despair.

Emily, compelled by unseen forces, led the group to a grand hall adorned with a twisted chandelier that cast eerie patterns of light. In the center stood a forgotten altar, covered in cryptic symbols. The air thickened with a spectral presence, and the friends felt the weight of unseen eyes upon them.

As Emily approached the altar, the whispers intensified, forming a cacophony that echoed through the mansion. Visions of ancient rituals played out before the friends, a tapestry of eldritch ceremonies and sacrificial rites. The Goatman's curse, woven into the very fabric of the mansion, revealed its darkest secrets.

Mark, his skepticism now replaced by a growing dread, watched as the spectral energy coalesced around Emily. Shadows danced upon the walls, forming grotesque figures that seemed to writhe in agony. The grand hall became a theater for the unfolding nightmare, with the friends as unwilling actors in a cosmic play.

The rest of the group, caught in the spectral current, stood as witnesses to the ancient forces that manipulated their destinies. The Goatman, now a looming presence within the grand hall, revealed itself with a spectral radiance. The air crackled with an otherworldly electricity as the friends braced themselves for the climax of the haunting spectacle.

Emily, her eyes now reflecting the eerie glow of the altar, spoke words that resonated with ancient power. The symbols etched into

the stone seemed to come alive, glowing brighter with each incantation. The grand hall pulsed with a spectral energy, and the friends felt the very fabric of reality unraveling around them.

A rift, a tear in the fabric of the supernatural, opened before the altar. From the depths emerged the Goatman, its form flickering with a malevolent radiance. The friends, now faced with the spectral entity, felt a chill that transcended the physical realm. The Goatman's laughter, a haunting melody, echoed through the grand hall.

The friends, caught in the grip of the Goatman's curse, were now mere pawns in its cosmic machinations. The mansion, a stage for the unfolding nightmare, seemed to warp and contort with the weight of ancient malevolence. Shadows, now animated with spectral life, closed in around the group, forming a suffocating shroud.

The Goatman, its voice echoing through the halls, spoke of cosmic bargains and the inevitable descent into darkness. The grand hall became a battleground for the friends' sanity as the Goatman's words clawed at the edges of their minds. The spectral currents, now a tempest of unseen forces, whipped through the mansion with an otherworldly fury.

As the friends stood before the altar, a choice loomed in the shadows—an offering to the Goatman or a futile attempt to defy the cosmic forces that bound them. The air crackled with an impending doom, and the grand hall seemed to hold its breath in anticipation of the friends' decision.

Emily, now a conduit for the Goatman's curse, faced the friends with hollow eyes. The whispers, once a dissonant symphony, became a unified chorus urging them toward the inevitable. The spectral threads tightened, pulling the friends into the cosmic dance that awaited its final act within the haunted mansion.

The friends, their fates entwined with the Goatman's curse, stood at the precipice of their own unraveling. The grand hall, a

silent witness to centuries of spectral torment, seemed to echo with the cries of lost souls and the laughter of an entity that defied mortal understanding.

The twisted trails, once a path through the haunted woods, now extended into the very fabric of their existence. The spectral alliance, an unbreakable bond, bound them to the Goatman's curse with an inescapable resolve. The friends, now faced with a choice that would seal their destinies, braced themselves for the next chapter in the cosmic nightmare that unfolded within the walls of the haunted mansion.

Chapter 13: Pact with the Shadows

The grand hall, now a stage for the unfolding cosmic drama, held its breath as the friends stood before the ancient altar. The Goatman, its spectral form flickering with malevolent radiance, loomed over them like a puppeteer orchestrating the final act of a nightmarish play. The air crackled with ethereal energy, and shadows clung to the walls, whispering tales of ancient pacts and unspeakable horrors.

Emily, a conduit for the Goatman's curse, raised her arms as if guided by unseen hands. The symbols on the altar pulsed with an otherworldly glow, and the friends felt the spectral currents intensify. The grand hall seemed to warp, its dimensions shifting in response to the cosmic forces at play. The Goatman's laughter echoed through the mansion, a haunting melody that heralded the imminent climax.

The friends, ensnared by the spectral alliance, felt the weight of the Goatman's gaze upon them. Unseen threads tightened, binding them to the ancient curse that now permeated the very fabric of the mansion. Mark, tormented by doubt and the shadows of betrayal, struggled to comprehend the unfolding nightmare. The grand hall, once a sanctuary of opulence, now exuded a malevolent aura that seeped into the marrow of their bones.

As Emily spoke the incantations, the spectral energy coalesced into a swirling vortex above the altar. The rift, a tear in the fabric of reality, widened, revealing glimpses of a cosmic void that defied mortal comprehension. The Goatman's voice, now a chorus of haunting whispers, echoed through the rift, speaking of forbidden knowledge and the inevitability of their entanglement with the supernatural.

The friends, caught in the grip of the Goatman's curse, felt an inexorable pull toward the cosmic void. Shadows danced upon the edges of the rift, forming grotesque figures that seemed to beckon them into the unknown. The grand hall, now a gateway to cosmic horrors, awaited the friends' choice—submit to the Goatman's influence or defy the cosmic forces that sought to unravel their existence.

Mark, his mind a tempest of conflicting emotions, looked to the other friends. Their faces mirrored the uncertainty that gnawed at his sanity. The Goatman's laughter, a maddening cacophony, intensified as the rift pulsed with an otherworldly glow. The decision, an irreversible pact with the shadows, loomed before them like a specter of doom.

Emily, her eyes hollow and distant, uttered words that seemed to resonate with the very fabric of the supernatural. The friends, compelled by unseen forces, stepped closer to the rift. The grand hall seemed to blur, its boundaries dissolving as the spectral energies surged around them.

Suddenly, the mansion trembled as if in response to an ancient power. The Goatman's laughter, once triumphant, faltered for a moment. The friends, caught in the grip of the cosmic tempest, felt a shift in the spectral currents. The rift, now a pulsating maw, cast an eerie glow upon their faces.

A voice, neither human nor spectral, reverberated through the grand hall—a lamentation that spoke of cosmic balance and the

consequences of meddling with forces beyond mortal understanding. The Goatman, its spectral form recoiling as if struck by an unseen force, hissed with an otherworldly fury.

The friends, momentarily released from the ethereal trance, found themselves standing at the precipice of the rift. The grand hall, now a battleground between cosmic entities, seemed to hold its breath in anticipation of the friends' next move.

Mark, his rational mind clashing with the supernatural forces that surrounded him, hesitated. The Goatman's curse, now weakened but far from defeated, still pulsed through the mansion. Shadows, like tendrils of malevolence, reached out from the walls, whispering promises of forbidden knowledge and unspeakable power.

The other friends, their faces etched with the struggle of internal conflicts, looked to Mark as if seeking guidance. The grand hall, a silent witness to their existential torment, seemed to echo with the cries of lost souls and the laughter of entities that defied mortal comprehension.

In that moment of hesitation, the Goatman's laughter resurged with a renewed malevolence. The spectral currents, like an invisible tide, surged forward, pulling the friends closer to the rift. Shadows clung to them, entwining with the unseen threads that bound them to the ancient curse.

Emily, still under the influence of the Goatman's influence, stepped closer to the rift. The grand hall, now a surreal tableau of cosmic conflict, seemed to warp and contort with the weight of ancient malevolence. The air, thick with the residue of spectral energy, clung to them as a suffocating shroud.

Mark, torn between defiance and the allure of forbidden power, felt the weight of the Goatman's gaze upon him. The rift, a gateway to the unknown, beckoned with a promise of cosmic revelations.

The friends, now at the mercy of supernatural forces, stood on the brink of a choice that would seal their destinies.

As Emily extended her hand toward the rift, the grand hall vibrated with an otherworldly resonance. The Goatman, its form flickering with a desperate fury, hissed with a spectral voice that echoed through the very fabric of the mansion. The friends, caught in the cosmic struggle, felt a surge of unseen forces that threatened to tear their souls asunder.

A voice, ancient and authoritative, cut through the chaos. It spoke of cosmic balance and the need for mortals to resist the temptations that lurked within the shadows. The rift, now a swirling maelstrom of spectral energy, seemed to respond to the authoritative voice.

The Goatman's laughter waned, replaced by an eerie silence. The friends, their minds still entangled in the ethereal web, witnessed the rift's transformation. The cosmic void, once a gateway to the unknown, now shimmered with a tranquil luminescence. Shadows receded, revealing the grand hall in its original state.

The friends, released from the spectral trance, found themselves standing in the mansion's grand hall. The Goatman, its presence diminished but not vanquished, lingered at the periphery of their perception. The air, now devoid of the suffocating spectral shroud, held a sense of uneasy calm.

The authoritative voice, a guiding force that had intervened in the cosmic struggle, echoed through the mansion. It spoke of the friends' resilience in the face of cosmic temptation and the importance of maintaining the delicate balance between the mortal realm and the supernatural. The grand hall, now free from the oppressive malevolence that had gripped it, seemed to regain a semblance of its former opulence. Paintings on the walls, once twisted depictions of torment, now appeared as mere artistic renderings. The dilapidated

mansion, bathed in an otherworldly glow, retained an eerie beauty that hinted at a history shrouded in mystery.

The friends, their senses returning to them, exchanged uncertain glances. The Goatman, a diminished presence, retreated further into the shadows, its spectral form flickering like a dying ember. The authoritative voice continued to resonate, guiding the friends toward a newfound understanding of the cosmic forces that governed their existence.

Mark, his mind a battlefield between reason and supernatural influence, struggled to reconcile the surreal events that had unfolded. The grand hall, once a chamber of horrors, now felt almost serene. The spectral currents, while still present, seemed to ebb away, leaving behind an uneasy calm.

The friends, guided by the authoritative voice, explored the mansion with a newfound sense of purpose. Rooms that had once harbored spectral terrors now revealed forgotten artifacts and relics of a bygone era. The Goatman's curse, now a fading echo, no longer held the mansion in its suffocating grip.

As they ventured deeper into the mansion, the authoritative voice spoke of ancient rituals, cosmic guardians, and the delicate balance that must be maintained to prevent the malevolence of the supernatural from overwhelming the mortal realm. The friends, their minds now attuned to the guiding force, began to understand the significance of their journey.

In a forgotten library, they discovered tomes that chronicled the history of the Goatman—a tragic entity bound by an unholy alliance forged in the shadows of cosmic realms. The authoritative voice explained that the friends' defiance had disrupted the spectral equilibrium, offering a chance to tip the balance away from the malevolence that had plagued the haunted woods.

Mark, grappling with the revelations, felt a weight lifting from his shoulders. The Goatman, now a vanquished specter, no longer held sway over his mind. The friends, united by their shared struggle, delved deeper into the mansion's secrets, guided by the authoritative voice toward a resolution that would safeguard both the mortal and supernatural realms.

In a chamber hidden beneath the mansion, they discovered an ancient artifact—an amulet pulsating with ethereal energy. The authoritative voice explained that the amulet had the power to seal the remnants of the Goatman's curse and restore balance to the haunted woods. The friends, now entrusted with a cosmic responsibility, prepared for a final confrontation.

The grand hall, once witness to cosmic struggles, became a staging ground for the friends' decisive act. The amulet, held by Emily, radiated with a soothing luminescence. The Goatman, its diminished form lingering in the shadows, hissed with a fading defiance.

As Emily approached the spectral remnants of the Goatman's curse, the authoritative voice guided her in a ritual of sealing. Symbols etched into the floor glowed with an otherworldly radiance. The friends, standing in a circle around the amulet, channeled their collective energy into the cosmic task before them.

The mansion trembled as the ritual unfolded, and the Goatman's laughter echoed one last time through the grand hall. Shadows, now devoid of malevolence, danced with a newfound serenity. The friends, their resolve unbroken, witnessed the ethereal currents converging toward the amulet, sealing the remnants of the Goatman's curse within its crystalline core.

A blinding light enveloped the grand hall, and the mansion seemed to transcend the boundaries of time and space. The friends felt a cosmic energy surging through them, connecting them to the very essence of the supernatural. The authoritative voice, now a

benevolent guide, spoke of the friends' triumph over cosmic malevolence and the restoration of equilibrium.

As the light subsided, the grand hall returned to its former state of faded grandeur. The Goatman, its spectral form extinguished, became a mere memory. The haunted woods, once a realm of cosmic nightmares, seemed to breathe with newfound vitality. The friends, now free from the spectral alliance that had bound them, emerged from the mansion with a sense of accomplishment.

The authoritative voice, a fading echo, spoke its final words of gratitude and guidance. The friends, forever changed by their ordeal, walked out of the haunted woods into the moonlit night. The spectral currents, now a gentle breeze, whispered tales of ancient struggles and cosmic resolutions.

As they exited the woods, the haunted realm seemed to recede into the shadows. The Goatman's curse, sealed within the amulet, no longer held dominion over the supernatural enclave. The friends, marked by their journey through cosmic horrors, carried the weight of their experiences as a testament to the delicate balance between the mortal and supernatural realms.

The haunted woods, now a tranquil grove bathed in moonlight, stood as a testament to the friends' resilience. The spectral alliance, once a malevolent force, had been disrupted, and the cosmic equilibrium restored. The friends, forever bonded by their shared struggle, left the haunted woods behind, their footsteps echoing with the echoes of ancient tales and the triumphant resolution of cosmic mysteries.

As they ventured further from the haunted woods, the moonlit path guided them back to the realm of the living. The friends, still processing the surreal events, found solace in the gentle rustle of leaves and the calming night breeze. The amulet, now a relic of

their cosmic triumph, radiated with a subtle glow, a testament to the balance they had restored.

The authoritative voice, its echoes fading into the night, left the friends with a lingering sense of purpose. The haunted mansion, once a chamber of spectral horrors, disappeared from their view. The spectral currents, now harmonized with the natural energies of the world, whispered tales of ancient guardians and cosmic safeguards.

Mark, his mind now free from the haunting influence, looked at his friends with a mixture of relief and gratitude. The journey through the haunted woods had forged bonds that transcended the boundaries of the mundane. The friends, forever changed by their cosmic ordeal, shared an unspoken understanding that went beyond the realm of mortal comprehension.

As they walked, the moon casting a silver glow on their path, the friends reflected on the cosmic mysteries they had encountered. The haunted woods, once a realm of malevolence, had become a sanctuary of cosmic balance. The amulet, now a symbol of their resilience, dangled from Emily's neck, a reminder of the unseen forces that bound them together.

In the distance, the haunted woods receded into the night, its secrets hidden once more within the shadows. The friends, now free from the spectral alliance, emerged into the world with a newfound appreciation for the delicate interplay between the known and the unknown. The cosmic forces, once a source of terror, had become guardians of a delicate equilibrium.

Days turned into nights, and the friends continued their journey, forever marked by the spectral ordeal. The haunted woods, now a distant memory, left an indelible imprint on their souls. The amulet, a silent guardian against malevolence, resonated with the cosmic energies that flowed through their veins.

As they reached the outskirts of a nearby town, the friends paused to gaze back at the moonlit horizon. The haunted woods, a realm of cosmic nightmares, remained hidden in the distance. The amulet, now a talisman of cosmic balance, glowed with a reassuring warmth.

The friends, bound by the shared secrets of the supernatural, moved forward into the tapestry of their lives. The authoritative voice, a distant echo, whispered final words of guidance, fading into the realm of forgotten cosmic tales. The haunted mansion, once a chamber of horrors, became a relic in their collective memory.

The moon, a silent witness to their cosmic journey, cast its light upon the friends as they continued their way. The spectral currents, now a gentle presence, whispered tales of ancient guardians watching over the boundaries between realms. The friends, now guardians in their own right, carried the weight of their cosmic triumph as they embraced the unknown that lay ahead.

The moonlit night, with its secrets and mysteries, enveloped the friends in a comforting embrace. The haunted woods, once a crucible of terror, became a distant chapter in the ever-expanding cosmic narrative. The friends, forever intertwined by the unseen threads of their shared ordeal, moved forward into the mysteries that awaited them, their footsteps echoing with the echoes of ancient tales and the triumphant resolution of cosmic enigmas.

Chapter 14: Echoes of the Unknown

The town at the outskirts offered a semblance of normalcy, but the friends couldn't shake the echoes of the haunted woods that lingered in the recesses of their minds. The amulet, now a silent guardian against unseen forces, emitted a subtle glow as they navigated the streets. The authoritative voice, a distant whisper, continued to guide them with cryptic assurances.

In the heart of the town, they stumbled upon an ancient bookstore. The shelves were lined with weathered tomes containing forgotten knowledge of the supernatural. The friends, still haunted by their cosmic journey, felt an irresistible pull toward the musty volumes that hinted at untold mysteries.

As they delved into the books, the words on the pages seemed to come alive, recounting tales of forgotten rituals, eldritch entities, and the delicate balance that tethered the mortal and supernatural realms. The amulet, attuned to the ancient energies, pulsed with an otherworldly resonance as if acknowledging the truths within the pages.

One particular book caught their attention—an ancient grimoire that spoke of cosmic gateways and the consequences of disrupting the equilibrium between realms. The authoritative voice, now a comforting presence, guided them to a passage that foretold of a looming cosmic disturbance tied to their recent ordeal.

The friends, gripped by a sense of urgency, sought answers from the cryptic text. The grimoire spoke of a cosmic entity known as the Veilstitcher—an ancient force responsible for mending the fabric of reality when disrupted by mortal meddling. The disrupted equilibrium in the haunted woods had awakened the Veilstitcher, and its influence now extended beyond the spectral enclave.

A foreboding realization set in—the friends' actions in the haunted woods had not only disrupted the Goatman's curse but had also set in motion a cosmic chain reaction. The Veilstitcher, a guardian of the cosmic balance, now sought to mend the fabric of reality by any means necessary.

The town, once a refuge, now became a battleground between the Veilstitcher's influence and the friends' struggle for understanding. Shadows seemed to dance with a newfound malevolence, and

the air vibrated with an otherworldly tension. The authoritative voice, now urgent, guided the friends toward a cosmic reckoning.

As night fell, the friends found themselves drawn to an abandoned mansion on the outskirts of the town—a structure that resonated with the cosmic energies emanating from the awakened Veilstitcher. The amulet, now glowing with an intensity that mirrored the urgency of their mission, led them through the moonlit streets toward the looming edifice.

The mansion, a spectral relic like the one in the haunted woods, exuded an ethereal glow. The Veilstitcher's influence seemed to warp the very fabric of reality within its walls. The friends, their minds attuned to the cosmic energies, hesitated at the threshold, knowing that their actions within might determine the fate of both the mortal and supernatural realms.

As they entered, the mansion revealed itself as a nexus of cosmic energies. The authoritative voice, now resonating with a somber tone, explained that the Veilstitcher, once a dormant guardian, had been stirred by the friends' disruption of the cosmic equilibrium. The mansion, a convergence point of realities, now stood as a battleground for their cosmic destiny.

The rooms within the mansion, adorned with symbols that pulsed with cosmic significance, told tales of forgotten rituals and eldritch pacts. Shadows, animated by the Veilstitcher's influence, seemed to observe the intruders with an ominous awareness. The friends, guided by the amulet and the authoritative voice, navigated the twisting corridors toward the heart of the cosmic disturbance.

In a grand chamber, they discovered an ancient portal—a tear in the fabric of reality itself. The Veilstitcher, a spectral entity with threads of cosmic energy weaving around it, stood at the center. The authoritative voice, now a desperate plea, urged the friends to

confront the awakened guardian and seek a resolution that could prevent the unraveling of reality.

The friends, their minds burdened by the weight of cosmic responsibility, faced the Veilstitcher. Its presence, a maelstrom of spectral energies, seemed to scrutinize their very essence. The amulet, now radiating with an otherworldly brilliance, resonated with the Veilstitcher's influence.

The authoritative voice spoke of a cosmic choice—a pact with the Veilstitcher to mend the fabric of reality or a defiance that could unleash untold cosmic consequences. The friends, bound by the unseen threads of their shared journey, exchanged uneasy glances as the Veilstitcher's influence pulsed around them.

Emily, still attuned to the cosmic currents, stepped forward with a sense of purpose. The amulet, now a conduit for cosmic energies, seemed to respond to her presence. The Veilstitcher, its spectral form shifting with an otherworldly grace, communicated in a language of cosmic vibrations that transcended mortal comprehension.

As Emily spoke, her words resonated with the Veilstitcher's energies. The symbols around the portal glowed with an ethereal luminescence, and the grand chamber seemed to ripple with unseen forces. The friends, caught between cosmic choices, felt the weight of their destinies hanging in the balance.

The Veilstitcher, now engaged in a cosmic dialogue, revealed the consequences of its awakening. Reality, torn by the disruption in the haunted woods, threatened to unravel unless a cosmic pact was forged. The friends, their minds a battleground between mortal instincts and cosmic responsibilities, listened to the Veilstitcher's revelations.

Mark, still grappling with the echoes of the haunted woods, questioned the Veilstitcher's motives. The authoritative voice, now a spectral whisper, explained that the awakened guardian sought to

preserve the delicate balance disrupted by mortal interference. The Veilstitcher's influence, while imposing, was a necessary force to prevent cosmic chaos.

The friends, now faced with an impossible choice, deliberated their next move. The Veilstitcher, its spectral form exuding a sense of inevitability, awaited their decision. The amulet, a silent witness to the cosmic drama, pulsed with an intensity that mirrored the urgency of the situation.

As the friends reached a collective decision, the Veilstitcher's influence intensified. The grand chamber seemed to tremble with unseen forces as cosmic energies converged around the portal. Shadows, now imbued with the guardian's essence, danced along the walls, casting grotesque silhouettes.

The Veilstitcher, its spectral form resonating with a somber luminescence, spoke words that transcended mortal comprehension. The friends, guided by the authoritative voice and the amulet's influence, entered into a cosmic pact with the awakened guardian. The symbols on the portal glowed brighter, and reality seemed to shift as the pact was forged.

The town outside, once caught in the grip of the Veilstitcher's influence, returned to a semblance of normalcy. The cosmic energies, now harmonized by the friends' choice, resonated with a tranquil hum. The mansion, a nexus of cosmic disturbances, faded into the shadows as the portal closed behind them.

The authoritative voice, a fading echo, expressed gratitude for the friends' sacrifice in preserving the cosmic equilibrium. The amulet, now a symbol of their cosmic pact, emitted a subdued glow. The Veilstitcher's influence, while still present, now felt more like a benevolent current flowing through the friends' veins. The cosmic energies, once turbulent, settled into a harmonious resonance that connected the mortal and supernatural realms.

The friends, their minds still echoing with the cosmic dialogue, emerged from the grand chamber. The mansion, now devoid of spectral disturbances, felt like a sanctuary of forgotten cosmic truths. The town, released from the Veilstitcher's influence, embraced a serene calm that hinted at the delicate balance that had been restored.

As the friends walked through the moonlit streets, the amulet pulsed with a gentle radiance. The authoritative voice, now a comforting whisper, spoke of the friends' role as guardians of the cosmic equilibrium. The Veilstitcher, its spectral presence lingering in the background, communicated an unspoken assurance that their sacrifice had averted a cosmic catastrophe.

Days turned into nights, and the friends found themselves drawn to the ancient bookstore once again. The tomes that had once spoken of cosmic disturbances now revealed passages about cosmic guardians and the delicate dance between realms. The friends, now more attuned to the cosmic energies, sought further understanding of their newfound responsibilities.

In the bookstore, they discovered a hidden chamber that housed an ancient artifact—a celestial map that depicted the interconnected realms of existence. The authoritative voice guided them to specific constellations that represented cosmic gateways and unseen forces that governed the fabric of reality.

As the friends studied the celestial map, the Veilstitcher's influence resonated with the symbols, creating an ethereal connection between the mortal and supernatural realms. The amulet, now an instrument of cosmic awareness, hummed with a resonant frequency that mirrored the cosmic energies depicted on the map.

The authoritative voice explained that the friends, having forged a cosmic pact with the Veilstitcher, now held the key to maintaining the delicate balance between realms. Their journey, once a

harrowing ordeal, had transformed into a cosmic responsibility to safeguard the cosmic equilibrium.

Guided by the celestial map and the amulet, the friends embarked on a journey that transcended the boundaries of the known. They visited ancient sites, long-forgotten temples, and mystical landscapes that resonated with cosmic energies. The Veilstitcher's influence, now a guiding force, revealed hidden truths about the interconnected nature of existence.

In their cosmic travels, the friends encountered otherworldly entities—guardians, cosmic spirits, and ethereal beings that watched over the boundaries between realms. Each encounter deepened their understanding of the cosmic forces at play and reinforced the importance of their role as guardians of the equilibrium.

The celestial map, now a cosmic compass, led them to a sacred grove bathed in starlight. The Veilstitcher's influence pulsed through the ancient trees, and the amulet resonated with a sublime luminescence. The authoritative voice, now a guiding presence, spoke of a cosmic convergence that required the friends' attention.

In the heart of the sacred grove, a cosmic portal shimmered with an otherworldly radiance. The symbols on the portal echoed the constellations on the celestial map. The friends, their minds attuned to the Veilstitcher's influence, recognized the significance of the cosmic convergence.

As they approached the portal, the Veilstitcher's spectral form materialized, its presence now a harmonious dance of cosmic energies. The amulet, imbued with the friends' cosmic journey, resonated with the portal's energies. The authoritative voice spoke of a cosmic event that would test their resolve and strengthen the bonds between realms.

The friends, guided by their newfound cosmic awareness, stepped through the portal. The celestial map, now a guide through the

cosmic convergence, revealed a breathtaking tapestry of interconnected realms. The Veilstitcher's influence, once a source of cosmic disturbance, now merged seamlessly with the cosmic currents that flowed through the tapestry.

As they traversed the cosmic convergence, the friends encountered celestial phenomena—shifting realities, ethereal landscapes, and manifestations of cosmic energies that transcended mortal comprehension. The amulet, now a conduit for their shared cosmic journey, pulsed with a vibrant energy that mirrored the celestial wonders around them.

The authoritative voice, a guiding presence in the cosmic expanse, explained the friends' role in maintaining the delicate balance between realms during the convergence. The Veilstitcher, its spectral form intertwining with the cosmic currents, communicated an unspoken assurance that their cosmic pact had prepared them for this pivotal moment.

In the cosmic tapestry, the friends witnessed the Veilstitcher's influence harmonizing with other cosmic guardians. The celestial convergence, a sublime dance of energies, echoed with the echoes of ancient tales and cosmic resolutions. The friends, now guardians of the equilibrium, embraced their role with a sense of cosmic purpose.

As the cosmic convergence reached its zenith, the friends felt a profound connection to the very fabric of existence. The Veilstitcher's influence, now a benevolent force, guided them through the celestial wonders. The amulet, a symbol of their cosmic journey, radiated with a brilliance that mirrored the cosmic energies that flowed through the tapestry.

As the friends emerged from the cosmic convergence, they found themselves back in the sacred grove bathed in starlight. The portal closed behind them, leaving a lingering sense of cosmic awareness. The Veilstitcher's spectral form, now a distant presence, conveyed

a silent gratitude for the friends' guardianship of the cosmic equilibrium.

The celestial map, still in their possession, revealed new constellations that represented the friends' cosmic journey. The authoritative voice, a fading echo, spoke of the friends' transformation from seekers of the unknown to guardians of cosmic balance. The amulet, now a relic imbued with cosmic energies, pulsed with a steady resonance.

The friends, forever changed by their cosmic ordeal, looked to the night sky with a newfound understanding. The echoes of the unknown, once a source of terror, now whispered tales of cosmic guardianship and the delicate dance between realms. The Veilstitcher's influence, though distant, remained a guiding force in their cosmic journey.

As the friends ventured back into the mortal realm, the town at the outskirts welcomed them with a tranquil calm. The echoes of the haunted woods and the cosmic convergence became part of their collective memory. The amulet, now a timeless artifact, symbolized their connection to the cosmic forces that governed existence.

The Veilstitcher, a guardian in the cosmic expanse, continued its silent vigil over the delicate balance between realms. The friends, now stewards of the equilibrium, embraced their cosmic responsibilities with a sense of purpose. The cosmic tapestry, woven with threads of celestial wonders, echoed with the echoes of ancient tales and the triumphant resolution of cosmic enigmas.

Guided by the celestial map, the friends embarked on a journey to further understand and strengthen their cosmic abilities. The amulet, now an integral part of their existence, resonated with the energies of the interconnected realms. The Veilstitcher's influence, though no longer a constant presence, lingered as a silent assurance in the background.

As they delved into their newfound cosmic awareness, the friends discovered hidden sanctuaries and ancient sites where the fabric of reality seemed thin. Each encounter with cosmic phenomena deepened their understanding of the delicate balance they upheld. The celestial map, now a well-worn guide, led them to forgotten realms where cosmic secrets awaited revelation.

The friends encountered other guardians—ethereal beings who watched over specific aspects of the cosmic equilibrium. These cosmic sentinels imparted ancient wisdom and shared tales of cosmic struggles that transcended mortal lifetimes. The amulet, responding to the cosmic revelations, pulsed with an ethereal glow that mirrored the wisdom they gained.

In one such realm, the friends faced a cosmic trial—an otherworldly challenge that tested their resilience and understanding of the interconnected tapestry. The Veilstitcher's influence, once again a guiding force, whispered encouragement as the friends navigated through shifting realities and celestial puzzles. The amulet, a source of cosmic strength, resonated with a brilliance that defied mortal comprehension.

As they emerged victorious from the cosmic trial, the friends felt a surge of cosmic energy coursing through them. The celestial map, now adorned with new constellations, reflected their triumph. The Veilstitcher's spectral form, a distant but benevolent presence, communicated a silent acknowledgment of their growth as cosmic stewards.

The friends, now attuned to the cosmic rhythms, realized that their journey had become a perpetual quest to maintain the balance between realms. The Veilstitcher's influence guided them toward cosmic disturbances that threatened to disrupt the delicate equilibrium. The amulet, a cosmic compass, pulsed with urgency as the friends embraced their roles as cosmic guardians.

In one particularly perilous encounter, the friends faced an entity that sought to unravel the threads of reality. The cosmic disturbance, a malevolent force that defied comprehension, manifested in shifting shadows and ethereal echoes. The Veilstitcher's influence, now an active guide, directed the friends in a cosmic battle against the encroaching chaos.

As the friends confronted the cosmic disturbance, the amulet resonated with a fierce brilliance. The celestial map, now animated with cosmic energies, revealed the weaknesses in the malevolent force. Guided by the Veilstitcher's influence, the friends channeled their cosmic abilities to weave threads of stability into the fabric of reality.

The cosmic battle unfolded in a surreal dance of energies, with the friends wielding the amulet as a conduit for their newfound cosmic powers. The Veilstitcher's spectral form, a silent overseer, observed their efforts with a sense of approval. The celestial map, now a source of tactical insight, guided the friends through the intricate maneuvers needed to restore cosmic equilibrium.

As the malevolent force recoiled under the friends' cosmic onslaught, the cosmic disturbance began to dissipate. The Veilstitcher's influence, intertwined with the amulet's radiant glow, sealed the weakened threads of reality. The friends, exhausted but triumphant, stood amidst the cosmic aftermath, their cosmic abilities now more refined and potent.

The Veilstitcher's spectral form approached, its essence resonating with a profound serenity. The amulet, still glowing with the aftermath of the cosmic battle, conveyed a sense of fulfillment. The celestial map, though marked by the recent cosmic disturbance, hinted at the friends' ongoing journey as cosmic guardians.

As the friends left the disrupted realm, the Veilstitcher's influence lingered as a silent companion. The amulet, now a vessel of cosmic

energies, pulsed with a steady rhythm. The celestial map, enriched by the recent experiences, reflected the intricate dance of cosmic forces that shaped their cosmic journey.

In the wake of the cosmic battle, the friends continued their exploration of interconnected realms. The Veilstitcher's influence, though less prominent, remained a guiding force in their cosmic endeavors. The amulet, now a symbol of their cosmic mastery, resonated with a harmonious energy that connected them to the very essence of the cosmic tapestry.

The friends' travels took them to celestial landscapes, ancient observatories, and cosmic sanctuaries where the boundaries between realms blurred. The Veilstitcher's influence guided them toward cosmic phenomena that demanded their attention. The amulet, now an instrument of cosmic balance, pulsed with an ethereal glow as they upheld their cosmic responsibilities.

Through their cosmic journey, the friends encountered beings of cosmic wisdom and entities that embodied the intricate dance of existence. The Veilstitcher's spectral form, though distant, communicated a sense of approval as the friends navigated through celestial wonders and unearthed forgotten truths.

As the friends embraced their roles as cosmic guardians, the Veilstitcher's influence gradually withdrew, leaving them with a sense of empowerment and cosmic purpose. The amulet, now an artifact infused with cosmic energies, became a symbol of their journey—an enduring testament to their triumphs over cosmic disturbances.

The celestial map, adorned with constellations representing their cosmic victories, guided the friends toward new realms and cosmic challenges. The echoes of the unknown, once a source of terror, now whispered tales of cosmic guardianship and the delicate dance between realms. The friends, forever bound by their shared cosmic

journey, embraced the ongoing mysteries that awaited them in the interconnected tapestry of existence.

As the friends ventured further into the cosmic unknown, the Veilstitcher's spectral form faded into the cosmic expanse, its influence becoming a timeless part of their cosmic legacy. The amulet, a luminous beacon of cosmic mastery, pulsed with the echoes of ancient tales and the triumphant resolution of cosmic enigmas. The celestial map, now a guide through the cosmic realms, unfolded new constellations that beckoned the friends toward their next cosmic adventure—a perpetual odyssey that transcended the boundaries of the known and embraced the infinite possibilities of the cosmic tapestry.

Chapter 15: Cosmic Odyssey

Guided by the celestial map, the friends embarked on a cosmic odyssey that traversed realms beyond mortal comprehension. The interconnected tapestry of existence unfolded before them, revealing celestial wonders, ethereal landscapes, and cosmic phenomena that defied explanation.

The Veilstitcher's influence, though a distant echo, resonated in the cosmic energies that enveloped the friends. The amulet, a radiant beacon of their cosmic mastery, pulsed with an ever-present glow. The celestial map, now adorned with constellations representing their cosmic victories, guided them toward new frontiers in the cosmic expanse.

Their cosmic journey led them to an astral city suspended in the fabric of reality—a nexus where cosmic beings congregated to exchange wisdom and share tales of cosmic struggles. The friends, now revered as cosmic guardians, were welcomed into the celestial enclave. The Veilstitcher's influence, a silent companion, conveyed a sense of pride in their cosmic achievements.

In the astral city, the friends encountered beings of transcendent wisdom—entities that embodied the very essence of cosmic existence. The Veilstitcher's spectral form, though unseen, communicated with the celestial beings in a language of cosmic vibrations. The amulet, resonating with the celestial energies, marked the friends as stewards of the delicate balance between realms.

As they communed with cosmic sages and explored the astral city's ethereal architecture, the friends learned of ancient prophecies that foretold cosmic challenges yet to come. The celestial map, now revealing constellations depicting future cosmic disturbances, guided them toward their next cosmic mission.

The Veilstitcher's influence, now a guiding force in their cosmic endeavors, urged the friends to embrace their roles as cosmic guardians with renewed determination. The amulet, a conduit for cosmic energies, hummed with a harmonious resonance that mirrored the celestial symphony around them.

Their cosmic odyssey led them to a realm where time flowed in paradoxical currents and spatial dimensions intertwined. The celestial map, now navigating through temporal anomalies, revealed cosmic disturbances that threatened to disrupt the cosmic equilibrium. The Veilstitcher's influence, though subtle, guided the friends toward a cosmic anomaly that transcended the boundaries of temporal understanding.

As they entered the realm of temporal paradoxes, the friends encountered echoes of past, present, and future cosmic events. The Veilstitcher's spectral form, now a temporal observer, guided them through the intricacies of temporal anomalies. The amulet, attuned to the temporal energies, pulsed with a rhythmic cadence that marked the ebb and flow of cosmic time.

In their cosmic exploration, the friends faced temporal challenges that tested their understanding of the interconnected tapestry. The

celestial map, now a guide through the temporal labyrinth, revealed constellations representing pivotal moments in cosmic history. The Veilstitcher's influence, intertwined with the amulet's radiant glow, whispered insights into the delicate dance between temporal forces.

As they navigated through temporal currents and faced paradoxical trials, the friends felt the weight of cosmic responsibility. The Veilstitcher's spectral form, a temporal overseer, communicated a sense of urgency in preserving the cosmic equilibrium across all timelines. The amulet, a temporal anchor, resonated with a steady frequency that harmonized with the cosmic time stream.

Their triumph over temporal challenges marked a pivotal moment in their cosmic journey. The Veilstitcher's influence, though bound by temporal constraints, conveyed a sense of approval. The amulet, now a temporal artifact, bore the imprints of their cosmic victories in the temporal realm.

The celestial map, enriched by their experiences in the realm of temporal paradoxes, guided the friends toward new frontiers in the cosmic tapestry. The Veilstitcher's spectral form, though distant, remained a silent companion in their cosmic odyssey. The amulet, now a relic infused with temporal energies, pulsed with the echoes of ancient tales and the triumphant resolution of temporal enigmas.

As the friends ventured further into the cosmic unknown, the celestial map unfolded new constellations representing uncharted realms. The Veilstitcher's influence, now a timeless presence, guided them toward cosmic phenomena that transcended mortal understanding. The amulet, an ever-present source of cosmic awareness, resonated with a luminous brilliance that mirrored the cosmic wonders around them.

Their cosmic odyssey continued, weaving through realms of surreal beauty, cosmic challenges, and ancient mysteries. The Veilstitcher's spectral form, now an ethereal companion, communicated

a sense of purpose in their ongoing quest to uphold the delicate balance between realms. The amulet, a cosmic talisman, pulsed with an enduring glow that marked the friends as eternal stewards of the cosmic equilibrium.

As the friends embraced the infinite possibilities of the cosmic tapestry, the echoes of the unknown whispered tales of cosmic guardianship and the intricate dance between realms. The Veilstitcher's influence, though timeless, remained an ever-watchful guide in their perpetual cosmic adventure. The amulet, a radiant symbol of their cosmic journey, continued to resonate with the echoes of ancient tales and the triumphant resolution of cosmic enigmas.

In the vast expanse of the interconnected tapestry, the friends' cosmic odyssey unfolded like an eternal saga—an ongoing exploration of the unknown, a journey that transcended the boundaries of the known, and a testament to the enduring bond between mortal souls and the cosmic forces that shaped their destinies.

Chapter 15: The Abyss of Cosmic Dread

As the friends delved deeper into the cosmic expanse, guided by the celestial map, they sensed an ominous shift in the fabric of reality. The Veilstitcher's influence, once a reassuring presence, now vibrated with an undercurrent of cosmic dread. The amulet, usually radiant with cosmic energies, flickered with an unsettling uncertainty as they approached a realm shrouded in cosmic shadows.

The astral city, which had once welcomed them as revered cosmic guardians, now revealed a darker underbelly. Celestial beings, their ethereal forms distorted by an unseen malevolence, whispered foreboding prophecies of an impending cosmic catastrophe. The Veilstitcher's spectral form, still present but veiled in cosmic dread, communicated a sense of urgency that sent shivers through the friends' cosmic awareness.

The celestial map, now marked by constellations that seemed to writhe with cosmic unease, directed them toward an abyssal rift—an anomaly in the fabric of existence that emitted an unsettling resonance. As they approached the cosmic abyss, the amulet pulsed with an erratic energy, reflecting the growing cosmic disturbance that threatened to unravel the delicate balance between realms.

As they entered the abyssal rift, the friends felt an overwhelming sense of existential dread. The Veilstitcher's influence, usually a guiding force, now manifested as haunting whispers that echoed through the cosmic void. Shadows danced with a malevolent glee, and the celestial map, once a source of guidance, seemed to lead them deeper into the cosmic abyss.

In the depths of the rift, the friends encountered cosmic horrors that defied mortal comprehension. Entities of cosmic malevolence, their forms twisted by the abyssal energies, sought to consume the very essence of their cosmic being. The Veilstitcher's spectral form, dimmed by the cosmic dread, conveyed a silent plea for the friends to resist the encroaching darkness.

The amulet, struggling against the oppressive forces of the abyss, emitted flashes of dim light that barely illuminated the cosmic horrors that lurked in the shadows. The celestial map, now distorted by the abyssal energies, led the friends through maddening labyrinths where reality itself seemed to unravel.

As they faced the cosmic horrors, the friends felt the weight of existential terror bearing down upon them. The Veilstitcher's spectral form, now a flickering beacon in the cosmic abyss, urged them to confront the source of the malevolence that threatened to rupture the fabric of reality. The amulet, their only source of cosmic defense, resonated with the desperate pulses of their fear-stricken hearts.

In their cosmic struggle against the abyssal forces, the friends discovered ancient ruins—remnants of a forgotten civilization that

had succumbed to the same cosmic dread. The celestial map, though tainted by the abyssal energies, revealed inscriptions that spoke of rituals to appease eldritch entities and the consequences of cosmic disturbances left unchecked.

The Veilstitcher's spectral form, now dimmed by the encroaching darkness, communicated the dire implications of the abyssal rift's existence. If not sealed, it threatened to become a cosmic tear that could unleash unspeakable horrors upon the interconnected tapestry. The friends, gripped by terror and determination, understood the gravity of their cosmic mission.

As they ventured deeper into the ruins, the abyssal energies twisted the very fabric of reality. Cosmic echoes whispered tales of the doomed civilization that had once thrived in the cosmic abyss. The amulet, now a fragile shield against the abyssal forces, flickered with the desperate hope that the friends could prevent a similar fate.

In the heart of the ruins, the friends discovered a cosmic altar—a focal point for the abyssal energies that pulsed through the rift. Eldritch symbols adorned the altar, resonating with malevolence that sent shivers down their spines. The celestial map, now a guide through the madness, directed them toward a cosmic ritual that could seal the abyssal rift and avert the impending cosmic catastrophe.

As they prepared to enact the ritual, the friends felt the oppressive weight of the abyssal energies bearing down upon them. Whispers of cosmic horrors echoed in their minds, and the Veilstitcher's spectral form, barely visible amidst the cosmic dread, communicated the urgency of completing the ritual before the fabric of reality unraveled completely.

The amulet, now strained to its cosmic limits, emitted a feeble glow as the friends channeled their cosmic abilities into the ritual. Shadows, animated by the abyssal forces, writhed in protest as the

celestial map guided them through the intricate steps of the cosmic sealing. The Veilstitcher's spectral form, though barely discernible, resonated with the friends' determination to defy the encroaching cosmic dread.

In the midst of the ritual, the friends felt the cosmic abyss resisting their efforts. Eldritch energies surged, threatening to overwhelm their sanity. The Veilstitcher's influence, now a beacon in the cosmic storm, lent its spectral strength to their cosmic struggle. The amulet, teetering on the brink of cosmic exhaustion, emitted a final burst of radiant light that merged with the celestial energies of the sealing ritual.

As the last cosmic incantation echoed through the ruins, a profound stillness settled over the abyssal rift. The cosmic dread that had permeated the very fabric of reality began to recede. The Veilstitcher's spectral form, now visible in a dim luminescence, conveyed a silent acknowledgment of the friends' success in averting the cosmic catastrophe.

The amulet, though dimmed and worn, retained a subdued glow—a testament to the friends' resilience against the abyssal forces. The celestial map, now cleared of the malevolent constellations, revealed a new cosmic equilibrium that mirrored the triumph over the cosmic dread that had threatened to consume the interconnected tapestry.

As the friends emerged from the ruins, the abyssal rift sealed behind them, the Veilstitcher's spectral form regained its ethereal brilliance. The amulet, though scarred by the cosmic struggle, pulsed with a renewed vitality. The celestial map, now restored to its cosmic clarity, guided them toward realms untouched by the malevolent forces that had lurked in the cosmic abyss.

The friends, forever changed by their harrowing encounter with the abyssal forces, continued their cosmic odyssey with a heightened

awareness of the cosmic horrors that lurked in the vast expanse. The Veilstitcher's influence, now a vigilant guardian, accompanied them as a guiding force. The amulet, a resilient artifact that bore the scars of their cosmic ordeal, resonated with a luminous brilliance that symbolized their triumph over the abyssal dread.

The celestial map, once tainted by malevolence, now guided the friends toward realms where cosmic wonders awaited discovery. The echoes of the unknown, though still haunting, whispered tales of cosmic resilience and the indomitable spirit that defied the abyssal forces. The friends, forever entwined by the shared horrors they had faced, embraced the mysteries that awaited them in the uncharted territories of the interconnected tapestry.

Their cosmic odyssey, now marked by the echoes of cosmic dread and triumphant resilience, unfolded like a cosmic epic—an eternal saga that transcended mortal fears and celebrated the enduring bond between mortal souls and the cosmic forces that shaped their destinies.

Chapter 16: Shadows of the Celestial Betrayal

As the friends ventured further into the cosmic unknown, guided by the celestial map, they found themselves in a realm cloaked in unsettling shadows. The Veilstitcher's influence, though a constant presence, seemed to waver as they approached an ancient observatory atop a desolate cosmic peak. The amulet, typically radiant with cosmic energies, emitted a dim glow that reflected the ominous atmosphere that pervaded the celestial landscape.

The observatory, a structure that bore witness to eons of cosmic phenomena, now echoed with whispers of a celestial betrayal that had cast a dark shadow over the interconnected tapestry. The Veilstitcher's spectral form, a silhouette against the cosmic gloom, communicated a tale of treachery that had resonated through the celestial realms.

The celestial map, now displaying constellations that seemed to writhe in cosmic agony, directed the friends toward the heart of the celestial betrayal. As they ascended the cosmic peak, the shadows deepened, and the amulet pulsed with a disconcerting rhythm that mirrored the cosmic unease.

In the observatory's inner sanctum, the friends discovered a cosmic artifact—a relic of ancient power that had been corrupted by the tendrils of celestial betrayal. Eldritch symbols adorned the artifact, resonating with malevolence that sent shivers down their spines. The Veilstitcher's influence, though shrouded in cosmic sorrow, urged them to unravel the mysteries of the celestial betrayal that had tainted the very essence of the interconnected tapestry.

As the friends examined the corrupted artifact, the shadows within the observatory seemed to come alive. Cosmic entities, twisted by the influence of celestial betrayal, materialized in ghostly forms. The Veilstitcher's spectral form, now obscured by the cosmic gloom, whispered warnings of the malevolent entities that guarded the secrets of the celestial betrayal.

The amulet, sensing the encroaching cosmic malevolence, emitted a protective aura that shielded the friends from the ghostly entities' influence. The celestial map, though distorted by the shadows, revealed inscriptions that chronicled the ancient pact that had led to the celestial betrayal and the cosmic consequences that followed.

In their exploration of the observatory, the friends faced spectral guardians—entities that embodied the malevolent echoes of celestial betrayal. Shadows danced with a haunting grace as the Veilstitcher's influence guided them through cosmic trials that tested their resolve. The amulet, a luminous beacon against the cosmic darkness, resonated with a determination to uncover the truth behind the celestial betrayal.

As they delved deeper into the observatory's mysteries, the whispers of the celestial betrayal grew more pronounced. The Veilstitcher's spectral form, now a spectral guide in the cosmic shadows, conveyed a sense of cosmic sorrow that mirrored the anguish of ancient cosmic entities. The amulet, their only defense against the encroaching malevolence, flickered with a resilient glow that defied the cosmic despair.

In the observatory's inner chambers, the friends uncovered an ancient cosmic chronicle—an illuminated manuscript that chronicled the events leading to the celestial betrayal. The celestial map, now revealing constellations that depicted cosmic alliances shattered by treachery, guided them through the cosmic revelations that awaited.

The Veilstitcher's influence, though shrouded in cosmic sorrow, narrated a tale of celestial beings bound by a sacred covenant to uphold the cosmic equilibrium. Betrayal, driven by cosmic ambition, had fractured the bonds of trust and unleashed cosmic disturbances that reverberated through the interconnected tapestry.

As the friends immersed themselves in the cosmic chronicle, they witnessed cosmic battles, treacherous alliances, and the tragic fall of celestial beings consumed by their desires for power. The celestial map, now marked by constellations that depicted the celestial betrayal in vivid detail, guided them toward the heart of the observatory where the corrupted artifact held the key to understanding the cosmic transgressions.

In the inner sanctum, the friends faced a spectral guardian—an embodiment of the celestial betrayal that had tainted the artifact with malevolent energies. The Veilstitcher's spectral form, now a solemn observer, conveyed a sense of sorrow as the friends confronted the echoes of ancient cosmic treachery. The amulet, resonating with the cosmic revelations, emitted a luminous glow that mirrored the

friends' determination to cleanse the artifact and unravel the mysteries of the celestial betrayal.

The celestial map, now pulsating with the cosmic consequences of the ancient transgressions, guided the friends through a ritual to purify the corrupted artifact. Shadows writhed with resistance, and the spectral guardian unleashed cosmic energies in a desperate attempt to prevent the redemption of the tainted relic. The Veilstitcher's influence, though veiled in cosmic sorrow, whispered words of encouragement as the friends channeled their cosmic abilities into the purification ritual.

In the midst of the cosmic struggle, the artifact resonated with celestial energies, and the shadows within the observatory recoiled. The Veilstitcher's spectral form, now visible in a dim luminescence, conveyed a sense of approval as the purification ritual reached its zenith. The amulet, though strained by the cosmic exertion, emitted a final burst of radiant light that merged with the purified energies of the artifact.

As the celestial energies enveloped the observatory, a profound stillness settled over the cosmic peak. The shadows dissipated, and the celestial map, now cleared of the malevolent constellations, revealed a new cosmic equilibrium that reflected the friends' triumph over the celestial betrayal. The Veilstitcher's spectral form, though still tinged with cosmic sorrow, conveyed a silent acknowledgment of their success in redeeming the corrupted artifact.

The amulet, though scarred by the cosmic struggle, retained a subdued glow—a testament to the friends' resilience against the malevolent forces of celestial betrayal. The celestial map, now restored to its cosmic clarity, guided them toward realms where the echoes of ancient treachery had been silenced.

As the friends emerged from the observatory, the celestial betrayal purged behind them, the Veilstitcher's spectral form regained

its ethereal brilliance. The amulet, though dimmed and worn, pulsed with a renewed vitality. The celestial map, now cleared of the malevolent constellations, guided them toward new frontiers in the interconnected tapestry.

The friends, forever changed by their harrowing encounter with the celestial betrayal, continued their cosmic odyssey with a heightened awareness of the cosmic transgressions that could threaten the delicate balance between realms. The Veilstitcher's influence, now a vigilant guardian, accompanied them as a guiding force. The amulet, a resilient artifact that bore the scars of their cosmic ordeal, resonated with a luminous brilliance that symbolized their triumph over the shadows of ancient treachery.

The celestial map, once tainted by malevolence, now guided the friends toward realms where cosmic wonders awaited discovery. The echoes of the unknown, though still haunting, whispered tales of cosmic resilience and the indomitable spirit that defied the shadows of celestial betrayal. The friends, forever entwined by the shared horrors they had faced, embraced the mysteries that awaited them in the uncharted territories of the interconnected tapestry.

Their cosmic odyssey, now marked by the echoes of celestial betrayal and triumphant resilience, unfolded like a cosmic epic—an eternal saga that transcended mortal fears and celebrated the enduring bond between mortal souls and the cosmic forces that shaped their destinies.

Chapter 17: Whispers of the Cosmic Abyss

As the friends continued their cosmic odyssey, guided by the celestial map, they found themselves drawn to a realm shrouded in enigmatic whispers—the remnants of cosmic echoes that hinted at an ancient cosmic abyss. The Veilstitcher's influence, a vigilant guardian, resonated with a somber resonance as they approached the threshold of this mysterious cosmic chasm. The amulet, though

usually radiant with cosmic energies, emitted an ethereal glow that reflected the unsettling atmosphere surrounding the abyss.

The celestial map, now marked by constellations that seemed to ripple like cosmic waves, directed the friends toward the edge of the cosmic abyss. As they descended into its depths, the shadows deepened, and the amulet pulsed with an eerie luminosity that mirrored the cosmic uncertainties that lay ahead.

In the cosmic abyss, the friends encountered surreal landscapes where the fabric of reality seemed to unravel. Ethereal whispers, echoing from the depths of the abyss, conveyed tales of ancient cosmic entities that had succumbed to the allure of forbidden knowledge. The Veilstitcher's spectral form, now a solemn guide, warned of the cosmic perils that lurked in the abyssal depths.

As they navigated through the cosmic echoes, the friends faced spectral manifestations—entities born from the lingering remnants of cosmic entities that had unraveled in the abyss. Shadows danced with an otherworldly grace, and the celestial map, now flickering with cosmic uncertainties, guided them through trials that tested their resilience against the cosmic abyss.

The Veilstitcher's influence, though a steadfast companion, communicated a sense of caution as the friends delved deeper into the cosmic unknown. The amulet, their cosmic beacon, emitted a protective aura that shielded them from the haunting forces that sought to entice them into the cosmic abyss's alluring depths.

In the heart of the abyss, the friends discovered an ancient cosmic library—a repository of forbidden knowledge that had driven cosmic entities to madness. Eldritch tomes, adorned with celestial symbols, whispered cosmic secrets that reverberated through the friends' consciousness. The celestial map, now etched with constellations depicting cosmic entities succumbing to the abyssal allure, guided them through the cosmic archives.

The Veilstitcher's spectral form, now a spectral librarian, communicated the dire consequences of delving too deeply into the forbidden knowledge within the cosmic library. The amulet, resonating with the echoes of cosmic entities lost to the abyss, pulsed with a cautionary rhythm that mirrored the friends' trepidation.

As they deciphered the celestial symbols within the tomes, the friends uncovered the tale of an ancient cosmic entity—an entity that had sought to unravel the mysteries of the cosmos but had succumbed to the cosmic abyss's seductive whispers. The celestial map, now revealing constellations that mirrored the entity's descent into madness, guided them toward the entity's resting place within the abyss.

The Veilstitcher's influence, now a solemn guide in the cosmic library, urged the friends to tread carefully as they approached the entity's lair. Shadows, animated by the abyssal energies, seemed to writhe with anticipation, and the amulet emitted a subdued glow that signaled their entry into the heart of the cosmic abyss.

In the presence of the ancient cosmic entity, echoes of madness reverberated through the abyss. The entity's spectral form, twisted by the allure of forbidden knowledge, manifested in surreal splendor. The Veilstitcher's spectral form, a spectral witness to the entity's tragic fate, communicated the profound sorrow that accompanied the entity's descent into the cosmic abyss.

The friends, now confronted by the entity's spectral manifestation, felt the weight of cosmic madness bearing down upon them. The celestial map, now depicting constellations that mirrored the entity's cosmic unraveling, guided them through a cosmic trial that tested their sanity. The amulet, their only defense against the abyssal forces, emitted a protective aura that resonated with a determination to resist the cosmic allure.

In their cosmic struggle against the entity's spectral manifestation, the friends uncovered the cosmic truths that had driven the entity to madness. Forbidden knowledge, woven into the very fabric of the cosmic abyss, whispered cosmic secrets that defied mortal comprehension. The Veilstitcher's spectral form, a witness to the unfolding cosmic drama, conveyed a sense of empathy for the entity's tragic journey.

The amulet, attuned to the cosmic revelations, emitted pulses of resonant light that harmonized with the celestial map's guidance. As the friends faced the entity's spectral manifestation, the cosmic abyss seemed to echo with the collective sorrow of entities lost to the seductive whispers of forbidden knowledge.

In a moment of cosmic clarity, the friends realized that the only way to quell the entity's spectral madness was to weave threads of cosmic understanding into the fabric of the abyss. The Veilstitcher's spectral form, now a spectral weaver, guided them through a cosmic ritual that sought to restore the entity's fractured consciousness.

As they channeled their cosmic abilities into the ritual, the cosmic abyss responded with an ethereal symphony. Shadows, once animated by madness, now danced with a melancholic grace. The celestial map, now pulsating with threads of cosmic understanding, guided the friends through the intricate maneuvers needed to mend the entity's cosmic essence.

In the cosmic aftermath of the ritual, the entity's spectral manifestation transformed. Madness gave way to a serene luminescence, and the abyssal energies seemed to retreat. The Veilstitcher's influence, now a cosmic weaver of understanding, conveyed a sense of resolution as the friends witnessed the entity's spectral form find peace within the cosmic abyss.

The amulet, though worn by the cosmic struggle, emitted a radiant glow that mirrored the friends' triumph over the abyssal allure.

The celestial map, now cleared of constellations depicting madness, revealed a new cosmic equilibrium that reflected the friends' ability to navigate the cosmic abyss and emerge unscathed.

As the friends ascended from the cosmic abyss, the Veilstitcher's spectral form regained its ethereal brilliance. The amulet, though scarred by the cosmic ordeal, pulsed with a renewed vitality. The celestial map, now cleared of the cosmic uncertainties, guided them toward new frontiers in the interconnected tapestry.

The friends, forever changed by their harrowing encounter with the cosmic abyss, continued their cosmic odyssey with a heightened awareness of the cosmic perils that lurked in the vast expanse. The Veilstitcher's influence, now a cosmic weaver of understanding, accompanied them as a guiding force. The amulet, a resilient artifact that bore the scars of their cosmic ordeal, resonated with a luminous brilliance that symbolized their triumph over the shadows of the cosmic abyss.

The celestial map, once tainted by cosmic uncertainties, now guided the friends toward realms where cosmic wonders awaited discovery. The echoes of the unknown, though still haunting, whispered tales of cosmic resilience and the indomitable spirit that defied the allure of the cosmic abyss. The friends, forever entwined by the shared horrors they had faced, embraced the mysteries that awaited them in the uncharted territories of the interconnected tapestry.

Their cosmic odyssey, now marked by the echoes of the cosmic abyss and triumphant resilience, unfolded like a cosmic epic—an eternal saga that transcended mortal fears and celebrated the enduring bond between mortal souls and the cosmic forces that shaped their destinies.

Chapter 18: Symphony of Celestial Woe

As the friends continued their cosmic journey, guided by the celestial map, they found themselves drawn to a realm where celestial

forces clashed in a symphony of woe. The Veilstitcher's influence, ever watchful, resonated with a sense of foreboding as they approached an ethereal battleground where cosmic entities engaged in an otherworldly conflict. The amulet, typically radiant with cosmic energies, flickered with an ominous luminosity that mirrored the discordant atmosphere surrounding the celestial battleground.

The celestial map, now marked by constellations that seemed to clash in celestial strife, directed the friends toward the epicenter of the cosmic conflict. As they ventured deeper into the celestial battleground, the cosmic energies pulsated with an unsettling intensity, and the amulet emitted an erratic glow that reflected the cosmic turbulence that surrounded them.

In the midst of the celestial clash, the friends witnessed cosmic entities locked in a dance of ethereal combat. Celestial beings, once guardians of cosmic harmony, now clashed in discordant symphonies that reverberated through the interconnected tapestry. The Veilstitcher's spectral form, a spectral witness to the celestial woe, communicated a tale of ancient grievances that had ignited the cosmic conflict.

The celestial map, now revealing constellations that depicted celestial entities entwined in celestial strife, guided the friends through the celestial battleground. Shadows danced with malevolent glee, and the amulet emitted a protective aura that shielded them from the cosmic energies unleashed in the celestial clash.

As they navigated through the cosmic battlefield, the friends encountered spectral remnants—echoes of celestial entities consumed by the warring energies. The Veilstitcher's influence, though a vigilant observer, conveyed a sense of cosmic sorrow as the friends witnessed the tragic consequences of the celestial conflict. The amulet, their cosmic protector, resonated with a determination to understand the origins of the celestial woe.

In the heart of the celestial battleground, the friends discovered an ancient cosmic artifact—a relic of power that had become a focal point for the warring energies. Eldritch symbols adorned the artifact, resonating with the echoes of ancient grievances that fueled the celestial conflict. The celestial map, now etched with constellations that depicted the artifact's role in the celestial strife, guided them toward understanding the artifact's significance.

The Veilstitcher's spectral form, now a spectral historian, communicated the cosmic tale of how the artifact had become a catalyst for the celestial woe. Betrayals, vendettas, and cosmic vendettas had intertwined in a cosmic dance that threatened to unravel the very fabric of the interconnected tapestry. The amulet, resonating with the cosmic revelations, emitted a luminescent glow that mirrored the friends' determination to quell the celestial conflict.

As they approached the cosmic artifact, the friends faced celestial guardians—entities consumed by the warring energies that emanated from the relic. Shadows, animated by ancient grievances, seemed to materialize in ethereal forms, and the Veilstitcher's spectral form guided them through trials that tested their resolve against the celestial woe.

The amulet, their cosmic defense, emitted a protective aura that shimmered with radiant light. The celestial map, now pulsating with constellations that depicted the celestial guardians in moments of cosmic despair, guided the friends through the celestial trials. The Veilstitcher's influence, though tinged with cosmic sorrow, urged them to confront the spectral remnants and restore cosmic harmony.

In their cosmic struggle against the celestial guardians, the friends uncovered the origins of the ancient vendettas that had fueled the celestial conflict. Betrayals, forged alliances, and cosmic vendettas had intertwined in a cosmic dance that threatened to consume the

celestial battleground. The Veilstitcher's spectral form, a witness to the unfolding cosmic drama, conveyed a sense of urgency as the friends unraveled the cosmic grievances that fueled the celestial woe.

The amulet, attuned to the cosmic revelations, emitted pulses of resonant light that harmonized with the celestial map's guidance. As the friends faced the celestial guardians, the cosmic energies seemed to shift in response to their cosmic understanding. Shadows, once animated by warring energies, now flickered with moments of celestial harmony.

In a pivotal moment of the celestial struggle, the friends realized that the only way to quell the celestial conflict was to sever the ties that bound the ancient vendettas. The Veilstitcher's spectral form, now a cosmic arbitrator, guided them through a celestial ritual that sought to break the cosmic cycles of vengeance and restore the celestial entities' understanding.

As they channeled their cosmic abilities into the ritual, the cosmic energies responded with an ethereal symphony. Shadows, once animated by ancient grievances, now danced in a harmonious ballet. The celestial map, now pulsating with threads of cosmic understanding, guided the friends through the intricate maneuvers needed to mend the celestial entities' fractured consciousness.

In the cosmic aftermath of the ritual, the celestial guardians transformed. The cosmic vendettas that had fueled their spectral existence seemed to dissipate, and the celestial energies responded with a serene luminescence. The Veilstitcher's influence, now a cosmic mediator, conveyed a sense of resolution as the friends witnessed the celestial entities find peace within the cosmic battleground.

The amulet, though worn by the cosmic struggle, emitted a radiant glow that mirrored the friends' triumph over the celestial woe. The celestial map, now cleared of constellations depicting discord, revealed a new cosmic equilibrium that reflected the friends'

ability to mediate the celestial conflict and bring about a cosmic understanding.

As the friends ascended from the celestial battleground, the Veilstitcher's spectral form regained its ethereal brilliance. The amulet, though scarred by the cosmic ordeal, pulsed with a renewed vitality. The celestial map, now cleared of the cosmic disharmony, guided them toward new frontiers in the interconnected tapestry.

The friends, forever changed by their harrowing encounter with the celestial woe, continued their cosmic odyssey with a heightened awareness of the cosmic perils that lurked in the vast expanse. The Veilstitcher's influence, now a cosmic mediator, accompanied them as a guiding force. The amulet, a resilient artifact that bore the scars of their cosmic ordeal, resonated with a luminous brilliance that symbolized their triumph over the discordant echoes of the celestial woe.

The celestial map, once tainted by cosmic disharmony, now guided the friends toward realms where cosmic wonders awaited discovery. The echoes of the unknown, though still haunting, whispered tales of cosmic resilience and the indomitable spirit that defied the discord of the celestial woe. The friends, forever entwined by the shared horrors they had faced, embraced the mysteries that awaited them in the uncharted territories of the interconnected tapestry.

Their cosmic odyssey, now marked by the echoes of the celestial woe and triumphant resilience, unfolded like a cosmic epic—an eternal saga that transcended mortal fears and celebrated the enduring bond between mortal souls and the cosmic forces that shaped their destinies.

Chapter 19: The Veil's Unraveling

In the wake of their triumph over the celestial woe, the friends felt a profound shift in the cosmic fabric as the celestial map guided them towards the heart of an impending cosmic catastrophe. The

Veilstitcher's influence, though a steadfast companion, resonated with an urgency that transcended the cosmic echoes. The amulet, usually radiant with cosmic energies, emitted a flickering glow that mirrored the unsettling atmosphere surrounding them.

The celestial map, now marked by constellations that seemed to spiral in cosmic distress, directed the friends towards an ancient cosmic observatory—a place where the threads of reality and the cosmic veil converged. As they approached the observatory, the shadows deepened, and the amulet pulsed with an ominous luminosity that hinted at the cosmic perils that awaited them.

In the observatory's sacred chambers, the friends discovered an ancient cosmic artifact—an unraveling veil that bound the threads of the interconnected tapestry. Eldritch symbols adorned the artifact, resonating with an unsettling energy that sent shivers down their spines. The Veilstitcher's spectral form, now a solemn guide, communicated a tale of cosmic imbalance that threatened to rupture the very fabric of reality.

The celestial map, now etched with constellations that depicted the cosmic veil's unraveling, guided the friends through the cosmic observatory. Shadows danced with malevolent glee, and the amulet emitted a protective aura that shielded them from the cosmic disturbances that emanated from the artifact.

As they explored the observatory's depths, the friends faced cosmic guardians—entities tasked with protecting the artifact that held the threads of the cosmic veil. The Veilstitcher's influence, though tinged with cosmic sorrow, urged them to confront the guardians and understand the source of the cosmic imbalance. The amulet, their cosmic shield, resonated with a determination to prevent the impending catastrophe.

In the heart of the observatory, the friends discovered celestial inscriptions that chronicled the artifact's role in maintaining the

cosmic equilibrium. The celestial map, now revealing constellations that depicted the threads of reality woven into the cosmic veil, guided them towards an understanding of the artifact's significance. The Veilstitcher's spectral form, now a cosmic historian, conveyed the dire consequences of the cosmic veil's unraveling.

As they deciphered the celestial inscriptions, the friends learned of an ancient cosmic entity—the Weaver of Realms—who had crafted the cosmic veil to ensure the harmony of the interconnected tapestry. Betrayals and vendettas had driven the cosmic entity to an abyss of despair, leading to a cosmic curse that now threatened to shatter the delicate threads of reality.

The Veilstitcher's spectral form, now a cosmic weaver, guided the friends through a ritual to commune with the Weaver of Realms and understand the cosmic curse that had befallen the artifact. The amulet, resonating with the cosmic revelations, emitted a luminescent glow that mirrored the friends' determination to mend the unraveling cosmic veil.

As they channeled their cosmic abilities into the ritual, the cosmic observatory responded with ethereal energies. Shadows, once animated by cosmic imbalance, now seemed to waver in a cosmic dance. The celestial map, now pulsating with threads of cosmic understanding, guided the friends through the intricate maneuvers needed to commune with the Weaver of Realms.

In the cosmic communion, the friends glimpsed the Weaver of Realms—a spectral entity consumed by cosmic despair. The Veilstitcher's spectral form, now a compassionate guide, urged them to unravel the cosmic curse that bound the Weaver and restore balance to the interconnected tapestry. The amulet, attuned to the cosmic revelations, emitted pulses of resonant light that harmonized with the celestial map's guidance.

As the friends faced the Weaver of Realms, the cosmic entity conveyed the tale of its descent into cosmic despair. Betrayals and vendettas had shattered the cosmic harmony it sought to maintain, leading to a curse that now threatened to unravel the very fabric of reality. The Veilstitcher's influence, now a cosmic mediator, urged the friends to break the chains of despair and restore hope to the Weaver.

In a pivotal moment of cosmic communion, the friends realized that the only way to mend the cosmic veil was to heal the Weaver of Realms' cosmic despair. The Veilstitcher's spectral form, now a cosmic healer, guided them through a celestial ritual that sought to break the cosmic curse and bring solace to the beleaguered cosmic entity.

As they channeled their cosmic abilities into the ritual, the cosmic observatory responded with an ethereal symphony. Shadows, once animated by cosmic despair, now seemed to waver in a harmonious ballet. The celestial map, now pulsating with threads of cosmic understanding, guided the friends through the intricate maneuvers needed to heal the Weaver of Realms.

In the cosmic aftermath of the ritual, the Weaver of Realms' spectral form transformed. Despair gave way to a serene luminescence, and the cosmic energies responded with a harmonious resonance. The Veilstitcher's influence, now a cosmic healer, conveyed a sense of resolution as the friends witnessed the Weaver find peace within the cosmic observatory.

The amulet, though worn by the cosmic struggle, emitted a radiant glow that mirrored the friends' triumph over the cosmic despair. The celestial map, now cleared of constellations depicting the cosmic curse, revealed a new cosmic equilibrium that reflected the friends' ability to mend the unraveling threads of the cosmic veil.

As the friends ascended from the cosmic observatory, the Veilstitcher's spectral form regained its ethereal brilliance. The amulet, though scarred by the cosmic ordeal, pulsed with a renewed vitality. The celestial map, now cleared of the cosmic imbalance, guided them toward new frontiers in the interconnected tapestry.

The friends, forever changed by their harrowing encounter with the unraveling cosmic veil, continued their cosmic odyssey with a heightened awareness of the cosmic perils that lurked in the vast expanse. The Veilstitcher's influence, now a cosmic healer, accompanied them as a guiding force. The amulet, a resilient artifact that bore the scars of their cosmic ordeal, resonated with a luminous brilliance that symbolized their triumph over the cosmic despair.

The celestial map, once tainted by cosmic imbalance, now guided the friends toward realms where cosmic wonders awaited discovery. The echoes of the unknown, though still haunting, whispered tales of cosmic resilience and the indomitable spirit that defied the cosmic despair. The friends, forever entwined by the shared horrors they had faced, embraced the mysteries that awaited them in the uncharted territories of the interconnected tapestry.

Their cosmic odyssey, now marked by the mending of the cosmic veil and triumphant resilience, unfolded like a cosmic epic—an eternal saga that transcended mortal fears and celebrated the enduring bond between mortal souls and the cosmic forces that shaped their destinies.

As the friends ventured forth from the cosmic observatory, a newfound clarity enveloped the interconnected tapestry. The Veilstitcher's spectral form, once a guardian in cosmic despair, radiated with a luminous brilliance that mirrored the cosmic healing they had achieved. The amulet, though marked by the trials of unraveling cosmic threads, retained a resilient glow—a testament to their ability to mend the cosmic veil.

The celestial map, now cleared of constellations depicting imbalance, guided the friends towards realms where cosmic wonders awaited discovery. The echoes of the unknown, though still haunting, whispered tales of cosmic resilience and the indomitable spirit that defied the cosmic despair. The friends, forever entwined by the shared horrors they had faced, embraced the mysteries that awaited them in the uncharted territories of the interconnected tapestry.

Their cosmic odyssey, now marked by the mending of the cosmic veil and triumphant resilience, unfolded like a cosmic epic—an eternal saga that transcended mortal fears and celebrated the enduring bond between mortal souls and the cosmic forces that shaped their destinies.

As they ventured into unexplored cosmic realms, the friends encountered celestial wonders that seemed to shimmer with a renewed vitality. The Veilstitcher's influence, now a beacon of cosmic healing, guided them through realms where echoes of their cosmic deeds resonated with celestial echoes. The amulet, a cosmic artifact infused with the power of mended threads, pulsed with a rhythmic glow that echoed the harmony they had restored.

The celestial map, now revealing constellations that depicted the friends as cosmic healers, guided them towards realms where their presence was needed. Shadows, once animated by cosmic despair, now seemed to retreat in the wake of their cosmic healing. The friends, now custodians of celestial balance, embraced their role in preserving the interconnected tapestry.

In their cosmic journey, the friends encountered celestial beings whose threads of reality had frayed. The Veilstitcher's spectral form, now a cosmic guide in mending, urged them to extend their healing touch to those ensnared by cosmic disarray. The amulet, resonating with the threads of cosmic understanding, emitted a gentle glow that mirrored their commitment to restoring celestial harmony.

As they traversed through realms touched by cosmic imbalance, the friends faced cosmic trials that tested their newfound abilities as healers of the interconnected tapestry. The Veilstitcher's influence, now a cosmic mentor, guided them through rituals that sought to mend the threads of reality and restore balance to celestial entities caught in the throes of cosmic disarray.

The amulet, a conduit of cosmic energies, emitted pulses of healing light that harmonized with the celestial map's guidance. Shadows, once animated by cosmic despair, now seemed to dissipate as the friends embraced their cosmic roles as healers. The echoes of their cosmic deeds reverberated through the interconnected tapestry, leaving a trail of celestial balance in their wake.

In a celestial sanctuary, the friends encountered a cosmic entity—a guardian of the celestial realms whose threads of reality had become entangled in cosmic disarray. The Veilstitcher's spectral form, now a cosmic healer, communicated with the entity in a language of cosmic understanding. The amulet, resonating with the threads of mended reality, emitted a soothing aura that calmed the entity's cosmic unrest.

As the friends performed a cosmic ritual to heal the guardian's threads, the celestial sanctuary responded with ethereal energies. The Veilstitcher's influence, now a cosmic conductor, guided them through the intricate maneuvers needed to mend the celestial guardian's frayed threads. The amulet, attuned to the cosmic revelations, emitted pulses of resonant light that harmonized with the celestial map's guidance.

In the cosmic aftermath of the ritual, the celestial guardian's spectral form transformed. Threads once entangled in cosmic disarray now shimmered with a serene luminescence. The Veilstitcher's influence, now a cosmic healer, conveyed a sense of fulfillment as

the friends witnessed the guardian find peace within the celestial sanctuary.

The amulet, though worn by the cosmic struggle, emitted a radiant glow that mirrored the friends' triumph as cosmic healers. The celestial map, now cleared of constellations depicting cosmic disarray, revealed a new cosmic equilibrium that reflected the friends' ability to extend their healing touch to the interconnected tapestry.

As the friends continued their cosmic journey, the Veilstitcher's spectral form, now a cosmic mentor, guided them towards realms where celestial entities awaited their healing touch. The amulet, a beacon of cosmic balance, pulsed with a rhythmic glow that echoed the harmonious resonance they had restored. The celestial map, now revealing constellations that depicted the friends as cosmic healers, guided them towards realms where their presence was needed.

Their cosmic odyssey, now marked by the mending of celestial threads and triumphant resilience, unfolded like a cosmic epic—an eternal saga that transcended mortal fears and celebrated the enduring bond between mortal souls and the cosmic forces that shaped their destinies.

Chapter 20: The Cosmic Reckoning

In the final leg of their cosmic odyssey, the friends sensed a gathering cosmic storm—a tempest that threatened to unravel the very fabric of reality. The Veilstitcher's influence, a vigilant beacon, resonated with a profound urgency that transcended the echoes of their past encounters. The amulet, though resilient, emitted a pulsating glow that mirrored the unsettling cosmic energies that surrounded them.

The celestial map, now marked by constellations that seemed to writhe in cosmic distress, guided the friends towards the epicenter of the looming cosmic tempest. As they approached, the shadows deepened, and the cosmic storm manifested in swirling patterns of

ethereal chaos. The Veilstitcher's spectral form, now a harbinger of cosmic reckoning, communicated a dire prophecy of an ancient cosmic entity—the Stormweaver—whose fury threatened to engulf the interconnected tapestry.

In the heart of the cosmic storm, the friends confronted an ethereal vortex—a manifestation of the Stormweaver's wrath. Eldritch symbols adorned the vortex, resonating with an ominous energy that sent shivers down their spines. The celestial map, now etched with constellations that depicted the Stormweaver's fury, guided them towards understanding the origin of the cosmic tempest.

The Veilstitcher's spectral form, now a cosmic seer, revealed the tale of the Stormweaver—an ancient cosmic entity imprisoned by the threads of reality in ages past. Betrayals and vendettas had fueled the Stormweaver's rage, and its spectral essence now sought to unleash cosmic chaos upon the interconnected tapestry. The amulet, resonating with the cosmic revelations, emitted a luminescent glow that mirrored the friends' determination to quell the cosmic reckoning.

As they ventured into the heart of the cosmic vortex, the friends faced celestial guardians—entities corrupted by the Stormweaver's malevolent influence. The Veilstitcher's influence, though tinged with cosmic sorrow, urged them to confront the guardians and understand the depths of the cosmic tempest's power. The amulet, their cosmic shield, resonated with a determination to resist the impending catastrophe.

In the cosmic battleground, the friends encountered remnants of cosmic entities ensnared by the Stormweaver's malevolent influence. Shadows, animated by cosmic fury, seemed to writhe with an otherworldly malevolence. The Veilstitcher's spectral form guided them through trials that tested their resolve against the impending cosmic reckoning.

The celestial map, now revealing constellations that depicted the enslaved cosmic entities, guided the friends through the cosmic trials. The amulet, emitting a protective aura, shimmered with a resilient light that mirrored their commitment to resist the cosmic tempest's onslaught.

As they navigated through the cosmic chaos, the friends uncovered an ancient cosmic prison—an ethereal cage that held the Stormweaver's spectral essence. Eldritch symbols adorned the prison, resonating with the echoes of ancient grievances that fueled the cosmic reckoning. The celestial map, now etched with constellations that depicted the prison's significance, guided them towards understanding the key to subduing the Stormweaver's fury.

The Veilstitcher's spectral form, now a cosmic keybearer, communicated a ritual to unlock the prison and confront the Stormweaver. The amulet, resonating with the cosmic revelations, emitted a luminescent glow that mirrored the friends' determination to face the ancient cosmic entity. As they channeled their cosmic abilities into the ritual, the cosmic prison responded with an ethereal symphony.

Shadows, once animated by cosmic fury, now seemed to waver in a discordant ballet. The celestial map, now pulsating with threads of cosmic understanding, guided the friends through the intricate maneuvers needed to unlock the ancient prison. The Veilstitcher's influence, now a cosmic guide, urged them to unravel the Stormweaver's malevolent influence and restore balance to the interconnected tapestry.

In the cosmic aftermath of the ritual, the ancient prison released the Stormweaver's spectral essence. The friends, now confronted by the embodiment of cosmic fury, felt the weight of the impending reckoning bearing down upon them. The Veilstitcher's spectral form, now a cosmic defender, communicated a sense of urgency as the friends prepared to face the Stormweaver's wrath.

The celestial map, now depicting constellations that mirrored the Stormweaver's cosmic fury, guided the friends through a cosmic trial that tested their resilience against the impending reckoning. The amulet, their only defense against the cosmic tempest, emitted a protective aura that shimmered with a determination to resist the ancient entity's onslaught.

In their cosmic struggle against the Stormweaver's spectral essence, the friends uncovered the origins of the ancient grievances that had fueled the cosmic reckoning. Betrayals, vendettas, and cosmic vendettas had intertwined in a malevolent dance that threatened to consume the interconnected tapestry. The Veilstitcher's spectral form, a witness to the unfolding cosmic drama, conveyed a sense of urgency as the friends unraveled the ancient cosmic entity's malevolent influence.

The amulet, attuned to the cosmic revelations, emitted pulses of resonant light that harmonized with the celestial map's guidance. As the friends faced the Stormweaver's spectral essence, the cosmic tempest seemed to shift in response to their cosmic understanding. Shadows, once animated by cosmic fury, now flickered with moments of cosmic discord.

In a pivotal moment of the cosmic struggle, the friends realized that the only way to quell the Stormweaver's wrath was to break the chains of ancient grievances. The Veilstitcher's spectral form, now a cosmic arbitrator, guided them through a celestial ritual that sought to sever the cosmic cycles of vengeance and restore the ancient entity's fractured consciousness.

As they channeled their cosmic abilities into the ritual, the cosmic tempest responded with an ethereal symphony. Shadows, once animated by cosmic fury, now seemed to waver in a harmonious ballet. The celestial map, now pulsating with threads of cosmic

understanding, guided the friends through the intricate maneuvers needed to mend the Stormweaver's spectral essence.

In the cosmic aftermath of the ritual, the Stormweaver's spectral essence transformed. Fury gave way to a serene luminescence, and the cosmic tempest seemed to retreat. The Veilstitcher's influence, now a cosmic mediator, conveyed a sense of resolution as the friends witnessed the ancient entity find peace within the interconnected tapestry.

The amulet, though worn by the cosmic struggle, emitted a radiant glow that mirrored the friends' triumph over the impending reckoning. The celestial map, now cleared of constellations depicting discord, revealed a new cosmic equilibrium that reflected the friends' ability to confront the ancient cosmic entity and emerge unscathed.

As the friends ascended from the cosmic battleground, the Veilstitcher's spectral form regained its ethereal brilliance. The amulet, though scarred by the cosmic ordeal, pulsed with a renewed vitality. The celestial map, now cleared of the cosmic turmoil, guided them towards new frontiers in the interconnected tapestry.

The friends, forever changed by their harrowing encounter with the cosmic reckoning, continued their cosmic odyssey with a heightened awareness of the cosmic perils that lurked in the vast expanse. The Veilstitcher's influence, now a cosmic mediator, accompanied them as a guiding force. The amulet, a resilient artifact that bore the scars of their cosmic ordeal, resonated with a luminous brilliance that symbolized their triumph over the impending reckoning.

The celestial map, once tainted by the cosmic turmoil, now guided the friends toward realms where cosmic wonders awaited discovery. The echoes of the unknown, though still haunting, whispered tales of cosmic resilience and the indomitable spirit that defied the cosmic tempest. The friends, forever entwined by the shared

horrors they had faced, embraced the mysteries that awaited them in the uncharted territories of the interconnected tapestry.

Their cosmic odyssey, now marked by the triumphant resolution of the cosmic reckoning, unfolded like a cosmic epic—an eternal saga that transcended mortal fears and celebrated the enduring bond between mortal souls and the cosmic forces that shaped their destinies.

As they journeyed into the unexplored cosmic realms, the friends encountered celestial wonders that seemed to radiate with the echoes of their victorious struggle. The Veilstitcher's influence, now a beacon of cosmic resolution, guided them through realms where echoes of their cosmic deeds resonated with celestial echoes. The amulet, a cosmic artifact infused with the power of triumphant threads, pulsed with a rhythmic glow that echoed the harmony they had restored.

The celestial map, now revealing constellations that depicted the friends as cosmic defenders, guided them toward realms where their presence was needed. Shadows, once animated by cosmic fury, now seemed to retreat in the wake of their cosmic triumph. The friends, now guardians of celestial balance, embraced their role in preserving the interconnected tapestry.

In their cosmic journey, the friends encountered celestial beings whose threads of reality had been freed from the shackles of ancient grievances. The Veilstitcher's spectral form, now a cosmic liberator, urged them to extend their cosmic influence to those freed from the burden of cosmic turmoil. The amulet, resonating with the threads of triumphant reality, emitted a radiant glow that mirrored their commitment to safeguarding the celestial realms.

As they traversed through realms touched by cosmic liberation, the friends faced cosmic trials that tested their newfound abilities as defenders of the interconnected tapestry. The Veilstitcher's

influence, now a cosmic mentor, guided them through rituals that sought to fortify the threads of reality and preserve balance in celestial entities freed from ancient shackles.

The amulet, a conduit of cosmic energies, emitted pulses of protective light that harmonized with the celestial map's guidance. Shadows, once animated by cosmic turmoil, now seemed to dissipate as the friends embraced their cosmic roles as defenders. The echoes of their cosmic deeds reverberated through the interconnected tapestry, leaving a trail of celestial balance in their wake.

In a celestial sanctuary, the friends encountered a cosmic entity—a guardian of the celestial realms whose threads of reality had been freed from ancient shackles. The Veilstitcher's spectral form, now a cosmic liberator, communicated with the entity in a language of cosmic understanding. The amulet, resonating with the threads of triumphant reality, emitted a soothing aura that celebrated the entity's cosmic liberation.

As the friends reveled in the cosmic liberation, the celestial sanctuary responded with ethereal energies. The Veilstitcher's influence, now a cosmic conductor of harmony, guided them through the intricate maneuvers needed to celebrate the celestial guardian's newfound freedom. The amulet, attuned to the cosmic revelations, emitted pulses of resonant light that harmonized with the celestial map's guidance.

In the cosmic aftermath of the celebration, the celestial guardian's spectral form radiated with joy. Threads once bound by ancient grievances now shimmered with a serene luminescence. The Veilstitcher's influence, now a cosmic celebrant, conveyed a sense of fulfillment as the friends witnessed the guardian revel in newfound peace within the celestial sanctuary.

The amulet, though worn by the cosmic struggle, emitted a radiant glow that mirrored the friends' triumph as cosmic liberators.

The celestial map, now cleared of constellations depicting ancient shackles, revealed a new cosmic equilibrium that reflected the friends' ability to free celestial entities from the burden of cosmic turmoil.

As the friends continued their cosmic journey, the Veilstitcher's spectral form, now a cosmic celebrant, guided them toward realms where celestial entities awaited their liberating touch. The amulet, a beacon of cosmic liberation, pulsed with a rhythmic glow that echoed the joy they had spread. The celestial map, now revealing constellations that depicted the friends as cosmic liberators, guided them toward realms where their presence was needed.

Their cosmic odyssey, now marked by the celebration of cosmic liberation and triumphant resolution, unfolded like a cosmic epic—an eternal saga that transcended mortal fears and celebrated the enduring bond between mortal souls and the cosmic forces that shaped their destinies.

3 |

Stormweaver
The Goatman Lives
By
Doug Hensley
Table Of Contents

Chapter 1: The Unknown Encounter

- A group of friends on a camping trip
- Mysterious noises in the woods at night

Chapter 2: Whispering Shadows

- Strange occurrences escalate
- Unsettling whispers heard in the darkness

Chapter 3: The Legend Unveiled

- Local tales of the Goatman shared around the campfire
- Skepticism and unease among the group

Chapter 4: A Fateful Decision

- The group decides to investigate the legend

- Deep into the forest, the atmosphere thickens

Chapter 5: Signs of the Goatman

- Disturbing symbols and tracks discovered
- Tension grows as reality sets in

Chapter 6: Disappearing Act

- One member of the group goes missing
- Panic and fear grip the others

Chapter 7: Unholy Alliance

- Remaining friends unite to find the missing person
- A pact to face the Goatman together

Chapter 8: Haunting Memories

- Flashbacks reveal past encounters with the Goatman
- Characters confront their own fears

Chapter 9: Night of the Full Moon

- The group faces the Goatman for the first time
- A terrifying chase through the woods ensues

Chapter 10: The Goatman's Curse

- Survivor guilt and paranoia set in
- The Goatman's curse becomes evident

Chapter 11: The Unseen Stalker

- Unexplained phenomena haunt the group
- A feeling of being constantly watched

Chapter 12: The Goatman's Lair

- Discover a hidden lair deep in the woods
- A horrifying revelation awaits

Chapter 13: Descent into Madness

- Characters grapple with their sanity
- Unexplainable events intensify

Chapter 14: The Goatman's Call

- A hypnotic call draws the group deeper
- Internal conflicts escalate

Chapter 15: Sacrificial Night

- The group faces a choice to save themselves or succumb to the Goatman's curse
- Tension peaks as the night unfolds

Chapter 16: Midnight Ritual

- Ritualistic elements unfold
- The Goatman's power grows stronger

Chapter 17: The Final Confrontation

- Confrontation with the Goatman in a climactic battle
- Sacrifices made to break the curse

Chapter 18: Lingering Shadows

- The aftermath of the confrontation
- The group struggles to return to normalcy

Chapter 19: Epilogue of Fear

- Lingering fears and unanswered questions
- Hints that the Goatman may still be out there

Chapter 20: The Legend Lives On

- Closing with a new group stumbling upon the same legend
- The cycle continues, leaving the ending open-ended and unsettling

Chapter 1: The Unknown Encounter

The dense forest canopy loomed overhead, casting eerie shadows as the group of friends, led by the adventurous spirit of Mark, ventured deeper into the wilderness. A cool breeze rustled the leaves, creating an ominous symphony that echoed through the trees. Their laughter filled the air, a stark contrast to the quiet unease that settled with the setting sun.

As darkness embraced the forest, the friends gathered around a crackling campfire. The flickering flames danced to the rhythm of their hushed conversations. An unsettling feeling hung in the air,

unnoticed by most, except for Emily, who couldn't shake off the sensation that they were not alone.

Unknown to the group, distant whispers intertwined with the nocturnal symphony, carried by the wind. Mark, the leader of the expedition, dismissed them as the rustling of leaves or the murmur of the night creatures. Little did they know that these whispers were the first ominous notes of a malevolent tune.

As the night wore on, the friends shared stories, trying to drown out the disconcerting sounds around them. In the midst of laughter, a sudden silence fell upon the group, broken only by the distant howl of a lone wolf. They exchanged uneasy glances, their camaraderie momentarily fractured.

The crackling fire cast eerie shadows on the surrounding trees, creating grotesque shapes that seemed to watch the friends with malevolent intent. An inexplicable tension wrapped itself around them, tightening like a coil. Emily's gaze flickered nervously between the dancing flames and the dark recesses of the forest.

The once vibrant atmosphere now carried an undertone of dread. Mark, attempting to dispel the growing unease, suggested exploring the nearby trails. Reluctantly, the group ventured into the heart of the woods, guided only by dim flashlights that struggled to penetrate the thick darkness.

As they meandered through the labyrinthine paths, the night seemed to swallow them whole. The moon cast an eerie glow, revealing twisted branches that resembled skeletal fingers reaching out from the shadows. Unbeknownst to the friends, unseen eyes observed their every move.

The distant echoes of footsteps, not matching the rhythm of their own, reverberated through the night. A cold shiver ran down Emily's spine as she whispered to Mark, "Did you hear that?" He

dismissed it as their imagination playing tricks, but doubt lingered in his eyes.

The trail, once familiar, now felt like an ever-twisting maze. Panic set in as the friends realized they were lost. The forest seemed to conspire against them, distorting their perception of time and space. Anxiety gripped the group, amplifying the unsettling aura that clung to the night.

A blood-curdling scream shattered the silence, sending shock-waves through the group. Fear etched deep lines on their faces as they turned toward the source. In the suffocating darkness, a silhouette moved swiftly, disappearing among the gnarled trees.

Panic took hold, and the friends sprinted back towards the campsite, fueled by a primal instinct to survive. The once-familiar surroundings now felt alien and menacing. The forest, alive with unseen malevolence, seemed to mock their feeble attempts to escape.

The crackling campfire welcomed them back, but the safety it once provided now felt like a fragile illusion. The missing member, a specter in their midst, cast a long shadow over the group. The night, far from over, held secrets that would unravel as the friends clung to the flickering flames, unaware of the terror that awaited them in the heart of the haunted woods.

Chapter 2: Whispering Shadows

The remnants of their once-jovial campfire flickered in the oppressive darkness. Unsettled by the earlier scream, the friends huddled close, their faces etched with fear. Mark, the bravest among them, attempted to lighten the mood with nervous jokes, but the unease lingered like a thick fog.

As they sat in the ominous stillness, the haunting whispers returned. The friends exchanged anxious glances, realizing the sounds were more than mere forest murmurs. The words, though

unintelligible, seemed to crawl beneath their skin, instilling a primal fear that transcended rationality.

Emily, the most sensitive to the otherworldly, clutched her ears, desperate to block out the spectral voices. The whispers intertwined with the wind, creating an otherworldly melody that resonated through the haunted woods. Shadows danced menacingly, morphing into grotesque forms that seemed to mimic the torment in the friends' hearts.

Mark, determined to maintain a semblance of control, suggested investigating the source of the whispers. Armed with flashlights, the group ventured into the inky darkness, guided by the haunting voices that seemed to lead them deeper into the heart of the haunted woods.

The forest, now transformed into a realm of spectral uncertainty, played tricks on their senses. Trees twisted into nightmarish shapes, their branches reaching out like skeletal fingers. Each step felt like a descent into an abyss, and the whispers grew louder, forming an otherworldly chorus that resonated through the friends' minds.

A surreal fog enveloped the path, distorting reality. Shadows detached from the trees, taking on a sinister life of their own. Unseen eyes followed the group's every move, and the air became dense with an otherworldly energy that made it difficult to breathe.

Amidst the disorienting whispers, a distant figure materialized before them. The friends froze, their flashlights trembling in their hands. The silhouette seemed to flicker between the shadows, an elusive presence that defied comprehension. Panic gripped the group as the figure approached with an otherworldly grace.

With each step, the whispers intensified, revealing fragments of a haunting narrative. The legend of the Goatman, an entity that blurred the line between man and beast, echoed through the spectral voices. Dread tightened its grip on the friends as they realized

they were entangled in a story that surpassed the boundaries of the known.

A sudden gust of wind extinguished their flashlights, plunging them into pitch darkness. The whispers crescendoed into an unsettling cacophony, weaving a narrative that spoke of ancient curses and forbidden rituals. The friends stumbled blindly, guided only by the haunting voices that seemed to mock their feeble attempts to escape the encroaching nightmare.

As they fumbled through the labyrinthine paths, the forest itself seemed to conspire against them. Trees leaned menacingly, forming an impenetrable barrier that distorted their perception of space. Panic reached its zenith when the friends realized they were caught in a malevolent force beyond their understanding.

In the heart of the haunted woods, the whispers reached a deafening climax. The spectral figure, now a manifestation of pure terror, revealed itself as the harbinger of an ancient curse. The friends, paralyzed by fear, witnessed the birth of a nightmare that transcended the realm of the living.

The haunting voices echoed a chilling prophecy, sealing the friends' fate as pawns in a cosmic game. As the shadows enveloped them, the whispers faded into an ominous silence, leaving the group suspended in the chilling realization that they were now entwined with the legendary Goatman, and their journey into terror had only just begun.

Chapter 3: The Legend Unveiled

The haunted woods bore witness to the friends' descent into an abyss of fear, their breaths visible in the chilling air as they stood at the precipice of the unknown. Mark, the once-confident leader, now felt the weight of uncertainty press upon him, his eyes flickering nervously between the faces of his friends.

The chilling echoes of the Goatman's curse lingered, a sinister resonance that seeped into their very souls. As the group gathered around the remnants of their campfire, a shadowy figure materialized within the shifting shadows, a grotesque manifestation of the legend they had dismissed as mere folklore.

An air of disbelief hung heavy as the friends exchanged uneasy glances. Emily's wide eyes mirrored the terror reflected in the faces of the others. The whispers, now reduced to a haunting murmur, seemed to emanate from the very core of the forest, weaving a tapestry of dread that ensnared the group in an inescapable nightmare.

Against the backdrop of encroaching darkness, Mark attempted to rationalize the situation, attributing the spectral figure to mere illusions. However, the disconcerting reality betrayed his attempts at reassurance. The forest, alive with an otherworldly energy, pulsated with the ancient heartbeat of a malevolent force.

Doubt gnawed at the edges of the friends' minds as the whispers intensified. The spectral figure, now a tangible presence, beckoned them into the heart of the woods. The group, caught in the gravitational pull of an insidious force, hesitated on the brink of a decision that would seal their fate.

Reluctantly, they followed the elusive silhouette, their path illuminated by the pale glow of the moon. The forest, now a labyrinth of twisted shadows, seemed to breathe in tandem with the ethereal whispers that guided their journey. Unseen eyes observed their every move as they delved deeper into the legend that had come to life.

The friends stumbled upon an ancient clearing, adorned with eerie symbols etched into the earth. Mark, ever the skeptic, dismissed them as mere remnants of forgotten rituals. However, the others felt an otherworldly pull, an invisible thread connecting them to a malevolent past.

As the group examined the haunting symbols, the whispers coalesced into a narrative, recounting the tale of the Goatman—a creature that straddled the boundary between man and beast, a cursed entity bound by ancient rites. The friends, ensnared in the unfolding nightmare, now faced a reality that surpassed the confines of reason.

The spectral figure, a conduit of the Goatman's curse, revealed itself as a harbinger of impending doom. The friends, caught in the snare of a supernatural force, realized the legend was no mere folktale but a living nightmare that demanded their acknowledgment.

The moon cast an otherworldly glow upon the clearing as the group, paralyzed by a mixture of awe and terror, bore witness to the manifestation of the Goatman. A creature of nightmares stood before them, its eyes gleaming with an otherworldly intelligence that transcended the animalistic form it wore.

The atmosphere thickened with a palpable malevolence as the Goatman's presence dominated the clearing. Its form seemed to shift and contort, a grotesque dance that defied the laws of nature. The friends, gripped by an ancient fear, trembled as the Goatman spoke through the whispers, weaving a fate that intertwined with their very essence.

The friends, now bound by an unbreakable covenant, stood on the precipice of an unholy alliance. The Goatman, an embodiment of primordial terror, extended a spectral hand, inviting the group to embrace the curse that lurked within the shadows. Their destinies, forever altered, collided with the inexorable force of the legend, and the haunted woods echoed with the ominous laughter of a malevolent entity that reveled in the unfolding nightmare.

Chapter 4: A Fateful Decision

The haunted clearing pulsated with an otherworldly energy as the friends faced the enigmatic presence of the Goatman. The air

grew dense with the weight of an ancient curse, and the friends, caught between reason and the supernatural, found themselves at a crossroads that would define their destiny.

Mark, ever the voice of skepticism, hesitated. His logical mind resisted the pull of the unknown, urging him to reject the spectral hand that extended toward them. But the allure of the Goatman's power, shrouded in the whispers that echoed through the clearing, whispered promises of understanding and dominion over the mysterious forces that governed their existence.

Emily, sensitive to the ethereal currents, felt an irresistible draw. The whispers, now a seductive lullaby, caressed her consciousness, weaving visions of forbidden knowledge and a connection to realms beyond mortal comprehension. The choice lay before them, a perilous gambit that promised either enlightenment or descent into the abyss.

As the group teetered on the precipice of decision, the forest itself seemed to hold its breath. Unseen eyes observed their every move, and the shadows twisted in anticipation. The Goatman, a creature of the ancient woods, watched with an intelligence that transcended the animalistic facade it presented.

A cold wind whispered through the gnarled branches, carrying echoes of the past and the future. The choice, suspended in the eerie silence, would echo through the corridors of time, leaving an indelible mark on the souls of the friends who dared to confront the unknown.

In the midst of this spectral tableau, a memory surfaced in the recesses of Mark's mind—a childhood tale of a friend who disappeared in mysterious circumstances, whispered to be a victim of the Goatman's curse. The realization struck him like a bolt of lightning, igniting a primal fear that pulsed through his veins.

The haunting whispers morphed into chilling laughter, echoing Mark's internal turmoil. The Goatman, sensing the doubt, pressed its advantage, its eyes gleaming with an ancient malevolence. The clearing became a battleground of wills, where the tangible and intangible clashed in a dance of shadows.

As the friends deliberated, the forest responded to the rising tension. The ancient trees groaned, their branches contorting into grotesque forms. The whispers, now laced with impatience, intensified, urging the group to make their choice. The boundary between reality and nightmare blurred, and the friends found themselves ensnared in a surreal dreamscape.

Emily, tormented by the visions, trembled as conflicting emotions wrestled within her. The allure of forbidden knowledge clashed with an instinctual fear that warned of the consequences of tampering with forces beyond mortal understanding. The Goatman's eyes bore into her soul, a silent plea that transcended the limitations of spoken language.

Amidst the inner turmoil, a distant sound reverberated through the clearing—a mournful howl that cut through the spectral tension. The friends, momentarily distracted, turned toward the source. Shadows danced on the periphery of the clearing, and an unseen presence circled them like a predatory force.

The Goatman's form flickered, its patience wearing thin. The friends, aware of the imminent choice, felt the weight of the decision settle upon them like a suffocating cloak. The clearing, a stage for the cosmic drama, held its breath as the friends confronted the inevitable.

In a moment of collective resolve, the group stepped back from the outstretched hand of the Goatman. The whispers, now a discordant symphony of disappointment, echoed through the haunted

woods. The spectral figure, once a harbinger of alliance, recoiled into the shadows, its eyes aflame with an ancient ire.

As the friends retreated from the clearing, the forest sighed with relief. The ethereal tension dissipated, and the haunted woods returned to a semblance of stillness. The friends, marked by the encounter, stumbled back into the labyrinth of the forest, haunted by the knowledge that they had narrowly evaded a fate entwined with the Goatman's curse.

Yet, the shadows clung to their every step, and the whispers lingered, a reminder that the legend, far from defeated, awaited its next encounter with unsuspecting souls who dared to tread the boundary between the known and the supernatural. The night, pregnant with uncertainty, unfolded its mysteries as the friends navigated the haunted woods, forever changed by the fateful decision that spared them from the Goatman's insidious embrace.

T

Chapter 5: Signs of the Goatman

The haunted woods, having witnessed the friends' rejection of the Goatman's enticement, stirred with an ancient restlessness. The air crackled with latent energy as the group, still shaken from their encounter, navigated the twisting trails. The forest, once familiar, now seemed to shift and contort, its very essence reacting to the disturbance in the supernatural equilibrium.

Unspoken tension hung between the friends as they threaded through the labyrinth of shadows. The whispers, subdued but undeterred, lingered on the periphery of their consciousness. Emily, especially, felt the ethereal threads tugging at the edges of her sanity, weaving a tapestry of unnerving visions that threatened to unravel the fabric of her understanding.

A subtle rustling in the underbrush echoed through the stillness, sending a shiver down the spines of the friends. The forest seemed to

respond to their every step, alive with an unseen force that observed their every move. Paranoia took root, and the group cast nervous glances over their shoulders, half-expecting the Goatman's grotesque figure to materialize from the shadows.

Mark, burdened by the weight of his past and the consequences of the group's rejection, led the way with a furrowed brow. The once-confident leader now grappled with doubt, haunted by the memory of his childhood friend who had vanished into the clutches of the Goatman's curse. The forest, sensing his internal conflict, seemed to feed on his insecurities, twisting the trees into macabre forms that mirrored the tendrils of fear constricting his heart.

As they pressed forward, the trail revealed unsettling signs— twisted branches forming crude symbols, the earth marked with enigmatic patterns, and distant echoes that mimicked the mournful cries of the spectral creature they had narrowly evaded. The friends, unable to escape the omnipresent gaze of the haunted woods, exchanged wary glances as the realization dawned that the legend of the Goatman was far from a mere tale.

The group stumbled upon a clearing bathed in an eerie moonlit glow, its center dominated by a gnarled tree that bore the unmistakable markings of the supernatural. Emily, drawn by an invisible force, approached the ancient tree, her fingers tracing the symbols etched into its bark. The whispers, now a ghostly murmur, beckoned her to decipher the cryptic language of the Goatman's curse.

As Emily touched the symbols, the forest responded with a sudden surge of energy. The air crackled with an otherworldly charge, and the friends, captivated by a force beyond their control, witnessed the roots of the ancient tree twitch and writhe. The earth itself seemed to pulse with an unholy heartbeat as the symbols glowed with an ethereal light.

A ghostly apparition materialized before them, an echo of the Goatman's presence. Its eyes gleamed with an otherworldly intelligence, and a spectral voice resonated through the clearing. The friends, entranced by the unfolding spectacle, listened as the Goatman's tale unfolded—a story of ancient curses, forbidden pacts, and the insatiable hunger that bound it to the haunted woods.

As the spectral apparition spoke, the friends felt the tendrils of the Goatman's influence worming their way into their minds. Visions of torment and cosmic malevolence unfolded, weaving a narrative that blurred the boundaries between reality and nightmare. Emily, caught in the vortex of the supernatural revelation, glimpsed the unfathomable depths of the Goatman's ancient origins.

The whispers crescendoed, their words weaving an intricate web that ensnared the friends in a surreal dance of fate. The forest, now an extension of the Goatman's domain, pulsed with an ominous energy. The group, teetering on the precipice of enlightenment and damnation, faced the haunting reality that the legend had claimed them as unwilling participants in its insidious narrative.

In the midst of the ethereal revelation, a distant howl echoed through the clearing—a mournful cry that reverberated through the haunted woods. The spectral Goatman, its form flickering like a dying flame, receded into the shadows. The ancient tree, its roots once animated, settled into an eerie stillness.

The friends, released from the trance, stumbled backward, their minds reeling from the forbidden knowledge bestowed upon them. The clearing, now devoid of the Goatman's presence, returned to a deceptive calm. The haunted woods, however, retained the scars of their encounter, the symbols etched into the ancient tree serving as a chilling reminder that they were forever bound to the unfolding nightmare.

As the group retreated from the clearing, the forest whispered its secrets—a haunting lament that echoed through the shadows. The friends, marked by the signs of the Goatman, ventured deeper into the heart of the haunted woods, their destinies entwined with the ancient curse that refused to release its grip. The spectral whispers lingered, a spectral chorus that foretold of the terrors yet to unfold in the labyrinth of nightmares they now called home.

Chapter 6: Disappearing Act

The haunted woods, now saturated with the residual energy of the Goatman's revelation, clung to the friends like a suffocating shroud. The symbols etched into the ancient tree continued to glow with an otherworldly radiance, casting an eerie glow upon the path ahead. The air, thick with the weight of forbidden knowledge, pressed down on the group as they pressed forward, their fate intricately woven into the fabric of the supernatural.

Mark, haunted by the ghostly memories of his childhood friend's disappearance, felt an invisible force tugging at the edges of his consciousness. The whispers, once distant murmurs, now reverberated through his mind with an unsettling clarity. He strained to maintain composure, masking his internal turmoil behind a façade of false bravado. Unbeknownst to him, the haunted woods, sentient and malevolent, fed on his fear like a ravenous entity.

The trail, twisted and labyrinthine, seemed to shift with a will of its own. The friends, ensnared by the spectral threads that bound them to the Goatman's curse, navigated the surreal landscape with trepidation. The shadows played tricks on their senses, morphing into phantasmal shapes that seemed to watch with unseen eyes.

As the group delved deeper into the heart of the haunted woods, a palpable tension threaded through their camaraderie. Emily, marked by the spectral encounter at the ancient tree, felt an inexorable pull toward the unknown. The whispers, now a constant companion,

murmured secrets that transcended the realm of mortal understanding. Her eyes, once bright with curiosity, now reflected the unsettling wisdom bestowed upon her by the Goatman's revelation.

A distant howl echoed through the woods, a mournful cry that reverberated with a haunting resonance. The friends, halted by the spectral sound, exchanged uneasy glances. The Goatman's influence, a malevolent force that defied the natural order, now seemed to guide their every step. The path ahead, obscured by a foreboding mist, beckoned them into the heart of the supernatural enigma.

The trail, fraught with unseen perils, led the friends to a clearing bathed in an ethereal glow. A spectral figure materialized before them, its eyes gleaming with an otherworldly intelligence. The Goatman, a manifestation of cosmic dread, stood as a sentinel at the crossroads of their destiny.

In a voice that echoed through the haunted woods, the Goatman spoke, its words a haunting melody that resonated with the friends' deepest fears. The choices made, the destinies entwined, the group stood as unwitting participants in a cosmic drama that unfolded with a relentless momentum. The Goatman, a puppeteer of fate, reveled in the dance of shadows that played out in the haunted clearing.

As the spectral figure spoke, the surroundings warped into a surreal dreamscape. Reality and nightmare merged, and the friends found themselves suspended in a liminal space where time seemed to lose its meaning. Visions of the Goatman's cursed legacy unfolded—a tapestry of despair woven with threads of ancient malevolence.

Mark, tormented by memories of his lost friend, witnessed haunting scenes from the past. The woods became a theater of spectral apparitions, replaying moments of anguish and despair. The Goatman's voice, a spectral undertone, whispered forgotten secrets that clawed at the edges of his sanity.

Emily, sensitive to the ethereal currents, glimpsed glimpses of the future—a mosaic of tormented landscapes and spectral encounters. The haunted woods, now a maze of interconnected destinies, revealed a nightmarish tableau that unfolded with an inexorable inevitability.

As the visions played out, the friends, paralyzed by the supernatural revelation, became mere spectators in their own existential drama. The Goatman, a harbinger of cosmic terror, reveled in the torment it unleashed upon their minds. The clearing, a stage for the unfolding nightmare, pulsated with an otherworldly energy.

Suddenly, the visions ceased, and the friends, released from the spectral trance, found themselves standing in the clearing once more. The Goatman, its form flickering like a dying ember, faded into the shadows. The ancient tree, now devoid of the supernatural glow, stood as a silent witness to the cosmic theater that unfolded beneath its twisted branches.

The friends, disoriented and haunted by the echoes of the Goatman's revelations, staggered away from the clearing. The haunted woods, now a sentient labyrinth, seemed to rearrange itself, guiding the group deeper into the heart of the supernatural enigma.

As they pressed forward, a cold wind whispered through the twisted branches, carrying with it a chilling echo of the Goatman's laughter. The friends, caught in a cycle of existential dread, stumbled through the haunted woods, forever marked by the disappearing act that unfolded in the surreal clearing. The night, pregnant with cosmic uncertainty, stretched before them like an endless abyss, and the friends, ensnared by the spectral forces that governed their fate, plunged further into the inescapable nightmare that awaited in the shadowed depths of the ancient forest.

Chapter 7: Unholy Alliance

The haunted woods, now a realm of spectral uncertainty, closed in around the friends as they stumbled through the labyrinthine trails. The air was thick with an oppressive tension, and the whispers, once distant murmurs, reverberated through the trees with an unsettling urgency. Mark, Emily, and the rest of the group were mere pawns in a cosmic game, ensnared by the Goatman's curse, and each step they took seemed to propel them deeper into the heart of an insidious nightmare.

The trail, twisted and sinuous, led the friends to the edge of an ancient clearing. Moonlight filtered through the gnarled branches, casting an ethereal glow on the uneven ground. The clearing, marked by a series of grotesque symbols etched into the earth, seemed to pulse with a malevolent energy. Unseen eyes watched from the shadows as the friends hesitated at the threshold of the supernatural stage.

Emily, the once-curious soul now burdened by the weight of forbidden knowledge, felt an invisible force drawing her toward the center of the clearing. The whispers, now an incessant chorus, beckoned her to unravel the mysteries encoded in the symbols. A compulsion, an otherworldly pull, guided her steps as she approached the enigmatic patterns etched into the earth.

Mark, torn between the rational skepticism that had defined him and the growing influence of the Goatman's curse, cast wary glances at the symbols. The haunted woods, responsive to the internal struggles of the friends, seemed to warp and contort with a will of its own. Shadows danced in grotesque patterns, and the clearing became a stage for a supernatural spectacle.

The group, teetering on the brink of an abyss, gathered at the center of the clearing. Emily traced her fingers over the symbols, her touch unlocking a latent energy that pulsed through the earth. The whispers intensified, their spectral voices weaving a narrative

that echoed through the haunted woods—a tale of ancient alliances, cosmic conspiracies, and the inexorable dance between the living and the supernatural.

As Emily deciphered the symbols, the clearing transformed into a spectral panorama. Visions of the Goatman's cursed legacy unfolded, revealing a tapestry of intertwined destinies that stretched across epochs. The friends, now mere spectators in the cosmic drama, glimpsed fragments of the entity's tormented existence.

The Goatman, a creature bound by an unholy alliance with forces beyond mortal understanding, emerged as a tragic figure—a victim of a cosmic imbalance that demanded appeasement through unspeakable rituals and sacrifices. Its eyes, once gleaming with malevolence, now reflected a profound sadness that transcended the bestial form it wore.

The friends, ensnared in the unfolding revelation, witnessed scenes from the Goatman's past—a time when the ancient woods echoed with primal magic, and forbidden pacts were forged beneath the watchful gaze of eldritch entities. The haunted woods, a nexus of supernatural energies, became a stage for an age-old conflict that transcended the boundaries of time.

Mark, grappling with the conflicting forces that tore at his sanity, saw glimpses of the Goatman's interactions with lost souls—a spectral procession of individuals who had been entangled in the cosmic machinations of the ancient curse. The forest, a witness to centuries of suffering, whispered tales of tormented souls and unspeakable horrors that lurked in the shadowed depths.

The friends, released from the spectral visions, found themselves standing in the clearing once more. The symbols, now infused with a latent energy, pulsed with an otherworldly radiance. The Goatman, its form flickering between the grotesque and the tragic,

remained at the periphery of their perception, a spectral guardian of the haunted woods.

As the friends retreated from the clearing, a mournful howl echoed through the trees—a sound that transcended the natural world. The spectral alliance between the friends and the Goatman, forged by the revelation in the clearing, had sealed their destinies in an unholy covenant. The whispers, now a constant companion, guided them deeper into the labyrinth of the supernatural, their fates entwined with the spectral forces that governed the haunted woods.

The group, marked by the spectral encounter, pressed forward with a newfound awareness. The haunted woods, now an extension of the Goatman's domain, seemed to anticipate their every move. Shadows clung to the friends like a malevolent fog, and the air pulsed with an otherworldly energy that heightened the senses to the unseen threats that lurked in the shadows.

As they traversed the twisted trails, the group became acutely aware of an invisible tether connecting them to the Goatman's curse. The forest, alive with spectral currents, responded to their presence with a symphony of ethereal whispers. The alliance, forged in the clearing, propelled them toward a convergence of cosmic forces that awaited in the heart of the supernatural enigma.

The night, pregnant with uncertainty, stretched before the friends like an endless abyss. The haunted woods, a realm of shifting shadows and spectral whispers, beckoned them into the heart of the supernatural enigma. The Goatman, now an unseen puppeteer of their destinies, watched with an otherworldly intelligence as the group delved deeper into the spectral dance that awaited them in the shadowed depths.

Chapter 8: The Dance of Shadows

The haunted woods, now an extension of the Goatman's dominion, closed in around the friends as they ventured deeper into the labyrinth of shadows. The spectral alliance forged in the clearing bound them to the ancient curse, and with each step, the ethereal whispers seemed to guide their path. Mark, Emily, and the rest of the group were caught in a cosmic dance, their destinies entwined with the malevolent forces that governed the supernatural enigma.

The twisted trails led the friends to a secluded grove bathed in an otherworldly glow. Moonlight filtered through the gnarled branches, casting an ethereal pallor on the ground. The air crackled with latent energy, and the shadows played tricks on their senses. Unseen eyes observed their every move as the group hesitated at the edge of the spectral grove.

Emily, the unwitting conduit of forbidden knowledge, felt an invisible force pulling her toward the center of the grove. The whispers, now a spectral symphony, urged her to unravel the mysteries concealed within the ancient symbols etched into the earth. A compulsion, an otherworldly call, guided her steps as she approached the enigmatic patterns that pulsed with latent power.

Mark, torn between the skepticism that defined him and the growing influence of the Goatman's curse, cast wary glances at the symbols. The haunted woods, responsive to the internal struggles of the friends, seemed to warp and contort with a will of its own. Shadows danced in grotesque patterns, and the grove became a stage for a supernatural spectacle.

The rest of the group, caught in the gravitational pull of the Goatman's influence, gathered around Emily. The clearing, a nexus of spectral energies, hummed with an ominous resonance. Unseen forces coalesced, and the grove transformed into a gateway to the unknown.

As Emily traced her fingers over the symbols, the grove became a canvas for ethereal visions. The ancient curse, woven into the fabric of the haunted woods, unfolded before the friends like a nightmarish tapestry. The Goatman, a tragic figure shackled by an unholy alliance, emerged from the shadows, its form flickering with a spectral radiance.

The friends, ensnared in the unfolding revelation, witnessed scenes from the Goatman's existence—a journey through epochs marked by cosmic pacts, eldritch rituals, and the insatiable hunger that bound the entity to the supernatural realm. The grove, now a theater of spectral memories, echoed with the haunting cries of lost souls and the tormented echoes of ancient rites.

Mark, tormented by the conflicting forces that tore at his sanity, saw glimpses of the Goatman's interactions with souls who had been entangled in the cosmic machinations of the ancient curse. The forest, a silent witness to centuries of suffering, whispered tales of tormented spirits and unspeakable horrors that lurked in the shadowed depths.

Emily, sensitive to the ethereal currents, glimpsed fragments of the future—an ominous tableau that unfolded with an inexorable inevitability. The haunted woods, now a mosaic of interconnected destinies, revealed a nightmarish dance between the living and the spectral.

As the visions played out, the friends, released from the spectral trance, found themselves standing in the grove once more. The symbols, now infused with a latent energy, pulsed with an otherworldly radiance. The Goatman, its form flickering between the grotesque and the tragic, remained at the periphery of their perception, a spectral guardian of the haunted woods.

The friends, marked by the spectral encounter, retreated from the grove. The symbols, now charged with a malevolent force,

lingered in their consciousness like a haunting echo. The haunted woods, sentient and malevolent, responded to their presence with an unsettling intensity.

As the group pressed forward, the forest itself seemed to conspire against them. The twisted trails became a labyrinth, shifting with a will of their own. The spectral currents guided the friends deeper into the heart of the supernatural enigma, and the whispers, now an incessant chorus, reverberated through the haunted woods.

A sudden gust of wind whispered through the gnarled branches, carrying with it the mournful howl of the Goatman. The spectral alliance, forged in the grove, propelled the friends toward a convergence of cosmic forces that awaited in the shadowed depths. The night, fraught with unseen perils, stretched before them like an endless abyss, and the friends, ensnared by the spectral forces that governed their fate, plunged further into the inescapable dance of shadows that awaited in the ancient forest.

The twisted trails, illuminated by an otherworldly glow, led the group to the heart of the haunted woods. The whispers, now a cacophony of spectral voices, guided their every step, and the air pulsated with an ethereal energy that heightened the senses to the unseen threats that lurked in the shadows.

As the friends delved deeper, the forest itself seemed to morph into a surreal dreamscape. Trees contorted into nightmarish shapes, and the ground undulated like the surface of an otherworldly sea. Unseen eyes watched from the darkness, and the haunted woods, now a living entity, responded to their presence with a symphony of spectral echoes.

The group, now caught in a cosmic ballet, reached a clearing bathed in an otherworldly radiance. Symbols etched into the earth pulsed with an ancient power, and the whispers intensified, their spectral voices reaching a deafening crescendo. In the center of the

clearing stood a spectral figure—a manifestation of the Goatman's curse, its eyes gleaming with an otherworldly intelligence.

The friends, paralyzed by the unfolding spectacle, felt the air thicken with a malevolent force. The Goatman, now a puppeteer of their destinies, extended a spectral hand, inviting the group to join the cosmic dance. Mark, Emily, and the rest stood at the precipice of a choice that would seal their fate—a decision that transcended mortal understanding.

As the spectral figure beckoned, the haunted woods echoed with the haunting laughter of the Goatman. The friends, ensnared in the dance of shadows, stood at the nexus of the supernatural enigma, their destinies entwined with the ancient curse that governed the heart of the forest.

The night, fraught with cosmic uncertainty, stretched before the friends like an infinite canvas. The spectral grove, now a gateway to the unknown, beckoned them into the inescapable dance that awaited in the shadowed depths. The friends, marked by the ethereal revelations and the spectral alliance, plunged further into the heart of the haunted woods, where the Goatman's malevolent influence

Chapter 9: Pact with Shadows

The friends, standing on the precipice of the spectral clearing, felt the oppressive weight of the Goatman's influence bearing down upon them. The ethereal radiance cast an eerie glow on the symbols that pulsed with an otherworldly energy. The whispers, now an unrelenting cacophony, echoed through the haunted woods, urging the group to surrender to the cosmic dance that awaited.

Mark, the once-skeptical leader, hesitated, his eyes darting between the spectral figure and his companions. The forest, now a sentient entity, seemed to respond to his internal struggle, twisting the trees into grotesque forms that mirrored the tendrils of doubt

constricting his heart. Emily, sensitive to the ethereal currents, trembled as conflicting emotions wrestled within her.

The Goatman's eyes, gleaming with an ancient intelligence, bore into the souls of the friends. The haunted clearing became a battleground of wills, where the tangible and intangible clashed in a dance of shadows. Unseen forces whispered promises of enlightenment and power, luring the friends toward an unholy pact that defied the natural order.

In the face of the spectral invitation, the group felt a collective unease. The air crackled with tension, and the haunted woods, alive with spectral currents, seemed to conspire against them. The choice, a perilous gambit that promised either dominion over the supernatural or descent into eternal torment, hung in the balance.

As the friends deliberated, the grove transformed into a surreal dreamscape. Reality and nightmare merged, and the spectral figure at the center of the clearing became an ever-shifting enigma. The whispers, now a dissonant symphony, intensified, urging the group to embrace the Goatman's curse and become conduits for the malevolent forces that pulsed through the heart of the forest.

Emily, tormented by the conflicting forces that tugged at her soul, felt an irresistible pull toward the outstretched hand of the Goatman. The symbols etched into the earth seemed to respond to her internal turmoil, glowing with an intensity that mirrored the tumult within her consciousness. The friends, caught in the gravitational pull of an insidious force, stood at the crossroads of their destinies.

In a moment of collective resolve, the group stepped back from the spectral figure. The Goatman's eyes, once filled with a gleaming anticipation, narrowed with disappointment. The whispers, now a discordant lament, echoed through the haunted woods. The spectral figure, a harbinger of alliance, receded into the shadows, leaving

the friends standing in the clearing, marked by the weight of their choice.

The haunted woods, now a tapestry of shifting shadows and spectral echoes, responded to the rejection with a sinister sigh. The grove, once a gateway to the unknown, settled into an eerie stillness. The friends, released from the immediate threat, felt a mixture of relief and lingering dread.

As the group retreated from the clearing, the symbols etched into the earth seemed to pulse with a fading energy. The whispers, now reduced to a haunting murmur, lingered on the fringes of their consciousness. The haunted woods, while momentarily subdued, retained the scars of the friends' encounter, and the night unfolded with an ominous uncertainty.

The group, bound by the spectral alliance but defiant in the face of the Goatman's influence, ventured deeper into the labyrinth of shadows. The twisted trails, now a maze of spectral illusions, seemed to shift with a malevolent intent. The friends, caught in the ebb and flow of the supernatural currents, pressed forward with a cautious determination.

As they navigated the haunted woods, the spectral echoes intensified. Unseen eyes watched from the shadows, and the air became charged with an otherworldly energy. The friends, marked by the spectral encounter, felt the weight of the ancient curse lingering like a palpable presence. The night, pregnant with the unknown, whispered secrets that reverberated through the twisted branches.

Suddenly, a mournful howl echoed through the trees—a sound that transcended the natural world. The spectral alliance, though rejected in the clearing, continued to bind the friends to the Goatman's curse. The haunted woods, now a sentient entity, responded to their presence with an unsettling intensity.

The friends stumbled upon an ancient altar, hidden within the depths of the forest. The symbols engraved upon it mirrored those in the clearing, and the air pulsed with an otherworldly resonance. The whispers, now a siren's call, beckoned them to approach the altar, promising a communion with the supernatural forces that governed the haunted woods.

Mark, haunted by the memories of his lost friend and the consequences of the group's rejection, grappled with the inexorable pull toward the altar. The friends, caught between the desire for understanding and the fear of the unknown, hesitated at the threshold of the spectral enclave.

As they approached, the symbols on the altar glowed with an intensity that mirrored the ethereal currents within the haunted woods. The whispers, now a seductive melody, caressed their minds, weaving visions of power and transcendence. The Goatman's presence, though momentarily distant, lingered like a shadow cast upon the spectral canvas.

A choice loomed before the friends—a choice that would either cement their unholy alliance with the Goatman or cast them further into the abyss of the unknown. The haunted woods, alive with a malevolent energy, awaited the outcome of the cosmic dance that unfolded beneath its twisted canopy.

In a moment of collective hesitation, the friends stood at the edge of the altar, the symbols pulsating with an otherworldly radiance. The whispers, now a haunting serenade, reverberated through the haunted woods, weaving a narrative that transcended mortal understanding. The group, teetering on the brink of enlightenment and damnation, faced the haunting reality that the legend of the Goatman had claimed them as unwilling participants in its insidious narrative.

The night, draped in an ethereal mist, enveloped the friends as they stood at the crossroads of their destinies. The haunted woods, a realm of shifting shadows and spectral echoes, watched with an otherworldly intelligence as the group, bound by an unspoken pact, ventured further into the heart of the supernatural enigma. The night, now a canvas for the dance of shadows, whispered of terrors yet to unfold as the friends pressed forward, their footsteps echoing through the labyrinth of nightmares that awaited in the ancient forest.

Chapter 10: Veil of Shadows

The haunted woods, a labyrinth of shifting shadows and spectral echoes, enveloped the friends as they ventured deeper into the heart of the supernatural enigma. The spectral alliance, though rejected at the clearing, lingered like an unseen shroud, binding the group to the Goatman's curse. The twisted trails, now a maze of spectral illusions, seemed to warp with a malevolent intent, guiding the friends toward an unknown destination.

As the group pressed forward, the spectral echoes intensified. Unseen eyes watched from the shadows, and the air crackled with an otherworldly energy. The haunted woods, sentient and malevolent, responded to their presence with an unsettling intensity. The friends, marked by the spectral encounter, felt the weight of the ancient curse lingering like a palpable presence.

The whispers, once a dissonant symphony, now coalesced into a haunting serenade that reverberated through the twisted branches. Emily, sensitive to the ethereal currents, found herself caught in the ebb and flow of spectral energies. Visions of the Goatman's cursed legacy danced before her eyes—a tapestry of ancient alliances, forbidden pacts, and the insatiable hunger that bound the entity to the supernatural realm.

Mark, tormented by the memories of his lost friend and the consequences of their rejection, grappled with an internal struggle. The twisted trails seemed to twist with a will of their own, mirroring the tumult within his consciousness. The haunted woods, responsive to the friends' internal conflicts, conspired against them with a malevolent glee.

The friends stumbled upon an ancient altar, hidden within the depths of the forest. The symbols engraved upon it mirrored those in the clearing, and the air pulsed with an otherworldly resonance. The whispers, now a seductive melody, caressed their minds, weaving visions of power and transcendence. The Goatman's presence, though momentarily distant, lingered like a shadow cast upon the spectral canvas.

A choice loomed before the friends—a choice that would either cement their unholy alliance with the Goatman or cast them further into the abyss of the unknown. The haunted woods, alive with a malevolent energy, awaited the outcome of the cosmic dance that unfolded beneath its twisted canopy.

In a moment of collective hesitation, the friends stood at the edge of the altar, the symbols pulsating with an otherworldly radiance. The whispers, now a haunting serenade, reverberated through the haunted woods, weaving a narrative that transcended mortal understanding. The group, teetering on the brink of enlightenment and damnation, faced the haunting reality that the legend of the Goatman had claimed them as unwilling participants in its insidious narrative.

The night, draped in an ethereal mist, enveloped the friends as they stood at the crossroads of their destinies. The haunted woods, a realm of shifting shadows and spectral echoes, watched with an otherworldly intelligence as the group, bound by an unspoken pact, ventured further into the heart of the supernatural enigma. The

night, now a canvas for the dance of shadows, whispered of terrors yet to unfold as the friends pressed forward, their footsteps echoing through the labyrinth of nightmares that awaited in the ancient forest.

The twisted trails, illuminated by an otherworldly glow, led the group to the heart of the haunted woods. The whispers, now an incessant chorus, guided their every step, and the air pulsated with an ethereal energy that heightened the senses to the unseen threats that lurked in the shadows.

As the friends delved deeper, the forest itself seemed to morph into a surreal dreamscape. Trees contorted into nightmarish shapes, and the ground undulated like the surface of an otherworldly sea. Unseen eyes watched from the darkness, and the haunted woods, now a living entity, responded to their presence with a symphony of spectral echoes.

The group, now caught in a cosmic ballet, reached a clearing bathed in an otherworldly radiance. Symbols etched into the earth pulsed with an ancient power, and the whispers intensified, their spectral voices reaching a deafening crescendo. In the center of the clearing stood a spectral figure—a manifestation of the Goatman's curse, its eyes gleaming with an otherworldly intelligence.

The friends, paralyzed by the unfolding spectacle, felt the air thicken with a malevolent force. The Goatman, now a puppeteer of their destinies, extended a spectral hand, inviting the group to join the cosmic dance. Mark, Emily, and the rest stood at the precipice of a choice that would seal their fate—a decision that transcended mortal understanding.

As the spectral figure beckoned, the haunted woods echoed with the haunting laughter of the Goatman. The friends, ensnared in the dance of shadows, stood at the nexus of the supernatural enigma,

their destinies entwined with the ancient curse that governed the heart of the forest.

The night, fraught with cosmic uncertainty, stretched before the friends like an infinite canvas. The spectral grove, now a gateway to the unknown, beckoned them into the inescapable dance that awaited in the shadowed depths. The friends, marked by the ethereal revelations and the spectral alliance, plunged further into the heart of the haunted woods, where the Goatman's malevolent influence awaited.

The twisted trails, now a spectral tapestry, led the friends to a clearing bathed in an ethereal glow. Symbols etched into the earth pulsated with an otherworldly radiance, and the whispers, now a ghostly chorus, guided them to the center of the supernatural stage. The spectral figure, a manifestation of the Goatman's curse, awaited with eyes that gleamed with ancient knowledge.

In a moment of collective resolve, the friends stepped forward, surrendering to the cosmic dance that unfolded in the haunted clearing. The symbols, now infused with a latent energy, glowed with an intensity that mirrored the ethereal currents within the haunted woods. The whispers, a symphony of spectral voices, reached a crescendo, weaving a narrative that transcended mortal comprehension.

As the friends embraced the spectral invitation, the clearing transformed into a surreal dreamscape. Reality and nightmare merged, and the friends found themselves suspended in a liminal space where time seemed to lose its meaning. Visions of the Goatman's cursed legacy unfolded—a tapestry of intertwined destinies and cosmic malevolence.

Mark, tormented by the memories of his lost friend, witnessed haunting scenes from the past. The woods became a theater of spectral apparitions, replaying moments of anguish and despair. The

Goatman's voice, a spectral undertone, whispered forgotten secrets that clawed at the edges of his sanity.

Emily, sensitive to the ethereal currents, glimpsed fragments of the future—an ominous tableau that unfolded with an inexorable inevitability. The haunted woods, now a mosaic of interconnected destinies, revealed a nightmarish dance between the living and the spectral.

As the visions played out, the friends, paralyzed by the supernatural revelation, became mere spectators in their own existential drama. The Goatman, a harbinger of cosmic terror, reveled in the torment it unleashed upon their minds. The clearing, a stage for the unfolding nightmare, pulsated with an otherworldly energy.

Suddenly, the visions ceased, and the friends, released from the spectral trance, found themselves standing in the clearing once more. The Goatman, its form flickering like a

dying ember, faded into the shadows. The ancient tree, now devoid of the supernatural glow, stood as a silent witness to the cosmic theater that unfolded beneath its twisted branches.

The friends, disoriented and haunted by the echoes of the Goatman's revelations, stumbled away from the clearing. The haunted woods, now a sentient labyrinth, seemed to rearrange itself, guiding the group deeper into the heart of the supernatural enigma. The air, thick with the residue of spectral energy, clung to them like an intangible shroud.

As they pressed forward, a cold wind whispered through the twisted branches, carrying with it a chilling echo of the Goatman's laughter. The friends, caught in a cycle of existential dread, stumbled through the haunted woods, forever marked by the disappearing act that unfolded in the surreal clearing. The night, pregnant with cosmic uncertainty, stretched before them like an endless abyss.

The spectral alliance, rejected at the altar, continued to bind the friends to the Goatman's curse. The twisted trails, now a spectral tapestry, guided them with an otherworldly intelligence. Shadows clung to the group like a malevolent fog, and the air pulsed with an ethereal energy that heightened their senses to the unseen threats that lurked in the shadows.

As they traversed the haunted woods, the group became acutely aware of an invisible tether connecting them to the Goatman's curse. The forest, alive with spectral currents, responded to their presence with a symphony of ethereal whispers. The alliance, forged in the clearing, propelled them toward a convergence of cosmic forces that awaited in the heart of the supernatural enigma.

The night, fraught with unseen perils, stretched before the friends like an endless abyss. The haunted woods, a realm of shifting shadows and spectral whispers, beckoned them into the heart of the supernatural enigma. The Goatman, now an unseen puppeteer of their destinies, watched with an otherworldly intelligence as the group delved deeper into the spectral dance that awaited them in the shadowed depths.

The twisted trails, illuminated by an otherworldly glow, led the friends to an ancient ruin hidden within the depths of the haunted woods. The spectral echoes intensified, and the air crackled with an otherworldly energy. Unseen eyes watched from the darkness as the group hesitated at the threshold of the supernatural enclave.

Emily, sensitive to the ethereal currents, felt an invisible force drawing her toward the heart of the ruins. The whispers, now an incessant chorus, urged her to unravel the mysteries concealed within the ancient stones. A compulsion, an otherworldly pull, guided her steps as she approached the spectral threshold.

Mark, torn between rational skepticism and the growing influence of the Goatman's curse, cast wary glances at the ancient ruin.

The haunted woods, responsive to the internal struggles of the friends, seemed to warp and contort with a will of its own. Shadows danced in grotesque patterns, and the ruins became a stage for a supernatural spectacle.

The rest of the group, ensnared by the spectral forces that governed their fate, gathered around Emily. The ruins, a nexus of spectral energies, hummed with an ominous resonance. Unseen forces coalesced, and the ancient stones transformed into conduits for the ethereal currents that pulsed through the heart of the forest.

As Emily traced her fingers over the weathered stones, the ruins became a canvas for ethereal visions. The ancient curse, woven into the fabric of the haunted woods, unfolded before the friends like a nightmarish tapestry. The Goatman, a tragic figure shackled by an unholy alliance, emerged from the shadows, its form flickering with a spectral radiance.

The friends, ensnared in the unfolding revelation, witnessed scenes from the Goatman's existence—a journey through epochs marked by cosmic pacts, eldritch rituals, and the insatiable hunger that bound the entity to the supernatural realm. The ruins, now a theater of spectral memories, echoed with the haunting cries of lost souls and the tormented echoes of ancient rites.

Mark, tormented by the conflicting forces that tore at his sanity, saw glimpses of the Goatman's interactions with lost souls—a spectral procession of individuals who had been entangled in the cosmic machinations of the ancient curse. The forest, a silent witness to centuries of suffering, whispered tales of tormented spirits and unspeakable horrors that lurked in the shadowed depths.

Emily, sensitive to the ethereal currents, glimpsed fragments of the future—an ominous tableau that unfolded with an inexorable inevitability. The haunted woods, now a mosaic of interconnected

destinies, revealed a nightmarish dance between the living and the spectral.

As the visions played out, the friends, paralyzed by the supernatural revelation, became mere spectators in their own existential drama. The Goatman, a harbinger of cosmic terror, reveled in the torment it unleashed upon their minds. The ruins, a stage for the unfolding nightmare, pulsated with an otherworldly energy.

Suddenly, the visions ceased, and the friends, released from the spectral trance, found themselves standing in the ruins once more. The Goatman, its form flickering between the grotesque and the tragic, remained at the periphery of their perception, a spectral guardian of the haunted woods.

The friends, disoriented and haunted by the echoes of the Goatman's revelations, stumbled away from the ruins. The haunted woods, now a sentient labyrinth, seemed to rearrange itself, guiding the group deeper into the heart of the supernatural enigma. The air, thick with the residue of spectral energy, clung to them like an intangible shroud.

As they pressed forward, a cold wind whispered through the twisted branches, carrying with it a chilling echo of the Goatman's laughter. The friends, caught in a cycle of existential dread, stumbled through the haunted woods, forever marked by the disappearing act that unfolded in the surreal clearing. The night, pregnant with cosmic uncertainty, stretched before them like an endless abyss.

The spectral alliance, rejected at the ruins, continued to bind the friends to the Goatman's curse. The twisted trails, now a spectral tapestry, guided them with an otherworldly intelligence. Shadows clung to the group like a malevolent fog, and the air pulsed with an ethereal energy that heightened their senses to the unseen threats that lurked in the shadows.

As they traversed the haunted woods, the group became acutely aware of an invisible tether connecting them to the Goatman's curse. The forest, alive with spectral currents, responded to their presence with a symphony of ethereal whispers. The alliance, forged in the ruins, propelled them toward a convergence of cosmic forces that awaited in the heart of the supernatural enigma.

The night, fraught with unseen perils, stretched before the friends like an endless abyss. The haunted woods, a realm of shifting shadows and spectral whispers, beckoned them into the heart of the supernatural enigma. The Goatman, now an unseen puppeteer of their destinies, watched with an otherworldly intelligence as the group delved deeper into the spectral dance that awaited them in the shadowed depths.

The twisted trails, illuminated by an otherworldly glow, led the friends to an ancient grove concealed within the heart of the haunted woods. The spectral echoes intensified, and the air crackled with an otherworldly energy. Unseen eyes watched from the darkness as the group hesitated at the threshold of the supernatural enclave.

Emily, sensitive to the ethereal currents, felt an invisible force pulling her toward the center of the grove. The whispers, now an incessant chorus, urged her to unravel the mysteries concealed within the ancient trees. A compulsion, an otherworldly call, guided her steps as she approached the spectral threshold.

Mark, torn between rational skepticism and the growing influence of the Goatman's curse, cast wary glances at the ancient grove. The haunted woods, responsive to the internal struggles of the friends, seemed to warp and contort with a will of its own. Shadows danced in grotesque patterns, and the grove became a stage for a supernatural spectacle.

The rest of the group, ensnared by the spectral forces that governed their fate, gathered around Emily. The grove, a nexus

of spectral energies, hummed with an ominous resonance. Unseen forces coalesced, and the ancient trees transformed into conduits for the ethereal currents that pulsed through the heart of the forest.

As Emily traced her fingers over the gnarled bark, the grove became a canvas for ethereal visions. The ancient curse, woven into the fabric of the haunted woods, unfolded before the friends like a nightmarish tapestry. The Goatman, a tragic figure shackled by an unholy alliance, emerged from the shadows, its form flickering with a spectral radiance.

The friends, ensnared in the unfolding revelation, witnessed scenes from the Goatman's existence—a journey through epochs marked by cosmic pacts, eldritch rituals, and the insatiable hunger that bound the entity to the supernatural realm. The grove, now a theater of spectral memories, echoed with the haunting cries of lost souls and the tormented echoes of ancient rites.

Mark, tormented by the conflicting forces that tore at his sanity, saw glimpses of the Goatman's interactions with lost souls—a spectral procession of individuals who had been entangled in the cosmic machinations of the ancient curse. The forest, a silent witness to centuries of suffering, whispered tales of tormented spirits and unspeakable horrors that lurked in the shadowed depths.

Emily, sensitive to the ethereal currents, glimpsed fragments of the future—an ominous tableau that unfolded with an inexorable inevitability. The haunted woods, now a mosaic of interconnected destinies, revealed a nightmarish dance between the living and the spectral.

As the visions played out, the friends, paralyzed by the supernatural revelation, became mere spectators in their own existential drama. The Goatman, a harbinger of cosmic terror, reveled in the torment it unleashed upon their minds. The grove, a stage for the unfolding nightmare, pulsated with an otherworldly energy.

Suddenly, the visions ceased, and the friends, released from the spectral trance, found themselves standing in the grove once more. The Goatman, its form flickering between the grotesque and the tragic, remained at the periphery of their perception, a spectral guardian of the haunted woods.

The friends, disoriented and haunted by the echoes of the Goatman's revelations, stumbled away from the grove. The haunted woods, now a sentient labyrinth, seemed to rearrange itself, guiding the group deeper into the heart of the supernatural enigma. The air, thick with the residue of spectral energy, clung to them like an intangible shroud.

As they pressed forward, a cold wind whispered through the twisted branches, carrying with it a chilling echo of the Goatman's laughter. The friends, caught in a cycle of existential dread, stumbled through the haunted woods, forever marked by the disappearing act that unfolded in the surreal clearing. The night, pregnant with cosmic uncertainty, stretched before them like an endless abyss.

The spectral alliance, rejected at the grove, continued to bind the friends to the Goatman's curse. The twisted trails, now a spectral tapestry, guided them with an otherworldly intelligence. Shadows clung to the group like a malevolent fog, and the air pulsed with an ethereal energy that heightened their senses to the unseen threats that lurked in the shadows.

As they traversed the haunted woods, the group became acutely aware of

an invisible tether connecting them to the Goatman's curse. The forest, alive with spectral currents, responded to their presence with a symphony of ethereal whispers. The alliance, forged in the grove, propelled them toward a convergence of cosmic forces that awaited in the heart of the supernatural enigma.

The night, fraught with unseen perils, stretched before the friends like an endless abyss. The haunted woods, a realm of shifting shadows and spectral whispers, beckoned them into the heart of the supernatural enigma. The Goatman, now an unseen puppeteer of their destinies, watched with an otherworldly intelligence as the group delved deeper into the spectral dance that awaited them in the shadowed depths.

The twisted trails, illuminated by an otherworldly glow, led the friends to an ancient burial ground hidden within the heart of the haunted woods. The spectral echoes intensified, and the air crackled with an otherworldly energy. Unseen eyes watched from the darkness as the group hesitated at the threshold of the supernatural enclave.

Emily, sensitive to the ethereal currents, felt an invisible force pulling her toward the center of the burial ground. The whispers, now an incessant chorus, urged her to unravel the mysteries concealed within the ancient gravestones. A compulsion, an otherworldly call, guided her steps as she approached the spectral threshold.

Mark, torn between rational skepticism and the growing influence of the Goatman's curse, cast wary glances at the ancient burial ground. The haunted woods, responsive to the internal struggles of the friends, seemed to warp and contort with a will of its own. Shadows danced in grotesque patterns, and the burial ground became a stage for a supernatural spectacle.

The rest of the group, ensnared by the spectral forces that governed their fate, gathered around Emily. The burial ground, a nexus of spectral energies, hummed with an ominous resonance. Unseen forces coalesced, and the ancient gravestones transformed into conduits for the ethereal currents that pulsed through the heart of the forest.

As Emily traced her fingers over the weathered stones, the burial ground became a canvas for ethereal visions. The ancient curse, woven into the fabric of the haunted woods, unfolded before the friends like a nightmarish tapestry. The Goatman, a tragic figure shackled by an unholy alliance, emerged from the shadows, its form flickering with a spectral radiance.

The friends, ensnared in the unfolding revelation, witnessed scenes from the Goatman's existence—a journey through epochs marked by cosmic pacts, eldritch rituals, and the insatiable hunger that bound the entity to the supernatural realm. The burial ground, now a theater of spectral memories, echoed with the haunting cries of lost souls and the tormented echoes of ancient rites.

Mark, tormented by the conflicting forces that tore at his sanity, saw glimpses of the Goatman's interactions with lost souls—a spectral procession of individuals who had been entangled in the cosmic machinations of the ancient curse. The forest, a silent witness to centuries of suffering, whispered tales of tormented spirits and unspeakable horrors that lurked in the shadowed depths.

Emily, sensitive to the ethereal currents, glimpsed fragments of the future—an ominous tableau that unfolded with an inexorable inevitability. The haunted woods, now a mosaic of interconnected destinies, revealed a nightmarish dance between the living and the spectral.

As the visions played out, the friends, paralyzed by the supernatural revelation, became mere spectators in their own existential drama. The Goatman, a harbinger of cosmic terror, reveled in the torment it unleashed upon their minds. The burial ground, a stage for the unfolding nightmare, pulsated with an otherworldly energy.

Suddenly, the visions ceased, and the friends, released from the spectral trance, found themselves standing in the burial ground once more. The Goatman, its form flickering between the grotesque and

the tragic, remained at the periphery of their perception, a spectral guardian of the haunted woods.

The friends, disoriented and haunted by the echoes of the Goatman's revelations, stumbled away from the burial ground. The haunted woods, now a sentient labyrinth, seemed to rearrange itself, guiding the group deeper into the heart of the supernatural enigma. The air, thick with the residue of spectral energy, clung to them like an intangible shroud.

As they pressed forward, a cold wind whispered through the twisted branches, carrying with it a chilling echo of the Goatman's laughter. The friends, caught in a cycle of existential dread, stumbled through the haunted woods, forever marked by the disappearing act that unfolded in the surreal clearing. The night, pregnant with cosmic uncertainty, stretched before them like an endless abyss.

The spectral alliance, rejected at the burial ground, continued to bind the friends to the Goatman's curse. The twisted trails, now a spectral tapestry, guided them with an otherworldly intelligence. Shadows clung to the group like a malevolent fog, and the air pulsed with an ethereal energy that heightened their senses to the unseen threats that lurked in the shadows.

As they traversed the haunted woods, the group became acutely aware of an invisible tether connecting them to the Goatman's curse. The forest, alive with spectral currents, responded to their presence with a symphony of ethereal whispers. The alliance, forged in the burial ground, propelled them toward a convergence of cosmic forces that awaited in the heart of the supernatural enigma.

The night, fraught with unseen perils, stretched before the friends like an endless abyss. The haunted woods, a realm of shifting shadows and spectral whispers, beckoned them into the heart of the supernatural enigma. The Goatman, now an unseen puppeteer of their destinies, watched with an otherworldly intelligence as the

group delved deeper into the spectral dance that awaited them in the shadowed depths.

The twisted trails, illuminated by an otherworldly glow, led the friends to an ancient altar concealed within the heart of the haunted woods. The spectral echoes intensified, and the air crackled with an otherworldly energy. Unseen eyes watched from the darkness as the group hesitated at the threshold of the supernatural enclave.

Emily, sensitive to the ethereal currents, felt an invisible force pulling her toward the center of the altar. The whispers, now an incessant chorus, urged her to unravel the mysteries concealed within the ancient symbols. A compulsion, an otherworldly call, guided her steps as she approached the spectral threshold.

Mark, torn between rational skepticism and the growing influence of the Goatman's curse, cast wary glances at the ancient altar. The haunted woods, responsive to the internal struggles of the friends, seemed to warp and contort with a will of its own. Shadows danced in grotesque patterns, and the altar became a stage for a supernatural spectacle.

The rest of the group, ensnared by the spectral forces that governed their fate, gathered around Emily. The altar, a nexus of spectral energies, hummed with an ominous resonance. Unseen forces coalesced, and the ancient symbols transformed into conduits for the ethereal currents that pulsed through the heart of the forest.

As Emily traced her fingers over the weathered symbols, the altar became a canvas for ethereal visions. The ancient curse, woven into the fabric of the haunted woods, unfolded before the friends like a nightmarish tapestry. The Goatman, a tragic figure shackled by an unholy alliance, emerged from the shadows, its form flickering with a spectral radiance.

The friends, ensnared in the unfolding revelation, witnessed scenes from the Goatman's existence—a journey through epochs

marked by cosmic pacts, eldritch rituals, and the insatiable hunger that bound the entity to the supernatural realm. The altar, now a theater of spectral memories, echoed with the haunting cries of lost souls and the tormented echoes of ancient rites.

Mark, tormented by the conflicting forces that tore at his sanity, saw glimpses of the Goatman's interactions with lost souls—a spectral procession of individuals who had been entangled in the cosmic machinations of the ancient curse. The forest, a silent witness to centuries of suffering, whispered tales of tormented spirits and unspeakable horrors that lurked in the shadowed depths.

Emily, sensitive to the ethereal currents, glimpsed fragments of the future—an ominous tableau that unfolded with an inexorable inevitability. The haunted woods, now a mosaic of interconnected destinies, revealed a nightmarish dance between the living and the spectral.

As the visions played out, the friends, paralyzed by the supernatural revelation, became mere spectators in their own existential drama. The Goatman, a harbinger of cosmic terror, reveled in the torment it unleashed upon their minds. The altar, a stage for the unfolding nightmare, pulsated with an otherworldly energy.

Suddenly, the visions ceased, and the friends, released from the spectral trance, found themselves standing before the altar once more. The Goatman, its form flickering between the grotesque and the tragic, remained at the periphery of their perception, a spectral guardian of the haunted woods.

The friends, disoriented and haunted by the echoes of the Goatman's revelations, stumbled away from the altar. The haunted woods, now a sentient labyrinth, seemed to rearrange itself, guiding the group deeper into the heart of the supernatural enigma. The air, thick with the residue of spectral energy, clung to them like an intangible shroud.

As they pressed forward, a cold wind whispered through the twisted branches, carrying with it a chilling echo of the Goatman's laughter. The friends, caught in a cycle of existential dread, stumbled through the haunted woods, forever marked by the disappearing act that unfolded in the surreal clearing. The night, pregnant with cosmic uncertainty, stretched before them like an endless abyss.

The spectral alliance, rejected at the altar, continued to bind the friends to the Goatman's curse. The twisted trails, now a spectral tapestry, guided them with an otherworldly intelligence. Shadows clung to the group like a malevolent fog, and the air pulsed with an ethereal energy that heightened their senses to the unseen threats that lurked in the shadows.

As they traversed the haunted woods, the group became acutely aware of an invisible tether connecting them to the Goatman's curse. The forest, alive with spectral currents, responded to their presence with a symphony of ethereal whispers. The alliance, forged in the altar, propelled them toward a convergence of cosmic forces that awaited in the heart of the supernatural enigma.

Chapter 11: Echoes of Betrayal

The haunted woods, now pulsating with an otherworldly energy, closed in around the friends like a malevolent embrace. The spectral alliance, an invisible tether, bound them to the Goatman's curse, and the twisted trails led them deeper into the heart of the supernatural enigma. Each step resonated with an eerie echo, as if the forest itself whispered tales of ancient treacheries.

The air, thick with a palpable tension, seemed to vibrate with the echoes of spectral voices. Unseen eyes watched from the shadows, and the friends felt the weight of the Goatman's malevolent gaze upon them. Emily, still sensitive to the ethereal currents, shivered as the whispers intensified, weaving a narrative of betrayal and impending doom.

Mark, haunted by the memories of his lost friend and the shifting allegiances within the group, struggled to maintain a semblance of composure. The haunted woods, now a labyrinth of twisted shadows, seemed to mirror the turmoil within his mind. Visions of the Goatman's cursed legacy clashed with the reality of their journey, blurring the lines between nightmare and waking.

As the friends ventured further, the twisted trails guided them to an ancient grove bathed in an unnatural glow. The spectral echoes intensified, and the air crackled with an otherworldly energy. Symbols etched into the trees pulsed with an ethereal radiance, casting grotesque shadows that danced with a life of their own.

In the center of the grove stood a spectral figure—a manifestation of the Goatman's curse, its eyes gleaming with an otherworldly intelligence. The friends, transfixed by the haunting presence, felt the weight of an unspoken invitation. The grove, now a stage for a cosmic drama, beckoned them to confront the echoes of betrayal that lingered in the shadows.

Emily, driven by a compulsion she could not resist, approached the spectral figure. The whispers, now a dissonant symphony, reverberated through the grove, casting a haunting spell upon the group. The friends, their senses heightened by the spectral energy, became acutely aware of the invisible threads that connected them to the Goatman's curse.

As Emily reached out, the spectral figure extended a ghostly hand. A surge of ancient memories flooded her consciousness—a tapestry of betrayals and alliances that transcended mortal understanding. The Goatman's voice, a haunting undertone, whispered forgotten secrets that clawed at the edges of her sanity.

Mark, torn between the mistrust within the group and the allure of the Goatman's promises, grappled with an internal tempest. Shadows cast by the ethereal glow contorted into grotesque shapes,

mirroring the conflicting emotions that tormented him. The grove, now a battleground of spectral forces, awaited the resolution of the internal strife that threatened to tear the group apart.

The rest of the friends, ensnared by the spectral drama, watched with a mixture of fear and fascination. The grove, bathed in an otherworldly radiance, became a theater for the unfolding nightmare. The Goatman's laughter, a haunting melody, echoed through the ancient trees, marking the friends as unwilling participants in its cosmic play.

Suddenly, the spectral figure and Emily recoiled as if struck by an unseen force. The grove, now plunged into an eerie silence, seemed to hold its breath. The spectral alliance, momentarily disrupted, cast a shadow of uncertainty upon the friends.

A voice, neither human nor spectral, resonated through the grove—a chorus of ancient whispers that spoke of broken pacts and the consequences of defiance. The friends, still caught in the ethereal web, felt the weight of the Goatman's judgment looming over them.

The grove, once a sanctuary of spectral revelations, became a battleground between the friends and the malevolent forces that sought to manipulate their destinies. The twisted trails, now obscured by shifting shadows, led the group deeper into the heart of the haunted woods, where the echoes of betrayal whispered of darker truths yet to unfold.

As the friends pressed forward, the spectral alliance tightened its grip, binding them to the Goatman's curse with an unbreakable resolve. The haunted woods, now a realm of shifting shadows and unseen perils, seemed to anticipate their every move. Each step echoed with the weight of ancient choices, and the air pulsed with an otherworldly energy that foretold of imminent horrors.

The twisted trails, like serpentine veins, guided the friends to an ancient ruin hidden within the depths of the haunted woods.

Symbols etched into the stones glowed with an ethereal radiance, and the air hummed with a spectral resonance. Unseen eyes watched from the darkness, and the ruins became a threshold to the unknown.

As the friends hesitated at the entrance, the whispers intensified, forming a cacophony of spectral voices that spoke of forgotten oaths and the inevitable descent into darkness. Emily, still bearing the weight of the spectral revelation, felt a compulsion to unravel the mysteries concealed within the ruins.

Mark, his trust shattered by the echoes of betrayal, cast wary glances at the ancient stones. The haunted woods, now alive with a malevolent energy, seemed to pulse with the heartbeat of an ancient evil. Shadows danced upon the ruins, casting ominous shapes that hinted at the horrors waiting within.

The rest of the group, caught in the web of the Goatman's curse, gathered around Emily. The ruins, a nexus of spectral energies, beckoned them to confront the consequences of their choices. The ancient stones, infused with an otherworldly power, awaited the unfolding of a cosmic drama that transcended the boundaries of mortal understanding.

As Emily traced her fingers over the weathered symbols, the ruins became a canvas for ethereal visions. The ancient curse, woven into the fabric of the haunted woods, unfolded before the friends like a nightmarish tapestry. The Goatman, a tragic figure shackled by an unholy alliance, emerged from the shadows, its form flickering with a spectral radiance.

The friends, ensnared in the unfolding revelation, witnessed scenes from the Goatman's existence—a journey through epochs marked by cosmic pacts, eldritch rituals, and the insatiable hunger that bound the entity to the supernatural realm. The ruins, now a

theater of spectral memories, echoed with the haunting cries of lost souls and the tormented echoes of ancient rites.

Mark, tormented by the conflicting forces that tore at his sanity, saw glimpses of the Goatman's interactions with lost souls—a spectral procession of individuals who had been entangled in the cosmic machinations of the ancient curse. The forest, a silent witness to centuries of suffering, whispered tales of tormented spirits and unspeakable horrors that lurked in the shadowed depths.

Emily, sensitive to the ethereal currents, glimpsed fragments of the future—an ominous tableau that unfolded with an inexorable inevitability. The haunted woods, now a mosaic of interconnected destinies, revealed a nightmarish dance between the living and the spectral.

As the visions played out, the friends, paralyzed by the supernatural revelation, became mere spectators in their own existential drama. The Goatman, a harbinger of cosmic terror, reveled in the torment it unleashed upon their minds. The ruins, a stage for the unfolding nightmare, pulsated with an otherworldly energy.

Suddenly, the visions ceased, and the friends, released from the spectral trance, found themselves standing within the ancient ruins once more. The Goatman, its form flickering between the grotesque and the tragic, remained a spectral presence at the periphery of their perception. The ruins, now silent and foreboding, seemed to anticipate the next chapter in the cosmic drama.

The friends, shaken by the spectral revelations, exchanged uneasy glances. The twisted trails, like a river of shadows, beckoned them deeper into the heart of the haunted woods. The air, heavy with the residue of ethereal energy, clung to them as a constant reminder of the supernatural forces that governed their fate.

As they ventured forth, the ruins behind them, the haunted woods seemed to close in, its twisted branches forming an impenetrable

canopy above. Shadows danced along the gnarled trunks, and the ground beneath their feet pulsed with an otherworldly heartbeat. The friends, now bound by the unseen threads of the Goatman's curse, pressed on with a mixture of dread and determination.

The twisted trails led them to a clearing bathed in an eerie, spectral light. In the center stood an ancient altar, adorned with symbols that seemed to writhe and shift in the dim illumination. The air became charged with an unsettling energy, and the friends felt the weight of the Goatman's gaze upon them once more.

Emily, still influenced by the ethereal currents, approached the altar with a sense of inevitability. The whispers, now a haunting chorus, seemed to guide her every step. The friends, unable to resist the unseen forces that governed their journey, gathered around the ancient stone structure.

As Emily reached out to touch the symbols, the altar responded with a surge of spectral energy. Visions unfolded before her eyes— scenes of ancient rituals, cosmic pacts, and the intertwining destinies of those who had crossed paths with the Goatman. The friends, ensnared in the ethereal spectacle, witnessed the tragic tales of souls bound to an ancient curse.

Mark, his skepticism eroded by the relentless onslaught of supernatural revelations, saw the threads of fate weaving around the group. The haunted woods, now a stage for cosmic machinations, echoed with the tormented cries of lost souls and the spectral laughter of the Goatman. The air crackled with an ominous resonance, and the ground seemed to shift beneath their feet.

The rest of the group, caught in the spectral current, felt the altar's power enveloping them. Shadows danced upon their faces, mirroring the ancient struggles playing out in the unseen realms. The Goatman, a puppeteer of destinies, reveled in the unfolding

drama as the friends teetered on the precipice of their own cosmic unraveling.

A voice, echoing from the depths of the haunted woods, resonated through the clearing—a haunting lamentation that spoke of betrayal, cosmic bargains, and the unrelenting hunger that bound the Goatman to its cursed existence. The friends, now witnesses to the unfolding tragedy, felt the weight of their choices bearing down upon them.

Emily, guided by an otherworldly compulsion, spoke words that seemed to echo with ancient power. The symbols on the altar glowed brighter, and the spectral light enveloped the friends. The haunted woods, alive with the energy of forgotten pacts, seemed to respond to Emily's invocation, and the air crackled with an ethereal electricity.

The friends, now connected by an invisible web of fate, felt the boundaries between the living and the spectral blur. The clearing transformed into a surreal tableau—a nexus of cosmic energies that defied mortal comprehension. The Goatman, its spectral form looming large, became a focal point in the unfolding ritual.

As the spectral light reached its zenith, the haunted woods seemed to hold its breath. The air became charged with an otherworldly tension, and the friends braced themselves for the unknown. Shadows, twisted and contorted, converged upon the clearing, forming a veil between the mortal realm and the supernatural forces that lurked beyond.

Suddenly, the spectral light extinguished, plunging the clearing into darkness. The friends, disoriented and surrounded by an oppressive silence, found themselves standing in the aftermath of the ritual. The Goatman's laughter echoed through the haunted woods, mocking the futility of mortal endeavors.

The twisted trails, now obscured by the lingering shadows, beckoned the friends deeper into the heart of the supernatural enigma. The air, thick with the residue of spectral energies, clung to them as a spectral shroud. The haunted woods, a labyrinth of cosmic horrors, seemed to whisper tales of their impending doom.

As the friends pressed forward, the spectral alliance tightening its grip, they became unwitting participants in a nightmare woven from the threads of ancient curses and cosmic machinations. The Goatman, a spectral puppeteer, reveled in the torment it unleashed upon their minds. The haunted woods, a realm of shifting shadows and unseen perils, awaited the next chapter in the unfolding cosmic drama.

Chapter 12: Whispers in the Shadows

The twisted trails guided the friends through the haunted woods, a realm now saturated with the lingering echoes of the ritual. The air crackled with an unsettling energy, and the shadows seemed to writhe with a newfound malevolence. The Goatman's curse, an invisible tether, bound them tighter as they delved deeper into the heart of the supernatural enigma.

The friends, haunted by the spectral revelations and the unsettling ritual, pressed on with a sense of trepidation. Each step through the dense undergrowth echoed with an ominous resonance, and the twisted branches overhead formed a canopy that blocked out the moonlight. The darkness seemed to pulse with a life of its own, and unseen eyes watched their every move.

As they traversed the haunted woods, Mark's gaze darted nervously between the shifting shadows. The Goatman's laughter lingered in the air, a haunting reminder of their entanglement with cosmic forces beyond their understanding. Doubt gnawed at Mark's sanity, and the trust between the friends strained under the weight of unseen horrors.

Emily, still influenced by the ethereal currents, walked with a purpose that seemed guided by forces beyond her control. The whispers, now a dissonant symphony, surrounded her like a spectral aura. The friends, ensnared in the spectral web, followed Emily as the twisted trails led them to a clearing bathed in an otherworldly glow.

In the center of the clearing stood a dilapidated mansion, its decaying façade casting eerie shadows in the spectral light. The air hummed with a haunting melody, and the friends felt an inexplicable compulsion to enter the mansion. The Goatman's curse, now a palpable force, seemed to emanate from the ancient structure.

As they approached the mansion, its doors creaked open with a ghostly wail. The interior, shrouded in darkness, exuded a malevolent energy. Unseen whispers echoed through the halls, recounting the tragic tales of those who had crossed paths with the Goatman within these haunted walls.

The friends hesitated at the threshold, a silent acknowledgment of the impending horrors awaiting them. Emily, still under the influence of the spectral forces, stepped forward with an unwavering determination. The mansion seemed to welcome her, its walls pulsating with an unseen heartbeat.

As the friends entered, the doors slammed shut behind them, sealing their fate within the spectral confines of the mansion. The air grew colder, and the walls whispered tales of betrayal, sacrifice, and the unrelenting hunger that bound the Goatman to its cursed existence. Shadows danced along the corridors, casting grotesque silhouettes that seemed to mock the intruders.

The mansion, a labyrinth of forgotten memories and spectral horrors, unfolded its secrets with each creaking floorboard and echoing whisper. The friends, now prisoners of the spectral drama, ventured deeper into the heart of the ancient structure. The Goatman's

laughter, a sinister undertone, reverberated through the halls, guiding them toward an inevitable confrontation.

Rooms adorned with dusty relics told stories of a bygone era, where the mansion was once a place of decadence and opulence. Now, draped in an ethereal gloom, the grandeur had given way to a pervading sense of decay. Paintings on the walls seemed to watch the intruders with hollow eyes, capturing moments of torment and despair.

Emily, compelled by unseen forces, led the group to a grand hall adorned with a twisted chandelier that cast eerie patterns of light. In the center stood a forgotten altar, covered in cryptic symbols. The air thickened with a spectral presence, and the friends felt the weight of unseen eyes upon them.

As Emily approached the altar, the whispers intensified, forming a cacophony that echoed through the mansion. Visions of ancient rituals played out before the friends, a tapestry of eldritch ceremonies and sacrificial rites. The Goatman's curse, woven into the very fabric of the mansion, revealed its darkest secrets.

Mark, his skepticism now replaced by a growing dread, watched as the spectral energy coalesced around Emily. Shadows danced upon the walls, forming grotesque figures that seemed to writhe in agony. The grand hall became a theater for the unfolding nightmare, with the friends as unwilling actors in a cosmic play.

The rest of the group, caught in the spectral current, stood as witnesses to the ancient forces that manipulated their destinies. The Goatman, now a looming presence within the grand hall, revealed itself with a spectral radiance. The air crackled with an otherworldly electricity as the friends braced themselves for the climax of the haunting spectacle.

Emily, her eyes now reflecting the eerie glow of the altar, spoke words that resonated with ancient power. The symbols etched into

the stone seemed to come alive, glowing brighter with each incantation. The grand hall pulsed with a spectral energy, and the friends felt the very fabric of reality unraveling around them.

A rift, a tear in the fabric of the supernatural, opened before the altar. From the depths emerged the Goatman, its form flickering with a malevolent radiance. The friends, now faced with the spectral entity, felt a chill that transcended the physical realm. The Goatman's laughter, a haunting melody, echoed through the grand hall.

The friends, caught in the grip of the Goatman's curse, were now mere pawns in its cosmic machinations. The mansion, a stage for the unfolding nightmare, seemed to warp and contort with the weight of ancient malevolence. Shadows, now animated with spectral life, closed in around the group, forming a suffocating shroud.

The Goatman, its voice echoing through the halls, spoke of cosmic bargains and the inevitable descent into darkness. The grand hall became a battleground for the friends' sanity as the Goatman's words clawed at the edges of their minds. The spectral currents, now a tempest of unseen forces, whipped through the mansion with an otherworldly fury.

As the friends stood before the altar, a choice loomed in the shadows—an offering to the Goatman or a futile attempt to defy the cosmic forces that bound them. The air crackled with an impending doom, and the grand hall seemed to hold its breath in anticipation of the friends' decision.

Emily, now a conduit for the Goatman's curse, faced the friends with hollow eyes. The whispers, once a dissonant symphony, became a unified chorus urging them toward the inevitable. The spectral threads tightened, pulling the friends into the cosmic dance that awaited its final act within the haunted mansion.

The friends, their fates entwined with the Goatman's curse, stood at the precipice of their own unraveling. The grand hall, a

silent witness to centuries of spectral torment, seemed to echo with the cries of lost souls and the laughter of an entity that defied mortal understanding.

The twisted trails, once a path through the haunted woods, now extended into the very fabric of their existence. The spectral alliance, an unbreakable bond, bound them to the Goatman's curse with an inescapable resolve. The friends, now faced with a choice that would seal their destinies, braced themselves for the next chapter in the cosmic nightmare that unfolded within the walls of the haunted mansion.

Chapter 13: Pact with the Shadows

The grand hall, now a stage for the unfolding cosmic drama, held its breath as the friends stood before the ancient altar. The Goatman, its spectral form flickering with malevolent radiance, loomed over them like a puppeteer orchestrating the final act of a nightmarish play. The air crackled with ethereal energy, and shadows clung to the walls, whispering tales of ancient pacts and unspeakable horrors.

Emily, a conduit for the Goatman's curse, raised her arms as if guided by unseen hands. The symbols on the altar pulsed with an otherworldly glow, and the friends felt the spectral currents intensify. The grand hall seemed to warp, its dimensions shifting in response to the cosmic forces at play. The Goatman's laughter echoed through the mansion, a haunting melody that heralded the imminent climax.

The friends, ensnared by the spectral alliance, felt the weight of the Goatman's gaze upon them. Unseen threads tightened, binding them to the ancient curse that now permeated the very fabric of the mansion. Mark, tormented by doubt and the shadows of betrayal, struggled to comprehend the unfolding nightmare. The grand hall, once a sanctuary of opulence, now exuded a malevolent aura that seeped into the marrow of their bones.

As Emily spoke the incantations, the spectral energy coalesced into a swirling vortex above the altar. The rift, a tear in the fabric of reality, widened, revealing glimpses of a cosmic void that defied mortal comprehension. The Goatman's voice, now a chorus of haunting whispers, echoed through the rift, speaking of forbidden knowledge and the inevitability of their entanglement with the supernatural.

The friends, caught in the grip of the Goatman's curse, felt an inexorable pull toward the cosmic void. Shadows danced upon the edges of the rift, forming grotesque figures that seemed to beckon them into the unknown. The grand hall, now a gateway to cosmic horrors, awaited the friends' choice—submit to the Goatman's influence or defy the cosmic forces that sought to unravel their existence.

Mark, his mind a tempest of conflicting emotions, looked to the other friends. Their faces mirrored the uncertainty that gnawed at his sanity. The Goatman's laughter, a maddening cacophony, intensified as the rift pulsed with an otherworldly glow. The decision, an irreversible pact with the shadows, loomed before them like a specter of doom.

Emily, her eyes hollow and distant, uttered words that seemed to resonate with the very fabric of the supernatural. The friends, compelled by unseen forces, stepped closer to the rift. The grand hall seemed to blur, its boundaries dissolving as the spectral energies surged around them.

Suddenly, the mansion trembled as if in response to an ancient power. The Goatman's laughter, once triumphant, faltered for a moment. The friends, caught in the grip of the cosmic tempest, felt a shift in the spectral currents. The rift, now a pulsating maw, cast an eerie glow upon their faces.

A voice, neither human nor spectral, reverberated through the grand hall—a lamentation that spoke of cosmic balance and the

consequences of meddling with forces beyond mortal understanding. The Goatman, its spectral form recoiling as if struck by an unseen force, hissed with an otherworldly fury.

The friends, momentarily released from the ethereal trance, found themselves standing at the precipice of the rift. The grand hall, now a battleground between cosmic entities, seemed to hold its breath in anticipation of the friends' next move.

Mark, his rational mind clashing with the supernatural forces that surrounded him, hesitated. The Goatman's curse, now weakened but far from defeated, still pulsed through the mansion. Shadows, like tendrils of malevolence, reached out from the walls, whispering promises of forbidden knowledge and unspeakable power.

The other friends, their faces etched with the struggle of internal conflicts, looked to Mark as if seeking guidance. The grand hall, a silent witness to their existential torment, seemed to echo with the cries of lost souls and the laughter of entities that defied mortal comprehension.

In that moment of hesitation, the Goatman's laughter resurged with a renewed malevolence. The spectral currents, like an invisible tide, surged forward, pulling the friends closer to the rift. Shadows clung to them, entwining with the unseen threads that bound them to the ancient curse.

Emily, still under the influence of the Goatman's influence, stepped closer to the rift. The grand hall, now a surreal tableau of cosmic conflict, seemed to warp and contort with the weight of ancient malevolence. The air, thick with the residue of spectral energy, clung to them as a suffocating shroud.

Mark, torn between defiance and the allure of forbidden power, felt the weight of the Goatman's gaze upon him. The rift, a gateway to the unknown, beckoned with a promise of cosmic revelations.

The friends, now at the mercy of supernatural forces, stood on the brink of a choice that would seal their destinies.

As Emily extended her hand toward the rift, the grand hall vibrated with an otherworldly resonance. The Goatman, its form flickering with a desperate fury, hissed with a spectral voice that echoed through the very fabric of the mansion. The friends, caught in the cosmic struggle, felt a surge of unseen forces that threatened to tear their souls asunder.

A voice, ancient and authoritative, cut through the chaos. It spoke of cosmic balance and the need for mortals to resist the temptations that lurked within the shadows. The rift, now a swirling maelstrom of spectral energy, seemed to respond to the authoritative voice.

The Goatman's laughter waned, replaced by an eerie silence. The friends, their minds still entangled in the ethereal web, witnessed the rift's transformation. The cosmic void, once a gateway to the unknown, now shimmered with a tranquil luminescence. Shadows receded, revealing the grand hall in its original state.

The friends, released from the spectral trance, found themselves standing in the mansion's grand hall. The Goatman, its presence diminished but not vanquished, lingered at the periphery of their perception. The air, now devoid of the suffocating spectral shroud, held a sense of uneasy calm.

The authoritative voice, a guiding force that had intervened in the cosmic struggle, echoed through the mansion. It spoke of the friends' resilience in the face of cosmic temptation and the importance of maintaining the delicate balance between the mortal realm and the supernatural. The grand hall, now free from the oppressive malevolence that had gripped it, seemed to regain a semblance of its former opulence. Paintings on the walls, once twisted depictions of torment, now appeared as mere artistic renderings. The dilapidated

mansion, bathed in an otherworldly glow, retained an eerie beauty that hinted at a history shrouded in mystery.

The friends, their senses returning to them, exchanged uncertain glances. The Goatman, a diminished presence, retreated further into the shadows, its spectral form flickering like a dying ember. The authoritative voice continued to resonate, guiding the friends toward a newfound understanding of the cosmic forces that governed their existence.

Mark, his mind a battlefield between reason and supernatural influence, struggled to reconcile the surreal events that had unfolded. The grand hall, once a chamber of horrors, now felt almost serene. The spectral currents, while still present, seemed to ebb away, leaving behind an uneasy calm.

The friends, guided by the authoritative voice, explored the mansion with a newfound sense of purpose. Rooms that had once harbored spectral terrors now revealed forgotten artifacts and relics of a bygone era. The Goatman's curse, now a fading echo, no longer held the mansion in its suffocating grip.

As they ventured deeper into the mansion, the authoritative voice spoke of ancient rituals, cosmic guardians, and the delicate balance that must be maintained to prevent the malevolence of the supernatural from overwhelming the mortal realm. The friends, their minds now attuned to the guiding force, began to understand the significance of their journey.

In a forgotten library, they discovered tomes that chronicled the history of the Goatman—a tragic entity bound by an unholy alliance forged in the shadows of cosmic realms. The authoritative voice explained that the friends' defiance had disrupted the spectral equilibrium, offering a chance to tip the balance away from the malevolence that had plagued the haunted woods.

Mark, grappling with the revelations, felt a weight lifting from his shoulders. The Goatman, now a vanquished specter, no longer held sway over his mind. The friends, united by their shared struggle, delved deeper into the mansion's secrets, guided by the authoritative voice toward a resolution that would safeguard both the mortal and supernatural realms.

In a chamber hidden beneath the mansion, they discovered an ancient artifact—an amulet pulsating with ethereal energy. The authoritative voice explained that the amulet had the power to seal the remnants of the Goatman's curse and restore balance to the haunted woods. The friends, now entrusted with a cosmic responsibility, prepared for a final confrontation.

The grand hall, once witness to cosmic struggles, became a staging ground for the friends' decisive act. The amulet, held by Emily, radiated with a soothing luminescence. The Goatman, its diminished form lingering in the shadows, hissed with a fading defiance.

As Emily approached the spectral remnants of the Goatman's curse, the authoritative voice guided her in a ritual of sealing. Symbols etched into the floor glowed with an otherworldly radiance. The friends, standing in a circle around the amulet, channeled their collective energy into the cosmic task before them.

The mansion trembled as the ritual unfolded, and the Goatman's laughter echoed one last time through the grand hall. Shadows, now devoid of malevolence, danced with a newfound serenity. The friends, their resolve unbroken, witnessed the ethereal currents converging toward the amulet, sealing the remnants of the Goatman's curse within its crystalline core.

A blinding light enveloped the grand hall, and the mansion seemed to transcend the boundaries of time and space. The friends felt a cosmic energy surging through them, connecting them to the very essence of the supernatural. The authoritative voice, now a

benevolent guide, spoke of the friends' triumph over cosmic malevolence and the restoration of equilibrium.

As the light subsided, the grand hall returned to its former state of faded grandeur. The Goatman, its spectral form extinguished, became a mere memory. The haunted woods, once a realm of cosmic nightmares, seemed to breathe with newfound vitality. The friends, now free from the spectral alliance that had bound them, emerged from the mansion with a sense of accomplishment.

The authoritative voice, a fading echo, spoke its final words of gratitude and guidance. The friends, forever changed by their ordeal, walked out of the haunted woods into the moonlit night. The spectral currents, now a gentle breeze, whispered tales of ancient struggles and cosmic resolutions.

As they exited the woods, the haunted realm seemed to recede into the shadows. The Goatman's curse, sealed within the amulet, no longer held dominion over the supernatural enclave. The friends, marked by their journey through cosmic horrors, carried the weight of their experiences as a testament to the delicate balance between the mortal and supernatural realms.

The haunted woods, now a tranquil grove bathed in moonlight, stood as a testament to the friends' resilience. The spectral alliance, once a malevolent force, had been disrupted, and the cosmic equilibrium restored. The friends, forever bonded by their shared struggle, left the haunted woods behind, their footsteps echoing with the echoes of ancient tales and the triumphant resolution of cosmic mysteries.

As they ventured further from the haunted woods, the moonlit path guided them back to the realm of the living. The friends, still processing the surreal events, found solace in the gentle rustle of leaves and the calming night breeze. The amulet, now a relic of

their cosmic triumph, radiated with a subtle glow, a testament to the balance they had restored.

The authoritative voice, its echoes fading into the night, left the friends with a lingering sense of purpose. The haunted mansion, once a chamber of spectral horrors, disappeared from their view. The spectral currents, now harmonized with the natural energies of the world, whispered tales of ancient guardians and cosmic safeguards.

Mark, his mind now free from the haunting influence, looked at his friends with a mixture of relief and gratitude. The journey through the haunted woods had forged bonds that transcended the boundaries of the mundane. The friends, forever changed by their cosmic ordeal, shared an unspoken understanding that went beyond the realm of mortal comprehension.

As they walked, the moon casting a silver glow on their path, the friends reflected on the cosmic mysteries they had encountered. The haunted woods, once a realm of malevolence, had become a sanctuary of cosmic balance. The amulet, now a symbol of their resilience, dangled from Emily's neck, a reminder of the unseen forces that bound them together.

In the distance, the haunted woods receded into the night, its secrets hidden once more within the shadows. The friends, now free from the spectral alliance, emerged into the world with a newfound appreciation for the delicate interplay between the known and the unknown. The cosmic forces, once a source of terror, had become guardians of a delicate equilibrium.

Days turned into nights, and the friends continued their journey, forever marked by the spectral ordeal. The haunted woods, now a distant memory, left an indelible imprint on their souls. The amulet, a silent guardian against malevolence, resonated with the cosmic energies that flowed through their veins.

As they reached the outskirts of a nearby town, the friends paused to gaze back at the moonlit horizon. The haunted woods, a realm of cosmic nightmares, remained hidden in the distance. The amulet, now a talisman of cosmic balance, glowed with a reassuring warmth.

The friends, bound by the shared secrets of the supernatural, moved forward into the tapestry of their lives. The authoritative voice, a distant echo, whispered final words of guidance, fading into the realm of forgotten cosmic tales. The haunted mansion, once a chamber of horrors, became a relic in their collective memory.

The moon, a silent witness to their cosmic journey, cast its light upon the friends as they continued their way. The spectral currents, now a gentle presence, whispered tales of ancient guardians watching over the boundaries between realms. The friends, now guardians in their own right, carried the weight of their cosmic triumph as they embraced the unknown that lay ahead.

The moonlit night, with its secrets and mysteries, enveloped the friends in a comforting embrace. The haunted woods, once a crucible of terror, became a distant chapter in the ever-expanding cosmic narrative. The friends, forever intertwined by the unseen threads of their shared ordeal, moved forward into the mysteries that awaited them, their footsteps echoing with the echoes of ancient tales and the triumphant resolution of cosmic enigmas.

Chapter 14: Echoes of the Unknown

The town at the outskirts offered a semblance of normalcy, but the friends couldn't shake the echoes of the haunted woods that lingered in the recesses of their minds. The amulet, now a silent guardian against unseen forces, emitted a subtle glow as they navigated the streets. The authoritative voice, a distant whisper, continued to guide them with cryptic assurances.

In the heart of the town, they stumbled upon an ancient bookstore. The shelves were lined with weathered tomes containing forgotten knowledge of the supernatural. The friends, still haunted by their cosmic journey, felt an irresistible pull toward the musty volumes that hinted at untold mysteries.

As they delved into the books, the words on the pages seemed to come alive, recounting tales of forgotten rituals, eldritch entities, and the delicate balance that tethered the mortal and supernatural realms. The amulet, attuned to the ancient energies, pulsed with an otherworldly resonance as if acknowledging the truths within the pages.

One particular book caught their attention—an ancient grimoire that spoke of cosmic gateways and the consequences of disrupting the equilibrium between realms. The authoritative voice, now a comforting presence, guided them to a passage that foretold of a looming cosmic disturbance tied to their recent ordeal.

The friends, gripped by a sense of urgency, sought answers from the cryptic text. The grimoire spoke of a cosmic entity known as the Veilstitcher—an ancient force responsible for mending the fabric of reality when disrupted by mortal meddling. The disrupted equilibrium in the haunted woods had awakened the Veilstitcher, and its influence now extended beyond the spectral enclave.

A foreboding realization set in—the friends' actions in the haunted woods had not only disrupted the Goatman's curse but had also set in motion a cosmic chain reaction. The Veilstitcher, a guardian of the cosmic balance, now sought to mend the fabric of reality by any means necessary.

The town, once a refuge, now became a battleground between the Veilstitcher's influence and the friends' struggle for understanding. Shadows seemed to dance with a newfound malevolence, and

the air vibrated with an otherworldly tension. The authoritative voice, now urgent, guided the friends toward a cosmic reckoning.

As night fell, the friends found themselves drawn to an abandoned mansion on the outskirts of the town—a structure that resonated with the cosmic energies emanating from the awakened Veilstitcher. The amulet, now glowing with an intensity that mirrored the urgency of their mission, led them through the moonlit streets toward the looming edifice.

The mansion, a spectral relic like the one in the haunted woods, exuded an ethereal glow. The Veilstitcher's influence seemed to warp the very fabric of reality within its walls. The friends, their minds attuned to the cosmic energies, hesitated at the threshold, knowing that their actions within might determine the fate of both the mortal and supernatural realms.

As they entered, the mansion revealed itself as a nexus of cosmic energies. The authoritative voice, now resonating with a somber tone, explained that the Veilstitcher, once a dormant guardian, had been stirred by the friends' disruption of the cosmic equilibrium. The mansion, a convergence point of realities, now stood as a battleground for their cosmic destiny.

The rooms within the mansion, adorned with symbols that pulsed with cosmic significance, told tales of forgotten rituals and eldritch pacts. Shadows, animated by the Veilstitcher's influence, seemed to observe the intruders with an ominous awareness. The friends, guided by the amulet and the authoritative voice, navigated the twisting corridors toward the heart of the cosmic disturbance.

In a grand chamber, they discovered an ancient portal—a tear in the fabric of reality itself. The Veilstitcher, a spectral entity with threads of cosmic energy weaving around it, stood at the center. The authoritative voice, now a desperate plea, urged the friends to

confront the awakened guardian and seek a resolution that could prevent the unraveling of reality.

The friends, their minds burdened by the weight of cosmic responsibility, faced the Veilstitcher. Its presence, a maelstrom of spectral energies, seemed to scrutinize their very essence. The amulet, now radiating with an otherworldly brilliance, resonated with the Veilstitcher's influence.

The authoritative voice spoke of a cosmic choice—a pact with the Veilstitcher to mend the fabric of reality or a defiance that could unleash untold cosmic consequences. The friends, bound by the unseen threads of their shared journey, exchanged uneasy glances as the Veilstitcher's influence pulsed around them.

Emily, still attuned to the cosmic currents, stepped forward with a sense of purpose. The amulet, now a conduit for cosmic energies, seemed to respond to her presence. The Veilstitcher, its spectral form shifting with an otherworldly grace, communicated in a language of cosmic vibrations that transcended mortal comprehension.

As Emily spoke, her words resonated with the Veilstitcher's energies. The symbols around the portal glowed with an ethereal luminescence, and the grand chamber seemed to ripple with unseen forces. The friends, caught between cosmic choices, felt the weight of their destinies hanging in the balance.

The Veilstitcher, now engaged in a cosmic dialogue, revealed the consequences of its awakening. Reality, torn by the disruption in the haunted woods, threatened to unravel unless a cosmic pact was forged. The friends, their minds a battleground between mortal instincts and cosmic responsibilities, listened to the Veilstitcher's revelations.

Mark, still grappling with the echoes of the haunted woods, questioned the Veilstitcher's motives. The authoritative voice, now a spectral whisper, explained that the awakened guardian sought to

preserve the delicate balance disrupted by mortal interference. The Veilstitcher's influence, while imposing, was a necessary force to prevent cosmic chaos.

The friends, now faced with an impossible choice, deliberated their next move. The Veilstitcher, its spectral form exuding a sense of inevitability, awaited their decision. The amulet, a silent witness to the cosmic drama, pulsed with an intensity that mirrored the urgency of the situation.

As the friends reached a collective decision, the Veilstitcher's influence intensified. The grand chamber seemed to tremble with unseen forces as cosmic energies converged around the portal. Shadows, now imbued with the guardian's essence, danced along the walls, casting grotesque silhouettes.

The Veilstitcher, its spectral form resonating with a somber luminescence, spoke words that transcended mortal comprehension. The friends, guided by the authoritative voice and the amulet's influence, entered into a cosmic pact with the awakened guardian. The symbols on the portal glowed brighter, and reality seemed to shift as the pact was forged.

The town outside, once caught in the grip of the Veilstitcher's influence, returned to a semblance of normalcy. The cosmic energies, now harmonized by the friends' choice, resonated with a tranquil hum. The mansion, a nexus of cosmic disturbances, faded into the shadows as the portal closed behind them.

The authoritative voice, a fading echo, expressed gratitude for the friends' sacrifice in preserving the cosmic equilibrium. The amulet, now a symbol of their cosmic pact, emitted a subdued glow. The Veilstitcher's influence, while still present, now felt more like a benevolent current flowing through the friends' veins. The cosmic energies, once turbulent, settled into a harmonious resonance that connected the mortal and supernatural realms.

The friends, their minds still echoing with the cosmic dialogue, emerged from the grand chamber. The mansion, now devoid of spectral disturbances, felt like a sanctuary of forgotten cosmic truths. The town, released from the Veilstitcher's influence, embraced a serene calm that hinted at the delicate balance that had been restored.

As the friends walked through the moonlit streets, the amulet pulsed with a gentle radiance. The authoritative voice, now a comforting whisper, spoke of the friends' role as guardians of the cosmic equilibrium. The Veilstitcher, its spectral presence lingering in the background, communicated an unspoken assurance that their sacrifice had averted a cosmic catastrophe.

Days turned into nights, and the friends found themselves drawn to the ancient bookstore once again. The tomes that had once spoken of cosmic disturbances now revealed passages about cosmic guardians and the delicate dance between realms. The friends, now more attuned to the cosmic energies, sought further understanding of their newfound responsibilities.

In the bookstore, they discovered a hidden chamber that housed an ancient artifact—a celestial map that depicted the interconnected realms of existence. The authoritative voice guided them to specific constellations that represented cosmic gateways and unseen forces that governed the fabric of reality.

As the friends studied the celestial map, the Veilstitcher's influence resonated with the symbols, creating an ethereal connection between the mortal and supernatural realms. The amulet, now an instrument of cosmic awareness, hummed with a resonant frequency that mirrored the cosmic energies depicted on the map.

The authoritative voice explained that the friends, having forged a cosmic pact with the Veilstitcher, now held the key to maintaining the delicate balance between realms. Their journey, once a

harrowing ordeal, had transformed into a cosmic responsibility to safeguard the cosmic equilibrium.

Guided by the celestial map and the amulet, the friends embarked on a journey that transcended the boundaries of the known. They visited ancient sites, long-forgotten temples, and mystical landscapes that resonated with cosmic energies. The Veilstitcher's influence, now a guiding force, revealed hidden truths about the interconnected nature of existence.

In their cosmic travels, the friends encountered otherworldly entities—guardians, cosmic spirits, and ethereal beings that watched over the boundaries between realms. Each encounter deepened their understanding of the cosmic forces at play and reinforced the importance of their role as guardians of the equilibrium.

The celestial map, now a cosmic compass, led them to a sacred grove bathed in starlight. The Veilstitcher's influence pulsed through the ancient trees, and the amulet resonated with a sublime luminescence. The authoritative voice, now a guiding presence, spoke of a cosmic convergence that required the friends' attention.

In the heart of the sacred grove, a cosmic portal shimmered with an otherworldly radiance. The symbols on the portal echoed the constellations on the celestial map. The friends, their minds attuned to the Veilstitcher's influence, recognized the significance of the cosmic convergence.

As they approached the portal, the Veilstitcher's spectral form materialized, its presence now a harmonious dance of cosmic energies. The amulet, imbued with the friends' cosmic journey, resonated with the portal's energies. The authoritative voice spoke of a cosmic event that would test their resolve and strengthen the bonds between realms.

The friends, guided by their newfound cosmic awareness, stepped through the portal. The celestial map, now a guide through the

cosmic convergence, revealed a breathtaking tapestry of interconnected realms. The Veilstitcher's influence, once a source of cosmic disturbance, now merged seamlessly with the cosmic currents that flowed through the tapestry.

As they traversed the cosmic convergence, the friends encountered celestial phenomena—shifting realities, ethereal landscapes, and manifestations of cosmic energies that transcended mortal comprehension. The amulet, now a conduit for their shared cosmic journey, pulsed with a vibrant energy that mirrored the celestial wonders around them.

The authoritative voice, a guiding presence in the cosmic expanse, explained the friends' role in maintaining the delicate balance between realms during the convergence. The Veilstitcher, its spectral form intertwining with the cosmic currents, communicated an unspoken assurance that their cosmic pact had prepared them for this pivotal moment.

In the cosmic tapestry, the friends witnessed the Veilstitcher's influence harmonizing with other cosmic guardians. The celestial convergence, a sublime dance of energies, echoed with the echoes of ancient tales and cosmic resolutions. The friends, now guardians of the equilibrium, embraced their role with a sense of cosmic purpose.

As the cosmic convergence reached its zenith, the friends felt a profound connection to the very fabric of existence. The Veilstitcher's influence, now a benevolent force, guided them through the celestial wonders. The amulet, a symbol of their cosmic journey, radiated with a brilliance that mirrored the cosmic energies that flowed through the tapestry.

As the friends emerged from the cosmic convergence, they found themselves back in the sacred grove bathed in starlight. The portal closed behind them, leaving a lingering sense of cosmic awareness. The Veilstitcher's spectral form, now a distant presence, conveyed

a silent gratitude for the friends' guardianship of the cosmic equilibrium.

The celestial map, still in their possession, revealed new constellations that represented the friends' cosmic journey. The authoritative voice, a fading echo, spoke of the friends' transformation from seekers of the unknown to guardians of cosmic balance. The amulet, now a relic imbued with cosmic energies, pulsed with a steady resonance.

The friends, forever changed by their cosmic ordeal, looked to the night sky with a newfound understanding. The echoes of the unknown, once a source of terror, now whispered tales of cosmic guardianship and the delicate dance between realms. The Veilstitcher's influence, though distant, remained a guiding force in their cosmic journey.

As the friends ventured back into the mortal realm, the town at the outskirts welcomed them with a tranquil calm. The echoes of the haunted woods and the cosmic convergence became part of their collective memory. The amulet, now a timeless artifact, symbolized their connection to the cosmic forces that governed existence.

The Veilstitcher, a guardian in the cosmic expanse, continued its silent vigil over the delicate balance between realms. The friends, now stewards of the equilibrium, embraced their cosmic responsibilities with a sense of purpose. The cosmic tapestry, woven with threads of celestial wonders, echoed with the echoes of ancient tales and the triumphant resolution of cosmic enigmas.

Guided by the celestial map, the friends embarked on a journey to further understand and strengthen their cosmic abilities. The amulet, now an integral part of their existence, resonated with the energies of the interconnected realms. The Veilstitcher's influence, though no longer a constant presence, lingered as a silent assurance in the background.

As they delved into their newfound cosmic awareness, the friends discovered hidden sanctuaries and ancient sites where the fabric of reality seemed thin. Each encounter with cosmic phenomena deepened their understanding of the delicate balance they upheld. The celestial map, now a well-worn guide, led them to forgotten realms where cosmic secrets awaited revelation.

The friends encountered other guardians—ethereal beings who watched over specific aspects of the cosmic equilibrium. These cosmic sentinels imparted ancient wisdom and shared tales of cosmic struggles that transcended mortal lifetimes. The amulet, responding to the cosmic revelations, pulsed with an ethereal glow that mirrored the wisdom they gained.

In one such realm, the friends faced a cosmic trial—an otherworldly challenge that tested their resilience and understanding of the interconnected tapestry. The Veilstitcher's influence, once again a guiding force, whispered encouragement as the friends navigated through shifting realities and celestial puzzles. The amulet, a source of cosmic strength, resonated with a brilliance that defied mortal comprehension.

As they emerged victorious from the cosmic trial, the friends felt a surge of cosmic energy coursing through them. The celestial map, now adorned with new constellations, reflected their triumph. The Veilstitcher's spectral form, a distant but benevolent presence, communicated a silent acknowledgment of their growth as cosmic stewards.

The friends, now attuned to the cosmic rhythms, realized that their journey had become a perpetual quest to maintain the balance between realms. The Veilstitcher's influence guided them toward cosmic disturbances that threatened to disrupt the delicate equilibrium. The amulet, a cosmic compass, pulsed with urgency as the friends embraced their roles as cosmic guardians.

In one particularly perilous encounter, the friends faced an entity that sought to unravel the threads of reality. The cosmic disturbance, a malevolent force that defied comprehension, manifested in shifting shadows and ethereal echoes. The Veilstitcher's influence, now an active guide, directed the friends in a cosmic battle against the encroaching chaos.

As the friends confronted the cosmic disturbance, the amulet resonated with a fierce brilliance. The celestial map, now animated with cosmic energies, revealed the weaknesses in the malevolent force. Guided by the Veilstitcher's influence, the friends channeled their cosmic abilities to weave threads of stability into the fabric of reality.

The cosmic battle unfolded in a surreal dance of energies, with the friends wielding the amulet as a conduit for their newfound cosmic powers. The Veilstitcher's spectral form, a silent overseer, observed their efforts with a sense of approval. The celestial map, now a source of tactical insight, guided the friends through the intricate maneuvers needed to restore cosmic equilibrium.

As the malevolent force recoiled under the friends' cosmic onslaught, the cosmic disturbance began to dissipate. The Veilstitcher's influence, intertwined with the amulet's radiant glow, sealed the weakened threads of reality. The friends, exhausted but triumphant, stood amidst the cosmic aftermath, their cosmic abilities now more refined and potent.

The Veilstitcher's spectral form approached, its essence resonating with a profound serenity. The amulet, still glowing with the aftermath of the cosmic battle, conveyed a sense of fulfillment. The celestial map, though marked by the recent cosmic disturbance, hinted at the friends' ongoing journey as cosmic guardians.

As the friends left the disrupted realm, the Veilstitcher's influence lingered as a silent companion. The amulet, now a vessel of cosmic

energies, pulsed with a steady rhythm. The celestial map, enriched by the recent experiences, reflected the intricate dance of cosmic forces that shaped their cosmic journey.

In the wake of the cosmic battle, the friends continued their exploration of interconnected realms. The Veilstitcher's influence, though less prominent, remained a guiding force in their cosmic endeavors. The amulet, now a symbol of their cosmic mastery, resonated with a harmonious energy that connected them to the very essence of the cosmic tapestry.

The friends' travels took them to celestial landscapes, ancient observatories, and cosmic sanctuaries where the boundaries between realms blurred. The Veilstitcher's influence guided them toward cosmic phenomena that demanded their attention. The amulet, now an instrument of cosmic balance, pulsed with an ethereal glow as they upheld their cosmic responsibilities.

Through their cosmic journey, the friends encountered beings of cosmic wisdom and entities that embodied the intricate dance of existence. The Veilstitcher's spectral form, though distant, communicated a sense of approval as the friends navigated through celestial wonders and unearthed forgotten truths.

As the friends embraced their roles as cosmic guardians, the Veilstitcher's influence gradually withdrew, leaving them with a sense of empowerment and cosmic purpose. The amulet, now an artifact infused with cosmic energies, became a symbol of their journey—an enduring testament to their triumphs over cosmic disturbances.

The celestial map, adorned with constellations representing their cosmic victories, guided the friends toward new realms and cosmic challenges. The echoes of the unknown, once a source of terror, now whispered tales of cosmic guardianship and the delicate dance between realms. The friends, forever bound by their shared cosmic

journey, embraced the ongoing mysteries that awaited them in the interconnected tapestry of existence.

As the friends ventured further into the cosmic unknown, the Veilstitcher's spectral form faded into the cosmic expanse, its influence becoming a timeless part of their cosmic legacy. The amulet, a luminous beacon of cosmic mastery, pulsed with the echoes of ancient tales and the triumphant resolution of cosmic enigmas. The celestial map, now a guide through the cosmic realms, unfolded new constellations that beckoned the friends toward their next cosmic adventure—a perpetual odyssey that transcended the boundaries of the known and embraced the infinite possibilities of the cosmic tapestry.

Chapter 15: Cosmic Odyssey

Guided by the celestial map, the friends embarked on a cosmic odyssey that traversed realms beyond mortal comprehension. The interconnected tapestry of existence unfolded before them, revealing celestial wonders, ethereal landscapes, and cosmic phenomena that defied explanation.

The Veilstitcher's influence, though a distant echo, resonated in the cosmic energies that enveloped the friends. The amulet, a radiant beacon of their cosmic mastery, pulsed with an ever-present glow. The celestial map, now adorned with constellations representing their cosmic victories, guided them toward new frontiers in the cosmic expanse.

Their cosmic journey led them to an astral city suspended in the fabric of reality—a nexus where cosmic beings congregated to exchange wisdom and share tales of cosmic struggles. The friends, now revered as cosmic guardians, were welcomed into the celestial enclave. The Veilstitcher's influence, a silent companion, conveyed a sense of pride in their cosmic achievements.

In the astral city, the friends encountered beings of transcendent wisdom—entities that embodied the very essence of cosmic existence. The Veilstitcher's spectral form, though unseen, communicated with the celestial beings in a language of cosmic vibrations. The amulet, resonating with the celestial energies, marked the friends as stewards of the delicate balance between realms.

As they communed with cosmic sages and explored the astral city's ethereal architecture, the friends learned of ancient prophecies that foretold cosmic challenges yet to come. The celestial map, now revealing constellations depicting future cosmic disturbances, guided them toward their next cosmic mission.

The Veilstitcher's influence, now a guiding force in their cosmic endeavors, urged the friends to embrace their roles as cosmic guardians with renewed determination. The amulet, a conduit for cosmic energies, hummed with a harmonious resonance that mirrored the celestial symphony around them.

Their cosmic odyssey led them to a realm where time flowed in paradoxical currents and spatial dimensions intertwined. The celestial map, now navigating through temporal anomalies, revealed cosmic disturbances that threatened to disrupt the cosmic equilibrium. The Veilstitcher's influence, though subtle, guided the friends toward a cosmic anomaly that transcended the boundaries of temporal understanding.

As they entered the realm of temporal paradoxes, the friends encountered echoes of past, present, and future cosmic events. The Veilstitcher's spectral form, now a temporal observer, guided them through the intricacies of temporal anomalies. The amulet, attuned to the temporal energies, pulsed with a rhythmic cadence that marked the ebb and flow of cosmic time.

In their cosmic exploration, the friends faced temporal challenges that tested their understanding of the interconnected tapestry. The

celestial map, now a guide through the temporal labyrinth, revealed constellations representing pivotal moments in cosmic history. The Veilstitcher's influence, intertwined with the amulet's radiant glow, whispered insights into the delicate dance between temporal forces.

As they navigated through temporal currents and faced paradoxical trials, the friends felt the weight of cosmic responsibility. The Veilstitcher's spectral form, a temporal overseer, communicated a sense of urgency in preserving the cosmic equilibrium across all timelines. The amulet, a temporal anchor, resonated with a steady frequency that harmonized with the cosmic time stream.

Their triumph over temporal challenges marked a pivotal moment in their cosmic journey. The Veilstitcher's influence, though bound by temporal constraints, conveyed a sense of approval. The amulet, now a temporal artifact, bore the imprints of their cosmic victories in the temporal realm.

The celestial map, enriched by their experiences in the realm of temporal paradoxes, guided the friends toward new frontiers in the cosmic tapestry. The Veilstitcher's spectral form, though distant, remained a silent companion in their cosmic odyssey. The amulet, now a relic infused with temporal energies, pulsed with the echoes of ancient tales and the triumphant resolution of temporal enigmas.

As the friends ventured further into the cosmic unknown, the celestial map unfolded new constellations representing uncharted realms. The Veilstitcher's influence, now a timeless presence, guided them toward cosmic phenomena that transcended mortal understanding. The amulet, an ever-present source of cosmic awareness, resonated with a luminous brilliance that mirrored the cosmic wonders around them.

Their cosmic odyssey continued, weaving through realms of surreal beauty, cosmic challenges, and ancient mysteries. The Veilstitcher's spectral form, now an ethereal companion, communicated

a sense of purpose in their ongoing quest to uphold the delicate balance between realms. The amulet, a cosmic talisman, pulsed with an enduring glow that marked the friends as eternal stewards of the cosmic equilibrium.

As the friends embraced the infinite possibilities of the cosmic tapestry, the echoes of the unknown whispered tales of cosmic guardianship and the intricate dance between realms. The Veilstitcher's influence, though timeless, remained an ever-watchful guide in their perpetual cosmic adventure. The amulet, a radiant symbol of their cosmic journey, continued to resonate with the echoes of ancient tales and the triumphant resolution of cosmic enigmas.

In the vast expanse of the interconnected tapestry, the friends' cosmic odyssey unfolded like an eternal saga—an ongoing exploration of the unknown, a journey that transcended the boundaries of the known, and a testament to the enduring bond between mortal souls and the cosmic forces that shaped their destinies.

Chapter 15: The Abyss of Cosmic Dread

As the friends delved deeper into the cosmic expanse, guided by the celestial map, they sensed an ominous shift in the fabric of reality. The Veilstitcher's influence, once a reassuring presence, now vibrated with an undercurrent of cosmic dread. The amulet, usually radiant with cosmic energies, flickered with an unsettling uncertainty as they approached a realm shrouded in cosmic shadows.

The astral city, which had once welcomed them as revered cosmic guardians, now revealed a darker underbelly. Celestial beings, their ethereal forms distorted by an unseen malevolence, whispered foreboding prophecies of an impending cosmic catastrophe. The Veilstitcher's spectral form, still present but veiled in cosmic dread, communicated a sense of urgency that sent shivers through the friends' cosmic awareness.

The celestial map, now marked by constellations that seemed to writhe with cosmic unease, directed them toward an abyssal rift—an anomaly in the fabric of existence that emitted an unsettling resonance. As they approached the cosmic abyss, the amulet pulsed with an erratic energy, reflecting the growing cosmic disturbance that threatened to unravel the delicate balance between realms.

As they entered the abyssal rift, the friends felt an overwhelming sense of existential dread. The Veilstitcher's influence, usually a guiding force, now manifested as haunting whispers that echoed through the cosmic void. Shadows danced with a malevolent glee, and the celestial map, once a source of guidance, seemed to lead them deeper into the cosmic abyss.

In the depths of the rift, the friends encountered cosmic horrors that defied mortal comprehension. Entities of cosmic malevolence, their forms twisted by the abyssal energies, sought to consume the very essence of their cosmic being. The Veilstitcher's spectral form, dimmed by the cosmic dread, conveyed a silent plea for the friends to resist the encroaching darkness.

The amulet, struggling against the oppressive forces of the abyss, emitted flashes of dim light that barely illuminated the cosmic horrors that lurked in the shadows. The celestial map, now distorted by the abyssal energies, led the friends through maddening labyrinths where reality itself seemed to unravel.

As they faced the cosmic horrors, the friends felt the weight of existential terror bearing down upon them. The Veilstitcher's spectral form, now a flickering beacon in the cosmic abyss, urged them to confront the source of the malevolence that threatened to rupture the fabric of reality. The amulet, their only source of cosmic defense, resonated with the desperate pulses of their fear-stricken hearts.

In their cosmic struggle against the abyssal forces, the friends discovered ancient ruins—remnants of a forgotten civilization that

had succumbed to the same cosmic dread. The celestial map, though tainted by the abyssal energies, revealed inscriptions that spoke of rituals to appease eldritch entities and the consequences of cosmic disturbances left unchecked.

The Veilstitcher's spectral form, now dimmed by the encroaching darkness, communicated the dire implications of the abyssal rift's existence. If not sealed, it threatened to become a cosmic tear that could unleash unspeakable horrors upon the interconnected tapestry. The friends, gripped by terror and determination, understood the gravity of their cosmic mission.

As they ventured deeper into the ruins, the abyssal energies twisted the very fabric of reality. Cosmic echoes whispered tales of the doomed civilization that had once thrived in the cosmic abyss. The amulet, now a fragile shield against the abyssal forces, flickered with the desperate hope that the friends could prevent a similar fate.

In the heart of the ruins, the friends discovered a cosmic altar—a focal point for the abyssal energies that pulsed through the rift. Eldritch symbols adorned the altar, resonating with malevolence that sent shivers down their spines. The celestial map, now a guide through the madness, directed them toward a cosmic ritual that could seal the abyssal rift and avert the impending cosmic catastrophe.

As they prepared to enact the ritual, the friends felt the oppressive weight of the abyssal energies bearing down upon them. Whispers of cosmic horrors echoed in their minds, and the Veilstitcher's spectral form, barely visible amidst the cosmic dread, communicated the urgency of completing the ritual before the fabric of reality unraveled completely.

The amulet, now strained to its cosmic limits, emitted a feeble glow as the friends channeled their cosmic abilities into the ritual. Shadows, animated by the abyssal forces, writhed in protest as the

celestial map guided them through the intricate steps of the cosmic sealing. The Veilstitcher's spectral form, though barely discernible, resonated with the friends' determination to defy the encroaching cosmic dread.

In the midst of the ritual, the friends felt the cosmic abyss resisting their efforts. Eldritch energies surged, threatening to overwhelm their sanity. The Veilstitcher's influence, now a beacon in the cosmic storm, lent its spectral strength to their cosmic struggle. The amulet, teetering on the brink of cosmic exhaustion, emitted a final burst of radiant light that merged with the celestial energies of the sealing ritual.

As the last cosmic incantation echoed through the ruins, a profound stillness settled over the abyssal rift. The cosmic dread that had permeated the very fabric of reality began to recede. The Veilstitcher's spectral form, now visible in a dim luminescence, conveyed a silent acknowledgment of the friends' success in averting the cosmic catastrophe.

The amulet, though dimmed and worn, retained a subdued glow—a testament to the friends' resilience against the abyssal forces. The celestial map, now cleared of the malevolent constellations, revealed a new cosmic equilibrium that mirrored the triumph over the cosmic dread that had threatened to consume the interconnected tapestry.

As the friends emerged from the ruins, the abyssal rift sealed behind them, the Veilstitcher's spectral form regained its ethereal brilliance. The amulet, though scarred by the cosmic struggle, pulsed with a renewed vitality. The celestial map, now restored to its cosmic clarity, guided them toward realms untouched by the malevolent forces that had lurked in the cosmic abyss.

The friends, forever changed by their harrowing encounter with the abyssal forces, continued their cosmic odyssey with a heightened

awareness of the cosmic horrors that lurked in the vast expanse. The Veilstitcher's influence, now a vigilant guardian, accompanied them as a guiding force. The amulet, a resilient artifact that bore the scars of their cosmic ordeal, resonated with a luminous brilliance that symbolized their triumph over the abyssal dread.

The celestial map, once tainted by malevolence, now guided the friends toward realms where cosmic wonders awaited discovery. The echoes of the unknown, though still haunting, whispered tales of cosmic resilience and the indomitable spirit that defied the abyssal forces. The friends, forever entwined by the shared horrors they had faced, embraced the mysteries that awaited them in the uncharted territories of the interconnected tapestry.

Their cosmic odyssey, now marked by the echoes of cosmic dread and triumphant resilience, unfolded like a cosmic epic—an eternal saga that transcended mortal fears and celebrated the enduring bond between mortal souls and the cosmic forces that shaped their destinies.

Chapter 16: Shadows of the Celestial Betrayal

As the friends ventured further into the cosmic unknown, guided by the celestial map, they found themselves in a realm cloaked in unsettling shadows. The Veilstitcher's influence, though a constant presence, seemed to waver as they approached an ancient observatory atop a desolate cosmic peak. The amulet, typically radiant with cosmic energies, emitted a dim glow that reflected the ominous atmosphere that pervaded the celestial landscape.

The observatory, a structure that bore witness to eons of cosmic phenomena, now echoed with whispers of a celestial betrayal that had cast a dark shadow over the interconnected tapestry. The Veilstitcher's spectral form, a silhouette against the cosmic gloom, communicated a tale of treachery that had resonated through the celestial realms.

The celestial map, now displaying constellations that seemed to writhe in cosmic agony, directed the friends toward the heart of the celestial betrayal. As they ascended the cosmic peak, the shadows deepened, and the amulet pulsed with a disconcerting rhythm that mirrored the cosmic unease.

In the observatory's inner sanctum, the friends discovered a cosmic artifact—a relic of ancient power that had been corrupted by the tendrils of celestial betrayal. Eldritch symbols adorned the artifact, resonating with malevolence that sent shivers down their spines. The Veilstitcher's influence, though shrouded in cosmic sorrow, urged them to unravel the mysteries of the celestial betrayal that had tainted the very essence of the interconnected tapestry.

As the friends examined the corrupted artifact, the shadows within the observatory seemed to come alive. Cosmic entities, twisted by the influence of celestial betrayal, materialized in ghostly forms. The Veilstitcher's spectral form, now obscured by the cosmic gloom, whispered warnings of the malevolent entities that guarded the secrets of the celestial betrayal.

The amulet, sensing the encroaching cosmic malevolence, emitted a protective aura that shielded the friends from the ghostly entities' influence. The celestial map, though distorted by the shadows, revealed inscriptions that chronicled the ancient pact that had led to the celestial betrayal and the cosmic consequences that followed.

In their exploration of the observatory, the friends faced spectral guardians—entities that embodied the malevolent echoes of celestial betrayal. Shadows danced with a haunting grace as the Veilstitcher's influence guided them through cosmic trials that tested their resolve. The amulet, a luminous beacon against the cosmic darkness, resonated with a determination to uncover the truth behind the celestial betrayal.

As they delved deeper into the observatory's mysteries, the whispers of the celestial betrayal grew more pronounced. The Veilstitcher's spectral form, now a spectral guide in the cosmic shadows, conveyed a sense of cosmic sorrow that mirrored the anguish of ancient cosmic entities. The amulet, their only defense against the encroaching malevolence, flickered with a resilient glow that defied the cosmic despair.

In the observatory's inner chambers, the friends uncovered an ancient cosmic chronicle—an illuminated manuscript that chronicled the events leading to the celestial betrayal. The celestial map, now revealing constellations that depicted cosmic alliances shattered by treachery, guided them through the cosmic revelations that awaited.

The Veilstitcher's influence, though shrouded in cosmic sorrow, narrated a tale of celestial beings bound by a sacred covenant to uphold the cosmic equilibrium. Betrayal, driven by cosmic ambition, had fractured the bonds of trust and unleashed cosmic disturbances that reverberated through the interconnected tapestry.

As the friends immersed themselves in the cosmic chronicle, they witnessed cosmic battles, treacherous alliances, and the tragic fall of celestial beings consumed by their desires for power. The celestial map, now marked by constellations that depicted the celestial betrayal in vivid detail, guided them toward the heart of the observatory where the corrupted artifact held the key to understanding the cosmic transgressions.

In the inner sanctum, the friends faced a spectral guardian—an embodiment of the celestial betrayal that had tainted the artifact with malevolent energies. The Veilstitcher's spectral form, now a solemn observer, conveyed a sense of sorrow as the friends confronted the echoes of ancient cosmic treachery. The amulet, resonating with the cosmic revelations, emitted a luminous glow that mirrored the

friends' determination to cleanse the artifact and unravel the mysteries of the celestial betrayal.

The celestial map, now pulsating with the cosmic consequences
of the ancient transgressions, guided the friends through a ritual
to purify the corrupted artifact. Shadows writhed with resistance,
and the spectral guardian unleashed cosmic energies in a desperate attempt to prevent the redemption of the tainted relic. The
Veilstitcher's influence, though veiled in cosmic sorrow, whispered
words of encouragement as the friends channeled their cosmic abilities into the purification ritual.

In the midst of the cosmic struggle, the artifact resonated with
celestial energies, and the shadows within the observatory recoiled.
The Veilstitcher's spectral form, now visible in a dim luminescence,
conveyed a sense of approval as the purification ritual reached its
zenith. The amulet, though strained by the cosmic exertion, emitted
a final burst of radiant light that merged with the purified energies
of the artifact.

As the celestial energies enveloped the observatory, a profound
stillness settled over the cosmic peak. The shadows dissipated, and
the celestial map, now cleared of the malevolent constellations, revealed a new cosmic equilibrium that reflected the friends' triumph
over the celestial betrayal. The Veilstitcher's spectral form, though
still tinged with cosmic sorrow, conveyed a silent acknowledgment
of their success in redeeming the corrupted artifact.

The amulet, though scarred by the cosmic struggle, retained a
subdued glow—a testament to the friends' resilience against the malevolent forces of celestial betrayal. The celestial map, now restored
to its cosmic clarity, guided them toward realms where the echoes of
ancient treachery had been silenced.

As the friends emerged from the observatory, the celestial betrayal purged behind them, the Veilstitcher's spectral form regained

its ethereal brilliance. The amulet, though dimmed and worn, pulsed with a renewed vitality. The celestial map, now cleared of the malevolent constellations, guided them toward new frontiers in the interconnected tapestry.

The friends, forever changed by their harrowing encounter with the celestial betrayal, continued their cosmic odyssey with a heightened awareness of the cosmic transgressions that could threaten the delicate balance between realms. The Veilstitcher's influence, now a vigilant guardian, accompanied them as a guiding force. The amulet, a resilient artifact that bore the scars of their cosmic ordeal, resonated with a luminous brilliance that symbolized their triumph over the shadows of ancient treachery.

The celestial map, once tainted by malevolence, now guided the friends toward realms where cosmic wonders awaited discovery. The echoes of the unknown, though still haunting, whispered tales of cosmic resilience and the indomitable spirit that defied the shadows of celestial betrayal. The friends, forever entwined by the shared horrors they had faced, embraced the mysteries that awaited them in the uncharted territories of the interconnected tapestry.

Their cosmic odyssey, now marked by the echoes of celestial betrayal and triumphant resilience, unfolded like a cosmic epic—an eternal saga that transcended mortal fears and celebrated the enduring bond between mortal souls and the cosmic forces that shaped their destinies.

Chapter 17: Whispers of the Cosmic Abyss

As the friends continued their cosmic odyssey, guided by the celestial map, they found themselves drawn to a realm shrouded in enigmatic whispers—the remnants of cosmic echoes that hinted at an ancient cosmic abyss. The Veilstitcher's influence, a vigilant guardian, resonated with a somber resonance as they approached the threshold of this mysterious cosmic chasm. The amulet, though

usually radiant with cosmic energies, emitted an ethereal glow that reflected the unsettling atmosphere surrounding the abyss.

The celestial map, now marked by constellations that seemed to ripple like cosmic waves, directed the friends toward the edge of the cosmic abyss. As they descended into its depths, the shadows deepened, and the amulet pulsed with an eerie luminosity that mirrored the cosmic uncertainties that lay ahead.

In the cosmic abyss, the friends encountered surreal landscapes where the fabric of reality seemed to unravel. Ethereal whispers, echoing from the depths of the abyss, conveyed tales of ancient cosmic entities that had succumbed to the allure of forbidden knowledge. The Veilstitcher's spectral form, now a solemn guide, warned of the cosmic perils that lurked in the abyssal depths.

As they navigated through the cosmic echoes, the friends faced spectral manifestations—entities born from the lingering remnants of cosmic entities that had unraveled in the abyss. Shadows danced with an otherworldly grace, and the celestial map, now flickering with cosmic uncertainties, guided them through trials that tested their resilience against the cosmic abyss.

The Veilstitcher's influence, though a steadfast companion, communicated a sense of caution as the friends delved deeper into the cosmic unknown. The amulet, their cosmic beacon, emitted a protective aura that shielded them from the haunting forces that sought to entice them into the cosmic abyss's alluring depths.

In the heart of the abyss, the friends discovered an ancient cosmic library—a repository of forbidden knowledge that had driven cosmic entities to madness. Eldritch tomes, adorned with celestial symbols, whispered cosmic secrets that reverberated through the friends' consciousness. The celestial map, now etched with constellations depicting cosmic entities succumbing to the abyssal allure, guided them through the cosmic archives.

The Veilstitcher's spectral form, now a spectral librarian, communicated the dire consequences of delving too deeply into the forbidden knowledge within the cosmic library. The amulet, resonating with the echoes of cosmic entities lost to the abyss, pulsed with a cautionary rhythm that mirrored the friends' trepidation.

As they deciphered the celestial symbols within the tomes, the friends uncovered the tale of an ancient cosmic entity—an entity that had sought to unravel the mysteries of the cosmos but had succumbed to the cosmic abyss's seductive whispers. The celestial map, now revealing constellations that mirrored the entity's descent into madness, guided them toward the entity's resting place within the abyss.

The Veilstitcher's influence, now a solemn guide in the cosmic library, urged the friends to tread carefully as they approached the entity's lair. Shadows, animated by the abyssal energies, seemed to writhe with anticipation, and the amulet emitted a subdued glow that signaled their entry into the heart of the cosmic abyss.

In the presence of the ancient cosmic entity, echoes of madness reverberated through the abyss. The entity's spectral form, twisted by the allure of forbidden knowledge, manifested in surreal splendor. The Veilstitcher's spectral form, a spectral witness to the entity's tragic fate, communicated the profound sorrow that accompanied the entity's descent into the cosmic abyss.

The friends, now confronted by the entity's spectral manifestation, felt the weight of cosmic madness bearing down upon them. The celestial map, now depicting constellations that mirrored the entity's cosmic unraveling, guided them through a cosmic trial that tested their sanity. The amulet, their only defense against the abyssal forces, emitted a protective aura that resonated with a determination to resist the cosmic allure.

In their cosmic struggle against the entity's spectral manifestation, the friends uncovered the cosmic truths that had driven the entity to madness. Forbidden knowledge, woven into the very fabric of the cosmic abyss, whispered cosmic secrets that defied mortal comprehension. The Veilstitcher's spectral form, a witness to the unfolding cosmic drama, conveyed a sense of empathy for the entity's tragic journey.

The amulet, attuned to the cosmic revelations, emitted pulses of resonant light that harmonized with the celestial map's guidance. As the friends faced the entity's spectral manifestation, the cosmic abyss seemed to echo with the collective sorrow of entities lost to the seductive whispers of forbidden knowledge.

In a moment of cosmic clarity, the friends realized that the only way to quell the entity's spectral madness was to weave threads of cosmic understanding into the fabric of the abyss. The Veilstitcher's spectral form, now a spectral weaver, guided them through a cosmic ritual that sought to restore the entity's fractured consciousness.

As they channeled their cosmic abilities into the ritual, the cosmic abyss responded with an ethereal symphony. Shadows, once animated by madness, now danced with a melancholic grace. The celestial map, now pulsating with threads of cosmic understanding, guided the friends through the intricate maneuvers needed to mend the entity's cosmic essence.

In the cosmic aftermath of the ritual, the entity's spectral manifestation transformed. Madness gave way to a serene luminescence, and the abyssal energies seemed to retreat. The Veilstitcher's influence, now a cosmic weaver of understanding, conveyed a sense of resolution as the friends witnessed the entity's spectral form find peace within the cosmic abyss.

The amulet, though worn by the cosmic struggle, emitted a radiant glow that mirrored the friends' triumph over the abyssal allure.

The celestial map, now cleared of constellations depicting madness, revealed a new cosmic equilibrium that reflected the friends' ability to navigate the cosmic abyss and emerge unscathed.

As the friends ascended from the cosmic abyss, the Veilstitcher's spectral form regained its ethereal brilliance. The amulet, though scarred by the cosmic ordeal, pulsed with a renewed vitality. The celestial map, now cleared of the cosmic uncertainties, guided them toward new frontiers in the interconnected tapestry.

The friends, forever changed by their harrowing encounter with the cosmic abyss, continued their cosmic odyssey with a heightened awareness of the cosmic perils that lurked in the vast expanse. The Veilstitcher's influence, now a cosmic weaver of understanding, accompanied them as a guiding force. The amulet, a resilient artifact that bore the scars of their cosmic ordeal, resonated with a luminous brilliance that symbolized their triumph over the shadows of the cosmic abyss.

The celestial map, once tainted by cosmic uncertainties, now guided the friends toward realms where cosmic wonders awaited discovery. The echoes of the unknown, though still haunting, whispered tales of cosmic resilience and the indomitable spirit that defied the allure of the cosmic abyss. The friends, forever entwined by the shared horrors they had faced, embraced the mysteries that awaited them in the uncharted territories of the interconnected tapestry.

Their cosmic odyssey, now marked by the echoes of the cosmic abyss and triumphant resilience, unfolded like a cosmic epic—an eternal saga that transcended mortal fears and celebrated the enduring bond between mortal souls and the cosmic forces that shaped their destinies.

Chapter 18: Symphony of Celestial Woe

As the friends continued their cosmic journey, guided by the celestial map, they found themselves drawn to a realm where celestial

forces clashed in a symphony of woe. The Veilstitcher's influence, ever watchful, resonated with a sense of foreboding as they approached an ethereal battleground where cosmic entities engaged in an otherworldly conflict. The amulet, typically radiant with cosmic energies, flickered with an ominous luminosity that mirrored the discordant atmosphere surrounding the celestial battleground.

The celestial map, now marked by constellations that seemed to clash in celestial strife, directed the friends toward the epicenter of the cosmic conflict. As they ventured deeper into the celestial battleground, the cosmic energies pulsated with an unsettling intensity, and the amulet emitted an erratic glow that reflected the cosmic turbulence that surrounded them.

In the midst of the celestial clash, the friends witnessed cosmic entities locked in a dance of ethereal combat. Celestial beings, once guardians of cosmic harmony, now clashed in discordant symphonies that reverberated through the interconnected tapestry. The Veilstitcher's spectral form, a spectral witness to the celestial woe, communicated a tale of ancient grievances that had ignited the cosmic conflict.

The celestial map, now revealing constellations that depicted celestial entities entwined in celestial strife, guided the friends through the celestial battleground. Shadows danced with malevolent glee, and the amulet emitted a protective aura that shielded them from the cosmic energies unleashed in the celestial clash.

As they navigated through the cosmic battlefield, the friends encountered spectral remnants—echoes of celestial entities consumed by the warring energies. The Veilstitcher's influence, though a vigilant observer, conveyed a sense of cosmic sorrow as the friends witnessed the tragic consequences of the celestial conflict. The amulet, their cosmic protector, resonated with a determination to understand the origins of the celestial woe.

In the heart of the celestial battleground, the friends discovered an ancient cosmic artifact—a relic of power that had become a focal point for the warring energies. Eldritch symbols adorned the artifact, resonating with the echoes of ancient grievances that fueled the celestial conflict. The celestial map, now etched with constellations that depicted the artifact's role in the celestial strife, guided them toward understanding the artifact's significance.

The Veilstitcher's spectral form, now a spectral historian, communicated the cosmic tale of how the artifact had become a catalyst for the celestial woe. Betrayals, vendettas, and cosmic vendettas had intertwined in a cosmic dance that threatened to unravel the very fabric of the interconnected tapestry. The amulet, resonating with the cosmic revelations, emitted a luminescent glow that mirrored the friends' determination to quell the celestial conflict.

As they approached the cosmic artifact, the friends faced celestial guardians—entities consumed by the warring energies that emanated from the relic. Shadows, animated by ancient grievances, seemed to materialize in ethereal forms, and the Veilstitcher's spectral form guided them through trials that tested their resolve against the celestial woe.

The amulet, their cosmic defense, emitted a protective aura that shimmered with radiant light. The celestial map, now pulsating with constellations that depicted the celestial guardians in moments of cosmic despair, guided the friends through the celestial trials. The Veilstitcher's influence, though tinged with cosmic sorrow, urged them to confront the spectral remnants and restore cosmic harmony.

In their cosmic struggle against the celestial guardians, the friends uncovered the origins of the ancient vendettas that had fueled the celestial conflict. Betrayals, forged alliances, and cosmic vendettas had intertwined in a cosmic dance that threatened to consume the

celestial battleground. The Veilstitcher's spectral form, a witness to the unfolding cosmic drama, conveyed a sense of urgency as the friends unraveled the cosmic grievances that fueled the celestial woe.

The amulet, attuned to the cosmic revelations, emitted pulses of resonant light that harmonized with the celestial map's guidance. As the friends faced the celestial guardians, the cosmic energies seemed to shift in response to their cosmic understanding. Shadows, once animated by warring energies, now flickered with moments of celestial harmony.

In a pivotal moment of the celestial struggle, the friends realized that the only way to quell the celestial conflict was to sever the ties that bound the ancient vendettas. The Veilstitcher's spectral form, now a cosmic arbitrator, guided them through a celestial ritual that sought to break the cosmic cycles of vengeance and restore the celestial entities' understanding.

As they channeled their cosmic abilities into the ritual, the cosmic energies responded with an ethereal symphony. Shadows, once animated by ancient grievances, now danced in a harmonious ballet. The celestial map, now pulsating with threads of cosmic understanding, guided the friends through the intricate maneuvers needed to mend the celestial entities' fractured consciousness.

In the cosmic aftermath of the ritual, the celestial guardians transformed. The cosmic vendettas that had fueled their spectral existence seemed to dissipate, and the celestial energies responded with a serene luminescence. The Veilstitcher's influence, now a cosmic mediator, conveyed a sense of resolution as the friends witnessed the celestial entities find peace within the cosmic battleground.

The amulet, though worn by the cosmic struggle, emitted a radiant glow that mirrored the friends' triumph over the celestial woe. The celestial map, now cleared of constellations depicting discord, revealed a new cosmic equilibrium that reflected the friends'

ability to mediate the celestial conflict and bring about a cosmic understanding.

As the friends ascended from the celestial battleground, the Veilstitcher's spectral form regained its ethereal brilliance. The amulet, though scarred by the cosmic ordeal, pulsed with a renewed vitality. The celestial map, now cleared of the cosmic disharmony, guided them toward new frontiers in the interconnected tapestry.

The friends, forever changed by their harrowing encounter with the celestial woe, continued their cosmic odyssey with a heightened awareness of the cosmic perils that lurked in the vast expanse. The Veilstitcher's influence, now a cosmic mediator, accompanied them as a guiding force. The amulet, a resilient artifact that bore the scars of their cosmic ordeal, resonated with a luminous brilliance that symbolized their triumph over the discordant echoes of the celestial woe.

The celestial map, once tainted by cosmic disharmony, now guided the friends toward realms where cosmic wonders awaited discovery. The echoes of the unknown, though still haunting, whispered tales of cosmic resilience and the indomitable spirit that defied the discord of the celestial woe. The friends, forever entwined by the shared horrors they had faced, embraced the mysteries that awaited them in the uncharted territories of the interconnected tapestry.

Their cosmic odyssey, now marked by the echoes of the celestial woe and triumphant resilience, unfolded like a cosmic epic—an eternal saga that transcended mortal fears and celebrated the enduring bond between mortal souls and the cosmic forces that shaped their destinies.

Chapter 19: The Veil's Unraveling

In the wake of their triumph over the celestial woe, the friends felt a profound shift in the cosmic fabric as the celestial map guided them towards the heart of an impending cosmic catastrophe. The

Veilstitcher's influence, though a steadfast companion, resonated with an urgency that transcended the cosmic echoes. The amulet, usually radiant with cosmic energies, emitted a flickering glow that mirrored the unsettling atmosphere surrounding them.

The celestial map, now marked by constellations that seemed to spiral in cosmic distress, directed the friends towards an ancient cosmic observatory—a place where the threads of reality and the cosmic veil converged. As they approached the observatory, the shadows deepened, and the amulet pulsed with an ominous luminosity that hinted at the cosmic perils that awaited them.

In the observatory's sacred chambers, the friends discovered an ancient cosmic artifact—an unraveling veil that bound the threads of the interconnected tapestry. Eldritch symbols adorned the artifact, resonating with an unsettling energy that sent shivers down their spines. The Veilstitcher's spectral form, now a solemn guide, communicated a tale of cosmic imbalance that threatened to rupture the very fabric of reality.

The celestial map, now etched with constellations that depicted the cosmic veil's unraveling, guided the friends through the cosmic observatory. Shadows danced with malevolent glee, and the amulet emitted a protective aura that shielded them from the cosmic disturbances that emanated from the artifact.

As they explored the observatory's depths, the friends faced cosmic guardians—entities tasked with protecting the artifact that held the threads of the cosmic veil. The Veilstitcher's influence, though tinged with cosmic sorrow, urged them to confront the guardians and understand the source of the cosmic imbalance. The amulet, their cosmic shield, resonated with a determination to prevent the impending catastrophe.

In the heart of the observatory, the friends discovered celestial inscriptions that chronicled the artifact's role in maintaining the

cosmic equilibrium. The celestial map, now revealing constellations that depicted the threads of reality woven into the cosmic veil, guided them towards an understanding of the artifact's significance. The Veilstitcher's spectral form, now a cosmic historian, conveyed the dire consequences of the cosmic veil's unraveling.

As they deciphered the celestial inscriptions, the friends learned of an ancient cosmic entity—the Weaver of Realms—who had crafted the cosmic veil to ensure the harmony of the interconnected tapestry. Betrayals and vendettas had driven the cosmic entity to an abyss of despair, leading to a cosmic curse that now threatened to shatter the delicate threads of reality.

The Veilstitcher's spectral form, now a cosmic weaver, guided the friends through a ritual to commune with the Weaver of Realms and understand the cosmic curse that had befallen the artifact. The amulet, resonating with the cosmic revelations, emitted a luminescent glow that mirrored the friends' determination to mend the unraveling cosmic veil.

As they channeled their cosmic abilities into the ritual, the cosmic observatory responded with ethereal energies. Shadows, once animated by cosmic imbalance, now seemed to waver in a cosmic dance. The celestial map, now pulsating with threads of cosmic understanding, guided the friends through the intricate maneuvers needed to commune with the Weaver of Realms.

In the cosmic communion, the friends glimpsed the Weaver of Realms—a spectral entity consumed by cosmic despair. The Veilstitcher's spectral form, now a compassionate guide, urged them to unravel the cosmic curse that bound the Weaver and restore balance to the interconnected tapestry. The amulet, attuned to the cosmic revelations, emitted pulses of resonant light that harmonized with the celestial map's guidance.

As the friends faced the Weaver of Realms, the cosmic entity conveyed the tale of its descent into cosmic despair. Betrayals and vendettas had shattered the cosmic harmony it sought to maintain, leading to a curse that now threatened to unravel the very fabric of reality. The Veilstitcher's influence, now a cosmic mediator, urged the friends to break the chains of despair and restore hope to the Weaver.

In a pivotal moment of cosmic communion, the friends realized that the only way to mend the cosmic veil was to heal the Weaver of Realms' cosmic despair. The Veilstitcher's spectral form, now a cosmic healer, guided them through a celestial ritual that sought to break the cosmic curse and bring solace to the beleaguered cosmic entity.

As they channeled their cosmic abilities into the ritual, the cosmic observatory responded with an ethereal symphony. Shadows, once animated by cosmic despair, now seemed to waver in a harmonious ballet. The celestial map, now pulsating with threads of cosmic understanding, guided the friends through the intricate maneuvers needed to heal the Weaver of Realms.

In the cosmic aftermath of the ritual, the Weaver of Realms' spectral form transformed. Despair gave way to a serene luminescence, and the cosmic energies responded with a harmonious resonance. The Veilstitcher's influence, now a cosmic healer, conveyed a sense of resolution as the friends witnessed the Weaver find peace within the cosmic observatory.

The amulet, though worn by the cosmic struggle, emitted a radiant glow that mirrored the friends' triumph over the cosmic despair. The celestial map, now cleared of constellations depicting the cosmic curse, revealed a new cosmic equilibrium that reflected the friends' ability to mend the unraveling threads of the cosmic veil.

As the friends ascended from the cosmic observatory, the Veil-stitcher's spectral form regained its ethereal brilliance. The amulet, though scarred by the cosmic ordeal, pulsed with a renewed vitality. The celestial map, now cleared of the cosmic imbalance, guided them toward new frontiers in the interconnected tapestry.

The friends, forever changed by their harrowing encounter with the unraveling cosmic veil, continued their cosmic odyssey with a heightened awareness of the cosmic perils that lurked in the vast expanse. The Veilstitcher's influence, now a cosmic healer, accompanied them as a guiding force. The amulet, a resilient artifact that bore the scars of their cosmic ordeal, resonated with a luminous brilliance that symbolized their triumph over the cosmic despair.

The celestial map, once tainted by cosmic imbalance, now guided the friends toward realms where cosmic wonders awaited discovery. The echoes of the unknown, though still haunting, whispered tales of cosmic resilience and the indomitable spirit that defied the cosmic despair. The friends, forever entwined by the shared horrors they had faced, embraced the mysteries that awaited them in the uncharted territories of the interconnected tapestry.

Their cosmic odyssey, now marked by the mending of the cosmic veil and triumphant resilience, unfolded like a cosmic epic—an eternal saga that transcended mortal fears and celebrated the enduring bond between mortal souls and the cosmic forces that shaped their destinies.

As the friends ventured forth from the cosmic observatory, a newfound clarity enveloped the interconnected tapestry. The Veil-stitcher's spectral form, once a guardian in cosmic despair, radiated with a luminous brilliance that mirrored the cosmic healing they had achieved. The amulet, though marked by the trials of unraveling cosmic threads, retained a resilient glow—a testament to their ability to mend the cosmic veil.

The celestial map, now cleared of constellations depicting imbalance, guided the friends towards realms where cosmic wonders awaited discovery. The echoes of the unknown, though still haunting, whispered tales of cosmic resilience and the indomitable spirit that defied the cosmic despair. The friends, forever entwined by the shared horrors they had faced, embraced the mysteries that awaited them in the uncharted territories of the interconnected tapestry.

Their cosmic odyssey, now marked by the mending of the cosmic veil and triumphant resilience, unfolded like a cosmic epic—an eternal saga that transcended mortal fears and celebrated the enduring bond between mortal souls and the cosmic forces that shaped their destinies.

As they ventured into unexplored cosmic realms, the friends encountered celestial wonders that seemed to shimmer with a renewed vitality. The Veilstitcher's influence, now a beacon of cosmic healing, guided them through realms where echoes of their cosmic deeds resonated with celestial echoes. The amulet, a cosmic artifact infused with the power of mended threads, pulsed with a rhythmic glow that echoed the harmony they had restored.

The celestial map, now revealing constellations that depicted the friends as cosmic healers, guided them towards realms where their presence was needed. Shadows, once animated by cosmic despair, now seemed to retreat in the wake of their cosmic healing. The friends, now custodians of celestial balance, embraced their role in preserving the interconnected tapestry.

In their cosmic journey, the friends encountered celestial beings whose threads of reality had frayed. The Veilstitcher's spectral form, now a cosmic guide in mending, urged them to extend their healing touch to those ensnared by cosmic disarray. The amulet, resonating with the threads of cosmic understanding, emitted a gentle glow that mirrored their commitment to restoring celestial harmony.

As they traversed through realms touched by cosmic imbalance, the friends faced cosmic trials that tested their newfound abilities as healers of the interconnected tapestry. The Veilstitcher's influence, now a cosmic mentor, guided them through rituals that sought to mend the threads of reality and restore balance to celestial entities caught in the throes of cosmic disarray.

The amulet, a conduit of cosmic energies, emitted pulses of healing light that harmonized with the celestial map's guidance. Shadows, once animated by cosmic despair, now seemed to dissipate as the friends embraced their cosmic roles as healers. The echoes of their cosmic deeds reverberated through the interconnected tapestry, leaving a trail of celestial balance in their wake.

In a celestial sanctuary, the friends encountered a cosmic entity—a guardian of the celestial realms whose threads of reality had become entangled in cosmic disarray. The Veilstitcher's spectral form, now a cosmic healer, communicated with the entity in a language of cosmic understanding. The amulet, resonating with the threads of mended reality, emitted a soothing aura that calmed the entity's cosmic unrest.

As the friends performed a cosmic ritual to heal the guardian's threads, the celestial sanctuary responded with ethereal energies. The Veilstitcher's influence, now a cosmic conductor, guided them through the intricate maneuvers needed to mend the celestial guardian's frayed threads. The amulet, attuned to the cosmic revelations, emitted pulses of resonant light that harmonized with the celestial map's guidance.

In the cosmic aftermath of the ritual, the celestial guardian's spectral form transformed. Threads once entangled in cosmic disarray now shimmered with a serene luminescence. The Veilstitcher's influence, now a cosmic healer, conveyed a sense of fulfillment as

the friends witnessed the guardian find peace within the celestial sanctuary.

The amulet, though worn by the cosmic struggle, emitted a radiant glow that mirrored the friends' triumph as cosmic healers. The celestial map, now cleared of constellations depicting cosmic disarray, revealed a new cosmic equilibrium that reflected the friends' ability to extend their healing touch to the interconnected tapestry.

As the friends continued their cosmic journey, the Veilstitcher's spectral form, now a cosmic mentor, guided them towards realms where celestial entities awaited their healing touch. The amulet, a beacon of cosmic balance, pulsed with a rhythmic glow that echoed the harmonious resonance they had restored. The celestial map, now revealing constellations that depicted the friends as cosmic healers, guided them towards realms where their presence was needed.

Their cosmic odyssey, now marked by the mending of celestial threads and triumphant resilience, unfolded like a cosmic epic—an eternal saga that transcended mortal fears and celebrated the enduring bond between mortal souls and the cosmic forces that shaped their destinies.

Chapter 20: The Cosmic Reckoning

In the final leg of their cosmic odyssey, the friends sensed a gathering cosmic storm—a tempest that threatened to unravel the very fabric of reality. The Veilstitcher's influence, a vigilant beacon, resonated with a profound urgency that transcended the echoes of their past encounters. The amulet, though resilient, emitted a pulsating glow that mirrored the unsettling cosmic energies that surrounded them.

The celestial map, now marked by constellations that seemed to writhe in cosmic distress, guided the friends towards the epicenter of the looming cosmic tempest. As they approached, the shadows deepened, and the cosmic storm manifested in swirling patterns of

ethereal chaos. The Veilstitcher's spectral form, now a harbinger of cosmic reckoning, communicated a dire prophecy of an ancient cosmic entity—the Stormweaver—whose fury threatened to engulf the interconnected tapestry.

In the heart of the cosmic storm, the friends confronted an ethereal vortex—a manifestation of the Stormweaver's wrath. Eldritch symbols adorned the vortex, resonating with an ominous energy that sent shivers down their spines. The celestial map, now etched with constellations that depicted the Stormweaver's fury, guided them towards understanding the origin of the cosmic tempest.

The Veilstitcher's spectral form, now a cosmic seer, revealed the tale of the Stormweaver—an ancient cosmic entity imprisoned by the threads of reality in ages past. Betrayals and vendettas had fueled the Stormweaver's rage, and its spectral essence now sought to unleash cosmic chaos upon the interconnected tapestry. The amulet, resonating with the cosmic revelations, emitted a luminescent glow that mirrored the friends' determination to quell the cosmic reckoning.

As they ventured into the heart of the cosmic vortex, the friends faced celestial guardians—entities corrupted by the Stormweaver's malevolent influence. The Veilstitcher's influence, though tinged with cosmic sorrow, urged them to confront the guardians and understand the depths of the cosmic tempest's power. The amulet, their cosmic shield, resonated with a determination to resist the impending catastrophe.

In the cosmic battleground, the friends encountered remnants of cosmic entities ensnared by the Stormweaver's malevolent influence. Shadows, animated by cosmic fury, seemed to writhe with an other-worldly malevolence. The Veilstitcher's spectral form guided them through trials that tested their resolve against the impending cosmic reckoning.

The celestial map, now revealing constellations that depicted the enslaved cosmic entities, guided the friends through the cosmic trials. The amulet, emitting a protective aura, shimmered with a resilient light that mirrored their commitment to resist the cosmic tempest's onslaught.

As they navigated through the cosmic chaos, the friends uncovered an ancient cosmic prison—an ethereal cage that held the Stormweaver's spectral essence. Eldritch symbols adorned the prison, resonating with the echoes of ancient grievances that fueled the cosmic reckoning. The celestial map, now etched with constellations that depicted the prison's significance, guided them towards understanding the key to subduing the Stormweaver's fury.

The Veilstitcher's spectral form, now a cosmic keybearer, communicated a ritual to unlock the prison and confront the Stormweaver. The amulet, resonating with the cosmic revelations, emitted a luminescent glow that mirrored the friends' determination to face the ancient cosmic entity. As they channeled their cosmic abilities into the ritual, the cosmic prison responded with an ethereal symphony.

Shadows, once animated by cosmic fury, now seemed to waver in a discordant ballet. The celestial map, now pulsating with threads of cosmic understanding, guided the friends through the intricate maneuvers needed to unlock the ancient prison. The Veilstitcher's influence, now a cosmic guide, urged them to unravel the Stormweaver's malevolent influence and restore balance to the interconnected tapestry.

In the cosmic aftermath of the ritual, the ancient prison released the Stormweaver's spectral essence. The friends, now confronted by the embodiment of cosmic fury, felt the weight of the impending reckoning bearing down upon them. The Veilstitcher's spectral form, now a cosmic defender, communicated a sense of urgency as the friends prepared to face the Stormweaver's wrath.

The celestial map, now depicting constellations that mirrored the Stormweaver's cosmic fury, guided the friends through a cosmic trial that tested their resilience against the impending reckoning. The amulet, their only defense against the cosmic tempest, emitted a protective aura that shimmered with a determination to resist the ancient entity's onslaught.

In their cosmic struggle against the Stormweaver's spectral essence, the friends uncovered the origins of the ancient grievances that had fueled the cosmic reckoning. Betrayals, vendettas, and cosmic vendettas had intertwined in a malevolent dance that threatened to consume the interconnected tapestry. The Veilstitcher's spectral form, a witness to the unfolding cosmic drama, conveyed a sense of urgency as the friends unraveled the ancient cosmic entity's malevolent influence.

The amulet, attuned to the cosmic revelations, emitted pulses of resonant light that harmonized with the celestial map's guidance. As the friends faced the Stormweaver's spectral essence, the cosmic tempest seemed to shift in response to their cosmic understanding. Shadows, once animated by cosmic fury, now flickered with moments of cosmic discord.

In a pivotal moment of the cosmic struggle, the friends realized that the only way to quell the Stormweaver's wrath was to break the chains of ancient grievances. The Veilstitcher's spectral form, now a cosmic arbitrator, guided them through a celestial ritual that sought to sever the cosmic cycles of vengeance and restore the ancient entity's fractured consciousness.

As they channeled their cosmic abilities into the ritual, the cosmic tempest responded with an ethereal symphony. Shadows, once animated by cosmic fury, now seemed to waver in a harmonious ballet. The celestial map, now pulsating with threads of cosmic

understanding, guided the friends through the intricate maneuvers needed to mend the Stormweaver's spectral essence.

In the cosmic aftermath of the ritual, the Stormweaver's spectral essence transformed. Fury gave way to a serene luminescence, and the cosmic tempest seemed to retreat. The Veilstitcher's influence, now a cosmic mediator, conveyed a sense of resolution as the friends witnessed the ancient entity find peace within the interconnected tapestry.

The amulet, though worn by the cosmic struggle, emitted a radiant glow that mirrored the friends' triumph over the impending reckoning. The celestial map, now cleared of constellations depicting discord, revealed a new cosmic equilibrium that reflected the friends' ability to confront the ancient cosmic entity and emerge unscathed.

As the friends ascended from the cosmic battleground, the Veilstitcher's spectral form regained its ethereal brilliance. The amulet, though scarred by the cosmic ordeal, pulsed with a renewed vitality. The celestial map, now cleared of the cosmic turmoil, guided them towards new frontiers in the interconnected tapestry.

The friends, forever changed by their harrowing encounter with the cosmic reckoning, continued their cosmic odyssey with a heightened awareness of the cosmic perils that lurked in the vast expanse. The Veilstitcher's influence, now a cosmic mediator, accompanied them as a guiding force. The amulet, a resilient artifact that bore the scars of their cosmic ordeal, resonated with a luminous brilliance that symbolized their triumph over the impending reckoning.

The celestial map, once tainted by the cosmic turmoil, now guided the friends toward realms where cosmic wonders awaited discovery. The echoes of the unknown, though still haunting, whispered tales of cosmic resilience and the indomitable spirit that defied the cosmic tempest. The friends, forever entwined by the shared

horrors they had faced, embraced the mysteries that awaited them in the uncharted territories of the interconnected tapestry.

Their cosmic odyssey, now marked by the triumphant resolution of the cosmic reckoning, unfolded like a cosmic epic—an eternal saga that transcended mortal fears and celebrated the enduring bond between mortal souls and the cosmic forces that shaped their destinies.

As they journeyed into the unexplored cosmic realms, the friends encountered celestial wonders that seemed to radiate with the echoes of their victorious struggle. The Veilstitcher's influence, now a beacon of cosmic resolution, guided them through realms where echoes of their cosmic deeds resonated with celestial echoes. The amulet, a cosmic artifact infused with the power of triumphant threads, pulsed with a rhythmic glow that echoed the harmony they had restored.

The celestial map, now revealing constellations that depicted the friends as cosmic defenders, guided them toward realms where their presence was needed. Shadows, once animated by cosmic fury, now seemed to retreat in the wake of their cosmic triumph. The friends, now guardians of celestial balance, embraced their role in preserving the interconnected tapestry.

In their cosmic journey, the friends encountered celestial beings whose threads of reality had been freed from the shackles of ancient grievances. The Veilstitcher's spectral form, now a cosmic liberator, urged them to extend their cosmic influence to those freed from the burden of cosmic turmoil. The amulet, resonating with the threads of triumphant reality, emitted a radiant glow that mirrored their commitment to safeguarding the celestial realms.

As they traversed through realms touched by cosmic liberation, the friends faced cosmic trials that tested their newfound abilities as defenders of the interconnected tapestry. The Veilstitcher's

influence, now a cosmic mentor, guided them through rituals that sought to fortify the threads of reality and preserve balance in celestial entities freed from ancient shackles.

The amulet, a conduit of cosmic energies, emitted pulses of protective light that harmonized with the celestial map's guidance. Shadows, once animated by cosmic turmoil, now seemed to dissipate as the friends embraced their cosmic roles as defenders. The echoes of their cosmic deeds reverberated through the interconnected tapestry, leaving a trail of celestial balance in their wake.

In a celestial sanctuary, the friends encountered a cosmic entity—a guardian of the celestial realms whose threads of reality had been freed from ancient shackles. The Veilstitcher's spectral form, now a cosmic liberator, communicated with the entity in a language of cosmic understanding. The amulet, resonating with the threads of triumphant reality, emitted a soothing aura that celebrated the entity's cosmic liberation.

As the friends reveled in the cosmic liberation, the celestial sanctuary responded with ethereal energies. The Veilstitcher's influence, now a cosmic conductor of harmony, guided them through the intricate maneuvers needed to celebrate the celestial guardian's newfound freedom. The amulet, attuned to the cosmic revelations, emitted pulses of resonant light that harmonized with the celestial map's guidance.

In the cosmic aftermath of the celebration, the celestial guardian's spectral form radiated with joy. Threads once bound by ancient grievances now shimmered with a serene luminescence. The Veilstitcher's influence, now a cosmic celebrant, conveyed a sense of fulfillment as the friends witnessed the guardian revel in newfound peace within the celestial sanctuary.

The amulet, though worn by the cosmic struggle, emitted a radiant glow that mirrored the friends' triumph as cosmic liberators.

The celestial map, now cleared of constellations depicting ancient shackles, revealed a new cosmic equilibrium that reflected the friends' ability to free celestial entities from the burden of cosmic turmoil.

As the friends continued their cosmic journey, the Veilstitcher's spectral form, now a cosmic celebrant, guided them toward realms where celestial entities awaited their liberating touch. The amulet, a beacon of cosmic liberation, pulsed with a rhythmic glow that echoed the joy they had spread. The celestial map, now revealing constellations that depicted the friends as cosmic liberators, guided them toward realms where their presence was needed.

Their cosmic odyssey, now marked by the celebration of cosmic liberation and triumphant resolution, unfolded like a cosmic epic—an eternal saga that transcended mortal fears and celebrated the enduring bond between mortal souls and the cosmic forces that shaped their destinies.

Stormweaver
The Goatman Lives
By
Doug Hensley
Table Of Contents

Chapter 1: The Unknown Encounter

- A group of friends on a camping trip
- Mysterious noises in the woods at night

Chapter 2: Whispering Shadows

- Strange occurrences escalate
- Unsettling whispers heard in the darkness

Chapter 3: The Legend Unveiled

- Local tales of the Goatman shared around the campfire
- Skepticism and unease among the group

Chapter 4: A Fateful Decision

- The group decides to investigate the legend

- Deep into the forest, the atmosphere thickens

Chapter 5: Signs of the Goatman

- Disturbing symbols and tracks discovered
- Tension grows as reality sets in

Chapter 6: Disappearing Act

- One member of the group goes missing
- Panic and fear grip the others

Chapter 7: Unholy Alliance

- Remaining friends unite to find the missing person
- A pact to face the Goatman together

Chapter 8: Haunting Memories

- Flashbacks reveal past encounters with the Goatman
- Characters confront their own fears

Chapter 9: Night of the Full Moon

- The group faces the Goatman for the first time
- A terrifying chase through the woods ensues

Chapter 10: The Goatman's Curse

- Survivor guilt and paranoia set in
- The Goatman's curse becomes evident

Chapter 11: The Unseen Stalker

- Unexplained phenomena haunt the group
- A feeling of being constantly watched

Chapter 12: The Goatman's Lair

- Discover a hidden lair deep in the woods
- A horrifying revelation awaits

Chapter 13: Descent into Madness

- Characters grapple with their sanity
- Unexplainable events intensify

Chapter 14: The Goatman's Call

- A hypnotic call draws the group deeper
- Internal conflicts escalate

Chapter 15: Sacrificial Night

- The group faces a choice to save themselves or succumb to the Goatman's curse
- Tension peaks as the night unfolds

Chapter 16: Midnight Ritual

- Ritualistic elements unfold
- The Goatman's power grows stronger

Chapter 17: The Final Confrontation

- Confrontation with the Goatman in a climactic battle
- Sacrifices made to break the curse

Chapter 18: Lingering Shadows

- The aftermath of the confrontation
- The group struggles to return to normalcy

Chapter 19: Epilogue of Fear

- Lingering fears and unanswered questions
- Hints that the Goatman may still be out there

Chapter 20: The Legend Lives On

- Closing with a new group stumbling upon the same legend
- The cycle continues, leaving the ending open-ended and unsettling

Chapter 1: The Unknown Encounter

The dense forest canopy loomed overhead, casting eerie shadows as the group of friends, led by the adventurous spirit of Mark, ventured deeper into the wilderness. A cool breeze rustled the leaves, creating an ominous symphony that echoed through the trees. Their laughter filled the air, a stark contrast to the quiet unease that settled with the setting sun.

As darkness embraced the forest, the friends gathered around a crackling campfire. The flickering flames danced to the rhythm of their hushed conversations. An unsettling feeling hung in the air,

unnoticed by most, except for Emily, who couldn't shake off the sensation that they were not alone.

Unknown to the group, distant whispers intertwined with the nocturnal symphony, carried by the wind. Mark, the leader of the expedition, dismissed them as the rustling of leaves or the murmur of the night creatures. Little did they know that these whispers were the first ominous notes of a malevolent tune.

As the night wore on, the friends shared stories, trying to drown out the disconcerting sounds around them. In the midst of laughter, a sudden silence fell upon the group, broken only by the distant howl of a lone wolf. They exchanged uneasy glances, their camaraderie momentarily fractured.

The crackling fire cast eerie shadows on the surrounding trees, creating grotesque shapes that seemed to watch the friends with malevolent intent. An inexplicable tension wrapped itself around them, tightening like a coil. Emily's gaze flickered nervously between the dancing flames and the dark recesses of the forest.

The once vibrant atmosphere now carried an undertone of dread. Mark, attempting to dispel the growing unease, suggested exploring the nearby trails. Reluctantly, the group ventured into the heart of the woods, guided only by dim flashlights that struggled to penetrate the thick darkness.

As they meandered through the labyrinthine paths, the night seemed to swallow them whole. The moon cast an eerie glow, revealing twisted branches that resembled skeletal fingers reaching out from the shadows. Unbeknownst to the friends, unseen eyes observed their every move.

The distant echoes of footsteps, not matching the rhythm of their own, reverberated through the night. A cold shiver ran down Emily's spine as she whispered to Mark, "Did you hear that?" He

dismissed it as their imagination playing tricks, but doubt lingered in his eyes.

The trail, once familiar, now felt like an ever-twisting maze. Panic set in as the friends realized they were lost. The forest seemed to conspire against them, distorting their perception of time and space. Anxiety gripped the group, amplifying the unsettling aura that clung to the night.

A blood-curdling scream shattered the silence, sending shockwaves through the group. Fear etched deep lines on their faces as they turned toward the source. In the suffocating darkness, a silhouette moved swiftly, disappearing among the gnarled trees.

Panic took hold, and the friends sprinted back towards the campsite, fueled by a primal instinct to survive. The once-familiar surroundings now felt alien and menacing. The forest, alive with unseen malevolence, seemed to mock their feeble attempts to escape.

The crackling campfire welcomed them back, but the safety it once provided now felt like a fragile illusion. The missing member, a specter in their midst, cast a long shadow over the group. The night, far from over, held secrets that would unravel as the friends clung to the flickering flames, unaware of the terror that awaited them in the heart of the haunted woods.

Chapter 2: Whispering Shadows

The remnants of their once-jovial campfire flickered in the oppressive darkness. Unsettled by the earlier scream, the friends huddled close, their faces etched with fear. Mark, the bravest among them, attempted to lighten the mood with nervous jokes, but the unease lingered like a thick fog.

As they sat in the ominous stillness, the haunting whispers returned. The friends exchanged anxious glances, realizing the sounds were more than mere forest murmurs. The words, though

unintelligible, seemed to crawl beneath their skin, instilling a primal fear that transcended rationality.

Emily, the most sensitive to the otherworldly, clutched her ears, desperate to block out the spectral voices. The whispers intertwined with the wind, creating an otherworldly melody that resonated through the haunted woods. Shadows danced menacingly, morphing into grotesque forms that seemed to mimic the torment in the friends' hearts.

Mark, determined to maintain a semblance of control, suggested investigating the source of the whispers. Armed with flashlights, the group ventured into the inky darkness, guided by the haunting voices that seemed to lead them deeper into the heart of the haunted woods.

The forest, now transformed into a realm of spectral uncertainty, played tricks on their senses. Trees twisted into nightmarish shapes, their branches reaching out like skeletal fingers. Each step felt like a descent into an abyss, and the whispers grew louder, forming an otherworldly chorus that resonated through the friends' minds.

A surreal fog enveloped the path, distorting reality. Shadows detached from the trees, taking on a sinister life of their own. Unseen eyes followed the group's every move, and the air became dense with an otherworldly energy that made it difficult to breathe.

Amidst the disorienting whispers, a distant figure materialized before them. The friends froze, their flashlights trembling in their hands. The silhouette seemed to flicker between the shadows, an elusive presence that defied comprehension. Panic gripped the group as the figure approached with an otherworldly grace.

With each step, the whispers intensified, revealing fragments of a haunting narrative. The legend of the Goatman, an entity that blurred the line between man and beast, echoed through the spectral voices. Dread tightened its grip on the friends as they realized

they were entangled in a story that surpassed the boundaries of the known.

A sudden gust of wind extinguished their flashlights, plunging them into pitch darkness. The whispers crescendoed into an unsettling cacophony, weaving a narrative that spoke of ancient curses and forbidden rituals. The friends stumbled blindly, guided only by the haunting voices that seemed to mock their feeble attempts to escape the encroaching nightmare.

As they fumbled through the labyrinthine paths, the forest itself seemed to conspire against them. Trees leaned menacingly, forming an impenetrable barrier that distorted their perception of space. Panic reached its zenith when the friends realized they were caught in a malevolent force beyond their understanding.

In the heart of the haunted woods, the whispers reached a deafening climax. The spectral figure, now a manifestation of pure terror, revealed itself as the harbinger of an ancient curse. The friends, paralyzed by fear, witnessed the birth of a nightmare that transcended the realm of the living.

The haunting voices echoed a chilling prophecy, sealing the friends' fate as pawns in a cosmic game. As the shadows enveloped them, the whispers faded into an ominous silence, leaving the group suspended in the chilling realization that they were now entwined with the legendary Goatman, and their journey into terror had only just begun.

Chapter 3: The Legend Unveiled

The haunted woods bore witness to the friends' descent into an abyss of fear, their breaths visible in the chilling air as they stood at the precipice of the unknown. Mark, the once-confident leader, now felt the weight of uncertainty press upon him, his eyes flickering nervously between the faces of his friends.

The chilling echoes of the Goatman's curse lingered, a sinister resonance that seeped into their very souls. As the group gathered around the remnants of their campfire, a shadowy figure materialized within the shifting shadows, a grotesque manifestation of the legend they had dismissed as mere folklore.

An air of disbelief hung heavy as the friends exchanged uneasy glances. Emily's wide eyes mirrored the terror reflected in the faces of the others. The whispers, now reduced to a haunting murmur, seemed to emanate from the very core of the forest, weaving a tapestry of dread that ensnared the group in an inescapable nightmare.

Against the backdrop of encroaching darkness, Mark attempted to rationalize the situation, attributing the spectral figure to mere illusions. However, the disconcerting reality betrayed his attempts at reassurance. The forest, alive with an otherworldly energy, pulsated with the ancient heartbeat of a malevolent force.

Doubt gnawed at the edges of the friends' minds as the whispers intensified. The spectral figure, now a tangible presence, beckoned them into the heart of the woods. The group, caught in the gravitational pull of an insidious force, hesitated on the brink of a decision that would seal their fate.

Reluctantly, they followed the elusive silhouette, their path illuminated by the pale glow of the moon. The forest, now a labyrinth of twisted shadows, seemed to breathe in tandem with the ethereal whispers that guided their journey. Unseen eyes observed their every move as they delved deeper into the legend that had come to life.

The friends stumbled upon an ancient clearing, adorned with eerie symbols etched into the earth. Mark, ever the skeptic, dismissed them as mere remnants of forgotten rituals. However, the others felt an otherworldly pull, an invisible thread connecting them to a malevolent past.

As the group examined the haunting symbols, the whispers coalesced into a narrative, recounting the tale of the Goatman—a creature that straddled the boundary between man and beast, a cursed entity bound by ancient rites. The friends, ensnared in the unfolding nightmare, now faced a reality that surpassed the confines of reason.

The spectral figure, a conduit of the Goatman's curse, revealed itself as a harbinger of impending doom. The friends, caught in the snare of a supernatural force, realized the legend was no mere folktale but a living nightmare that demanded their acknowledgment.

The moon cast an otherworldly glow upon the clearing as the group, paralyzed by a mixture of awe and terror, bore witness to the manifestation of the Goatman. A creature of nightmares stood before them, its eyes gleaming with an otherworldly intelligence that transcended the animalistic form it wore.

The atmosphere thickened with a palpable malevolence as the Goatman's presence dominated the clearing. Its form seemed to shift and contort, a grotesque dance that defied the laws of nature. The friends, gripped by an ancient fear, trembled as the Goatman spoke through the whispers, weaving a fate that intertwined with their very essence.

The friends, now bound by an unbreakable covenant, stood on the precipice of an unholy alliance. The Goatman, an embodiment of primordial terror, extended a spectral hand, inviting the group to embrace the curse that lurked within the shadows. Their destinies, forever altered, collided with the inexorable force of the legend, and the haunted woods echoed with the ominous laughter of a malevolent entity that reveled in the unfolding nightmare.

Chapter 4: A Fateful Decision

The haunted clearing pulsated with an otherworldly energy as the friends faced the enigmatic presence of the Goatman. The air

grew dense with the weight of an ancient curse, and the friends, caught between reason and the supernatural, found themselves at a crossroads that would define their destiny.

Mark, ever the voice of skepticism, hesitated. His logical mind resisted the pull of the unknown, urging him to reject the spectral hand that extended toward them. But the allure of the Goatman's power, shrouded in the whispers that echoed through the clearing, whispered promises of understanding and dominion over the mysterious forces that governed their existence.

Emily, sensitive to the ethereal currents, felt an irresistible draw. The whispers, now a seductive lullaby, caressed her consciousness, weaving visions of forbidden knowledge and a connection to realms beyond mortal comprehension. The choice lay before them, a perilous gambit that promised either enlightenment or descent into the abyss.

As the group teetered on the precipice of decision, the forest itself seemed to hold its breath. Unseen eyes observed their every move, and the shadows twisted in anticipation. The Goatman, a creature of the ancient woods, watched with an intelligence that transcended the animalistic facade it presented.

A cold wind whispered through the gnarled branches, carrying echoes of the past and the future. The choice, suspended in the eerie silence, would echo through the corridors of time, leaving an indelible mark on the souls of the friends who dared to confront the unknown.

In the midst of this spectral tableau, a memory surfaced in the recesses of Mark's mind—a childhood tale of a friend who disappeared in mysterious circumstances, whispered to be a victim of the Goatman's curse. The realization struck him like a bolt of lightning, igniting a primal fear that pulsed through his veins.

The haunting whispers morphed into chilling laughter, echoing Mark's internal turmoil. The Goatman, sensing the doubt, pressed its advantage, its eyes gleaming with an ancient malevolence. The clearing became a battleground of wills, where the tangible and intangible clashed in a dance of shadows.

As the friends deliberated, the forest responded to the rising tension. The ancient trees groaned, their branches contorting into grotesque forms. The whispers, now laced with impatience, intensified, urging the group to make their choice. The boundary between reality and nightmare blurred, and the friends found themselves ensnared in a surreal dreamscape.

Emily, tormented by the visions, trembled as conflicting emotions wrestled within her. The allure of forbidden knowledge clashed with an instinctual fear that warned of the consequences of tampering with forces beyond mortal understanding. The Goatman's eyes bore into her soul, a silent plea that transcended the limitations of spoken language.

Amidst the inner turmoil, a distant sound reverberated through the clearing—a mournful howl that cut through the spectral tension. The friends, momentarily distracted, turned toward the source. Shadows danced on the periphery of the clearing, and an unseen presence circled them like a predatory force.

The Goatman's form flickered, its patience wearing thin. The friends, aware of the imminent choice, felt the weight of the decision settle upon them like a suffocating cloak. The clearing, a stage for the cosmic drama, held its breath as the friends confronted the inevitable.

In a moment of collective resolve, the group stepped back from the outstretched hand of the Goatman. The whispers, now a discordant symphony of disappointment, echoed through the haunted

woods. The spectral figure, once a harbinger of alliance, recoiled into the shadows, its eyes aflame with an ancient ire.

As the friends retreated from the clearing, the forest sighed with relief. The ethereal tension dissipated, and the haunted woods returned to a semblance of stillness. The friends, marked by the encounter, stumbled back into the labyrinth of the forest, haunted by the knowledge that they had narrowly evaded a fate entwined with the Goatman's curse.

Yet, the shadows clung to their every step, and the whispers lingered, a reminder that the legend, far from defeated, awaited its next encounter with unsuspecting souls who dared to tread the boundary between the known and the supernatural. The night, pregnant with uncertainty, unfolded its mysteries as the friends navigated the haunted woods, forever changed by the fateful decision that spared them from the Goatman's insidious embrace.

T

Chapter 5: Signs of the Goatman

The haunted woods, having witnessed the friends' rejection of the Goatman's enticement, stirred with an ancient restlessness. The air crackled with latent energy as the group, still shaken from their encounter, navigated the twisting trails. The forest, once familiar, now seemed to shift and contort, its very essence reacting to the disturbance in the supernatural equilibrium.

Unspoken tension hung between the friends as they threaded through the labyrinth of shadows. The whispers, subdued but undeterred, lingered on the periphery of their consciousness. Emily, especially, felt the ethereal threads tugging at the edges of her sanity, weaving a tapestry of unnerving visions that threatened to unravel the fabric of her understanding.

A subtle rustling in the underbrush echoed through the stillness, sending a shiver down the spines of the friends. The forest seemed to

respond to their every step, alive with an unseen force that observed their every move. Paranoia took root, and the group cast nervous glances over their shoulders, half-expecting the Goatman's grotesque figure to materialize from the shadows.

Mark, burdened by the weight of his past and the consequences of the group's rejection, led the way with a furrowed brow. The once-confident leader now grappled with doubt, haunted by the memory of his childhood friend who had vanished into the clutches of the Goatman's curse. The forest, sensing his internal conflict, seemed to feed on his insecurities, twisting the trees into macabre forms that mirrored the tendrils of fear constricting his heart.

As they pressed forward, the trail revealed unsettling signs— twisted branches forming crude symbols, the earth marked with enigmatic patterns, and distant echoes that mimicked the mournful cries of the spectral creature they had narrowly evaded. The friends, unable to escape the omnipresent gaze of the haunted woods, exchanged wary glances as the realization dawned that the legend of the Goatman was far from a mere tale.

The group stumbled upon a clearing bathed in an eerie moonlit glow, its center dominated by a gnarled tree that bore the unmistakable markings of the supernatural. Emily, drawn by an invisible force, approached the ancient tree, her fingers tracing the symbols etched into its bark. The whispers, now a ghostly murmur, beckoned her to decipher the cryptic language of the Goatman's curse.

As Emily touched the symbols, the forest responded with a sudden surge of energy. The air crackled with an otherworldly charge, and the friends, captivated by a force beyond their control, witnessed the roots of the ancient tree twitch and writhe. The earth itself seemed to pulse with an unholy heartbeat as the symbols glowed with an ethereal light.

A ghostly apparition materialized before them, an echo of the Goatman's presence. Its eyes gleamed with an otherworldly intelligence, and a spectral voice resonated through the clearing. The friends, entranced by the unfolding spectacle, listened as the Goatman's tale unfolded—a story of ancient curses, forbidden pacts, and the insatiable hunger that bound it to the haunted woods.

As the spectral apparition spoke, the friends felt the tendrils of the Goatman's influence worming their way into their minds. Visions of torment and cosmic malevolence unfolded, weaving a narrative that blurred the boundaries between reality and nightmare. Emily, caught in the vortex of the supernatural revelation, glimpsed the unfathomable depths of the Goatman's ancient origins.

The whispers crescendoed, their words weaving an intricate web that ensnared the friends in a surreal dance of fate. The forest, now an extension of the Goatman's domain, pulsed with an ominous energy. The group, teetering on the precipice of enlightenment and damnation, faced the haunting reality that the legend had claimed them as unwilling participants in its insidious narrative.

In the midst of the ethereal revelation, a distant howl echoed through the clearing—a mournful cry that reverberated through the haunted woods. The spectral Goatman, its form flickering like a dying flame, receded into the shadows. The ancient tree, its roots once animated, settled into an eerie stillness.

The friends, released from the trance, stumbled backward, their minds reeling from the forbidden knowledge bestowed upon them. The clearing, now devoid of the Goatman's presence, returned to a deceptive calm. The haunted woods, however, retained the scars of their encounter, the symbols etched into the ancient tree serving as a chilling reminder that they were forever bound to the unfolding nightmare.

As the group retreated from the clearing, the forest whispered its secrets—a haunting lament that echoed through the shadows. The friends, marked by the signs of the Goatman, ventured deeper into the heart of the haunted woods, their destinies entwined with the ancient curse that refused to release its grip. The spectral whispers lingered, a spectral chorus that foretold of the terrors yet to unfold in the labyrinth of nightmares they now called home.

Chapter 6: Disappearing Act

The haunted woods, now saturated with the residual energy of the Goatman's revelation, clung to the friends like a suffocating shroud. The symbols etched into the ancient tree continued to glow with an otherworldly radiance, casting an eerie glow upon the path ahead. The air, thick with the weight of forbidden knowledge, pressed down on the group as they pressed forward, their fate intricately woven into the fabric of the supernatural.

Mark, haunted by the ghostly memories of his childhood friend's disappearance, felt an invisible force tugging at the edges of his consciousness. The whispers, once distant murmurs, now reverberated through his mind with an unsettling clarity. He strained to maintain composure, masking his internal turmoil behind a façade of false bravado. Unbeknownst to him, the haunted woods, sentient and malevolent, fed on his fear like a ravenous entity.

The trail, twisted and labyrinthine, seemed to shift with a will of its own. The friends, ensnared by the spectral threads that bound them to the Goatman's curse, navigated the surreal landscape with trepidation. The shadows played tricks on their senses, morphing into phantasmal shapes that seemed to watch with unseen eyes.

As the group delved deeper into the heart of the haunted woods, a palpable tension threaded through their camaraderie. Emily, marked by the spectral encounter at the ancient tree, felt an inexorable pull toward the unknown. The whispers, now a constant companion,

murmured secrets that transcended the realm of mortal understanding. Her eyes, once bright with curiosity, now reflected the unsettling wisdom bestowed upon her by the Goatman's revelation.

A distant howl echoed through the woods, a mournful cry that reverberated with a haunting resonance. The friends, halted by the spectral sound, exchanged uneasy glances. The Goatman's influence, a malevolent force that defied the natural order, now seemed to guide their every step. The path ahead, obscured by a foreboding mist, beckoned them into the heart of the supernatural enigma.

The trail, fraught with unseen perils, led the friends to a clearing bathed in an ethereal glow. A spectral figure materialized before them, its eyes gleaming with an otherworldly intelligence. The Goatman, a manifestation of cosmic dread, stood as a sentinel at the crossroads of their destiny.

In a voice that echoed through the haunted woods, the Goatman spoke, its words a haunting melody that resonated with the friends' deepest fears. The choices made, the destinies entwined, the group stood as unwitting participants in a cosmic drama that unfolded with a relentless momentum. The Goatman, a puppeteer of fate, reveled in the dance of shadows that played out in the haunted clearing.

As the spectral figure spoke, the surroundings warped into a surreal dreamscape. Reality and nightmare merged, and the friends found themselves suspended in a liminal space where time seemed to lose its meaning. Visions of the Goatman's cursed legacy unfolded—a tapestry of despair woven with threads of ancient malevolence.

Mark, tormented by memories of his lost friend, witnessed haunting scenes from the past. The woods became a theater of spectral apparitions, replaying moments of anguish and despair. The Goatman's voice, a spectral undertone, whispered forgotten secrets that clawed at the edges of his sanity.

Emily, sensitive to the ethereal currents, glimpsed glimpses of the future—a mosaic of tormented landscapes and spectral encounters. The haunted woods, now a maze of interconnected destinies, revealed a nightmarish tableau that unfolded with an inexorable inevitability.

As the visions played out, the friends, paralyzed by the supernatural revelation, became mere spectators in their own existential drama. The Goatman, a harbinger of cosmic terror, reveled in the torment it unleashed upon their minds. The clearing, a stage for the unfolding nightmare, pulsated with an otherworldly energy.

Suddenly, the visions ceased, and the friends, released from the spectral trance, found themselves standing in the clearing once more. The Goatman, its form flickering like a dying ember, faded into the shadows. The ancient tree, now devoid of the supernatural glow, stood as a silent witness to the cosmic theater that unfolded beneath its twisted branches.

The friends, disoriented and haunted by the echoes of the Goatman's revelations, staggered away from the clearing. The haunted woods, now a sentient labyrinth, seemed to rearrange itself, guiding the group deeper into the heart of the supernatural enigma.

As they pressed forward, a cold wind whispered through the twisted branches, carrying with it a chilling echo of the Goatman's laughter. The friends, caught in a cycle of existential dread, stumbled through the haunted woods, forever marked by the disappearing act that unfolded in the surreal clearing. The night, pregnant with cosmic uncertainty, stretched before them like an endless abyss, and the friends, ensnared by the spectral forces that governed their fate, plunged further into the inescapable nightmare that awaited in the shadowed depths of the ancient forest.

Chapter 7: Unholy Alliance

The haunted woods, now a realm of spectral uncertainty, closed in around the friends as they stumbled through the labyrinthine trails. The air was thick with an oppressive tension, and the whispers, once distant murmurs, reverberated through the trees with an unsettling urgency. Mark, Emily, and the rest of the group were mere pawns in a cosmic game, ensnared by the Goatman's curse, and each step they took seemed to propel them deeper into the heart of an insidious nightmare.

The trail, twisted and sinuous, led the friends to the edge of an ancient clearing. Moonlight filtered through the gnarled branches, casting an ethereal glow on the uneven ground. The clearing, marked by a series of grotesque symbols etched into the earth, seemed to pulse with a malevolent energy. Unseen eyes watched from the shadows as the friends hesitated at the threshold of the supernatural stage.

Emily, the once-curious soul now burdened by the weight of forbidden knowledge, felt an invisible force drawing her toward the center of the clearing. The whispers, now an incessant chorus, beckoned her to unravel the mysteries encoded in the symbols. A compulsion, an otherworldly pull, guided her steps as she approached the enigmatic patterns etched into the earth.

Mark, torn between the rational skepticism that had defined him and the growing influence of the Goatman's curse, cast wary glances at the symbols. The haunted woods, responsive to the internal struggles of the friends, seemed to warp and contort with a will of its own. Shadows danced in grotesque patterns, and the clearing became a stage for a supernatural spectacle.

The group, teetering on the brink of an abyss, gathered at the center of the clearing. Emily traced her fingers over the symbols, her touch unlocking a latent energy that pulsed through the earth. The whispers intensified, their spectral voices weaving a narrative

that echoed through the haunted woods—a tale of ancient alliances, cosmic conspiracies, and the inexorable dance between the living and the supernatural.

As Emily deciphered the symbols, the clearing transformed into a spectral panorama. Visions of the Goatman's cursed legacy unfolded, revealing a tapestry of intertwined destinies that stretched across epochs. The friends, now mere spectators in the cosmic drama, glimpsed fragments of the entity's tormented existence.

The Goatman, a creature bound by an unholy alliance with forces beyond mortal understanding, emerged as a tragic figure—a victim of a cosmic imbalance that demanded appeasement through unspeakable rituals and sacrifices. Its eyes, once gleaming with malevolence, now reflected a profound sadness that transcended the bestial form it wore.

The friends, ensnared in the unfolding revelation, witnessed scenes from the Goatman's past—a time when the ancient woods echoed with primal magic, and forbidden pacts were forged beneath the watchful gaze of eldritch entities. The haunted woods, a nexus of supernatural energies, became a stage for an age-old conflict that transcended the boundaries of time.

Mark, grappling with the conflicting forces that tore at his sanity, saw glimpses of the Goatman's interactions with lost souls—a spectral procession of individuals who had been entangled in the cosmic machinations of the ancient curse. The forest, a witness to centuries of suffering, whispered tales of tormented souls and unspeakable horrors that lurked in the shadowed depths.

The friends, released from the spectral visions, found themselves standing in the clearing once more. The symbols, now infused with a latent energy, pulsed with an otherworldly radiance. The Goatman, its form flickering between the grotesque and the tragic,

remained at the periphery of their perception, a spectral guardian of the haunted woods.

As the friends retreated from the clearing, a mournful howl echoed through the trees—a sound that transcended the natural world. The spectral alliance between the friends and the Goatman, forged by the revelation in the clearing, had sealed their destinies in an unholy covenant. The whispers, now a constant companion, guided them deeper into the labyrinth of the supernatural, their fates entwined with the spectral forces that governed the haunted woods.

The group, marked by the spectral encounter, pressed forward with a newfound awareness. The haunted woods, now an extension of the Goatman's domain, seemed to anticipate their every move. Shadows clung to the friends like a malevolent fog, and the air pulsed with an otherworldly energy that heightened the senses to the unseen threats that lurked in the shadows.

As they traversed the twisted trails, the group became acutely aware of an invisible tether connecting them to the Goatman's curse. The forest, alive with spectral currents, responded to their presence with a symphony of ethereal whispers. The alliance, forged in the clearing, propelled them toward a convergence of cosmic forces that awaited in the heart of the supernatural enigma.

The night, pregnant with uncertainty, stretched before the friends like an endless abyss. The haunted woods, a realm of shifting shadows and spectral whispers, beckoned them into the heart of the supernatural enigma. The Goatman, now an unseen puppeteer of their destinies, watched with an otherworldly intelligence as the group delved deeper into the spectral dance that awaited them in the shadowed depths.

Chapter 8: The Dance of Shadows

The haunted woods, now an extension of the Goatman's dominion, closed in around the friends as they ventured deeper into the
labyrinth of shadows. The spectral alliance forged in the clearing
bound them to the ancient curse, and with each step, the ethereal
whispers seemed to guide their path. Mark, Emily, and the rest of the
group were caught in a cosmic dance, their destinies entwined with
the malevolent forces that governed the supernatural enigma.

The twisted trails led the friends to a secluded grove bathed
in an otherworldly glow. Moonlight filtered through the gnarled
branches, casting an ethereal pallor on the ground. The air crackled
with latent energy, and the shadows played tricks on their senses.
Unseen eyes observed their every move as the group hesitated at the
edge of the spectral grove.

Emily, the unwitting conduit of forbidden knowledge, felt an
invisible force pulling her toward the center of the grove. The whispers, now a spectral symphony, urged her to unravel the mysteries
concealed within the ancient symbols etched into the earth. A compulsion, an otherworldly call, guided her steps as she approached the
enigmatic patterns that pulsed with latent power.

Mark, torn between the skepticism that defined him and the
growing influence of the Goatman's curse, cast wary glances at the
symbols. The haunted woods, responsive to the internal struggles
of the friends, seemed to warp and contort with a will of its own.
Shadows danced in grotesque patterns, and the grove became a stage
for a supernatural spectacle.

The rest of the group, caught in the gravitational pull of the
Goatman's influence, gathered around Emily. The clearing, a nexus
of spectral energies, hummed with an ominous resonance. Unseen
forces coalesced, and the grove transformed into a gateway to the
unknown.

As Emily traced her fingers over the symbols, the grove became a canvas for ethereal visions. The ancient curse, woven into the fabric of the haunted woods, unfolded before the friends like a nightmarish tapestry. The Goatman, a tragic figure shackled by an unholy alliance, emerged from the shadows, its form flickering with a spectral radiance.

The friends, ensnared in the unfolding revelation, witnessed scenes from the Goatman's existence—a journey through epochs marked by cosmic pacts, eldritch rituals, and the insatiable hunger that bound the entity to the supernatural realm. The grove, now a theater of spectral memories, echoed with the haunting cries of lost souls and the tormented echoes of ancient rites.

Mark, tormented by the conflicting forces that tore at his sanity, saw glimpses of the Goatman's interactions with souls who had been entangled in the cosmic machinations of the ancient curse. The forest, a silent witness to centuries of suffering, whispered tales of tormented spirits and unspeakable horrors that lurked in the shadowed depths.

Emily, sensitive to the ethereal currents, glimpsed fragments of the future—an ominous tableau that unfolded with an inexorable inevitability. The haunted woods, now a mosaic of interconnected destinies, revealed a nightmarish dance between the living and the spectral.

As the visions played out, the friends, released from the spectral trance, found themselves standing in the grove once more. The symbols, now infused with a latent energy, pulsed with an otherworldly radiance. The Goatman, its form flickering between the grotesque and the tragic, remained at the periphery of their perception, a spectral guardian of the haunted woods.

The friends, marked by the spectral encounter, retreated from the grove. The symbols, now charged with a malevolent force,

lingered in their consciousness like a haunting echo. The haunted woods, sentient and malevolent, responded to their presence with an unsettling intensity.

As the group pressed forward, the forest itself seemed to conspire against them. The twisted trails became a labyrinth, shifting with a will of their own. The spectral currents guided the friends deeper into the heart of the supernatural enigma, and the whispers, now an incessant chorus, reverberated through the haunted woods.

A sudden gust of wind whispered through the gnarled branches, carrying with it the mournful howl of the Goatman. The spectral alliance, forged in the grove, propelled the friends toward a convergence of cosmic forces that awaited in the shadowed depths. The night, fraught with unseen perils, stretched before them like an endless abyss, and the friends, ensnared by the spectral forces that governed their fate, plunged further into the inescapable dance of shadows that awaited in the ancient forest.

The twisted trails, illuminated by an otherworldly glow, led the group to the heart of the haunted woods. The whispers, now a cacophony of spectral voices, guided their every step, and the air pulsated with an ethereal energy that heightened the senses to the unseen threats that lurked in the shadows.

As the friends delved deeper, the forest itself seemed to morph into a surreal dreamscape. Trees contorted into nightmarish shapes, and the ground undulated like the surface of an otherworldly sea. Unseen eyes watched from the darkness, and the haunted woods, now a living entity, responded to their presence with a symphony of spectral echoes.

The group, now caught in a cosmic ballet, reached a clearing bathed in an otherworldly radiance. Symbols etched into the earth pulsed with an ancient power, and the whispers intensified, their spectral voices reaching a deafening crescendo. In the center of the

clearing stood a spectral figure—a manifestation of the Goatman's curse, its eyes gleaming with an otherworldly intelligence.

The friends, paralyzed by the unfolding spectacle, felt the air thicken with a malevolent force. The Goatman, now a puppeteer of their destinies, extended a spectral hand, inviting the group to join the cosmic dance. Mark, Emily, and the rest stood at the precipice of a choice that would seal their fate—a decision that transcended mortal understanding.

As the spectral figure beckoned, the haunted woods echoed with the haunting laughter of the Goatman. The friends, ensnared in the dance of shadows, stood at the nexus of the supernatural enigma, their destinies entwined with the ancient curse that governed the heart of the forest.

The night, fraught with cosmic uncertainty, stretched before the friends like an infinite canvas. The spectral grove, now a gateway to the unknown, beckoned them into the inescapable dance that awaited in the shadowed depths. The friends, marked by the ethereal revelations and the spectral alliance, plunged further into the heart of the haunted woods, where the Goatman's malevolent influence

Chapter 9: Pact with Shadows

The friends, standing on the precipice of the spectral clearing, felt the oppressive weight of the Goatman's influence bearing down upon them. The ethereal radiance cast an eerie glow on the symbols that pulsed with an otherworldly energy. The whispers, now an unrelenting cacophony, echoed through the haunted woods, urging the group to surrender to the cosmic dance that awaited.

Mark, the once-skeptical leader, hesitated, his eyes darting between the spectral figure and his companions. The forest, now a sentient entity, seemed to respond to his internal struggle, twisting the trees into grotesque forms that mirrored the tendrils of doubt

constricting his heart. Emily, sensitive to the ethereal currents, trembled as conflicting emotions wrestled within her.

The Goatman's eyes, gleaming with an ancient intelligence, bore into the souls of the friends. The haunted clearing became a battleground of wills, where the tangible and intangible clashed in a dance of shadows. Unseen forces whispered promises of enlightenment and power, luring the friends toward an unholy pact that defied the natural order.

In the face of the spectral invitation, the group felt a collective unease. The air crackled with tension, and the haunted woods, alive with spectral currents, seemed to conspire against them. The choice, a perilous gambit that promised either dominion over the supernatural or descent into eternal torment, hung in the balance.

As the friends deliberated, the grove transformed into a surreal dreamscape. Reality and nightmare merged, and the spectral figure at the center of the clearing became an ever-shifting enigma. The whispers, now a dissonant symphony, intensified, urging the group to embrace the Goatman's curse and become conduits for the malevolent forces that pulsed through the heart of the forest.

Emily, tormented by the conflicting forces that tugged at her soul, felt an irresistible pull toward the outstretched hand of the Goatman. The symbols etched into the earth seemed to respond to her internal turmoil, glowing with an intensity that mirrored the tumult within her consciousness. The friends, caught in the gravitational pull of an insidious force, stood at the crossroads of their destinies.

In a moment of collective resolve, the group stepped back from the spectral figure. The Goatman's eyes, once filled with a gleaming anticipation, narrowed with disappointment. The whispers, now a discordant lament, echoed through the haunted woods. The spectral figure, a harbinger of alliance, receded into the shadows, leaving

the friends standing in the clearing, marked by the weight of their choice.

The haunted woods, now a tapestry of shifting shadows and spectral echoes, responded to the rejection with a sinister sigh. The grove, once a gateway to the unknown, settled into an eerie stillness. The friends, released from the immediate threat, felt a mixture of relief and lingering dread.

As the group retreated from the clearing, the symbols etched into the earth seemed to pulse with a fading energy. The whispers, now reduced to a haunting murmur, lingered on the fringes of their consciousness. The haunted woods, while momentarily subdued, retained the scars of the friends' encounter, and the night unfolded with an ominous uncertainty.

The group, bound by the spectral alliance but defiant in the face of the Goatman's influence, ventured deeper into the labyrinth of shadows. The twisted trails, now a maze of spectral illusions, seemed to shift with a malevolent intent. The friends, caught in the ebb and flow of the supernatural currents, pressed forward with a cautious determination.

As they navigated the haunted woods, the spectral echoes intensified. Unseen eyes watched from the shadows, and the air became charged with an otherworldly energy. The friends, marked by the spectral encounter, felt the weight of the ancient curse lingering like a palpable presence. The night, pregnant with the unknown, whispered secrets that reverberated through the twisted branches.

Suddenly, a mournful howl echoed through the trees—a sound that transcended the natural world. The spectral alliance, though rejected in the clearing, continued to bind the friends to the Goatman's curse. The haunted woods, now a sentient entity, responded to their presence with an unsettling intensity.

The friends stumbled upon an ancient altar, hidden within the depths of the forest. The symbols engraved upon it mirrored those in the clearing, and the air pulsed with an otherworldly resonance. The whispers, now a siren's call, beckoned them to approach the altar, promising a communion with the supernatural forces that governed the haunted woods.

Mark, haunted by the memories of his lost friend and the consequences of the group's rejection, grappled with the inexorable pull toward the altar. The friends, caught between the desire for understanding and the fear of the unknown, hesitated at the threshold of the spectral enclave.

As they approached, the symbols on the altar glowed with an intensity that mirrored the ethereal currents within the haunted woods. The whispers, now a seductive melody, caressed their minds, weaving visions of power and transcendence. The Goatman's presence, though momentarily distant, lingered like a shadow cast upon the spectral canvas.

A choice loomed before the friends—a choice that would either cement their unholy alliance with the Goatman or cast them further into the abyss of the unknown. The haunted woods, alive with a malevolent energy, awaited the outcome of the cosmic dance that unfolded beneath its twisted canopy.

In a moment of collective hesitation, the friends stood at the edge of the altar, the symbols pulsating with an otherworldly radiance. The whispers, now a haunting serenade, reverberated through the haunted woods, weaving a narrative that transcended mortal understanding. The group, teetering on the brink of enlightenment and damnation, faced the haunting reality that the legend of the Goatman had claimed them as unwilling participants in its insidious narrative.

The night, draped in an ethereal mist, enveloped the friends as they stood at the crossroads of their destinies. The haunted woods, a realm of shifting shadows and spectral echoes, watched with an otherworldly intelligence as the group, bound by an unspoken pact, ventured further into the heart of the supernatural enigma. The night, now a canvas for the dance of shadows, whispered of terrors yet to unfold as the friends pressed forward, their footsteps echoing through the labyrinth of nightmares that awaited in the ancient forest.

Chapter 10: Veil of Shadows

The haunted woods, a labyrinth of shifting shadows and spectral echoes, enveloped the friends as they ventured deeper into the heart of the supernatural enigma. The spectral alliance, though rejected at the clearing, lingered like an unseen shroud, binding the group to the Goatman's curse. The twisted trails, now a maze of spectral illusions, seemed to warp with a malevolent intent, guiding the friends toward an unknown destination.

As the group pressed forward, the spectral echoes intensified. Unseen eyes watched from the shadows, and the air crackled with an otherworldly energy. The haunted woods, sentient and malevolent, responded to their presence with an unsettling intensity. The friends, marked by the spectral encounter, felt the weight of the ancient curse lingering like a palpable presence.

The whispers, once a dissonant symphony, now coalesced into a haunting serenade that reverberated through the twisted branches. Emily, sensitive to the ethereal currents, found herself caught in the ebb and flow of spectral energies. Visions of the Goatman's cursed legacy danced before her eyes—a tapestry of ancient alliances, forbidden pacts, and the insatiable hunger that bound the entity to the supernatural realm.

Mark, tormented by the memories of his lost friend and the consequences of their rejection, grappled with an internal struggle. The twisted trails seemed to twist with a will of their own, mirroring the tumult within his consciousness. The haunted woods, responsive to the friends' internal conflicts, conspired against them with a malevolent glee.

The friends stumbled upon an ancient altar, hidden within the depths of the forest. The symbols engraved upon it mirrored those in the clearing, and the air pulsed with an otherworldly resonance. The whispers, now a seductive melody, caressed their minds, weaving visions of power and transcendence. The Goatman's presence, though momentarily distant, lingered like a shadow cast upon the spectral canvas.

A choice loomed before the friends—a choice that would either cement their unholy alliance with the Goatman or cast them further into the abyss of the unknown. The haunted woods, alive with a malevolent energy, awaited the outcome of the cosmic dance that unfolded beneath its twisted canopy.

In a moment of collective hesitation, the friends stood at the edge of the altar, the symbols pulsating with an otherworldly radiance. The whispers, now a haunting serenade, reverberated through the haunted woods, weaving a narrative that transcended mortal understanding. The group, teetering on the brink of enlightenment and damnation, faced the haunting reality that the legend of the Goatman had claimed them as unwilling participants in its insidious narrative.

The night, draped in an ethereal mist, enveloped the friends as they stood at the crossroads of their destinies. The haunted woods, a realm of shifting shadows and spectral echoes, watched with an otherworldly intelligence as the group, bound by an unspoken pact, ventured further into the heart of the supernatural enigma. The

night, now a canvas for the dance of shadows, whispered of terrors yet to unfold as the friends pressed forward, their footsteps echoing through the labyrinth of nightmares that awaited in the ancient forest.

The twisted trails, illuminated by an otherworldly glow, led the group to the heart of the haunted woods. The whispers, now an incessant chorus, guided their every step, and the air pulsated with an ethereal energy that heightened the senses to the unseen threats that lurked in the shadows.

As the friends delved deeper, the forest itself seemed to morph into a surreal dreamscape. Trees contorted into nightmarish shapes, and the ground undulated like the surface of an otherworldly sea. Unseen eyes watched from the darkness, and the haunted woods, now a living entity, responded to their presence with a symphony of spectral echoes.

The group, now caught in a cosmic ballet, reached a clearing bathed in an otherworldly radiance. Symbols etched into the earth pulsed with an ancient power, and the whispers intensified, their spectral voices reaching a deafening crescendo. In the center of the clearing stood a spectral figure—a manifestation of the Goatman's curse, its eyes gleaming with an otherworldly intelligence.

The friends, paralyzed by the unfolding spectacle, felt the air thicken with a malevolent force. The Goatman, now a puppeteer of their destinies, extended a spectral hand, inviting the group to join the cosmic dance. Mark, Emily, and the rest stood at the precipice of a choice that would seal their fate—a decision that transcended mortal understanding.

As the spectral figure beckoned, the haunted woods echoed with the haunting laughter of the Goatman. The friends, ensnared in the dance of shadows, stood at the nexus of the supernatural enigma,

their destinies entwined with the ancient curse that governed the heart of the forest.

The night, fraught with cosmic uncertainty, stretched before the friends like an infinite canvas. The spectral grove, now a gateway to the unknown, beckoned them into the inescapable dance that awaited in the shadowed depths. The friends, marked by the ethereal revelations and the spectral alliance, plunged further into the heart of the haunted woods, where the Goatman's malevolent influence awaited.

The twisted trails, now a spectral tapestry, led the friends to a clearing bathed in an ethereal glow. Symbols etched into the earth pulsated with an otherworldly radiance, and the whispers, now a ghostly chorus, guided them to the center of the supernatural stage. The spectral figure, a manifestation of the Goatman's curse, awaited with eyes that gleamed with ancient knowledge.

In a moment of collective resolve, the friends stepped forward, surrendering to the cosmic dance that unfolded in the haunted clearing. The symbols, now infused with a latent energy, glowed with an intensity that mirrored the ethereal currents within the haunted woods. The whispers, a symphony of spectral voices, reached a crescendo, weaving a narrative that transcended mortal comprehension.

As the friends embraced the spectral invitation, the clearing transformed into a surreal dreamscape. Reality and nightmare merged, and the friends found themselves suspended in a liminal space where time seemed to lose its meaning. Visions of the Goatman's cursed legacy unfolded—a tapestry of intertwined destinies and cosmic malevolence.

Mark, tormented by the memories of his lost friend, witnessed haunting scenes from the past. The woods became a theater of spectral apparitions, replaying moments of anguish and despair. The

Goatman's voice, a spectral undertone, whispered forgotten secrets that clawed at the edges of his sanity.

Emily, sensitive to the ethereal currents, glimpsed fragments of the future—an ominous tableau that unfolded with an inexorable inevitability. The haunted woods, now a mosaic of interconnected destinies, revealed a nightmarish dance between the living and the spectral.

As the visions played out, the friends, paralyzed by the supernatural revelation, became mere spectators in their own existential drama. The Goatman, a harbinger of cosmic terror, reveled in the torment it unleashed upon their minds. The clearing, a stage for the unfolding nightmare, pulsated with an otherworldly energy.

Suddenly, the visions ceased, and the friends, released from the spectral trance, found themselves standing in the clearing once more. The Goatman, its form flickering like a

dying ember, faded into the shadows. The ancient tree, now devoid of the supernatural glow, stood as a silent witness to the cosmic theater that unfolded beneath its twisted branches.

The friends, disoriented and haunted by the echoes of the Goatman's revelations, stumbled away from the clearing. The haunted woods, now a sentient labyrinth, seemed to rearrange itself, guiding the group deeper into the heart of the supernatural enigma. The air, thick with the residue of spectral energy, clung to them like an intangible shroud.

As they pressed forward, a cold wind whispered through the twisted branches, carrying with it a chilling echo of the Goatman's laughter. The friends, caught in a cycle of existential dread, stumbled through the haunted woods, forever marked by the disappearing act that unfolded in the surreal clearing. The night, pregnant with cosmic uncertainty, stretched before them like an endless abyss.

The spectral alliance, rejected at the altar, continued to bind the friends to the Goatman's curse. The twisted trails, now a spectral tapestry, guided them with an otherworldly intelligence. Shadows clung to the group like a malevolent fog, and the air pulsed with an ethereal energy that heightened their senses to the unseen threats that lurked in the shadows.

As they traversed the haunted woods, the group became acutely aware of an invisible tether connecting them to the Goatman's curse. The forest, alive with spectral currents, responded to their presence with a symphony of ethereal whispers. The alliance, forged in the clearing, propelled them toward a convergence of cosmic forces that awaited in the heart of the supernatural enigma.

The night, fraught with unseen perils, stretched before the friends like an endless abyss. The haunted woods, a realm of shifting shadows and spectral whispers, beckoned them into the heart of the supernatural enigma. The Goatman, now an unseen puppeteer of their destinies, watched with an otherworldly intelligence as the group delved deeper into the spectral dance that awaited them in the shadowed depths.

The twisted trails, illuminated by an otherworldly glow, led the friends to an ancient ruin hidden within the depths of the haunted woods. The spectral echoes intensified, and the air crackled with an otherworldly energy. Unseen eyes watched from the darkness as the group hesitated at the threshold of the supernatural enclave.

Emily, sensitive to the ethereal currents, felt an invisible force drawing her toward the heart of the ruins. The whispers, now an incessant chorus, urged her to unravel the mysteries concealed within the ancient stones. A compulsion, an otherworldly pull, guided her steps as she approached the spectral threshold.

Mark, torn between rational skepticism and the growing influence of the Goatman's curse, cast wary glances at the ancient ruin.

The haunted woods, responsive to the internal struggles of the friends, seemed to warp and contort with a will of its own. Shadows danced in grotesque patterns, and the ruins became a stage for a supernatural spectacle.

The rest of the group, ensnared by the spectral forces that governed their fate, gathered around Emily. The ruins, a nexus of spectral energies, hummed with an ominous resonance. Unseen forces coalesced, and the ancient stones transformed into conduits for the ethereal currents that pulsed through the heart of the forest.

As Emily traced her fingers over the weathered stones, the ruins became a canvas for ethereal visions. The ancient curse, woven into the fabric of the haunted woods, unfolded before the friends like a nightmarish tapestry. The Goatman, a tragic figure shackled by an unholy alliance, emerged from the shadows, its form flickering with a spectral radiance.

The friends, ensnared in the unfolding revelation, witnessed scenes from the Goatman's existence—a journey through epochs marked by cosmic pacts, eldritch rituals, and the insatiable hunger that bound the entity to the supernatural realm. The ruins, now a theater of spectral memories, echoed with the haunting cries of lost souls and the tormented echoes of ancient rites.

Mark, tormented by the conflicting forces that tore at his sanity, saw glimpses of the Goatman's interactions with lost souls—a spectral procession of individuals who had been entangled in the cosmic machinations of the ancient curse. The forest, a silent witness to centuries of suffering, whispered tales of tormented spirits and unspeakable horrors that lurked in the shadowed depths.

Emily, sensitive to the ethereal currents, glimpsed fragments of the future—an ominous tableau that unfolded with an inexorable inevitability. The haunted woods, now a mosaic of interconnected

destinies, revealed a nightmarish dance between the living and the spectral.

As the visions played out, the friends, paralyzed by the supernatural revelation, became mere spectators in their own existential drama. The Goatman, a harbinger of cosmic terror, reveled in the torment it unleashed upon their minds. The ruins, a stage for the unfolding nightmare, pulsated with an otherworldly energy.

Suddenly, the visions ceased, and the friends, released from the spectral trance, found themselves standing in the ruins once more. The Goatman, its form flickering between the grotesque and the tragic, remained at the periphery of their perception, a spectral guardian of the haunted woods.

The friends, disoriented and haunted by the echoes of the Goatman's revelations, stumbled away from the ruins. The haunted woods, now a sentient labyrinth, seemed to rearrange itself, guiding the group deeper into the heart of the supernatural enigma. The air, thick with the residue of spectral energy, clung to them like an intangible shroud.

As they pressed forward, a cold wind whispered through the twisted branches, carrying with it a chilling echo of the Goatman's laughter. The friends, caught in a cycle of existential dread, stumbled through the haunted woods, forever marked by the disappearing act that unfolded in the surreal clearing. The night, pregnant with cosmic uncertainty, stretched before them like an endless abyss.

The spectral alliance, rejected at the ruins, continued to bind the friends to the Goatman's curse. The twisted trails, now a spectral tapestry, guided them with an otherworldly intelligence. Shadows clung to the group like a malevolent fog, and the air pulsed with an ethereal energy that heightened their senses to the unseen threats that lurked in the shadows.

As they traversed the haunted woods, the group became acutely aware of an invisible tether connecting them to the Goatman's curse. The forest, alive with spectral currents, responded to their presence with a symphony of ethereal whispers. The alliance, forged in the ruins, propelled them toward a convergence of cosmic forces that awaited in the heart of the supernatural enigma.

The night, fraught with unseen perils, stretched before the friends like an endless abyss. The haunted woods, a realm of shifting shadows and spectral whispers, beckoned them into the heart of the supernatural enigma. The Goatman, now an unseen puppeteer of their destinies, watched with an otherworldly intelligence as the group delved deeper into the spectral dance that awaited them in the shadowed depths.

The twisted trails, illuminated by an otherworldly glow, led the friends to an ancient grove concealed within the heart of the haunted woods. The spectral echoes intensified, and the air crackled with an otherworldly energy. Unseen eyes watched from the darkness as the group hesitated at the threshold of the supernatural enclave.

Emily, sensitive to the ethereal currents, felt an invisible force pulling her toward the center of the grove. The whispers, now an incessant chorus, urged her to unravel the mysteries concealed within the ancient trees. A compulsion, an otherworldly call, guided her steps as she approached the spectral threshold.

Mark, torn between rational skepticism and the growing influence of the Goatman's curse, cast wary glances at the ancient grove. The haunted woods, responsive to the internal struggles of the friends, seemed to warp and contort with a will of its own. Shadows danced in grotesque patterns, and the grove became a stage for a supernatural spectacle.

The rest of the group, ensnared by the spectral forces that governed their fate, gathered around Emily. The grove, a nexus

of spectral energies, hummed with an ominous resonance. Unseen forces coalesced, and the ancient trees transformed into conduits for the ethereal currents that pulsed through the heart of the forest.

As Emily traced her fingers over the gnarled bark, the grove became a canvas for ethereal visions. The ancient curse, woven into the fabric of the haunted woods, unfolded before the friends like a nightmarish tapestry. The Goatman, a tragic figure shackled by an unholy alliance, emerged from the shadows, its form flickering with a spectral radiance.

The friends, ensnared in the unfolding revelation, witnessed scenes from the Goatman's existence—a journey through epochs marked by cosmic pacts, eldritch rituals, and the insatiable hunger that bound the entity to the supernatural realm. The grove, now a theater of spectral memories, echoed with the haunting cries of lost souls and the tormented echoes of ancient rites.

Mark, tormented by the conflicting forces that tore at his sanity, saw glimpses of the Goatman's interactions with lost souls—a spectral procession of individuals who had been entangled in the cosmic machinations of the ancient curse. The forest, a silent witness to centuries of suffering, whispered tales of tormented spirits and unspeakable horrors that lurked in the shadowed depths.

Emily, sensitive to the ethereal currents, glimpsed fragments of the future—an ominous tableau that unfolded with an inexorable inevitability. The haunted woods, now a mosaic of interconnected destinies, revealed a nightmarish dance between the living and the spectral.

As the visions played out, the friends, paralyzed by the supernatural revelation, became mere spectators in their own existential drama. The Goatman, a harbinger of cosmic terror, reveled in the torment it unleashed upon their minds. The grove, a stage for the unfolding nightmare, pulsated with an otherworldly energy.

Suddenly, the visions ceased, and the friends, released from the spectral trance, found themselves standing in the grove once more. The Goatman, its form flickering between the grotesque and the tragic, remained at the periphery of their perception, a spectral guardian of the haunted woods.

The friends, disoriented and haunted by the echoes of the Goatman's revelations, stumbled away from the grove. The haunted woods, now a sentient labyrinth, seemed to rearrange itself, guiding the group deeper into the heart of the supernatural enigma. The air, thick with the residue of spectral energy, clung to them like an intangible shroud.

As they pressed forward, a cold wind whispered through the twisted branches, carrying with it a chilling echo of the Goatman's laughter. The friends, caught in a cycle of existential dread, stumbled through the haunted woods, forever marked by the disappearing act that unfolded in the surreal clearing. The night, pregnant with cosmic uncertainty, stretched before them like an endless abyss.

The spectral alliance, rejected at the grove, continued to bind the friends to the Goatman's curse. The twisted trails, now a spectral tapestry, guided them with an otherworldly intelligence. Shadows clung to the group like a malevolent fog, and the air pulsed with an ethereal energy that heightened their senses to the unseen threats that lurked in the shadows.

As they traversed the haunted woods, the group became acutely aware of

an invisible tether connecting them to the Goatman's curse. The forest, alive with spectral currents, responded to their presence with a symphony of ethereal whispers. The alliance, forged in the grove, propelled them toward a convergence of cosmic forces that awaited in the heart of the supernatural enigma.

The night, fraught with unseen perils, stretched before the friends like an endless abyss. The haunted woods, a realm of shifting shadows and spectral whispers, beckoned them into the heart of the supernatural enigma. The Goatman, now an unseen puppeteer of their destinies, watched with an otherworldly intelligence as the group delved deeper into the spectral dance that awaited them in the shadowed depths.

The twisted trails, illuminated by an otherworldly glow, led the friends to an ancient burial ground hidden within the heart of the haunted woods. The spectral echoes intensified, and the air crackled with an otherworldly energy. Unseen eyes watched from the darkness as the group hesitated at the threshold of the supernatural enclave.

Emily, sensitive to the ethereal currents, felt an invisible force pulling her toward the center of the burial ground. The whispers, now an incessant chorus, urged her to unravel the mysteries concealed within the ancient gravestones. A compulsion, an otherworldly call, guided her steps as she approached the spectral threshold.

Mark, torn between rational skepticism and the growing influence of the Goatman's curse, cast wary glances at the ancient burial ground. The haunted woods, responsive to the internal struggles of the friends, seemed to warp and contort with a will of its own. Shadows danced in grotesque patterns, and the burial ground became a stage for a supernatural spectacle.

The rest of the group, ensnared by the spectral forces that governed their fate, gathered around Emily. The burial ground, a nexus of spectral energies, hummed with an ominous resonance. Unseen forces coalesced, and the ancient gravestones transformed into conduits for the ethereal currents that pulsed through the heart of the forest.

As Emily traced her fingers over the weathered stones, the burial ground became a canvas for ethereal visions. The ancient curse, woven into the fabric of the haunted woods, unfolded before the friends like a nightmarish tapestry. The Goatman, a tragic figure shackled by an unholy alliance, emerged from the shadows, its form flickering with a spectral radiance.

The friends, ensnared in the unfolding revelation, witnessed scenes from the Goatman's existence—a journey through epochs marked by cosmic pacts, eldritch rituals, and the insatiable hunger that bound the entity to the supernatural realm. The burial ground, now a theater of spectral memories, echoed with the haunting cries of lost souls and the tormented echoes of ancient rites.

Mark, tormented by the conflicting forces that tore at his sanity, saw glimpses of the Goatman's interactions with lost souls—a spectral procession of individuals who had been entangled in the cosmic machinations of the ancient curse. The forest, a silent witness to centuries of suffering, whispered tales of tormented spirits and unspeakable horrors that lurked in the shadowed depths.

Emily, sensitive to the ethereal currents, glimpsed fragments of the future—an ominous tableau that unfolded with an inexorable inevitability. The haunted woods, now a mosaic of interconnected destinies, revealed a nightmarish dance between the living and the spectral.

As the visions played out, the friends, paralyzed by the supernatural revelation, became mere spectators in their own existential drama. The Goatman, a harbinger of cosmic terror, reveled in the torment it unleashed upon their minds. The burial ground, a stage for the unfolding nightmare, pulsated with an otherworldly energy.

Suddenly, the visions ceased, and the friends, released from the spectral trance, found themselves standing in the burial ground once more. The Goatman, its form flickering between the grotesque and

the tragic, remained at the periphery of their perception, a spectral guardian of the haunted woods.

The friends, disoriented and haunted by the echoes of the Goatman's revelations, stumbled away from the burial ground. The haunted woods, now a sentient labyrinth, seemed to rearrange itself, guiding the group deeper into the heart of the supernatural enigma. The air, thick with the residue of spectral energy, clung to them like an intangible shroud.

As they pressed forward, a cold wind whispered through the twisted branches, carrying with it a chilling echo of the Goatman's laughter. The friends, caught in a cycle of existential dread, stumbled through the haunted woods, forever marked by the disappearing act that unfolded in the surreal clearing. The night, pregnant with cosmic uncertainty, stretched before them like an endless abyss.

The spectral alliance, rejected at the burial ground, continued to bind the friends to the Goatman's curse. The twisted trails, now a spectral tapestry, guided them with an otherworldly intelligence. Shadows clung to the group like a malevolent fog, and the air pulsed with an ethereal energy that heightened their senses to the unseen threats that lurked in the shadows.

As they traversed the haunted woods, the group became acutely aware of an invisible tether connecting them to the Goatman's curse. The forest, alive with spectral currents, responded to their presence with a symphony of ethereal whispers. The alliance, forged in the burial ground, propelled them toward a convergence of cosmic forces that awaited in the heart of the supernatural enigma.

The night, fraught with unseen perils, stretched before the friends like an endless abyss. The haunted woods, a realm of shifting shadows and spectral whispers, beckoned them into the heart of the supernatural enigma. The Goatman, now an unseen puppeteer of their destinies, watched with an otherworldly intelligence as the

group delved deeper into the spectral dance that awaited them in the shadowed depths.

The twisted trails, illuminated by an otherworldly glow, led the friends to an ancient altar concealed within the heart of the haunted woods. The spectral echoes intensified, and the air crackled with an otherworldly energy. Unseen eyes watched from the darkness as the group hesitated at the threshold of the supernatural enclave.

Emily, sensitive to the ethereal currents, felt an invisible force pulling her toward the center of the altar. The whispers, now an incessant chorus, urged her to unravel the mysteries concealed within the ancient symbols. A compulsion, an otherworldly call, guided her steps as she approached the spectral threshold.

Mark, torn between rational skepticism and the growing influence of the Goatman's curse, cast wary glances at the ancient altar. The haunted woods, responsive to the internal struggles of the friends, seemed to warp and contort with a will of its own. Shadows danced in grotesque patterns, and the altar became a stage for a supernatural spectacle.

The rest of the group, ensnared by the spectral forces that governed their fate, gathered around Emily. The altar, a nexus of spectral energies, hummed with an ominous resonance. Unseen forces coalesced, and the ancient symbols transformed into conduits for the ethereal currents that pulsed through the heart of the forest.

As Emily traced her fingers over the weathered symbols, the altar became a canvas for ethereal visions. The ancient curse, woven into the fabric of the haunted woods, unfolded before the friends like a nightmarish tapestry. The Goatman, a tragic figure shackled by an unholy alliance, emerged from the shadows, its form flickering with a spectral radiance.

The friends, ensnared in the unfolding revelation, witnessed scenes from the Goatman's existence—a journey through epochs

marked by cosmic pacts, eldritch rituals, and the insatiable hunger that bound the entity to the supernatural realm. The altar, now a theater of spectral memories, echoed with the haunting cries of lost souls and the tormented echoes of ancient rites.

Mark, tormented by the conflicting forces that tore at his sanity, saw glimpses of the Goatman's interactions with lost souls—a spectral procession of individuals who had been entangled in the cosmic machinations of the ancient curse. The forest, a silent witness to centuries of suffering, whispered tales of tormented spirits and unspeakable horrors that lurked in the shadowed depths.

Emily, sensitive to the ethereal currents, glimpsed fragments of the future—an ominous tableau that unfolded with an inexorable inevitability. The haunted woods, now a mosaic of interconnected destinies, revealed a nightmarish dance between the living and the spectral.

As the visions played out, the friends, paralyzed by the supernatural revelation, became mere spectators in their own existential drama. The Goatman, a harbinger of cosmic terror, reveled in the torment it unleashed upon their minds. The altar, a stage for the unfolding nightmare, pulsated with an otherworldly energy.

Suddenly, the visions ceased, and the friends, released from the spectral trance, found themselves standing before the altar once more. The Goatman, its form flickering between the grotesque and the tragic, remained at the periphery of their perception, a spectral guardian of the haunted woods.

The friends, disoriented and haunted by the echoes of the Goatman's revelations, stumbled away from the altar. The haunted woods, now a sentient labyrinth, seemed to rearrange itself, guiding the group deeper into the heart of the supernatural enigma. The air, thick with the residue of spectral energy, clung to them like an intangible shroud.

As they pressed forward, a cold wind whispered through the twisted branches, carrying with it a chilling echo of the Goatman's laughter. The friends, caught in a cycle of existential dread, stumbled through the haunted woods, forever marked by the disappearing act that unfolded in the surreal clearing. The night, pregnant with cosmic uncertainty, stretched before them like an endless abyss.

The spectral alliance, rejected at the altar, continued to bind the friends to the Goatman's curse. The twisted trails, now a spectral tapestry, guided them with an otherworldly intelligence. Shadows clung to the group like a malevolent fog, and the air pulsed with an ethereal energy that heightened their senses to the unseen threats that lurked in the shadows.

As they traversed the haunted woods, the group became acutely aware of an invisible tether connecting them to the Goatman's curse. The forest, alive with spectral currents, responded to their presence with a symphony of ethereal whispers. The alliance, forged in the altar, propelled them toward a convergence of cosmic forces that awaited in the heart of the supernatural enigma.

Chapter 11: Echoes of Betrayal

The haunted woods, now pulsating with an otherworldly energy, closed in around the friends like a malevolent embrace. The spectral alliance, an invisible tether, bound them to the Goatman's curse, and the twisted trails led them deeper into the heart of the supernatural enigma. Each step resonated with an eerie echo, as if the forest itself whispered tales of ancient treacheries.

The air, thick with a palpable tension, seemed to vibrate with the echoes of spectral voices. Unseen eyes watched from the shadows, and the friends felt the weight of the Goatman's malevolent gaze upon them. Emily, still sensitive to the ethereal currents, shivered as the whispers intensified, weaving a narrative of betrayal and impending doom.

Mark, haunted by the memories of his lost friend and the shifting allegiances within the group, struggled to maintain a semblance of composure. The haunted woods, now a labyrinth of twisted shadows, seemed to mirror the turmoil within his mind. Visions of the Goatman's cursed legacy clashed with the reality of their journey, blurring the lines between nightmare and waking.

As the friends ventured further, the twisted trails guided them to an ancient grove bathed in an unnatural glow. The spectral echoes intensified, and the air crackled with an otherworldly energy. Symbols etched into the trees pulsed with an ethereal radiance, casting grotesque shadows that danced with a life of their own.

In the center of the grove stood a spectral figure—a manifestation of the Goatman's curse, its eyes gleaming with an otherworldly intelligence. The friends, transfixed by the haunting presence, felt the weight of an unspoken invitation. The grove, now a stage for a cosmic drama, beckoned them to confront the echoes of betrayal that lingered in the shadows.

Emily, driven by a compulsion she could not resist, approached the spectral figure. The whispers, now a dissonant symphony, reverberated through the grove, casting a haunting spell upon the group. The friends, their senses heightened by the spectral energy, became acutely aware of the invisible threads that connected them to the Goatman's curse.

As Emily reached out, the spectral figure extended a ghostly hand. A surge of ancient memories flooded her consciousness—a tapestry of betrayals and alliances that transcended mortal understanding. The Goatman's voice, a haunting undertone, whispered forgotten secrets that clawed at the edges of her sanity.

Mark, torn between the mistrust within the group and the allure of the Goatman's promises, grappled with an internal tempest. Shadows cast by the ethereal glow contorted into grotesque shapes,

mirroring the conflicting emotions that tormented him. The grove, now a battleground of spectral forces, awaited the resolution of the internal strife that threatened to tear the group apart.

The rest of the friends, ensnared by the spectral drama, watched with a mixture of fear and fascination. The grove, bathed in an otherworldly radiance, became a theater for the unfolding nightmare. The Goatman's laughter, a haunting melody, echoed through the ancient trees, marking the friends as unwilling participants in its cosmic play.

Suddenly, the spectral figure and Emily recoiled as if struck by an unseen force. The grove, now plunged into an eerie silence, seemed to hold its breath. The spectral alliance, momentarily disrupted, cast a shadow of uncertainty upon the friends.

A voice, neither human nor spectral, resonated through the grove—a chorus of ancient whispers that spoke of broken pacts and the consequences of defiance. The friends, still caught in the ethereal web, felt the weight of the Goatman's judgment looming over them.

The grove, once a sanctuary of spectral revelations, became a battleground between the friends and the malevolent forces that sought to manipulate their destinies. The twisted trails, now obscured by shifting shadows, led the group deeper into the heart of the haunted woods, where the echoes of betrayal whispered of darker truths yet to unfold.

As the friends pressed forward, the spectral alliance tightened its grip, binding them to the Goatman's curse with an unbreakable resolve. The haunted woods, now a realm of shifting shadows and unseen perils, seemed to anticipate their every move. Each step echoed with the weight of ancient choices, and the air pulsed with an otherworldly energy that foretold of imminent horrors.

The twisted trails, like serpentine veins, guided the friends to an ancient ruin hidden within the depths of the haunted woods.

Symbols etched into the stones glowed with an ethereal radiance, and the air hummed with a spectral resonance. Unseen eyes watched from the darkness, and the ruins became a threshold to the unknown.

As the friends hesitated at the entrance, the whispers intensified, forming a cacophony of spectral voices that spoke of forgotten oaths and the inevitable descent into darkness. Emily, still bearing the weight of the spectral revelation, felt a compulsion to unravel the mysteries concealed within the ruins.

Mark, his trust shattered by the echoes of betrayal, cast wary glances at the ancient stones. The haunted woods, now alive with a malevolent energy, seemed to pulse with the heartbeat of an ancient evil. Shadows danced upon the ruins, casting ominous shapes that hinted at the horrors waiting within.

The rest of the group, caught in the web of the Goatman's curse, gathered around Emily. The ruins, a nexus of spectral energies, beckoned them to confront the consequences of their choices. The ancient stones, infused with an otherworldly power, awaited the unfolding of a cosmic drama that transcended the boundaries of mortal understanding.

As Emily traced her fingers over the weathered symbols, the ruins became a canvas for ethereal visions. The ancient curse, woven into the fabric of the haunted woods, unfolded before the friends like a nightmarish tapestry. The Goatman, a tragic figure shackled by an unholy alliance, emerged from the shadows, its form flickering with a spectral radiance.

The friends, ensnared in the unfolding revelation, witnessed scenes from the Goatman's existence—a journey through epochs marked by cosmic pacts, eldritch rituals, and the insatiable hunger that bound the entity to the supernatural realm. The ruins, now a

theater of spectral memories, echoed with the haunting cries of lost souls and the tormented echoes of ancient rites.

Mark, tormented by the conflicting forces that tore at his sanity, saw glimpses of the Goatman's interactions with lost souls—a spectral procession of individuals who had been entangled in the cosmic machinations of the ancient curse. The forest, a silent witness to centuries of suffering, whispered tales of tormented spirits and unspeakable horrors that lurked in the shadowed depths.

Emily, sensitive to the ethereal currents, glimpsed fragments of the future—an ominous tableau that unfolded with an inexorable inevitability. The haunted woods, now a mosaic of interconnected destinies, revealed a nightmarish dance between the living and the spectral.

As the visions played out, the friends, paralyzed by the supernatural revelation, became mere spectators in their own existential drama. The Goatman, a harbinger of cosmic terror, reveled in the torment it unleashed upon their minds. The ruins, a stage for the unfolding nightmare, pulsated with an otherworldly energy.

Suddenly, the visions ceased, and the friends, released from the spectral trance, found themselves standing within the ancient ruins once more. The Goatman, its form flickering between the grotesque and the tragic, remained a spectral presence at the periphery of their perception. The ruins, now silent and foreboding, seemed to anticipate the next chapter in the cosmic drama.

The friends, shaken by the spectral revelations, exchanged uneasy glances. The twisted trails, like a river of shadows, beckoned them deeper into the heart of the haunted woods. The air, heavy with the residue of ethereal energy, clung to them as a constant reminder of the supernatural forces that governed their fate.

As they ventured forth, the ruins behind them, the haunted woods seemed to close in, its twisted branches forming an impenetrable

canopy above. Shadows danced along the gnarled trunks, and the ground beneath their feet pulsed with an otherworldly heartbeat. The friends, now bound by the unseen threads of the Goatman's curse, pressed on with a mixture of dread and determination.

The twisted trails led them to a clearing bathed in an eerie, spectral light. In the center stood an ancient altar, adorned with symbols that seemed to writhe and shift in the dim illumination. The air became charged with an unsettling energy, and the friends felt the weight of the Goatman's gaze upon them once more.

Emily, still influenced by the ethereal currents, approached the altar with a sense of inevitability. The whispers, now a haunting chorus, seemed to guide her every step. The friends, unable to resist the unseen forces that governed their journey, gathered around the ancient stone structure.

As Emily reached out to touch the symbols, the altar responded with a surge of spectral energy. Visions unfolded before her eyes—scenes of ancient rituals, cosmic pacts, and the intertwining destinies of those who had crossed paths with the Goatman. The friends, ensnared in the ethereal spectacle, witnessed the tragic tales of souls bound to an ancient curse.

Mark, his skepticism eroded by the relentless onslaught of supernatural revelations, saw the threads of fate weaving around the group. The haunted woods, now a stage for cosmic machinations, echoed with the tormented cries of lost souls and the spectral laughter of the Goatman. The air crackled with an ominous resonance, and the ground seemed to shift beneath their feet.

The rest of the group, caught in the spectral current, felt the altar's power enveloping them. Shadows danced upon their faces, mirroring the ancient struggles playing out in the unseen realms. The Goatman, a puppeteer of destinies, reveled in the unfolding

drama as the friends teetered on the precipice of their own cosmic unraveling.

A voice, echoing from the depths of the haunted woods, resonated through the clearing—a haunting lamentation that spoke of betrayal, cosmic bargains, and the unrelenting hunger that bound the Goatman to its cursed existence. The friends, now witnesses to the unfolding tragedy, felt the weight of their choices bearing down upon them.

Emily, guided by an otherworldly compulsion, spoke words that seemed to echo with ancient power. The symbols on the altar glowed brighter, and the spectral light enveloped the friends. The haunted woods, alive with the energy of forgotten pacts, seemed to respond to Emily's invocation, and the air crackled with an ethereal electricity.

The friends, now connected by an invisible web of fate, felt the boundaries between the living and the spectral blur. The clearing transformed into a surreal tableau—a nexus of cosmic energies that defied mortal comprehension. The Goatman, its spectral form looming large, became a focal point in the unfolding ritual.

As the spectral light reached its zenith, the haunted woods seemed to hold its breath. The air became charged with an otherworldly tension, and the friends braced themselves for the unknown. Shadows, twisted and contorted, converged upon the clearing, forming a veil between the mortal realm and the supernatural forces that lurked beyond.

Suddenly, the spectral light extinguished, plunging the clearing into darkness. The friends, disoriented and surrounded by an oppressive silence, found themselves standing in the aftermath of the ritual. The Goatman's laughter echoed through the haunted woods, mocking the futility of mortal endeavors.

The twisted trails, now obscured by the lingering shadows, beckoned the friends deeper into the heart of the supernatural enigma. The air, thick with the residue of spectral energies, clung to them as a spectral shroud. The haunted woods, a labyrinth of cosmic horrors, seemed to whisper tales of their impending doom.

As the friends pressed forward, the spectral alliance tightening its grip, they became unwitting participants in a nightmare woven from the threads of ancient curses and cosmic machinations. The Goatman, a spectral puppeteer, reveled in the torment it unleashed upon their minds. The haunted woods, a realm of shifting shadows and unseen perils, awaited the next chapter in the unfolding cosmic drama.

Chapter 12: Whispers in the Shadows

The twisted trails guided the friends through the haunted woods, a realm now saturated with the lingering echoes of the ritual. The air crackled with an unsettling energy, and the shadows seemed to writhe with a newfound malevolence. The Goatman's curse, an invisible tether, bound them tighter as they delved deeper into the heart of the supernatural enigma.

The friends, haunted by the spectral revelations and the unsettling ritual, pressed on with a sense of trepidation. Each step through the dense undergrowth echoed with an ominous resonance, and the twisted branches overhead formed a canopy that blocked out the moonlight. The darkness seemed to pulse with a life of its own, and unseen eyes watched their every move.

As they traversed the haunted woods, Mark's gaze darted nervously between the shifting shadows. The Goatman's laughter lingered in the air, a haunting reminder of their entanglement with cosmic forces beyond their understanding. Doubt gnawed at Mark's sanity, and the trust between the friends strained under the weight of unseen horrors.

Emily, still influenced by the ethereal currents, walked with a purpose that seemed guided by forces beyond her control. The whispers, now a dissonant symphony, surrounded her like a spectral aura. The friends, ensnared in the spectral web, followed Emily as the twisted trails led them to a clearing bathed in an otherworldly glow.

In the center of the clearing stood a dilapidated mansion, its decaying façade casting eerie shadows in the spectral light. The air hummed with a haunting melody, and the friends felt an inexplicable compulsion to enter the mansion. The Goatman's curse, now a palpable force, seemed to emanate from the ancient structure.

As they approached the mansion, its doors creaked open with a ghostly wail. The interior, shrouded in darkness, exuded a malevolent energy. Unseen whispers echoed through the halls, recounting the tragic tales of those who had crossed paths with the Goatman within these haunted walls.

The friends hesitated at the threshold, a silent acknowledgment of the impending horrors awaiting them. Emily, still under the influence of the spectral forces, stepped forward with an unwavering determination. The mansion seemed to welcome her, its walls pulsating with an unseen heartbeat.

As the friends entered, the doors slammed shut behind them, sealing their fate within the spectral confines of the mansion. The air grew colder, and the walls whispered tales of betrayal, sacrifice, and the unrelenting hunger that bound the Goatman to its cursed existence. Shadows danced along the corridors, casting grotesque silhouettes that seemed to mock the intruders.

The mansion, a labyrinth of forgotten memories and spectral horrors, unfolded its secrets with each creaking floorboard and echoing whisper. The friends, now prisoners of the spectral drama, ventured deeper into the heart of the ancient structure. The Goatman's

laughter, a sinister undertone, reverberated through the halls, guiding them toward an inevitable confrontation.

Rooms adorned with dusty relics told stories of a bygone era, where the mansion was once a place of decadence and opulence. Now, draped in an ethereal gloom, the grandeur had given way to a pervading sense of decay. Paintings on the walls seemed to watch the intruders with hollow eyes, capturing moments of torment and despair.

Emily, compelled by unseen forces, led the group to a grand hall adorned with a twisted chandelier that cast eerie patterns of light. In the center stood a forgotten altar, covered in cryptic symbols. The air thickened with a spectral presence, and the friends felt the weight of unseen eyes upon them.

As Emily approached the altar, the whispers intensified, forming a cacophony that echoed through the mansion. Visions of ancient rituals played out before the friends, a tapestry of eldritch ceremonies and sacrificial rites. The Goatman's curse, woven into the very fabric of the mansion, revealed its darkest secrets.

Mark, his skepticism now replaced by a growing dread, watched as the spectral energy coalesced around Emily. Shadows danced upon the walls, forming grotesque figures that seemed to writhe in agony. The grand hall became a theater for the unfolding nightmare, with the friends as unwilling actors in a cosmic play.

The rest of the group, caught in the spectral current, stood as witnesses to the ancient forces that manipulated their destinies. The Goatman, now a looming presence within the grand hall, revealed itself with a spectral radiance. The air crackled with an otherworldly electricity as the friends braced themselves for the climax of the haunting spectacle.

Emily, her eyes now reflecting the eerie glow of the altar, spoke words that resonated with ancient power. The symbols etched into

the stone seemed to come alive, glowing brighter with each incantation. The grand hall pulsed with a spectral energy, and the friends felt the very fabric of reality unraveling around them.

A rift, a tear in the fabric of the supernatural, opened before the altar. From the depths emerged the Goatman, its form flickering with a malevolent radiance. The friends, now faced with the spectral entity, felt a chill that transcended the physical realm. The Goatman's laughter, a haunting melody, echoed through the grand hall.

The friends, caught in the grip of the Goatman's curse, were now mere pawns in its cosmic machinations. The mansion, a stage for the unfolding nightmare, seemed to warp and contort with the weight of ancient malevolence. Shadows, now animated with spectral life, closed in around the group, forming a suffocating shroud.

The Goatman, its voice echoing through the halls, spoke of cosmic bargains and the inevitable descent into darkness. The grand hall became a battleground for the friends' sanity as the Goatman's words clawed at the edges of their minds. The spectral currents, now a tempest of unseen forces, whipped through the mansion with an otherworldly fury.

As the friends stood before the altar, a choice loomed in the shadows—an offering to the Goatman or a futile attempt to defy the cosmic forces that bound them. The air crackled with an impending doom, and the grand hall seemed to hold its breath in anticipation of the friends' decision.

Emily, now a conduit for the Goatman's curse, faced the friends with hollow eyes. The whispers, once a dissonant symphony, became a unified chorus urging them toward the inevitable. The spectral threads tightened, pulling the friends into the cosmic dance that awaited its final act within the haunted mansion.

The friends, their fates entwined with the Goatman's curse, stood at the precipice of their own unraveling. The grand hall, a

silent witness to centuries of spectral torment, seemed to echo with the cries of lost souls and the laughter of an entity that defied mortal understanding.

The twisted trails, once a path through the haunted woods, now extended into the very fabric of their existence. The spectral alliance, an unbreakable bond, bound them to the Goatman's curse with an inescapable resolve. The friends, now faced with a choice that would seal their destinies, braced themselves for the next chapter in the cosmic nightmare that unfolded within the walls of the haunted mansion.

Chapter 13: Pact with the Shadows

The grand hall, now a stage for the unfolding cosmic drama, held its breath as the friends stood before the ancient altar. The Goatman, its spectral form flickering with malevolent radiance, loomed over them like a puppeteer orchestrating the final act of a nightmarish play. The air crackled with ethereal energy, and shadows clung to the walls, whispering tales of ancient pacts and unspeakable horrors.

Emily, a conduit for the Goatman's curse, raised her arms as if guided by unseen hands. The symbols on the altar pulsed with an otherworldly glow, and the friends felt the spectral currents intensify. The grand hall seemed to warp, its dimensions shifting in response to the cosmic forces at play. The Goatman's laughter echoed through the mansion, a haunting melody that heralded the imminent climax.

The friends, ensnared by the spectral alliance, felt the weight of the Goatman's gaze upon them. Unseen threads tightened, binding them to the ancient curse that now permeated the very fabric of the mansion. Mark, tormented by doubt and the shadows of betrayal, struggled to comprehend the unfolding nightmare. The grand hall, once a sanctuary of opulence, now exuded a malevolent aura that seeped into the marrow of their bones.

As Emily spoke the incantations, the spectral energy coalesced into a swirling vortex above the altar. The rift, a tear in the fabric of reality, widened, revealing glimpses of a cosmic void that defied mortal comprehension. The Goatman's voice, now a chorus of haunting whispers, echoed through the rift, speaking of forbidden knowledge and the inevitability of their entanglement with the supernatural.

The friends, caught in the grip of the Goatman's curse, felt an inexorable pull toward the cosmic void. Shadows danced upon the edges of the rift, forming grotesque figures that seemed to beckon them into the unknown. The grand hall, now a gateway to cosmic horrors, awaited the friends' choice—submit to the Goatman's influence or defy the cosmic forces that sought to unravel their existence.

Mark, his mind a tempest of conflicting emotions, looked to the other friends. Their faces mirrored the uncertainty that gnawed at his sanity. The Goatman's laughter, a maddening cacophony, intensified as the rift pulsed with an otherworldly glow. The decision, an irreversible pact with the shadows, loomed before them like a specter of doom.

Emily, her eyes hollow and distant, uttered words that seemed to resonate with the very fabric of the supernatural. The friends, compelled by unseen forces, stepped closer to the rift. The grand hall seemed to blur, its boundaries dissolving as the spectral energies surged around them.

Suddenly, the mansion trembled as if in response to an ancient power. The Goatman's laughter, once triumphant, faltered for a moment. The friends, caught in the grip of the cosmic tempest, felt a shift in the spectral currents. The rift, now a pulsating maw, cast an eerie glow upon their faces.

A voice, neither human nor spectral, reverberated through the grand hall—a lamentation that spoke of cosmic balance and the

consequences of meddling with forces beyond mortal understanding. The Goatman, its spectral form recoiling as if struck by an unseen force, hissed with an otherworldly fury.

The friends, momentarily released from the ethereal trance, found themselves standing at the precipice of the rift. The grand hall, now a battleground between cosmic entities, seemed to hold its breath in anticipation of the friends' next move.

Mark, his rational mind clashing with the supernatural forces that surrounded him, hesitated. The Goatman's curse, now weakened but far from defeated, still pulsed through the mansion. Shadows, like tendrils of malevolence, reached out from the walls, whispering promises of forbidden knowledge and unspeakable power.

The other friends, their faces etched with the struggle of internal conflicts, looked to Mark as if seeking guidance. The grand hall, a silent witness to their existential torment, seemed to echo with the cries of lost souls and the laughter of entities that defied mortal comprehension.

In that moment of hesitation, the Goatman's laughter resurged with a renewed malevolence. The spectral currents, like an invisible tide, surged forward, pulling the friends closer to the rift. Shadows clung to them, entwining with the unseen threads that bound them to the ancient curse.

Emily, still under the influence of the Goatman's influence, stepped closer to the rift. The grand hall, now a surreal tableau of cosmic conflict, seemed to warp and contort with the weight of ancient malevolence. The air, thick with the residue of spectral energy, clung to them as a suffocating shroud.

Mark, torn between defiance and the allure of forbidden power, felt the weight of the Goatman's gaze upon him. The rift, a gateway to the unknown, beckoned with a promise of cosmic revelations.

The friends, now at the mercy of supernatural forces, stood on the brink of a choice that would seal their destinies.

As Emily extended her hand toward the rift, the grand hall vibrated with an otherworldly resonance. The Goatman, its form flickering with a desperate fury, hissed with a spectral voice that echoed through the very fabric of the mansion. The friends, caught in the cosmic struggle, felt a surge of unseen forces that threatened to tear their souls asunder.

A voice, ancient and authoritative, cut through the chaos. It spoke of cosmic balance and the need for mortals to resist the temptations that lurked within the shadows. The rift, now a swirling maelstrom of spectral energy, seemed to respond to the authoritative voice.

The Goatman's laughter waned, replaced by an eerie silence. The friends, their minds still entangled in the ethereal web, witnessed the rift's transformation. The cosmic void, once a gateway to the unknown, now shimmered with a tranquil luminescence. Shadows receded, revealing the grand hall in its original state.

The friends, released from the spectral trance, found themselves standing in the mansion's grand hall. The Goatman, its presence diminished but not vanquished, lingered at the periphery of their perception. The air, now devoid of the suffocating spectral shroud, held a sense of uneasy calm.

The authoritative voice, a guiding force that had intervened in the cosmic struggle, echoed through the mansion. It spoke of the friends' resilience in the face of cosmic temptation and the importance of maintaining the delicate balance between the mortal realm and the supernatural. The grand hall, now free from the oppressive malevolence that had gripped it, seemed to regain a semblance of its former opulence. Paintings on the walls, once twisted depictions of torment, now appeared as mere artistic renderings. The dilapidated

mansion, bathed in an otherworldly glow, retained an eerie beauty that hinted at a history shrouded in mystery.

The friends, their senses returning to them, exchanged uncertain glances. The Goatman, a diminished presence, retreated further into the shadows, its spectral form flickering like a dying ember. The authoritative voice continued to resonate, guiding the friends toward a newfound understanding of the cosmic forces that governed their existence.

Mark, his mind a battlefield between reason and supernatural influence, struggled to reconcile the surreal events that had unfolded. The grand hall, once a chamber of horrors, now felt almost serene. The spectral currents, while still present, seemed to ebb away, leaving behind an uneasy calm.

The friends, guided by the authoritative voice, explored the mansion with a newfound sense of purpose. Rooms that had once harbored spectral terrors now revealed forgotten artifacts and relics of a bygone era. The Goatman's curse, now a fading echo, no longer held the mansion in its suffocating grip.

As they ventured deeper into the mansion, the authoritative voice spoke of ancient rituals, cosmic guardians, and the delicate balance that must be maintained to prevent the malevolence of the supernatural from overwhelming the mortal realm. The friends, their minds now attuned to the guiding force, began to understand the significance of their journey.

In a forgotten library, they discovered tomes that chronicled the history of the Goatman—a tragic entity bound by an unholy alliance forged in the shadows of cosmic realms. The authoritative voice explained that the friends' defiance had disrupted the spectral equilibrium, offering a chance to tip the balance away from the malevolence that had plagued the haunted woods.

Mark, grappling with the revelations, felt a weight lifting from his shoulders. The Goatman, now a vanquished specter, no longer held sway over his mind. The friends, united by their shared struggle, delved deeper into the mansion's secrets, guided by the authoritative voice toward a resolution that would safeguard both the mortal and supernatural realms.

In a chamber hidden beneath the mansion, they discovered an ancient artifact—an amulet pulsating with ethereal energy. The authoritative voice explained that the amulet had the power to seal the remnants of the Goatman's curse and restore balance to the haunted woods. The friends, now entrusted with a cosmic responsibility, prepared for a final confrontation.

The grand hall, once witness to cosmic struggles, became a staging ground for the friends' decisive act. The amulet, held by Emily, radiated with a soothing luminescence. The Goatman, its diminished form lingering in the shadows, hissed with a fading defiance.

As Emily approached the spectral remnants of the Goatman's curse, the authoritative voice guided her in a ritual of sealing. Symbols etched into the floor glowed with an otherworldly radiance. The friends, standing in a circle around the amulet, channeled their collective energy into the cosmic task before them.

The mansion trembled as the ritual unfolded, and the Goatman's laughter echoed one last time through the grand hall. Shadows, now devoid of malevolence, danced with a newfound serenity. The friends, their resolve unbroken, witnessed the ethereal currents converging toward the amulet, sealing the remnants of the Goatman's curse within its crystalline core.

A blinding light enveloped the grand hall, and the mansion seemed to transcend the boundaries of time and space. The friends felt a cosmic energy surging through them, connecting them to the very essence of the supernatural. The authoritative voice, now a

benevolent guide, spoke of the friends' triumph over cosmic malevolence and the restoration of equilibrium.

As the light subsided, the grand hall returned to its former state of faded grandeur. The Goatman, its spectral form extinguished, became a mere memory. The haunted woods, once a realm of cosmic nightmares, seemed to breathe with newfound vitality. The friends, now free from the spectral alliance that had bound them, emerged from the mansion with a sense of accomplishment.

The authoritative voice, a fading echo, spoke its final words of gratitude and guidance. The friends, forever changed by their ordeal, walked out of the haunted woods into the moonlit night. The spectral currents, now a gentle breeze, whispered tales of ancient struggles and cosmic resolutions.

As they exited the woods, the haunted realm seemed to recede into the shadows. The Goatman's curse, sealed within the amulet, no longer held dominion over the supernatural enclave. The friends, marked by their journey through cosmic horrors, carried the weight of their experiences as a testament to the delicate balance between the mortal and supernatural realms.

The haunted woods, now a tranquil grove bathed in moonlight, stood as a testament to the friends' resilience. The spectral alliance, once a malevolent force, had been disrupted, and the cosmic equilibrium restored. The friends, forever bonded by their shared struggle, left the haunted woods behind, their footsteps echoing with the echoes of ancient tales and the triumphant resolution of cosmic mysteries.

As they ventured further from the haunted woods, the moonlit path guided them back to the realm of the living. The friends, still processing the surreal events, found solace in the gentle rustle of leaves and the calming night breeze. The amulet, now a relic of

their cosmic triumph, radiated with a subtle glow, a testament to the balance they had restored.

The authoritative voice, its echoes fading into the night, left the friends with a lingering sense of purpose. The haunted mansion, once a chamber of spectral horrors, disappeared from their view. The spectral currents, now harmonized with the natural energies of the world, whispered tales of ancient guardians and cosmic safeguards.

Mark, his mind now free from the haunting influence, looked at his friends with a mixture of relief and gratitude. The journey through the haunted woods had forged bonds that transcended the boundaries of the mundane. The friends, forever changed by their cosmic ordeal, shared an unspoken understanding that went beyond the realm of mortal comprehension.

As they walked, the moon casting a silver glow on their path, the friends reflected on the cosmic mysteries they had encountered. The haunted woods, once a realm of malevolence, had become a sanctuary of cosmic balance. The amulet, now a symbol of their resilience, dangled from Emily's neck, a reminder of the unseen forces that bound them together.

In the distance, the haunted woods receded into the night, its secrets hidden once more within the shadows. The friends, now free from the spectral alliance, emerged into the world with a newfound appreciation for the delicate interplay between the known and the unknown. The cosmic forces, once a source of terror, had become guardians of a delicate equilibrium.

Days turned into nights, and the friends continued their journey, forever marked by the spectral ordeal. The haunted woods, now a distant memory, left an indelible imprint on their souls. The amulet, a silent guardian against malevolence, resonated with the cosmic energies that flowed through their veins.

As they reached the outskirts of a nearby town, the friends paused to gaze back at the moonlit horizon. The haunted woods, a realm of cosmic nightmares, remained hidden in the distance. The amulet, now a talisman of cosmic balance, glowed with a reassuring warmth.

The friends, bound by the shared secrets of the supernatural, moved forward into the tapestry of their lives. The authoritative voice, a distant echo, whispered final words of guidance, fading into the realm of forgotten cosmic tales. The haunted mansion, once a chamber of horrors, became a relic in their collective memory.

The moon, a silent witness to their cosmic journey, cast its light upon the friends as they continued their way. The spectral currents, now a gentle presence, whispered tales of ancient guardians watching over the boundaries between realms. The friends, now guardians in their own right, carried the weight of their cosmic triumph as they embraced the unknown that lay ahead.

The moonlit night, with its secrets and mysteries, enveloped the friends in a comforting embrace. The haunted woods, once a crucible of terror, became a distant chapter in the ever-expanding cosmic narrative. The friends, forever intertwined by the unseen threads of their shared ordeal, moved forward into the mysteries that awaited them, their footsteps echoing with the echoes of ancient tales and the triumphant resolution of cosmic enigmas.

Chapter 14: Echoes of the Unknown

The town at the outskirts offered a semblance of normalcy, but the friends couldn't shake the echoes of the haunted woods that lingered in the recesses of their minds. The amulet, now a silent guardian against unseen forces, emitted a subtle glow as they navigated the streets. The authoritative voice, a distant whisper, continued to guide them with cryptic assurances.

In the heart of the town, they stumbled upon an ancient bookstore. The shelves were lined with weathered tomes containing forgotten knowledge of the supernatural. The friends, still haunted by their cosmic journey, felt an irresistible pull toward the musty volumes that hinted at untold mysteries.

As they delved into the books, the words on the pages seemed to come alive, recounting tales of forgotten rituals, eldritch entities, and the delicate balance that tethered the mortal and supernatural realms. The amulet, attuned to the ancient energies, pulsed with an otherworldly resonance as if acknowledging the truths within the pages.

One particular book caught their attention—an ancient grimoire that spoke of cosmic gateways and the consequences of disrupting the equilibrium between realms. The authoritative voice, now a comforting presence, guided them to a passage that foretold of a looming cosmic disturbance tied to their recent ordeal.

The friends, gripped by a sense of urgency, sought answers from the cryptic text. The grimoire spoke of a cosmic entity known as the Veilstitcher—an ancient force responsible for mending the fabric of reality when disrupted by mortal meddling. The disrupted equilibrium in the haunted woods had awakened the Veilstitcher, and its influence now extended beyond the spectral enclave.

A foreboding realization set in—the friends' actions in the haunted woods had not only disrupted the Goatman's curse but had also set in motion a cosmic chain reaction. The Veilstitcher, a guardian of the cosmic balance, now sought to mend the fabric of reality by any means necessary.

The town, once a refuge, now became a battleground between the Veilstitcher's influence and the friends' struggle for understanding. Shadows seemed to dance with a newfound malevolence, and

the air vibrated with an otherworldly tension. The authoritative voice, now urgent, guided the friends toward a cosmic reckoning.

As night fell, the friends found themselves drawn to an abandoned mansion on the outskirts of the town—a structure that resonated with the cosmic energies emanating from the awakened Veilstitcher. The amulet, now glowing with an intensity that mirrored the urgency of their mission, led them through the moonlit streets toward the looming edifice.

The mansion, a spectral relic like the one in the haunted woods, exuded an ethereal glow. The Veilstitcher's influence seemed to warp the very fabric of reality within its walls. The friends, their minds attuned to the cosmic energies, hesitated at the threshold, knowing that their actions within might determine the fate of both the mortal and supernatural realms.

As they entered, the mansion revealed itself as a nexus of cosmic energies. The authoritative voice, now resonating with a somber tone, explained that the Veilstitcher, once a dormant guardian, had been stirred by the friends' disruption of the cosmic equilibrium. The mansion, a convergence point of realities, now stood as a battleground for their cosmic destiny.

The rooms within the mansion, adorned with symbols that pulsed with cosmic significance, told tales of forgotten rituals and eldritch pacts. Shadows, animated by the Veilstitcher's influence, seemed to observe the intruders with an ominous awareness. The friends, guided by the amulet and the authoritative voice, navigated the twisting corridors toward the heart of the cosmic disturbance.

In a grand chamber, they discovered an ancient portal—a tear in the fabric of reality itself. The Veilstitcher, a spectral entity with threads of cosmic energy weaving around it, stood at the center. The authoritative voice, now a desperate plea, urged the friends to

confront the awakened guardian and seek a resolution that could prevent the unraveling of reality.

The friends, their minds burdened by the weight of cosmic responsibility, faced the Veilstitcher. Its presence, a maelstrom of spectral energies, seemed to scrutinize their very essence. The amulet, now radiating with an otherworldly brilliance, resonated with the Veilstitcher's influence.

The authoritative voice spoke of a cosmic choice—a pact with the Veilstitcher to mend the fabric of reality or a defiance that could unleash untold cosmic consequences. The friends, bound by the unseen threads of their shared journey, exchanged uneasy glances as the Veilstitcher's influence pulsed around them.

Emily, still attuned to the cosmic currents, stepped forward with a sense of purpose. The amulet, now a conduit for cosmic energies, seemed to respond to her presence. The Veilstitcher, its spectral form shifting with an otherworldly grace, communicated in a language of cosmic vibrations that transcended mortal comprehension.

As Emily spoke, her words resonated with the Veilstitcher's energies. The symbols around the portal glowed with an ethereal luminescence, and the grand chamber seemed to ripple with unseen forces. The friends, caught between cosmic choices, felt the weight of their destinies hanging in the balance.

The Veilstitcher, now engaged in a cosmic dialogue, revealed the consequences of its awakening. Reality, torn by the disruption in the haunted woods, threatened to unravel unless a cosmic pact was forged. The friends, their minds a battleground between mortal instincts and cosmic responsibilities, listened to the Veilstitcher's revelations.

Mark, still grappling with the echoes of the haunted woods, questioned the Veilstitcher's motives. The authoritative voice, now a spectral whisper, explained that the awakened guardian sought to

preserve the delicate balance disrupted by mortal interference. The Veilstitcher's influence, while imposing, was a necessary force to prevent cosmic chaos.

The friends, now faced with an impossible choice, deliberated their next move. The Veilstitcher, its spectral form exuding a sense of inevitability, awaited their decision. The amulet, a silent witness to the cosmic drama, pulsed with an intensity that mirrored the urgency of the situation.

As the friends reached a collective decision, the Veilstitcher's influence intensified. The grand chamber seemed to tremble with unseen forces as cosmic energies converged around the portal. Shadows, now imbued with the guardian's essence, danced along the walls, casting grotesque silhouettes.

The Veilstitcher, its spectral form resonating with a somber luminescence, spoke words that transcended mortal comprehension. The friends, guided by the authoritative voice and the amulet's influence, entered into a cosmic pact with the awakened guardian. The symbols on the portal glowed brighter, and reality seemed to shift as the pact was forged.

The town outside, once caught in the grip of the Veilstitcher's influence, returned to a semblance of normalcy. The cosmic energies, now harmonized by the friends' choice, resonated with a tranquil hum. The mansion, a nexus of cosmic disturbances, faded into the shadows as the portal closed behind them.

The authoritative voice, a fading echo, expressed gratitude for the friends' sacrifice in preserving the cosmic equilibrium. The amulet, now a symbol of their cosmic pact, emitted a subdued glow. The Veilstitcher's influence, while still present, now felt more like a benevolent current flowing through the friends' veins. The cosmic energies, once turbulent, settled into a harmonious resonance that connected the mortal and supernatural realms.

The friends, their minds still echoing with the cosmic dialogue, emerged from the grand chamber. The mansion, now devoid of spectral disturbances, felt like a sanctuary of forgotten cosmic truths. The town, released from the Veilstitcher's influence, embraced a serene calm that hinted at the delicate balance that had been restored.

As the friends walked through the moonlit streets, the amulet pulsed with a gentle radiance. The authoritative voice, now a comforting whisper, spoke of the friends' role as guardians of the cosmic equilibrium. The Veilstitcher, its spectral presence lingering in the background, communicated an unspoken assurance that their sacrifice had averted a cosmic catastrophe.

Days turned into nights, and the friends found themselves drawn to the ancient bookstore once again. The tomes that had once spoken of cosmic disturbances now revealed passages about cosmic guardians and the delicate dance between realms. The friends, now more attuned to the cosmic energies, sought further understanding of their newfound responsibilities.

In the bookstore, they discovered a hidden chamber that housed an ancient artifact—a celestial map that depicted the interconnected realms of existence. The authoritative voice guided them to specific constellations that represented cosmic gateways and unseen forces that governed the fabric of reality.

As the friends studied the celestial map, the Veilstitcher's influence resonated with the symbols, creating an ethereal connection between the mortal and supernatural realms. The amulet, now an instrument of cosmic awareness, hummed with a resonant frequency that mirrored the cosmic energies depicted on the map.

The authoritative voice explained that the friends, having forged a cosmic pact with the Veilstitcher, now held the key to maintaining the delicate balance between realms. Their journey, once a

harrowing ordeal, had transformed into a cosmic responsibility to safeguard the cosmic equilibrium.

Guided by the celestial map and the amulet, the friends embarked on a journey that transcended the boundaries of the known. They visited ancient sites, long-forgotten temples, and mystical landscapes that resonated with cosmic energies. The Veilstitcher's influence, now a guiding force, revealed hidden truths about the interconnected nature of existence.

In their cosmic travels, the friends encountered otherworldly entities—guardians, cosmic spirits, and ethereal beings that watched over the boundaries between realms. Each encounter deepened their understanding of the cosmic forces at play and reinforced the importance of their role as guardians of the equilibrium.

The celestial map, now a cosmic compass, led them to a sacred grove bathed in starlight. The Veilstitcher's influence pulsed through the ancient trees, and the amulet resonated with a sublime luminescence. The authoritative voice, now a guiding presence, spoke of a cosmic convergence that required the friends' attention.

In the heart of the sacred grove, a cosmic portal shimmered with an otherworldly radiance. The symbols on the portal echoed the constellations on the celestial map. The friends, their minds attuned to the Veilstitcher's influence, recognized the significance of the cosmic convergence.

As they approached the portal, the Veilstitcher's spectral form materialized, its presence now a harmonious dance of cosmic energies. The amulet, imbued with the friends' cosmic journey, resonated with the portal's energies. The authoritative voice spoke of a cosmic event that would test their resolve and strengthen the bonds between realms.

The friends, guided by their newfound cosmic awareness, stepped through the portal. The celestial map, now a guide through the

cosmic convergence, revealed a breathtaking tapestry of interconnected realms. The Veilstitcher's influence, once a source of cosmic disturbance, now merged seamlessly with the cosmic currents that flowed through the tapestry.

As they traversed the cosmic convergence, the friends encountered celestial phenomena—shifting realities, ethereal landscapes, and manifestations of cosmic energies that transcended mortal comprehension. The amulet, now a conduit for their shared cosmic journey, pulsed with a vibrant energy that mirrored the celestial wonders around them.

The authoritative voice, a guiding presence in the cosmic expanse, explained the friends' role in maintaining the delicate balance between realms during the convergence. The Veilstitcher, its spectral form intertwining with the cosmic currents, communicated an unspoken assurance that their cosmic pact had prepared them for this pivotal moment.

In the cosmic tapestry, the friends witnessed the Veilstitcher's influence harmonizing with other cosmic guardians. The celestial convergence, a sublime dance of energies, echoed with the echoes of ancient tales and cosmic resolutions. The friends, now guardians of the equilibrium, embraced their role with a sense of cosmic purpose.

As the cosmic convergence reached its zenith, the friends felt a profound connection to the very fabric of existence. The Veilstitcher's influence, now a benevolent force, guided them through the celestial wonders. The amulet, a symbol of their cosmic journey, radiated with a brilliance that mirrored the cosmic energies that flowed through the tapestry.

As the friends emerged from the cosmic convergence, they found themselves back in the sacred grove bathed in starlight. The portal closed behind them, leaving a lingering sense of cosmic awareness. The Veilstitcher's spectral form, now a distant presence, conveyed

a silent gratitude for the friends' guardianship of the cosmic equilibrium.

The celestial map, still in their possession, revealed new constellations that represented the friends' cosmic journey. The authoritative voice, a fading echo, spoke of the friends' transformation from seekers of the unknown to guardians of cosmic balance. The amulet, now a relic imbued with cosmic energies, pulsed with a steady resonance.

The friends, forever changed by their cosmic ordeal, looked to the night sky with a newfound understanding. The echoes of the unknown, once a source of terror, now whispered tales of cosmic guardianship and the delicate dance between realms. The Veilstitcher's influence, though distant, remained a guiding force in their cosmic journey.

As the friends ventured back into the mortal realm, the town at the outskirts welcomed them with a tranquil calm. The echoes of the haunted woods and the cosmic convergence became part of their collective memory. The amulet, now a timeless artifact, symbolized their connection to the cosmic forces that governed existence.

The Veilstitcher, a guardian in the cosmic expanse, continued its silent vigil over the delicate balance between realms. The friends, now stewards of the equilibrium, embraced their cosmic responsibilities with a sense of purpose. The cosmic tapestry, woven with threads of celestial wonders, echoed with the echoes of ancient tales and the triumphant resolution of cosmic enigmas.

Guided by the celestial map, the friends embarked on a journey to further understand and strengthen their cosmic abilities. The amulet, now an integral part of their existence, resonated with the energies of the interconnected realms. The Veilstitcher's influence, though no longer a constant presence, lingered as a silent assurance in the background.

As they delved into their newfound cosmic awareness, the friends discovered hidden sanctuaries and ancient sites where the fabric of reality seemed thin. Each encounter with cosmic phenomena deepened their understanding of the delicate balance they upheld. The celestial map, now a well-worn guide, led them to forgotten realms where cosmic secrets awaited revelation.

The friends encountered other guardians—ethereal beings who watched over specific aspects of the cosmic equilibrium. These cosmic sentinels imparted ancient wisdom and shared tales of cosmic struggles that transcended mortal lifetimes. The amulet, responding to the cosmic revelations, pulsed with an ethereal glow that mirrored the wisdom they gained.

In one such realm, the friends faced a cosmic trial—an otherworldly challenge that tested their resilience and understanding of the interconnected tapestry. The Veilstitcher's influence, once again a guiding force, whispered encouragement as the friends navigated through shifting realities and celestial puzzles. The amulet, a source of cosmic strength, resonated with a brilliance that defied mortal comprehension.

As they emerged victorious from the cosmic trial, the friends felt a surge of cosmic energy coursing through them. The celestial map, now adorned with new constellations, reflected their triumph. The Veilstitcher's spectral form, a distant but benevolent presence, communicated a silent acknowledgment of their growth as cosmic stewards.

The friends, now attuned to the cosmic rhythms, realized that their journey had become a perpetual quest to maintain the balance between realms. The Veilstitcher's influence guided them toward cosmic disturbances that threatened to disrupt the delicate equilibrium. The amulet, a cosmic compass, pulsed with urgency as the friends embraced their roles as cosmic guardians.

In one particularly perilous encounter, the friends faced an entity that sought to unravel the threads of reality. The cosmic disturbance, a malevolent force that defied comprehension, manifested in shifting shadows and ethereal echoes. The Veilstitcher's influence, now an active guide, directed the friends in a cosmic battle against the encroaching chaos.

As the friends confronted the cosmic disturbance, the amulet resonated with a fierce brilliance. The celestial map, now animated with cosmic energies, revealed the weaknesses in the malevolent force. Guided by the Veilstitcher's influence, the friends channeled their cosmic abilities to weave threads of stability into the fabric of reality.

The cosmic battle unfolded in a surreal dance of energies, with the friends wielding the amulet as a conduit for their newfound cosmic powers. The Veilstitcher's spectral form, a silent overseer, observed their efforts with a sense of approval. The celestial map, now a source of tactical insight, guided the friends through the intricate maneuvers needed to restore cosmic equilibrium.

As the malevolent force recoiled under the friends' cosmic onslaught, the cosmic disturbance began to dissipate. The Veilstitcher's influence, intertwined with the amulet's radiant glow, sealed the weakened threads of reality. The friends, exhausted but triumphant, stood amidst the cosmic aftermath, their cosmic abilities now more refined and potent.

The Veilstitcher's spectral form approached, its essence resonating with a profound serenity. The amulet, still glowing with the aftermath of the cosmic battle, conveyed a sense of fulfillment. The celestial map, though marked by the recent cosmic disturbance, hinted at the friends' ongoing journey as cosmic guardians.

As the friends left the disrupted realm, the Veilstitcher's influence lingered as a silent companion. The amulet, now a vessel of cosmic

energies, pulsed with a steady rhythm. The celestial map, enriched by the recent experiences, reflected the intricate dance of cosmic forces that shaped their cosmic journey.

In the wake of the cosmic battle, the friends continued their exploration of interconnected realms. The Veilstitcher's influence, though less prominent, remained a guiding force in their cosmic endeavors. The amulet, now a symbol of their cosmic mastery, resonated with a harmonious energy that connected them to the very essence of the cosmic tapestry.

The friends' travels took them to celestial landscapes, ancient observatories, and cosmic sanctuaries where the boundaries between realms blurred. The Veilstitcher's influence guided them toward cosmic phenomena that demanded their attention. The amulet, now an instrument of cosmic balance, pulsed with an ethereal glow as they upheld their cosmic responsibilities.

Through their cosmic journey, the friends encountered beings of cosmic wisdom and entities that embodied the intricate dance of existence. The Veilstitcher's spectral form, though distant, communicated a sense of approval as the friends navigated through celestial wonders and unearthed forgotten truths.

As the friends embraced their roles as cosmic guardians, the Veilstitcher's influence gradually withdrew, leaving them with a sense of empowerment and cosmic purpose. The amulet, now an artifact infused with cosmic energies, became a symbol of their journey—an enduring testament to their triumphs over cosmic disturbances.

The celestial map, adorned with constellations representing their cosmic victories, guided the friends toward new realms and cosmic challenges. The echoes of the unknown, once a source of terror, now whispered tales of cosmic guardianship and the delicate dance between realms. The friends, forever bound by their shared cosmic

journey, embraced the ongoing mysteries that awaited them in the interconnected tapestry of existence.

As the friends ventured further into the cosmic unknown, the Veilstitcher's spectral form faded into the cosmic expanse, its influence becoming a timeless part of their cosmic legacy. The amulet, a luminous beacon of cosmic mastery, pulsed with the echoes of ancient tales and the triumphant resolution of cosmic enigmas. The celestial map, now a guide through the cosmic realms, unfolded new constellations that beckoned the friends toward their next cosmic adventure—a perpetual odyssey that transcended the boundaries of the known and embraced the infinite possibilities of the cosmic tapestry.

Chapter 15: Cosmic Odyssey

Guided by the celestial map, the friends embarked on a cosmic odyssey that traversed realms beyond mortal comprehension. The interconnected tapestry of existence unfolded before them, revealing celestial wonders, ethereal landscapes, and cosmic phenomena that defied explanation.

The Veilstitcher's influence, though a distant echo, resonated in the cosmic energies that enveloped the friends. The amulet, a radiant beacon of their cosmic mastery, pulsed with an ever-present glow. The celestial map, now adorned with constellations representing their cosmic victories, guided them toward new frontiers in the cosmic expanse.

Their cosmic journey led them to an astral city suspended in the fabric of reality—a nexus where cosmic beings congregated to exchange wisdom and share tales of cosmic struggles. The friends, now revered as cosmic guardians, were welcomed into the celestial enclave. The Veilstitcher's influence, a silent companion, conveyed a sense of pride in their cosmic achievements.

In the astral city, the friends encountered beings of transcendent wisdom—entities that embodied the very essence of cosmic existence. The Veilstitcher's spectral form, though unseen, communicated with the celestial beings in a language of cosmic vibrations. The amulet, resonating with the celestial energies, marked the friends as stewards of the delicate balance between realms.

As they communed with cosmic sages and explored the astral city's ethereal architecture, the friends learned of ancient prophecies that foretold cosmic challenges yet to come. The celestial map, now revealing constellations depicting future cosmic disturbances, guided them toward their next cosmic mission.

The Veilstitcher's influence, now a guiding force in their cosmic endeavors, urged the friends to embrace their roles as cosmic guardians with renewed determination. The amulet, a conduit for cosmic energies, hummed with a harmonious resonance that mirrored the celestial symphony around them.

Their cosmic odyssey led them to a realm where time flowed in paradoxical currents and spatial dimensions intertwined. The celestial map, now navigating through temporal anomalies, revealed cosmic disturbances that threatened to disrupt the cosmic equilibrium. The Veilstitcher's influence, though subtle, guided the friends toward a cosmic anomaly that transcended the boundaries of temporal understanding.

As they entered the realm of temporal paradoxes, the friends encountered echoes of past, present, and future cosmic events. The Veilstitcher's spectral form, now a temporal observer, guided them through the intricacies of temporal anomalies. The amulet, attuned to the temporal energies, pulsed with a rhythmic cadence that marked the ebb and flow of cosmic time.

In their cosmic exploration, the friends faced temporal challenges that tested their understanding of the interconnected tapestry. The

celestial map, now a guide through the temporal labyrinth, revealed constellations representing pivotal moments in cosmic history. The Veilstitcher's influence, intertwined with the amulet's radiant glow, whispered insights into the delicate dance between temporal forces.

As they navigated through temporal currents and faced paradoxical trials, the friends felt the weight of cosmic responsibility. The Veilstitcher's spectral form, a temporal overseer, communicated a sense of urgency in preserving the cosmic equilibrium across all timelines. The amulet, a temporal anchor, resonated with a steady frequency that harmonized with the cosmic time stream.

Their triumph over temporal challenges marked a pivotal moment in their cosmic journey. The Veilstitcher's influence, though bound by temporal constraints, conveyed a sense of approval. The amulet, now a temporal artifact, bore the imprints of their cosmic victories in the temporal realm.

The celestial map, enriched by their experiences in the realm of temporal paradoxes, guided the friends toward new frontiers in the cosmic tapestry. The Veilstitcher's spectral form, though distant, remained a silent companion in their cosmic odyssey. The amulet, now a relic infused with temporal energies, pulsed with the echoes of ancient tales and the triumphant resolution of temporal enigmas.

As the friends ventured further into the cosmic unknown, the celestial map unfolded new constellations representing uncharted realms. The Veilstitcher's influence, now a timeless presence, guided them toward cosmic phenomena that transcended mortal understanding. The amulet, an ever-present source of cosmic awareness, resonated with a luminous brilliance that mirrored the cosmic wonders around them.

Their cosmic odyssey continued, weaving through realms of surreal beauty, cosmic challenges, and ancient mysteries. The Veilstitcher's spectral form, now an ethereal companion, communicated

a sense of purpose in their ongoing quest to uphold the delicate balance between realms. The amulet, a cosmic talisman, pulsed with an enduring glow that marked the friends as eternal stewards of the cosmic equilibrium.

As the friends embraced the infinite possibilities of the cosmic tapestry, the echoes of the unknown whispered tales of cosmic guardianship and the intricate dance between realms. The Veilstitcher's influence, though timeless, remained an ever-watchful guide in their perpetual cosmic adventure. The amulet, a radiant symbol of their cosmic journey, continued to resonate with the echoes of ancient tales and the triumphant resolution of cosmic enigmas.

In the vast expanse of the interconnected tapestry, the friends' cosmic odyssey unfolded like an eternal saga—an ongoing exploration of the unknown, a journey that transcended the boundaries of the known, and a testament to the enduring bond between mortal souls and the cosmic forces that shaped their destinies.

Chapter 15: The Abyss of Cosmic Dread

As the friends delved deeper into the cosmic expanse, guided by the celestial map, they sensed an ominous shift in the fabric of reality. The Veilstitcher's influence, once a reassuring presence, now vibrated with an undercurrent of cosmic dread. The amulet, usually radiant with cosmic energies, flickered with an unsettling uncertainty as they approached a realm shrouded in cosmic shadows.

The astral city, which had once welcomed them as revered cosmic guardians, now revealed a darker underbelly. Celestial beings, their ethereal forms distorted by an unseen malevolence, whispered foreboding prophecies of an impending cosmic catastrophe. The Veilstitcher's spectral form, still present but veiled in cosmic dread, communicated a sense of urgency that sent shivers through the friends' cosmic awareness.

The celestial map, now marked by constellations that seemed to writhe with cosmic unease, directed them toward an abyssal rift—an anomaly in the fabric of existence that emitted an unsettling resonance. As they approached the cosmic abyss, the amulet pulsed with an erratic energy, reflecting the growing cosmic disturbance that threatened to unravel the delicate balance between realms.

As they entered the abyssal rift, the friends felt an overwhelming sense of existential dread. The Veilstitcher's influence, usually a guiding force, now manifested as haunting whispers that echoed through the cosmic void. Shadows danced with a malevolent glee, and the celestial map, once a source of guidance, seemed to lead them deeper into the cosmic abyss.

In the depths of the rift, the friends encountered cosmic horrors that defied mortal comprehension. Entities of cosmic malevolence, their forms twisted by the abyssal energies, sought to consume the very essence of their cosmic being. The Veilstitcher's spectral form, dimmed by the cosmic dread, conveyed a silent plea for the friends to resist the encroaching darkness.

The amulet, struggling against the oppressive forces of the abyss, emitted flashes of dim light that barely illuminated the cosmic horrors that lurked in the shadows. The celestial map, now distorted by the abyssal energies, led the friends through maddening labyrinths where reality itself seemed to unravel.

As they faced the cosmic horrors, the friends felt the weight of existential terror bearing down upon them. The Veilstitcher's spectral form, now a flickering beacon in the cosmic abyss, urged them to confront the source of the malevolence that threatened to rupture the fabric of reality. The amulet, their only source of cosmic defense, resonated with the desperate pulses of their fear-stricken hearts.

In their cosmic struggle against the abyssal forces, the friends discovered ancient ruins—remnants of a forgotten civilization that

had succumbed to the same cosmic dread. The celestial map, though tainted by the abyssal energies, revealed inscriptions that spoke of rituals to appease eldritch entities and the consequences of cosmic disturbances left unchecked.

The Veilstitcher's spectral form, now dimmed by the encroaching darkness, communicated the dire implications of the abyssal rift's existence. If not sealed, it threatened to become a cosmic tear that could unleash unspeakable horrors upon the interconnected tapestry. The friends, gripped by terror and determination, understood the gravity of their cosmic mission.

As they ventured deeper into the ruins, the abyssal energies twisted the very fabric of reality. Cosmic echoes whispered tales of the doomed civilization that had once thrived in the cosmic abyss. The amulet, now a fragile shield against the abyssal forces, flickered with the desperate hope that the friends could prevent a similar fate.

In the heart of the ruins, the friends discovered a cosmic altar—a focal point for the abyssal energies that pulsed through the rift. Eldritch symbols adorned the altar, resonating with malevolence that sent shivers down their spines. The celestial map, now a guide through the madness, directed them toward a cosmic ritual that could seal the abyssal rift and avert the impending cosmic catastrophe.

As they prepared to enact the ritual, the friends felt the oppressive weight of the abyssal energies bearing down upon them. Whispers of cosmic horrors echoed in their minds, and the Veilstitcher's spectral form, barely visible amidst the cosmic dread, communicated the urgency of completing the ritual before the fabric of reality unraveled completely.

The amulet, now strained to its cosmic limits, emitted a feeble glow as the friends channeled their cosmic abilities into the ritual. Shadows, animated by the abyssal forces, writhed in protest as the

celestial map guided them through the intricate steps of the cosmic sealing. The Veilstitcher's spectral form, though barely discernible, resonated with the friends' determination to defy the encroaching cosmic dread.

In the midst of the ritual, the friends felt the cosmic abyss resisting their efforts. Eldritch energies surged, threatening to overwhelm their sanity. The Veilstitcher's influence, now a beacon in the cosmic storm, lent its spectral strength to their cosmic struggle. The amulet, teetering on the brink of cosmic exhaustion, emitted a final burst of radiant light that merged with the celestial energies of the sealing ritual.

As the last cosmic incantation echoed through the ruins, a profound stillness settled over the abyssal rift. The cosmic dread that had permeated the very fabric of reality began to recede. The Veilstitcher's spectral form, now visible in a dim luminescence, conveyed a silent acknowledgment of the friends' success in averting the cosmic catastrophe.

The amulet, though dimmed and worn, retained a subdued glow—a testament to the friends' resilience against the abyssal forces. The celestial map, now cleared of the malevolent constellations, revealed a new cosmic equilibrium that mirrored the triumph over the cosmic dread that had threatened to consume the interconnected tapestry.

As the friends emerged from the ruins, the abyssal rift sealed behind them, the Veilstitcher's spectral form regained its ethereal brilliance. The amulet, though scarred by the cosmic struggle, pulsed with a renewed vitality. The celestial map, now restored to its cosmic clarity, guided them toward realms untouched by the malevolent forces that had lurked in the cosmic abyss.

The friends, forever changed by their harrowing encounter with the abyssal forces, continued their cosmic odyssey with a heightened

awareness of the cosmic horrors that lurked in the vast expanse. The Veilstitcher's influence, now a vigilant guardian, accompanied them as a guiding force. The amulet, a resilient artifact that bore the scars of their cosmic ordeal, resonated with a luminous brilliance that symbolized their triumph over the abyssal dread.

The celestial map, once tainted by malevolence, now guided the friends toward realms where cosmic wonders awaited discovery. The echoes of the unknown, though still haunting, whispered tales of cosmic resilience and the indomitable spirit that defied the abyssal forces. The friends, forever entwined by the shared horrors they had faced, embraced the mysteries that awaited them in the uncharted territories of the interconnected tapestry.

Their cosmic odyssey, now marked by the echoes of cosmic dread and triumphant resilience, unfolded like a cosmic epic—an eternal saga that transcended mortal fears and celebrated the enduring bond between mortal souls and the cosmic forces that shaped their destinies.

Chapter 16: Shadows of the Celestial Betrayal

As the friends ventured further into the cosmic unknown, guided by the celestial map, they found themselves in a realm cloaked in unsettling shadows. The Veilstitcher's influence, though a constant presence, seemed to waver as they approached an ancient observatory atop a desolate cosmic peak. The amulet, typically radiant with cosmic energies, emitted a dim glow that reflected the ominous atmosphere that pervaded the celestial landscape.

The observatory, a structure that bore witness to eons of cosmic phenomena, now echoed with whispers of a celestial betrayal that had cast a dark shadow over the interconnected tapestry. The Veilstitcher's spectral form, a silhouette against the cosmic gloom, communicated a tale of treachery that had resonated through the celestial realms.

The celestial map, now displaying constellations that seemed to writhe in cosmic agony, directed the friends toward the heart of the celestial betrayal. As they ascended the cosmic peak, the shadows deepened, and the amulet pulsed with a disconcerting rhythm that mirrored the cosmic unease.

In the observatory's inner sanctum, the friends discovered a cosmic artifact—a relic of ancient power that had been corrupted by the tendrils of celestial betrayal. Eldritch symbols adorned the artifact, resonating with malevolence that sent shivers down their spines. The Veilstitcher's influence, though shrouded in cosmic sorrow, urged them to unravel the mysteries of the celestial betrayal that had tainted the very essence of the interconnected tapestry.

As the friends examined the corrupted artifact, the shadows within the observatory seemed to come alive. Cosmic entities, twisted by the influence of celestial betrayal, materialized in ghostly forms. The Veilstitcher's spectral form, now obscured by the cosmic gloom, whispered warnings of the malevolent entities that guarded the secrets of the celestial betrayal.

The amulet, sensing the encroaching cosmic malevolence, emitted a protective aura that shielded the friends from the ghostly entities' influence. The celestial map, though distorted by the shadows, revealed inscriptions that chronicled the ancient pact that had led to the celestial betrayal and the cosmic consequences that followed.

In their exploration of the observatory, the friends faced spectral guardians—entities that embodied the malevolent echoes of celestial betrayal. Shadows danced with a haunting grace as the Veilstitcher's influence guided them through cosmic trials that tested their resolve. The amulet, a luminous beacon against the cosmic darkness, resonated with a determination to uncover the truth behind the celestial betrayal.

As they delved deeper into the observatory's mysteries, the whispers of the celestial betrayal grew more pronounced. The Veilstitcher's spectral form, now a spectral guide in the cosmic shadows, conveyed a sense of cosmic sorrow that mirrored the anguish of ancient cosmic entities. The amulet, their only defense against the encroaching malevolence, flickered with a resilient glow that defied the cosmic despair.

In the observatory's inner chambers, the friends uncovered an ancient cosmic chronicle—an illuminated manuscript that chronicled the events leading to the celestial betrayal. The celestial map, now revealing constellations that depicted cosmic alliances shattered by treachery, guided them through the cosmic revelations that awaited.

The Veilstitcher's influence, though shrouded in cosmic sorrow, narrated a tale of celestial beings bound by a sacred covenant to uphold the cosmic equilibrium. Betrayal, driven by cosmic ambition, had fractured the bonds of trust and unleashed cosmic disturbances that reverberated through the interconnected tapestry.

As the friends immersed themselves in the cosmic chronicle, they witnessed cosmic battles, treacherous alliances, and the tragic fall of celestial beings consumed by their desires for power. The celestial map, now marked by constellations that depicted the celestial betrayal in vivid detail, guided them toward the heart of the observatory where the corrupted artifact held the key to understanding the cosmic transgressions.

In the inner sanctum, the friends faced a spectral guardian—an embodiment of the celestial betrayal that had tainted the artifact with malevolent energies. The Veilstitcher's spectral form, now a solemn observer, conveyed a sense of sorrow as the friends confronted the echoes of ancient cosmic treachery. The amulet, resonating with the cosmic revelations, emitted a luminous glow that mirrored the

friends' determination to cleanse the artifact and unravel the mysteries of the celestial betrayal.

The celestial map, now pulsating with the cosmic consequences
of the ancient transgressions, guided the friends through a ritual
to purify the corrupted artifact. Shadows writhed with resistance,
and the spectral guardian unleashed cosmic energies in a desperate attempt to prevent the redemption of the tainted relic. The
Veilstitcher's influence, though veiled in cosmic sorrow, whispered
words of encouragement as the friends channeled their cosmic abilities into the purification ritual.

In the midst of the cosmic struggle, the artifact resonated with
celestial energies, and the shadows within the observatory recoiled.
The Veilstitcher's spectral form, now visible in a dim luminescence,
conveyed a sense of approval as the purification ritual reached its
zenith. The amulet, though strained by the cosmic exertion, emitted
a final burst of radiant light that merged with the purified energies
of the artifact.

As the celestial energies enveloped the observatory, a profound
stillness settled over the cosmic peak. The shadows dissipated, and
the celestial map, now cleared of the malevolent constellations, revealed a new cosmic equilibrium that reflected the friends' triumph
over the celestial betrayal. The Veilstitcher's spectral form, though
still tinged with cosmic sorrow, conveyed a silent acknowledgment
of their success in redeeming the corrupted artifact.

The amulet, though scarred by the cosmic struggle, retained a
subdued glow—a testament to the friends' resilience against the malevolent forces of celestial betrayal. The celestial map, now restored
to its cosmic clarity, guided them toward realms where the echoes of
ancient treachery had been silenced.

As the friends emerged from the observatory, the celestial betrayal purged behind them, the Veilstitcher's spectral form regained

its ethereal brilliance. The amulet, though dimmed and worn, pulsed with a renewed vitality. The celestial map, now cleared of the malevolent constellations, guided them toward new frontiers in the interconnected tapestry.

The friends, forever changed by their harrowing encounter with the celestial betrayal, continued their cosmic odyssey with a heightened awareness of the cosmic transgressions that could threaten the delicate balance between realms. The Veilstitcher's influence, now a vigilant guardian, accompanied them as a guiding force. The amulet, a resilient artifact that bore the scars of their cosmic ordeal, resonated with a luminous brilliance that symbolized their triumph over the shadows of ancient treachery.

The celestial map, once tainted by malevolence, now guided the friends toward realms where cosmic wonders awaited discovery. The echoes of the unknown, though still haunting, whispered tales of cosmic resilience and the indomitable spirit that defied the shadows of celestial betrayal. The friends, forever entwined by the shared horrors they had faced, embraced the mysteries that awaited them in the uncharted territories of the interconnected tapestry.

Their cosmic odyssey, now marked by the echoes of celestial betrayal and triumphant resilience, unfolded like a cosmic epic—an eternal saga that transcended mortal fears and celebrated the enduring bond between mortal souls and the cosmic forces that shaped their destinies.

Chapter 17: Whispers of the Cosmic Abyss

As the friends continued their cosmic odyssey, guided by the celestial map, they found themselves drawn to a realm shrouded in enigmatic whispers—the remnants of cosmic echoes that hinted at an ancient cosmic abyss. The Veilstitcher's influence, a vigilant guardian, resonated with a somber resonance as they approached the threshold of this mysterious cosmic chasm. The amulet, though

usually radiant with cosmic energies, emitted an ethereal glow that reflected the unsettling atmosphere surrounding the abyss.

The celestial map, now marked by constellations that seemed to ripple like cosmic waves, directed the friends toward the edge of the cosmic abyss. As they descended into its depths, the shadows deepened, and the amulet pulsed with an eerie luminosity that mirrored the cosmic uncertainties that lay ahead.

In the cosmic abyss, the friends encountered surreal landscapes where the fabric of reality seemed to unravel. Ethereal whispers, echoing from the depths of the abyss, conveyed tales of ancient cosmic entities that had succumbed to the allure of forbidden knowledge. The Veilstitcher's spectral form, now a solemn guide, warned of the cosmic perils that lurked in the abyssal depths.

As they navigated through the cosmic echoes, the friends faced spectral manifestations—entities born from the lingering remnants of cosmic entities that had unraveled in the abyss. Shadows danced with an otherworldly grace, and the celestial map, now flickering with cosmic uncertainties, guided them through trials that tested their resilience against the cosmic abyss.

The Veilstitcher's influence, though a steadfast companion, communicated a sense of caution as the friends delved deeper into the cosmic unknown. The amulet, their cosmic beacon, emitted a protective aura that shielded them from the haunting forces that sought to entice them into the cosmic abyss's alluring depths.

In the heart of the abyss, the friends discovered an ancient cosmic library—a repository of forbidden knowledge that had driven cosmic entities to madness. Eldritch tomes, adorned with celestial symbols, whispered cosmic secrets that reverberated through the friends' consciousness. The celestial map, now etched with constellations depicting cosmic entities succumbing to the abyssal allure, guided them through the cosmic archives.

The Veilstitcher's spectral form, now a spectral librarian, communicated the dire consequences of delving too deeply into the forbidden knowledge within the cosmic library. The amulet, resonating with the echoes of cosmic entities lost to the abyss, pulsed with a cautionary rhythm that mirrored the friends' trepidation.

As they deciphered the celestial symbols within the tomes, the friends uncovered the tale of an ancient cosmic entity—an entity that had sought to unravel the mysteries of the cosmos but had succumbed to the cosmic abyss's seductive whispers. The celestial map, now revealing constellations that mirrored the entity's descent into madness, guided them toward the entity's resting place within the abyss.

The Veilstitcher's influence, now a solemn guide in the cosmic library, urged the friends to tread carefully as they approached the entity's lair. Shadows, animated by the abyssal energies, seemed to writhe with anticipation, and the amulet emitted a subdued glow that signaled their entry into the heart of the cosmic abyss.

In the presence of the ancient cosmic entity, echoes of madness reverberated through the abyss. The entity's spectral form, twisted by the allure of forbidden knowledge, manifested in surreal splendor. The Veilstitcher's spectral form, a spectral witness to the entity's tragic fate, communicated the profound sorrow that accompanied the entity's descent into the cosmic abyss.

The friends, now confronted by the entity's spectral manifestation, felt the weight of cosmic madness bearing down upon them. The celestial map, now depicting constellations that mirrored the entity's cosmic unraveling, guided them through a cosmic trial that tested their sanity. The amulet, their only defense against the abyssal forces, emitted a protective aura that resonated with a determination to resist the cosmic allure.

In their cosmic struggle against the entity's spectral manifestation, the friends uncovered the cosmic truths that had driven the entity to madness. Forbidden knowledge, woven into the very fabric of the cosmic abyss, whispered cosmic secrets that defied mortal comprehension. The Veilstitcher's spectral form, a witness to the unfolding cosmic drama, conveyed a sense of empathy for the entity's tragic journey.

The amulet, attuned to the cosmic revelations, emitted pulses of resonant light that harmonized with the celestial map's guidance. As the friends faced the entity's spectral manifestation, the cosmic abyss seemed to echo with the collective sorrow of entities lost to the seductive whispers of forbidden knowledge.

In a moment of cosmic clarity, the friends realized that the only way to quell the entity's spectral madness was to weave threads of cosmic understanding into the fabric of the abyss. The Veilstitcher's spectral form, now a spectral weaver, guided them through a cosmic ritual that sought to restore the entity's fractured consciousness.

As they channeled their cosmic abilities into the ritual, the cosmic abyss responded with an ethereal symphony. Shadows, once animated by madness, now danced with a melancholic grace. The celestial map, now pulsating with threads of cosmic understanding, guided the friends through the intricate maneuvers needed to mend the entity's cosmic essence.

In the cosmic aftermath of the ritual, the entity's spectral manifestation transformed. Madness gave way to a serene luminescence, and the abyssal energies seemed to retreat. The Veilstitcher's influence, now a cosmic weaver of understanding, conveyed a sense of resolution as the friends witnessed the entity's spectral form find peace within the cosmic abyss.

The amulet, though worn by the cosmic struggle, emitted a radiant glow that mirrored the friends' triumph over the abyssal allure.

The celestial map, now cleared of constellations depicting madness, revealed a new cosmic equilibrium that reflected the friends' ability to navigate the cosmic abyss and emerge unscathed.

As the friends ascended from the cosmic abyss, the Veilstitcher's spectral form regained its ethereal brilliance. The amulet, though scarred by the cosmic ordeal, pulsed with a renewed vitality. The celestial map, now cleared of the cosmic uncertainties, guided them toward new frontiers in the interconnected tapestry.

The friends, forever changed by their harrowing encounter with the cosmic abyss, continued their cosmic odyssey with a heightened awareness of the cosmic perils that lurked in the vast expanse. The Veilstitcher's influence, now a cosmic weaver of understanding, accompanied them as a guiding force. The amulet, a resilient artifact that bore the scars of their cosmic ordeal, resonated with a luminous brilliance that symbolized their triumph over the shadows of the cosmic abyss.

The celestial map, once tainted by cosmic uncertainties, now guided the friends toward realms where cosmic wonders awaited discovery. The echoes of the unknown, though still haunting, whispered tales of cosmic resilience and the indomitable spirit that defied the allure of the cosmic abyss. The friends, forever entwined by the shared horrors they had faced, embraced the mysteries that awaited them in the uncharted territories of the interconnected tapestry.

Their cosmic odyssey, now marked by the echoes of the cosmic abyss and triumphant resilience, unfolded like a cosmic epic—an eternal saga that transcended mortal fears and celebrated the enduring bond between mortal souls and the cosmic forces that shaped their destinies.

Chapter 18: Symphony of Celestial Woe

As the friends continued their cosmic journey, guided by the celestial map, they found themselves drawn to a realm where celestial

forces clashed in a symphony of woe. The Veilstitcher's influence, ever watchful, resonated with a sense of foreboding as they approached an ethereal battleground where cosmic entities engaged in an otherworldly conflict. The amulet, typically radiant with cosmic energies, flickered with an ominous luminosity that mirrored the discordant atmosphere surrounding the celestial battleground.

The celestial map, now marked by constellations that seemed to clash in celestial strife, directed the friends toward the epicenter of the cosmic conflict. As they ventured deeper into the celestial battleground, the cosmic energies pulsated with an unsettling intensity, and the amulet emitted an erratic glow that reflected the cosmic turbulence that surrounded them.

In the midst of the celestial clash, the friends witnessed cosmic entities locked in a dance of ethereal combat. Celestial beings, once guardians of cosmic harmony, now clashed in discordant symphonies that reverberated through the interconnected tapestry. The Veilstitcher's spectral form, a spectral witness to the celestial woe, communicated a tale of ancient grievances that had ignited the cosmic conflict.

The celestial map, now revealing constellations that depicted celestial entities entwined in celestial strife, guided the friends through the celestial battleground. Shadows danced with malevolent glee, and the amulet emitted a protective aura that shielded them from the cosmic energies unleashed in the celestial clash.

As they navigated through the cosmic battlefield, the friends encountered spectral remnants—echoes of celestial entities consumed by the warring energies. The Veilstitcher's influence, though a vigilant observer, conveyed a sense of cosmic sorrow as the friends witnessed the tragic consequences of the celestial conflict. The amulet, their cosmic protector, resonated with a determination to understand the origins of the celestial woe.

In the heart of the celestial battleground, the friends discovered an ancient cosmic artifact—a relic of power that had become a focal point for the warring energies. Eldritch symbols adorned the artifact, resonating with the echoes of ancient grievances that fueled the celestial conflict. The celestial map, now etched with constellations that depicted the artifact's role in the celestial strife, guided them toward understanding the artifact's significance.

The Veilstitcher's spectral form, now a spectral historian, communicated the cosmic tale of how the artifact had become a catalyst for the celestial woe. Betrayals, vendettas, and cosmic vendettas had intertwined in a cosmic dance that threatened to unravel the very fabric of the interconnected tapestry. The amulet, resonating with the cosmic revelations, emitted a luminescent glow that mirrored the friends' determination to quell the celestial conflict.

As they approached the cosmic artifact, the friends faced celestial guardians—entities consumed by the warring energies that emanated from the relic. Shadows, animated by ancient grievances, seemed to materialize in ethereal forms, and the Veilstitcher's spectral form guided them through trials that tested their resolve against the celestial woe.

The amulet, their cosmic defense, emitted a protective aura that shimmered with radiant light. The celestial map, now pulsating with constellations that depicted the celestial guardians in moments of cosmic despair, guided the friends through the celestial trials. The Veilstitcher's influence, though tinged with cosmic sorrow, urged them to confront the spectral remnants and restore cosmic harmony.

In their cosmic struggle against the celestial guardians, the friends uncovered the origins of the ancient vendettas that had fueled the celestial conflict. Betrayals, forged alliances, and cosmic vendettas had intertwined in a cosmic dance that threatened to consume the

celestial battleground. The Veilstitcher's spectral form, a witness to the unfolding cosmic drama, conveyed a sense of urgency as the friends unraveled the cosmic grievances that fueled the celestial woe.

The amulet, attuned to the cosmic revelations, emitted pulses of resonant light that harmonized with the celestial map's guidance. As the friends faced the celestial guardians, the cosmic energies seemed to shift in response to their cosmic understanding. Shadows, once animated by warring energies, now flickered with moments of celestial harmony.

In a pivotal moment of the celestial struggle, the friends realized that the only way to quell the celestial conflict was to sever the ties that bound the ancient vendettas. The Veilstitcher's spectral form, now a cosmic arbitrator, guided them through a celestial ritual that sought to break the cosmic cycles of vengeance and restore the celestial entities' understanding.

As they channeled their cosmic abilities into the ritual, the cosmic energies responded with an ethereal symphony. Shadows, once animated by ancient grievances, now danced in a harmonious ballet. The celestial map, now pulsating with threads of cosmic understanding, guided the friends through the intricate maneuvers needed to mend the celestial entities' fractured consciousness.

In the cosmic aftermath of the ritual, the celestial guardians transformed. The cosmic vendettas that had fueled their spectral existence seemed to dissipate, and the celestial energies responded with a serene luminescence. The Veilstitcher's influence, now a cosmic mediator, conveyed a sense of resolution as the friends witnessed the celestial entities find peace within the cosmic battleground.

The amulet, though worn by the cosmic struggle, emitted a radiant glow that mirrored the friends' triumph over the celestial woe. The celestial map, now cleared of constellations depicting discord, revealed a new cosmic equilibrium that reflected the friends'

ability to mediate the celestial conflict and bring about a cosmic understanding.

As the friends ascended from the celestial battleground, the Veilstitcher's spectral form regained its ethereal brilliance. The amulet, though scarred by the cosmic ordeal, pulsed with a renewed vitality. The celestial map, now cleared of the cosmic disharmony, guided them toward new frontiers in the interconnected tapestry.

The friends, forever changed by their harrowing encounter with the celestial woe, continued their cosmic odyssey with a heightened awareness of the cosmic perils that lurked in the vast expanse. The Veilstitcher's influence, now a cosmic mediator, accompanied them as a guiding force. The amulet, a resilient artifact that bore the scars of their cosmic ordeal, resonated with a luminous brilliance that symbolized their triumph over the discordant echoes of the celestial woe.

The celestial map, once tainted by cosmic disharmony, now guided the friends toward realms where cosmic wonders awaited discovery. The echoes of the unknown, though still haunting, whispered tales of cosmic resilience and the indomitable spirit that defied the discord of the celestial woe. The friends, forever entwined by the shared horrors they had faced, embraced the mysteries that awaited them in the uncharted territories of the interconnected tapestry.

Their cosmic odyssey, now marked by the echoes of the celestial woe and triumphant resilience, unfolded like a cosmic epic—an eternal saga that transcended mortal fears and celebrated the enduring bond between mortal souls and the cosmic forces that shaped their destinies.

Chapter 19: The Veil's Unraveling

In the wake of their triumph over the celestial woe, the friends felt a profound shift in the cosmic fabric as the celestial map guided them towards the heart of an impending cosmic catastrophe. The

Veilstitcher's influence, though a steadfast companion, resonated with an urgency that transcended the cosmic echoes. The amulet, usually radiant with cosmic energies, emitted a flickering glow that mirrored the unsettling atmosphere surrounding them.

The celestial map, now marked by constellations that seemed to spiral in cosmic distress, directed the friends towards an ancient cosmic observatory—a place where the threads of reality and the cosmic veil converged. As they approached the observatory, the shadows deepened, and the amulet pulsed with an ominous luminosity that hinted at the cosmic perils that awaited them.

In the observatory's sacred chambers, the friends discovered an ancient cosmic artifact—an unraveling veil that bound the threads of the interconnected tapestry. Eldritch symbols adorned the artifact, resonating with an unsettling energy that sent shivers down their spines. The Veilstitcher's spectral form, now a solemn guide, communicated a tale of cosmic imbalance that threatened to rupture the very fabric of reality.

The celestial map, now etched with constellations that depicted the cosmic veil's unraveling, guided the friends through the cosmic observatory. Shadows danced with malevolent glee, and the amulet emitted a protective aura that shielded them from the cosmic disturbances that emanated from the artifact.

As they explored the observatory's depths, the friends faced cosmic guardians—entities tasked with protecting the artifact that held the threads of the cosmic veil. The Veilstitcher's influence, though tinged with cosmic sorrow, urged them to confront the guardians and understand the source of the cosmic imbalance. The amulet, their cosmic shield, resonated with a determination to prevent the impending catastrophe.

In the heart of the observatory, the friends discovered celestial inscriptions that chronicled the artifact's role in maintaining the

cosmic equilibrium. The celestial map, now revealing constellations that depicted the threads of reality woven into the cosmic veil, guided them towards an understanding of the artifact's significance. The Veilstitcher's spectral form, now a cosmic historian, conveyed the dire consequences of the cosmic veil's unraveling.

As they deciphered the celestial inscriptions, the friends learned of an ancient cosmic entity—the Weaver of Realms—who had crafted the cosmic veil to ensure the harmony of the interconnected tapestry. Betrayals and vendettas had driven the cosmic entity to an abyss of despair, leading to a cosmic curse that now threatened to shatter the delicate threads of reality.

The Veilstitcher's spectral form, now a cosmic weaver, guided the friends through a ritual to commune with the Weaver of Realms and understand the cosmic curse that had befallen the artifact. The amulet, resonating with the cosmic revelations, emitted a luminescent glow that mirrored the friends' determination to mend the unraveling cosmic veil.

As they channeled their cosmic abilities into the ritual, the cosmic observatory responded with ethereal energies. Shadows, once animated by cosmic imbalance, now seemed to waver in a cosmic dance. The celestial map, now pulsating with threads of cosmic understanding, guided the friends through the intricate maneuvers needed to commune with the Weaver of Realms.

In the cosmic communion, the friends glimpsed the Weaver of Realms—a spectral entity consumed by cosmic despair. The Veilstitcher's spectral form, now a compassionate guide, urged them to unravel the cosmic curse that bound the Weaver and restore balance to the interconnected tapestry. The amulet, attuned to the cosmic revelations, emitted pulses of resonant light that harmonized with the celestial map's guidance.

As the friends faced the Weaver of Realms, the cosmic entity conveyed the tale of its descent into cosmic despair. Betrayals and vendettas had shattered the cosmic harmony it sought to maintain, leading to a curse that now threatened to unravel the very fabric of reality. The Veilstitcher's influence, now a cosmic mediator, urged the friends to break the chains of despair and restore hope to the Weaver.

In a pivotal moment of cosmic communion, the friends realized that the only way to mend the cosmic veil was to heal the Weaver of Realms' cosmic despair. The Veilstitcher's spectral form, now a cosmic healer, guided them through a celestial ritual that sought to break the cosmic curse and bring solace to the beleaguered cosmic entity.

As they channeled their cosmic abilities into the ritual, the cosmic observatory responded with an ethereal symphony. Shadows, once animated by cosmic despair, now seemed to waver in a harmonious ballet. The celestial map, now pulsating with threads of cosmic understanding, guided the friends through the intricate maneuvers needed to heal the Weaver of Realms.

In the cosmic aftermath of the ritual, the Weaver of Realms' spectral form transformed. Despair gave way to a serene luminescence, and the cosmic energies responded with a harmonious resonance. The Veilstitcher's influence, now a cosmic healer, conveyed a sense of resolution as the friends witnessed the Weaver find peace within the cosmic observatory.

The amulet, though worn by the cosmic struggle, emitted a radiant glow that mirrored the friends' triumph over the cosmic despair. The celestial map, now cleared of constellations depicting the cosmic curse, revealed a new cosmic equilibrium that reflected the friends' ability to mend the unraveling threads of the cosmic veil.

As the friends ascended from the cosmic observatory, the Veil-stitcher's spectral form regained its ethereal brilliance. The amulet, though scarred by the cosmic ordeal, pulsed with a renewed vitality. The celestial map, now cleared of the cosmic imbalance, guided them toward new frontiers in the interconnected tapestry.

The friends, forever changed by their harrowing encounter with the unraveling cosmic veil, continued their cosmic odyssey with a heightened awareness of the cosmic perils that lurked in the vast expanse. The Veilstitcher's influence, now a cosmic healer, accompanied them as a guiding force. The amulet, a resilient artifact that bore the scars of their cosmic ordeal, resonated with a luminous brilliance that symbolized their triumph over the cosmic despair.

The celestial map, once tainted by cosmic imbalance, now guided the friends toward realms where cosmic wonders awaited discovery. The echoes of the unknown, though still haunting, whispered tales of cosmic resilience and the indomitable spirit that defied the cosmic despair. The friends, forever entwined by the shared horrors they had faced, embraced the mysteries that awaited them in the uncharted territories of the interconnected tapestry.

Their cosmic odyssey, now marked by the mending of the cosmic veil and triumphant resilience, unfolded like a cosmic epic—an eternal saga that transcended mortal fears and celebrated the enduring bond between mortal souls and the cosmic forces that shaped their destinies.

As the friends ventured forth from the cosmic observatory, a newfound clarity enveloped the interconnected tapestry. The Veilstitcher's spectral form, once a guardian in cosmic despair, radiated with a luminous brilliance that mirrored the cosmic healing they had achieved. The amulet, though marked by the trials of unraveling cosmic threads, retained a resilient glow—a testament to their ability to mend the cosmic veil.

The celestial map, now cleared of constellations depicting imbalance, guided the friends towards realms where cosmic wonders awaited discovery. The echoes of the unknown, though still haunting, whispered tales of cosmic resilience and the indomitable spirit that defied the cosmic despair. The friends, forever entwined by the shared horrors they had faced, embraced the mysteries that awaited them in the uncharted territories of the interconnected tapestry.

Their cosmic odyssey, now marked by the mending of the cosmic veil and triumphant resilience, unfolded like a cosmic epic—an eternal saga that transcended mortal fears and celebrated the enduring bond between mortal souls and the cosmic forces that shaped their destinies.

As they ventured into unexplored cosmic realms, the friends encountered celestial wonders that seemed to shimmer with a renewed vitality. The Veilstitcher's influence, now a beacon of cosmic healing, guided them through realms where echoes of their cosmic deeds resonated with celestial echoes. The amulet, a cosmic artifact infused with the power of mended threads, pulsed with a rhythmic glow that echoed the harmony they had restored.

The celestial map, now revealing constellations that depicted the friends as cosmic healers, guided them towards realms where their presence was needed. Shadows, once animated by cosmic despair, now seemed to retreat in the wake of their cosmic healing. The friends, now custodians of celestial balance, embraced their role in preserving the interconnected tapestry.

In their cosmic journey, the friends encountered celestial beings whose threads of reality had frayed. The Veilstitcher's spectral form, now a cosmic guide in mending, urged them to extend their healing touch to those ensnared by cosmic disarray. The amulet, resonating with the threads of cosmic understanding, emitted a gentle glow that mirrored their commitment to restoring celestial harmony.

As they traversed through realms touched by cosmic imbalance, the friends faced cosmic trials that tested their newfound abilities as healers of the interconnected tapestry. The Veilstitcher's influence, now a cosmic mentor, guided them through rituals that sought to mend the threads of reality and restore balance to celestial entities caught in the throes of cosmic disarray.

The amulet, a conduit of cosmic energies, emitted pulses of healing light that harmonized with the celestial map's guidance. Shadows, once animated by cosmic despair, now seemed to dissipate as the friends embraced their cosmic roles as healers. The echoes of their cosmic deeds reverberated through the interconnected tapestry, leaving a trail of celestial balance in their wake.

In a celestial sanctuary, the friends encountered a cosmic entity—a guardian of the celestial realms whose threads of reality had become entangled in cosmic disarray. The Veilstitcher's spectral form, now a cosmic healer, communicated with the entity in a language of cosmic understanding. The amulet, resonating with the threads of mended reality, emitted a soothing aura that calmed the entity's cosmic unrest.

As the friends performed a cosmic ritual to heal the guardian's threads, the celestial sanctuary responded with ethereal energies. The Veilstitcher's influence, now a cosmic conductor, guided them through the intricate maneuvers needed to mend the celestial guardian's frayed threads. The amulet, attuned to the cosmic revelations, emitted pulses of resonant light that harmonized with the celestial map's guidance.

In the cosmic aftermath of the ritual, the celestial guardian's spectral form transformed. Threads once entangled in cosmic disarray now shimmered with a serene luminescence. The Veilstitcher's influence, now a cosmic healer, conveyed a sense of fulfillment as

the friends witnessed the guardian find peace within the celestial sanctuary.

The amulet, though worn by the cosmic struggle, emitted a radiant glow that mirrored the friends' triumph as cosmic healers. The celestial map, now cleared of constellations depicting cosmic disarray, revealed a new cosmic equilibrium that reflected the friends' ability to extend their healing touch to the interconnected tapestry.

As the friends continued their cosmic journey, the Veilstitcher's spectral form, now a cosmic mentor, guided them towards realms where celestial entities awaited their healing touch. The amulet, a beacon of cosmic balance, pulsed with a rhythmic glow that echoed the harmonious resonance they had restored. The celestial map, now revealing constellations that depicted the friends as cosmic healers, guided them towards realms where their presence was needed.

Their cosmic odyssey, now marked by the mending of celestial threads and triumphant resilience, unfolded like a cosmic epic—an eternal saga that transcended mortal fears and celebrated the enduring bond between mortal souls and the cosmic forces that shaped their destinies.

Chapter 20: The Cosmic Reckoning

In the final leg of their cosmic odyssey, the friends sensed a gathering cosmic storm—a tempest that threatened to unravel the very fabric of reality. The Veilstitcher's influence, a vigilant beacon, resonated with a profound urgency that transcended the echoes of their past encounters. The amulet, though resilient, emitted a pulsating glow that mirrored the unsettling cosmic energies that surrounded them.

The celestial map, now marked by constellations that seemed to writhe in cosmic distress, guided the friends towards the epicenter of the looming cosmic tempest. As they approached, the shadows deepened, and the cosmic storm manifested in swirling patterns of

ethereal chaos. The Veilstitcher's spectral form, now a harbinger of cosmic reckoning, communicated a dire prophecy of an ancient cosmic entity—the Stormweaver—whose fury threatened to engulf the interconnected tapestry.

In the heart of the cosmic storm, the friends confronted an ethereal vortex—a manifestation of the Stormweaver's wrath. Eldritch symbols adorned the vortex, resonating with an ominous energy that sent shivers down their spines. The celestial map, now etched with constellations that depicted the Stormweaver's fury, guided them towards understanding the origin of the cosmic tempest.

The Veilstitcher's spectral form, now a cosmic seer, revealed the tale of the Stormweaver—an ancient cosmic entity imprisoned by the threads of reality in ages past. Betrayals and vendettas had fueled the Stormweaver's rage, and its spectral essence now sought to unleash cosmic chaos upon the interconnected tapestry. The amulet, resonating with the cosmic revelations, emitted a luminescent glow that mirrored the friends' determination to quell the cosmic reckoning.

As they ventured into the heart of the cosmic vortex, the friends faced celestial guardians—entities corrupted by the Stormweaver's malevolent influence. The Veilstitcher's influence, though tinged with cosmic sorrow, urged them to confront the guardians and understand the depths of the cosmic tempest's power. The amulet, their cosmic shield, resonated with a determination to resist the impending catastrophe.

In the cosmic battleground, the friends encountered remnants of cosmic entities ensnared by the Stormweaver's malevolent influence. Shadows, animated by cosmic fury, seemed to writhe with an otherworldly malevolence. The Veilstitcher's spectral form guided them through trials that tested their resolve against the impending cosmic reckoning.

The celestial map, now revealing constellations that depicted the enslaved cosmic entities, guided the friends through the cosmic trials. The amulet, emitting a protective aura, shimmered with a resilient light that mirrored their commitment to resist the cosmic tempest's onslaught.

As they navigated through the cosmic chaos, the friends uncovered an ancient cosmic prison—an ethereal cage that held the Stormweaver's spectral essence. Eldritch symbols adorned the prison, resonating with the echoes of ancient grievances that fueled the cosmic reckoning. The celestial map, now etched with constellations that depicted the prison's significance, guided them towards understanding the key to subduing the Stormweaver's fury.

The Veilstitcher's spectral form, now a cosmic keybearer, communicated a ritual to unlock the prison and confront the Stormweaver. The amulet, resonating with the cosmic revelations, emitted a luminescent glow that mirrored the friends' determination to face the ancient cosmic entity. As they channeled their cosmic abilities into the ritual, the cosmic prison responded with an ethereal symphony.

Shadows, once animated by cosmic fury, now seemed to waver in a discordant ballet. The celestial map, now pulsating with threads of cosmic understanding, guided the friends through the intricate maneuvers needed to unlock the ancient prison. The Veilstitcher's influence, now a cosmic guide, urged them to unravel the Stormweaver's malevolent influence and restore balance to the interconnected tapestry.

In the cosmic aftermath of the ritual, the ancient prison released the Stormweaver's spectral essence. The friends, now confronted by the embodiment of cosmic fury, felt the weight of the impending reckoning bearing down upon them. The Veilstitcher's spectral form, now a cosmic defender, communicated a sense of urgency as the friends prepared to face the Stormweaver's wrath.

The celestial map, now depicting constellations that mirrored the Stormweaver's cosmic fury, guided the friends through a cosmic trial that tested their resilience against the impending reckoning. The amulet, their only defense against the cosmic tempest, emitted a protective aura that shimmered with a determination to resist the ancient entity's onslaught.

In their cosmic struggle against the Stormweaver's spectral essence, the friends uncovered the origins of the ancient grievances that had fueled the cosmic reckoning. Betrayals, vendettas, and cosmic vendettas had intertwined in a malevolent dance that threatened to consume the interconnected tapestry. The Veilstitcher's spectral form, a witness to the unfolding cosmic drama, conveyed a sense of urgency as the friends unraveled the ancient cosmic entity's malevolent influence.

The amulet, attuned to the cosmic revelations, emitted pulses of resonant light that harmonized with the celestial map's guidance. As the friends faced the Stormweaver's spectral essence, the cosmic tempest seemed to shift in response to their cosmic understanding. Shadows, once animated by cosmic fury, now flickered with moments of cosmic discord.

In a pivotal moment of the cosmic struggle, the friends realized that the only way to quell the Stormweaver's wrath was to break the chains of ancient grievances. The Veilstitcher's spectral form, now a cosmic arbitrator, guided them through a celestial ritual that sought to sever the cosmic cycles of vengeance and restore the ancient entity's fractured consciousness.

As they channeled their cosmic abilities into the ritual, the cosmic tempest responded with an ethereal symphony. Shadows, once animated by cosmic fury, now seemed to waver in a harmonious ballet. The celestial map, now pulsating with threads of cosmic

understanding, guided the friends through the intricate maneuvers needed to mend the Stormweaver's spectral essence.

In the cosmic aftermath of the ritual, the Stormweaver's spectral essence transformed. Fury gave way to a serene luminescence, and the cosmic tempest seemed to retreat. The Veilstitcher's influence, now a cosmic mediator, conveyed a sense of resolution as the friends witnessed the ancient entity find peace within the interconnected tapestry.

The amulet, though worn by the cosmic struggle, emitted a radiant glow that mirrored the friends' triumph over the impending reckoning. The celestial map, now cleared of constellations depicting discord, revealed a new cosmic equilibrium that reflected the friends' ability to confront the ancient cosmic entity and emerge unscathed.

As the friends ascended from the cosmic battleground, the Veilstitcher's spectral form regained its ethereal brilliance. The amulet, though scarred by the cosmic ordeal, pulsed with a renewed vitality. The celestial map, now cleared of the cosmic turmoil, guided them towards new frontiers in the interconnected tapestry.

The friends, forever changed by their harrowing encounter with the cosmic reckoning, continued their cosmic odyssey with a heightened awareness of the cosmic perils that lurked in the vast expanse. The Veilstitcher's influence, now a cosmic mediator, accompanied them as a guiding force. The amulet, a resilient artifact that bore the scars of their cosmic ordeal, resonated with a luminous brilliance that symbolized their triumph over the impending reckoning.

The celestial map, once tainted by the cosmic turmoil, now guided the friends toward realms where cosmic wonders awaited discovery. The echoes of the unknown, though still haunting, whispered tales of cosmic resilience and the indomitable spirit that defied the cosmic tempest. The friends, forever entwined by the shared

horrors they had faced, embraced the mysteries that awaited them in the uncharted territories of the interconnected tapestry.

Their cosmic odyssey, now marked by the triumphant resolution of the cosmic reckoning, unfolded like a cosmic epic—an eternal saga that transcended mortal fears and celebrated the enduring bond between mortal souls and the cosmic forces that shaped their destinies.

As they journeyed into the unexplored cosmic realms, the friends encountered celestial wonders that seemed to radiate with the echoes of their victorious struggle. The Veilstitcher's influence, now a beacon of cosmic resolution, guided them through realms where echoes of their cosmic deeds resonated with celestial echoes. The amulet, a cosmic artifact infused with the power of triumphant threads, pulsed with a rhythmic glow that echoed the harmony they had restored.

The celestial map, now revealing constellations that depicted the friends as cosmic defenders, guided them toward realms where their presence was needed. Shadows, once animated by cosmic fury, now seemed to retreat in the wake of their cosmic triumph. The friends, now guardians of celestial balance, embraced their role in preserving the interconnected tapestry.

In their cosmic journey, the friends encountered celestial beings whose threads of reality had been freed from the shackles of ancient grievances. The Veilstitcher's spectral form, now a cosmic liberator, urged them to extend their cosmic influence to those freed from the burden of cosmic turmoil. The amulet, resonating with the threads of triumphant reality, emitted a radiant glow that mirrored their commitment to safeguarding the celestial realms.

As they traversed through realms touched by cosmic liberation, the friends faced cosmic trials that tested their newfound abilities as defenders of the interconnected tapestry. The Veilstitcher's

influence, now a cosmic mentor, guided them through rituals that sought to fortify the threads of reality and preserve balance in celestial entities freed from ancient shackles.

The amulet, a conduit of cosmic energies, emitted pulses of protective light that harmonized with the celestial map's guidance. Shadows, once animated by cosmic turmoil, now seemed to dissipate as the friends embraced their cosmic roles as defenders. The echoes of their cosmic deeds reverberated through the interconnected tapestry, leaving a trail of celestial balance in their wake.

In a celestial sanctuary, the friends encountered a cosmic entity—a guardian of the celestial realms whose threads of reality had been freed from ancient shackles. The Veilstitcher's spectral form, now a cosmic liberator, communicated with the entity in a language of cosmic understanding. The amulet, resonating with the threads of triumphant reality, emitted a soothing aura that celebrated the entity's cosmic liberation.

As the friends reveled in the cosmic liberation, the celestial sanctuary responded with ethereal energies. The Veilstitcher's influence, now a cosmic conductor of harmony, guided them through the intricate maneuvers needed to celebrate the celestial guardian's newfound freedom. The amulet, attuned to the cosmic revelations, emitted pulses of resonant light that harmonized with the celestial map's guidance.

In the cosmic aftermath of the celebration, the celestial guardian's spectral form radiated with joy. Threads once bound by ancient grievances now shimmered with a serene luminescence. The Veilstitcher's influence, now a cosmic celebrant, conveyed a sense of fulfillment as the friends witnessed the guardian revel in newfound peace within the celestial sanctuary.

The amulet, though worn by the cosmic struggle, emitted a radiant glow that mirrored the friends' triumph as cosmic liberators.

The celestial map, now cleared of constellations depicting ancient shackles, revealed a new cosmic equilibrium that reflected the friends' ability to free celestial entities from the burden of cosmic turmoil.

As the friends continued their cosmic journey, the Veilstitcher's spectral form, now a cosmic celebrant, guided them toward realms where celestial entities awaited their liberating touch. The amulet, a beacon of cosmic liberation, pulsed with a rhythmic glow that echoed the joy they had spread. The celestial map, now revealing constellations that depicted the friends as cosmic liberators, guided them toward realms where their presence was needed.

Their cosmic odyssey, now marked by the celebration of cosmic liberation and triumphant resolution, unfolded like a cosmic epic—an eternal saga that transcended mortal fears and celebrated the enduring bond between mortal souls and the cosmic forces that shaped their destinies.